How Tory Governments Fall

ANTHONY SELDON is Founding Director of the
Institute of Contemporary British History.

KT-472-347

WITHDRAWN

How Tory Governments Fall

THE TORY PARTY
IN POWER
SINCE 1783

edited by Anthony Seldon

FontanaPress
An Imprint of HarperCollinsPublishers

Fontana Press
An Imprint of HarperCollins*Publishers*
77–85 Fulham Palace Road,
Hammersmith, London W6 8JB

This Fontana Press Original 1996
1 3 5 7 9 8 6 4 2

ISBN 0 00 686366-3

Photoset in Postscript Linotype Meridien by
Rowland Phototypesetting Ltd
Bury St Edmunds, Suffolk

Printed and bound in Great Britain by
Caledonian International
Book Manufacturing Ltd, Glasgow

This book is dedicated to all those who have written for or otherwise contributed to the activities of the Institute of Contemporary British History in its first ten years (1986–96). In particular, I would like to dedicate it to the two principal 'founding fathers', David Butler and Sir Frank Cooper, who along with David Severn and Lady (Olive) Wood helped Peter Hennessy and me establish the ICBH.

CONTENTS

ACKNOWLEDGEMENTS

The editor wishes to thank all his contributors, who endured his coaxing, prodding and perhaps over-prescriptive brief with exemplary good humour.

My colleagues at the Institute of Contemporary British History and St Dunstan's College have as always been a tower of support and stimulation. I am deeply grateful to the individuals who comprise both these outstanding organizations, and am very proud of my association with them.

Particular thanks to my collaborator on two books, Stuart Ball, for his intellectual input into this book, and also to my lifelong friend and mentor John Barnes, for his inspiration and genius on all matters concerned with the history of the right in Britain. The selfless guidance of both helped me not least in their comments on my introduction and conclusion.

Lewis Baston, my principal researcher on the biography of John Major, has been an enthusiastic presence throughout this book. I learnt much about the party and voting patterns from Russell Tillson. My editorial assistant and secretary Annemarie Weitzel has remarkably kept me and everyone else up to the mark. At HarperCollins the irrepressible duo of Philip Gwyn Jones and Toby Mundy proved again delightful and efficient partners while Caroline Hotblack put in sterling and sensitive work as picture researcher. Copy-editing was completed most effectively by Ian Gerrard, another Major researcher; Daniel Collings and Willian Gelling, both of Tonbridge School helped prepare the book for publication.

Finally, my thanks to my wife and young family for patience which would take two hundred years to repay.

ANTHONY SELDON
May 1996

LIST OF TABLES

The Tory Party in Power
1783–1996

Anthony Seldon

This book examines over two hundred years of the Tories in power. The party dominated the late eighteenth century, the start and end of the nineteenth century, and much of the twentieth century, and has been the most consistently successful political party not just in Britain but in the democratic world.

The post-1660 Restoration court of Charles II saw the first emergence of a 'Tory' faction, a group that became better defined after the Glorious Revolution of 1688 and the emergence of a Whig group to rival the Tories. By the last years of Queen Anne's reign from 1710 to 1714 the Tories had emerged triumphant, but British politics for fifty years after the 1720s was dominated by the Whigs.

This book settles on 1783 as its starting date, not because any clear set of Tory policies had emerged, but because December of that year saw the younger William Pitt become prime minister, and the beginning of a period of coalescence of attitudes and beliefs, spurred by the French Revolution, which were to define what the party stood for in the nineteenth century.

Ten periods of Tory dominance are described in the book. Authors were asked to address themselves to the nature of the party during the period in power they were describing: what was the basis of the Tories' initial election victory;

1

what were the unifying themes of policy during the period; what was the party's prevailing ideology; what interests were the Tories representing most closely during the period; what was the quality and the location of leadership (that is, to what extent was it collective); to what extent did any formal or informal partnership with another party exist, and how did it affect the substance of government policy. Authors were then asked to address themselves to the reasons for downfall, and were invited to consider nine factors in demise, as outlined in the Conclusion.

The Tory Party 1783–1996

The Tory Party has changed enormously over the two-hundred-year period examined. Pitt, Prime Minister from 1783 to 1801 and 1804 to 1806, called himself an independent Whig. Almost no members of Parliament called themselves 'Tories' until after the Great Reform Act of 1832, and MPs did not regard themselves as belonging to a cohesive and disciplined 'party', although the emergence of collective responsibility, not least under Lord Liverpool, enhanced the process. The 1832 Act accelerated the development of modern political parties, and established the principle that it would be success in general elections, rather than the will of the monarch, that would change parties in government. The Tories thus had a powerful spur to organize themselves as a party – to win general elections.

The power of the Crown, notably George III and George IV, to create and end ministries, and the looseness of the description 'Tory', are the defining characteristics of the first two chapters, by Jeremy Black and Norman Gash, covering the periods 1783–1806 and 1812–30. Defence of the position of the established Anglican Church, respect for the role of the monarchy and a strong stance in support of property, order and the landed interest – the legacy of the French Revolution – were the prevailing principles of the ministries in these periods. Liverpool's ministry from 1812

2

to 1827 saw a renewed emphasis on law and authority, a contempt for radicalism and populism, and a distrust of the Foxite Whigs. Support for the war against Napoleon from 1810 to 1815 was another common stance.

'Tory' was the description that came to be applied to Pitt and his successors, Portland (1807–9), Perceval (1809–12) and Liverpool. From 1830, 'Conservative' was the term increasingly used by the party's leaders. By 1834, Robert Peel referred in his Tamworth Manifesto to 'the great Conservative party', and after 1835 the term progressively replaced Tory as the common name to describe the party. The party began to break up after 1827, and after 1830 went into opposition, suffering a major defeat in the post-Reform Act election of 1832. It secured at most just 180 seats (the imprecise figure indicating the lack of coherence in the pre-Peel party), the lowest House of Commons representation in its history. After the mid-1830s and a brief period in office under Peel in 1834–35, the party gained in cohesion, and emerged in the 1841 general election as a group with a distinct identity. As Bruce Coleman shows in Chapter 3, skilful party management, utilizing the newly formed Carlton Club, divisions within the opposition and a reaction against radicalism and reform all fuelled the Conservative recovery between 1835 and 1841. These factors outweighed the importance of Peel's Tamworth Manifesto, which offered a moderate and reforming Conservatism, and was designed to woo disillusioned reformers from the ranks of the moderate Whigs. Too much can be made of the Peel government of 1841–46 being qualitatively 'new'. It did not mark the start of the Conservative Party, but rather another stage in its development. Peel preferred to see himself as leading a national rather than a factional group and the Country party aspect of many backbenchers remained. The broad stance of the Conservatives after 1841 was also recognizable from earlier manifestations: upholding of social order and property; maintenance of the position of the Crown and Church; opposition to reform agitation and to demands for 'democracy', and maintenance of the union with Ireland. Peel's reforming ministry came to an end in the split over the repeal of the Corn Laws in 1846, when he failed to carry his party with him on the need to abandon protection in favour of free trade.

Peel and his free-trade supporters separated from the Tories, and after Peel's death joined the Whigs, becoming one of the founding elements of the new Liberal Party after 1859. The protectionists, led by Stanley (later Lord Derby) from 1846 to 1868, became the true heirs of the Conservative tradition, and within a few years openly utilized the name 'Conservative'. It was to take twenty-eight years after 1846 before the party won a decisive general election victory, the longest period out of real power in its history. The appeal of the party narrowed at first, representing little more than the landed agricultural interest. The large and growing urban middle class and the business interest, the products of the rapidly progressing industrial revolution, were all but overlooked. The only occasions when the Conservatives were able to form fitful administrations, in 1852, 1858–59 and 1866–68, was when the Whig groupings divided among themselves.

John Vincent argues in Chapter 4 that divisions within the Liberals also explain in large part the Conservatives' great election victory in 1874. The two key points in the eclipse of the Liberal hegemony, according to Vincent, were the death of their popular leader Palmerston in October 1865, and 1870, when the Paris Commune reawakened fears of radicalism and unrest.

Election success over Gladstone in 1874 made Benjamin Disraeli prime minister. Although he had been leader in the House of Commons since 1852, it was not until February 1868 that he succeeded Lord Derby as party leader (and in the short term also as prime minister). Under him, the fortunes of the party were transformed. If Pitt defined what the Tory Party stood for, and Peel forged it into a parliamentary party, Disraeli helped make it a national party with a recognizably modern organization. In the debate over the Second Reform Act of 1866–67, Disraeli showed that the party was serious about wanting to govern, and in meeting rather than hiding from the challenges of a rapidly developing industrial country. In 1872, in speeches in Manchester and at Crystal Palace, Disraeli offered a withering attack on Gladstone and the unsettling legislation of his government since 1868. He also sketched out some thoughts on a Conservative programme, including the claim that the Conservatives were the patriotic party (thereby stealing the mantle of Palmerstone) and offering the promise of social improvement. This appeal to the working classes was central to making the Conservatives a national party. Disraeli began the process of broadening the appeal of the party beyond landed interests to business and the middle classes in the increasingly populated towns and suburbs. To mobilize these new classes of potential voters, Disraeli – or more specifically, those under him – created Conservative Central Office, the professional body of the party, and the beginnings of the National Union of Conservative and Constitutional Associations, to organize the voluntary party in the country.

Disraeli's government fell in 1880, and he died in the following year. The succession was disputed, but by 1885 Lord Salisbury had emerged as his successor. Defeated in the 1885 general election, Gladstone was back in government that November, but the Liberals then split over Irish Home Rule, helping to propel the Conservatives back into power in 1886. Fortified by the breakaway Liberal Unionists, a process astutely managed by Salisbury, the Conservatives dominated the next twenty years, and were only out of office for a brief spell between 1892 and 1895. These years saw the party's discipline and cohesion in Parliament greatly increased. Martin Pugh in Chapter 5 shows how precarious was the Conservatives' hold on power with the newly enfranchised electorates after the 1867 and 1884 Reform Acts, the latter almost doubling the electorate, from

3.15 million to 5.7 million. He shows how under Salisbury the party organization, galvanized by the Chief Agent, R. W. E. Middleton, and the Primrose League, established in 1883 to mobilize the wider electorate, were vital in securing the victories in 1886, 1895 and 1900. It was Salisbury, rather than Disraeli, who oversaw if not the first proposal then certainly the consummation of the marriage of the business interest, the towns and suburbs, with the Conservative Party. Central to this transition was the alliance between the Conservatives and the Liberal Unionists, led by Lord Hartington and Joseph Chamberlain. Many elements were also bound more strongly to the Tory Party as a consequence: Whig landowners, middle-class Anglicans, Noncomformists and even Roman Catholics came over to the Tory side. It also explains why the west midlands and Scotland quickly became Conservative after 1886. The serendipitous alliance with the Liberal Unionists – even though their numbers were not large – is central to understanding how the Conservatives were able to dominate British politics for the twenty years after 1886.

Salisbury's Conservative Party was clear about what it stood for: to the traditional nineteenth-century Tory pillars of monarchy, church, property, patriotism, were added empire and maintenance of the Union with Ireland. This menu was enough for the late-nineteenth-century palate, but the fast approaching twentieth century demanded more from its politicians. New economic, social and international pressures were threatening a seachange in the language of politics, with more activism sought from government than in the *laissez-faire* nineteenth century. Gladstone retired from politics in 1894, and his Liberal Party gave way to a new breed of interventionist 'New Liberals', such as H. H. Asquith and David Lloyd George, who increasingly made the running in domestic policy between 1906 and the outbreak of the First World War.

Salisbury resisted such change, which he regarded with deep suspicion. Innovations under his premiership, with

rare exceptions such as the system of elected local government, created in 1888, were enacted despite not because of
him. His nephew, A. J. Balfour, who succeeded him in 1902,
failed to give a clear lead on how to shape Conservatism
for the new century, and lost the initiative to Joseph Chamberlain who launched his Tariff Reform crusade, which
incorporated social reform, in 1903. Here was activism with
a vengeance, so strong that it cleft the Conservative Party
down the middle and was heavily responsible for the Liberal
landslide victory in 1906. The defeat, and the part tariff
reform was deemed to have played in it, set back the cause
of those who wanted the party to adopt a fresh set of policies. Balfour dithered on for five years until 1911; his successor, Andrew Bonar Law, put tariff reform on the
backburner, and opted to play the Orange card, a reactive
stance to stem the tide of Irish Home Rule. While he rallied
the party behind a common cause, he similarly failed to
provide a clear positive platform for the party to follow.

The 1906 defeat set in train a process which was to continue throughout the twentieth century. Loss of office at
the polls after a period in office or domination is followed
by a change in leader, a renovation of the party's organization and recasting of policy to align the party again with
changed voter preference. Once the much sought-after
office is recaptured, the party attempts to enact its new
policies and to retain popularity, two objectives not always
in tune with one another.

The new century was to provide a far more clement
seedbed for the Conservatives than the old. Having won
only four general elections on their own between 1832 and
1922, they have so dominated the period since 1900 that
it deserves the appellation 'the Conservative century'. Either
standing alone, or as the most powerful element in a
coalition, the party has held power for over seventy years
since its election victory in 1895. For much of the remaining
thirty years, its opponents have had but a fragile grip on
power. Only in three Parliaments did they secure significant

majorities, the Liberals in 1906–10, Labour in 1945–50 and again from 1966 to 1970. In contrast, it has been rare for Conservative ministries to lack a working majority.

This achievement is all the greater in the face of the challenges the party faced, eclipsing those of the nineteenth century: the rise of the mass Labour Party; full adult suffrage, including the vote for women and much easier registration procedures; a levelling of social hierarchy, precipitated by the First World War; the decline in the religious basis for voting and its potential replacement by class as the key determinant of choice; changes in the social, political and economic climate first in favour of interventionism and then away from it; direct challenges from militant trade unionism in the mid-1920s, early 1970s and mid-1980s; the partition of Ireland and membership of the European Community; a revolution in the technology of party communication; the loss of empire and Britain's absolute decline as a world power, and relative decline as an economic one. There is irony in this, as Michael Bentley notes in Chapter 7. Logic dictates that it should have been the nineteenth rather than the twentieth century that the Conservatives dominated, with voting in public under surveillance (until 1872), no death duties (until 1894), and a limited franchise based on property (until 1918).

Stuart Ball in Chapter 6 charts the stages by which the party crawled back to strength after its 1906 defeat, which left it with just 157 MPs. The two general elections of 1910 saw a significant recovery with 272 MPs on each occasion, insufficient, with Irish Nationalist and Labour support for the Liberals, for the Tories to regain power. It was the First World War which transformed the party's prospects, leading it back into office first under Asquith's coalition government from May 1915, with war disguising for the time being the party's lack of an agreed and distinctive domestic agenda beyond protectionism. Reorganization of the party, with a new post of party chairman created in 1911, facilitated the recovery. The ousting of Asquith in December 1916 and his replacement with a coalition government led by Lloyd George boosted the party's position again. Conservatives were now able to fill most of the key government posts, facilitated by the departure with Asquith of several prominent Liberal ministers. Conservatives now provided two-thirds of the coalition's support in the House of Commons, and Bonar Law was clearly the second figure in the government. His thinking about the challenges that would face government in the immediate postwar world chimed with Lloyd George's, and continuation of the coalition into peacetime seemed a matter of course. Armistice in November 1918 was followed by a general election in December, in which 523 MPs who supported the coalition were victorious, including an overwhelming Conservative slice with 382 MPs.

The tensions evident in the prewar Conservative Party, dormant during the war, surfaced again before long. Bonar Law retired as party leader because of illness in March 1921, to be succeeded by Austen Chamberlain, son of Joseph. Bonar Law had at least provided reassurance to Conservative MPs that Lloyd George, an increasingly mistrusted and autocratic figure, would not ride roughshod over Tory principles: Chamberlain held no such reassurance. Worse still, Conservative MPs had to swallow some bitter pills, including the abandonment of southern Ireland in the Anglo-Irish Treaty of 1921, and failure to legislate to limit trade union privileges or to reform the House of Lords, and restore some powers lost in 1911. Divisions in the party both in the country and in Parliament grew throughout 1922, with Lloyd George alienating both tariff reform and 'diehard' wings of the party, culminating in the Carlton Club meeting in October in which a majority of MPs voted against the Conservatives continuing in the coalition. Chamberlain at once resigned, and Bonar Law, summoned back into service, took over the leadership. In the ensuing election, in November 1922, the Conservatives were returned in a three-cornered fight (and 8 per cent less of the popular vote than in the 1910 elections) with 344 MPs.

9

The limpest period of Conservative office this century commenced. Several pro-coalition senior figures joined Chamberlain in refusing to serve in the new government. Bonar Law's leadership failed again to define a clear domestic platform for the party, and when his health finally collapsed in May 1923 Stanley Baldwin, the Chancellor of the Exchequer but a relative unknown, succeeded to the premiership. Baldwin's first major gambit to define a clear direction for the party was to revive Joseph Chamberlain's idea of tariff reform. But as Bonar Law had given a pledge that protectionism would not be introduced in the life of the Parliament, a general election, after only a year of office, was deemed necessary. The result saw the number of Conservative MPs fall to 258 (though the Tories' total number of votes was higher than in 1922), and a Labour government – the first – took office in January 1924. A strong Liberal performance with a newly reunited party accounted for the Conservative defeat in the election, but the failure of the leadership in 1922–23 to provide a clear direction contributed to the impression, as in the 1850s and 1860s, that the Conservatives were not a forward-looking party.

Baldwin's reputation, and the interwar position of the Conservative Party, were founded on his second government, from 1924 to 1929. The experience of the minority Labour government of January to October 1924 proved salutary: Baldwin sidelined protectionism, the ex-coalitionists rejoined the front bench, party organization and outlook were refreshed: the talk was of 'New Conservatism'. The 1924 general election saw the Conservatives returned to power with 412 MPs, and the Liberals crushed. Baldwin's achievements were to commit the party to social reform, as in the seminal Widows', Orphans' and Old Age Contributory Pensions Act of 1925; to extend the franchise, in the 1928 Equal Franchise Act, which lowered the voting age for women to twenty-one; economic rationalization, as in the 1926 Mining Industry Act; and a pragmatic accommodation with organized labour, in the Trade Disputes Act of 1927, which followed the 1926 General Strike. Talk of punitive anti-trade union legislation, in the air between 1918 and 1922, and which would have alienated working-class support, was shelved.

Defeat in 1929 owed less to a disenchantment with Baldwinian Conservatism, and its failures to secure disarmament or reduce unemployment, than to a revival of the Liberal Party. The number of three-cornered fights almost doubled, and there was a haemorrhaging of some Conservative support to the Liberals. The second Labour government, also a minority, lasted but two years. Financial crisis led to the formation of a National Government led by the former Labour Prime Minister Ramsay MacDonald, in which the Conservatives proved as dominant as they had been under the Lloyd George coalition of 1916–22. The Conservatives, fortunate to be out of office during the 1929–31 recession, cleverly exploited, with Neville Chamberlain to the fore, the Labour split in 1931.

Michael Bentley in Chapter 7 describes the puzzling period 1931–45 when the party was in government more as an administering force than a partisan political one. The National Government triumphed in the October 1931 general election, achieving 554 of the total of 615 MPs, with the Conservatives' share 473 MPs, their largest total this century. Bentley shows that with the need to appease the Simonite Liberals and National Labour largely in the past, 1935 marks the year when the National Government became more recognizably Tory, with Baldwin becoming Prime Minister on MacDonald's retirement in June 1935, and a Cabinet containing fifteen recognizable Tories out of a total of twenty-two. He sees the period from June 1935 until Baldwin's own retirement and succession of Neville Chamberlain in May 1937 as the peak of Tory ascendancy in the 1931–45 period. After 1937, Chamberlain's difficulties in dominating his party, and the crowding in of European affairs, increasingly obscured the Tory clarity of government. In May 1940 Churchill became Prime Minister, determined to put the interests and policy of the Conservative Party very much second to winning the war, and heading a new and genuinely coalition government, in which Labour (and Liberals) were key partners.

Did the National Governments take the country in a new interventionist direction, tackling social and economic problems in a constructive way, and anticipating the postwar settlement introduced by the Attlee government of 1945–51? Historians are still sharply divided on the subject. Much 'progressive' legislation was enacted certainly, including the Special Areas Act of 1934, the Education Act and extensions of national insurance in 1936, and cheap money was introduced in 1932 and agricultural marketing boards developed to alleviate some of the worst aspects of the depression that had beset Britain's farming industry between the wars. Bentley, however, is a sceptic in the debate about the radicalism of the National Government. He warns against seeing Conservatives in the National Government as being responsible for laying the foundations of the postwar welfare state and managed economy. Chamberlain, as Chancellor of the Exchequer from 1931 to 1937, was fiscally orthodox in the Gladstonian tradition: Keynesian policies, even if they had been a realistic option, Bentley argues, were not on the agenda. Measures were 'permissive' (in the Disraelian tradition) and minimalist, based on the means test. Concessions, such as help for unemployment in special areas, or restoration of unemployment benefits and salaries cut in 1931, were often to appease Liberal and Labour elements in the coalition. That said, the blend of free market economics with social reform was the brew that characterized Conservative policy for much of the postwar period.

On this reading, the Conservative Party in the first third of the century had begun, albeit in a piecemeal and grudging way, to adapt itself to the reality of a mass electorate. Many of the causes it championed were still overwhelmingly those of the nineteenth-century party: the monarchy (which

Baldwin had battled to save in the 1936 abdication crisis),
patriotism, the Church of England, agriculture and property.
Two pillars of the nineteenth-century party, however, had
come under attack in the interwar years, one fatally, the
other seeing merely the harbinger of change. Preservation
of the Union with all Ireland was sacrificed in the 1921
Act in which only Ulster was to remain within the United
Kingdom; Eire was to be kept in the Commonwealth, but
even that face-saver was rendered in effect meaningless in
the 1930s. The 1930s also witnessed the beginnings of progress towards the unpicking of the empire, with the growing
realization that India could not be kept indefinitely in the
empire against her will. The party's supporters meanwhile
had moved beyond the dwindling ranks of the landed classes
and the prosperous middle classes to include, at its height
in the 1930s, almost half the working class.

The party that lost the general election in 1945, and saw
its number of seats fall to its second worst total this century,
213, was one that had temporarily lost its way. Blamed for
failing to prepare the country adequately for war, the party's
organization was in disarray, its senior leadership unsyn-
chronized, and its domestic policies unconvincing. Recovery
after 1945 was rapid, however, with policy redefined under
the chairmanship of R. A. Butler at the Conservative
Research Department, candidate selection democratized in
the 'Maxwell-Fyfe' reforms, and the party organization
revamped under Lord Woolton (party chairman, 1946–55).
Power was almost clawed back in the general election of
February 1950, when the party secured 298 MPs, but ultimate success had to await the general election of October
1951, which the party won with a majority of seventeen
(despite polling 200,000 fewer votes than Labour).

John Turner in Chapter 8 describes what the Conservatives did with power which, with two general election
victories in 1955 and 1959 with increased majorities, they
retained until October 1964. These years saw the party
changing its policies more than in any other period in office.

No incremental fiddling with social policy here: the Conservatives significantly expanded the welfare state; financial orthodoxy at the Treasury was jettisoned in favour of Keynesian demand management policies in pursuit of economic growth; the empire was all but given away, and the party committed by its leadership to a future in Europe; nationalization of major parts of the economy was accepted as a fact of life, with the party in the early 1960s embarking on an unprecedented project of intervention in the economy; and the interests of property were extended to the ownership of even humble homes in the Conservatives' bid to build on their early attempts in the 1930s to create a property-owning democracy, and their desire to boost prosperity and possession of consumer durables.

Just as the evaporation of the Liberal vote in 1951 had brought the Conservatives to power, the revival of the Liberal vote helped to see the party off in a narrow general election contest in October 1964. The party replaced Sir Alec Douglas-Home (leader since 1963) with the non-public school Edward Heath in 1965, but no immediate dividends were to be had. The 1966 general election is the only occasion this century when the party has been out of power and the non-Conservative vote increased. The forced period in opposition gave Heath even longer to reformulate Conservative policy, and to enhance the party's organization. The fruit was victory in the June 1970 general election, with an overall majority of thirty.

Dennis Kavanagh analyses in Chapter 9 why the Heath government of 1970–74 failed to achieve its 'quiet revolution'. Heath set the party off in an elaborate direction. Trade unions were to be brought under a legal framework, the European Community was to be joined, and local government reformed. But Heath came up against powerful forces, both domestic and international, which knocked him off course. The record of the government easily fell prey to the increasingly pervasive New Right critique: unions were courted to a greater extent than practised by any Conser-

14

vative government before (or since); intervention in the economy reached unparalleled heights; social spending rose more than ever before; and new forms of bureaucracy were created in the NHS, local government and the civil service. Heath, it was alleged, did not even seem to particularly like the Conservative Party. Much of the New Right critique of Heath is overstated. As a premier, he is in more need of reappraisal than many. Nevertheless, his failure to court Tory MPs resulted in his ejection from the party leadership after he had lost the general elections of February and October 1974.

Mrs Thatcher, party leader from February 1975, and the saviour to whom the New Right turned, came like Heath from a grammar school background. She shared with her predecessor, too, little of the dread of radicalism that had characterized most Tory leaders from Pitt the Younger on. For Mrs Thatcher was a revolutionary, who saw her historic mission as a war on vested interests and structures that had accrued since the nineteenth century that impeded the operation of the free market. Her end, a minimal role for the state, was thus Tory, though her means of achieving it, radicalism, was not.

Ivor Crewe in Chapter 10 shows how her three consecutive election victories, unprecedented since Liverpool (1812–27), were made possible on between 42 and 44 per cent of the vote, less than the 48–50 per cent the party achieved in its three election victories of the 1950s. The distinctive features of the Thatcher era, he argues, namely her personal dominance over politics, her mission to change the political culture (which succeeded with the political classes but not with the general public) and her social and economic agenda, were the consequences, rather than the cause, of the Conservatives' electoral success.

Her determination to spread property ownership may not have created vast new legions of grateful Conservative voters, but it did alter the balance of interests in society. Ownership was encouraged in two ways: shareholding, which trebled from 7 per cent in 1979 to 25 per cent in 1991, and encouragement to home-ownership, which saw the proportion of households owning their own home rise from 52 per cent in 1979 to 66 per cent in 1989. Crewe estimates that the spread of home-ownership in the 1980s may have given the Conservatives an extra twenty to thirty seats, an effect that wore off in the recession of the early 1990s. A growing geographic divide was another feature of the Thatcher years. The Conservative Party had traditionally secured its support from the shires, the resorts and from the suburbs of large towns. The 1980s accelerated the trend of the party losing its MPs from large northern England cities and from Scotland: it became overwhelmingly the party of the prosperous south and south-east, though it has shown itself surprisingly resilient in rural areas in the north of England and the Midlands.

Crewe divides Major's premiership into two clear phases, 'Honeymoon' from 1990 to 1992, and 'Disintegration' from 1993. Black Wednesday, on 16 September 1992, when Britain left the European Exchange Rate Mechanism, was the turning-point. After that the Conservatives entered the deepest and longest electoral slump in modern British politics.

By the end of the twentieth century the Conservatives had certainly reached a turning-point. The traditional pillars of Conservative belief had all but withered away. Union with Ireland and empire had weakened their hold on the party before 1979, and were further watered down by the Downing Street Declaration of 1993 and the return to China of Hong Kong in 1997. Support for monarchy, the Church of England and the agricultural interests had become largely indistinct as defining characteristics of the Tories. Patriotism appeared (wrongly) to be under attack by the European Union policies of Heath and to a lesser extent Thatcher (until her Bruges speech *volte face*) and Major. Defence of existing constitutional arrangements had become a distinctive Tory position, albeit one which seemed increasingly isolated from the intellectual mainstream. Property remained the main element of continuity with the earlier party, but the property to be defended was no longer that of the landed gentry but of the manual worker who had bought his own council house.

Reasons for Conservative Dominance

The primary reason for Tory electoral success has been their pragmatism and passion for office, leading the party to be more adaptable to changes in voter preference than either of its two main rivals, the Liberals and Labour. The longest period in the wilderness was between 1846 and 1866, when the party seemed to have forgotten this instinct for office. Their brief tenures of power during this time, in 1852 and 1858–59, were caused not by positive Tory initiative but by the Whig coalitions falling apart. Periods out of office otherwise have not exceeded eleven years: 1830–41; 1880–85; 1905–15; 1929–31; 1945–51; 1964–70; 1974–79. Only two periods have seen the party out of office for longer than six years. The first came after the collapse of Liverpool's government following divisions over Catholic Emancipation and franchise reform and the party's shattering defeat in the post-Reform Act election of December 1832. It had still not formed itself as a cohesive parliamentary entity, and even then it was briefly in office for a few months in 1834–35. The second period, between December 1905 and May 1915, when Asquith invited the Conservatives to join his coalition government, was caused by the depth of the split over tariff reform, and all but came to an end after just four years, when in January 1910 the party won nearly 4 per cent more of the total vote than the Liberals, but received two fewer seats in the House of Commons. In opposition, the party has usually avoided recrimination, but quickly settled down purposefully to plotting strategy to regain office, seen conspicuously in the periods leading up to election victories in 1874, 1924, 1951, 1970 and 1979.

The Tories have often been seen as a party of consistent ideology and as defenders of core principles and interests. I am never convinced by this argument. What is remarkable about the Conservatives is not their ideological or interest tenacity but their willingness to jettison positions which no longer appeal: *laissez-faire*, the House of Lords, the Union with all Ireland, the empire, have all been abandoned when it suited the party, as to some extent have been the monarchy, the Church of England and the agricultural interest. Defence of private enterprise, private ownership and order are the only enduring Tory positions.

Only twice have opposition parties shown comparable adaptability. The Liberals reinvented themselves as New Liberals after 1906: the Great War and the Lloyd George–Asquith split after 1916 prevented the formula succeeding, though in all probability the Liberal adaptation came ten or fifteen years too late. Labour after its massive election defeat similarly reinvented itself under the leadership of Kinnock and Smith, finally blossoming forth as New Labour under Blair. It has yet to be shown whether New Labour will prove any more enduring than the limited success of the New Liberals.

The Tory Party's ability to appeal to all sectors of the electorate has been another important factor in their success. Peel's ministry from 1841 to 1846 saw important adaptations to industrialization and the middle-class voters enfranchised in 1832, introducing financial reforms to underpin Victorian capitalism, as well as legalizing trade unions and reducing some of the harsher barbs of employment in industry. Disraeli had shaped the Second Reform Act of 1867, and from 1874 to 1880 introduced important social reforms, especially in 1875. Too much can be claimed for the importance of these reforms in building up the body of grateful Tory voters; the changes were limited in scale, and had at best an uncertain effect on voting in subsequent elections. But they showed that the party was not content merely to react to events and to block reform, as appeared to be the case under the leadership of Derby from 1846 to 1868, Salisbury from 1885 to 1902 and Bonar Law from 1911 to 1921. Failure to offer a more positive platform impaired growth in the party's popularity under Derby and Bonar Law: Salisbury's inertia did not have a negative effect on election results because it was disguised by other factors, notably the cross-class appeal of empire and the Liberal Union split. Baldwin, Churchill (as peacetime premier from 1951 to 1955), Macmillan and Mrs Thatcher all governed in ways that broadened the appeal of the party in the light of economic and social changes in society. In the last analysis the Conservatives have been so successful because there have simply been greater numbers of potential voters for the Conservatives than for other parties during the twentieth century.

Comparative lack of schisms and the strength of party loyalty have meant that the Conservatives have rarely squandered their advantage. Only three major splits have occurred since 1832, over the repeal of the Corn Laws, tariff reform and Europe, each with considerable impact on the party's popularity. On the other hand, the party has capitalized on the splits of other parties; the Liberal Unionist windfall after 1886 helped keep the Tories in power for twenty years; the Lloyd George Liberals allowed the party to climb back to a position of dominance from 1916 to 1922; National Labour under MacDonald and the Simonite Liberals meant a winning electoral formula during 1931–40; and finally the split-off from Labour of the Social Democratic Party in 1981 helped Mrs Thatcher win handsome majorities in the 1983 and 1987 elections with lower percentages of the total vote than in 1979, when she won with a majority less than half the size. The third party vote tends to grow when the Tories are in office, as disillusioned middle classes, normally reluctant to cross the Rubicon and vote Labour, opt for the half-way house of the Liberals. The third party factor and split of the non-Conservative vote is a twentieth-century phenomenon. It has not always been the advantage it was in the 1980s; it damaged the party in elections after periods of Tory dominance in 1906 (aided by the Lib–Lab Pact), 1929, 1945, 1964 and 1974. Switches of the Liberal vote to the Conservatives after periods of Labour government may on the other hand have helped let the Tories back into government in 1924, 1951 and 1979.

Loyalty has traditionally permeated from the grass roots in the constituencies right up to the front bench. Less agitated by points of principle and procedure than certainly their Labour counterparts, and more given to feelings of deference for the leadership, Tory Party activists have for much of the period been content to toe the line. Where strong feelings at the top have broken the surface, as over the Fourth Party in the 1880s, the coalition from 1921 to 1924, India and appeasement in the 1930s, Suez in 1956 or Mrs Thatcher's monetarist economic policies in the 1980s, MPs and ministers have not crossed the floor to the other side. Some free-trade opponents of tariff reform did so in the 1900s, but they are the exception, as are opponents of the party's policy on Europe in the 1990s.

The Tories then are a party of instincts (above all for power) rather than of ideology. Many of their instincts chime naturally, indeed have been shaped by, those of the majority of the electorate. The party's dislike of extremism and preference for gradualism and moderation is one such popular instinct. The leadership behave in an upright and responsible manner: only in 1912–14 over Ulster can they be said to have acted in an unconstitutional manner. They appeal to common interest and national unity, and seem the natural choice for voters in time of national crisis or uncertainty, as during the First World War, the anxious 1930s or during the Cold War. Conservative leaders, whether Salisbury, Baldwin, Churchill or Macmillan, ooze reassurance: the front bench have often appeared 'safer' than whatever the opposition may happen to offer. The party's innate patriotism is another such instinct, initially stolen from Palmerston by Disraeli in the 1870s. From then until the 1940s it was clothed in the mantle of empire, as seen in the great imperial rallies in Victoria's Golden and Diamond Jubilees in 1887 and 1897, or in Noël Coward's 1931 hit musical *Cavalcade*. After the 1950s, patriotism effortlessly lost its imperial dimension, and became identified instead with strength in defence and resolute action in the face of foreign aggression, as in the 1982 Falklands War.

Organizational superiority has been apparent for much of the last two hundred years, and especially since the development of mass organization from the 1870s. This has meant the party has mostly been better able than other parties to deliver its voters. Through the agency of highly able organization men like J. E. Gorst, R. W. E. Middleton, J. C. C. Davidson and Lord Woolton, the Primrose League at the end of the nineteenth century, a willing party membership that peaked in the 1950s, and a greater number of professional party agents in constituencies than opposition parties could field, the Conservatives have usually been better than the Liberals or Labour at first enticing and then delivering voters in elections. From 1841, the party's first post-Reform Act election victory, the party has rarely been outdone at general elections in the strength of organization: this may well have tipped the result in close general elections as in 1874, 1895, 1935, 1951, 1970 and 1992, where superior organization in marginal constituencies could swing the result. More effective mastery of the arts of electioneering is also a Conservative asset, seen in a number of guises: opting to hold elections at harvest time when agricultural labourers would be less likely to cast their votes; being quicker to capitalize on the new techniques of radio, film, television, advertising agencies, opinion polling, direct mail, computers and information technology; and exploiting the windfall benefits from women, as party helpers from the 1880s and as voters after 1918, to plural voting with university seats before 1949.

Finally, the party has benefited from the support of the wealthiest elements in Britain: landowners in the nineteenth century, overlapping with support from business, finance and the professions from the end of the century, and the growing middle class in the twentieth century. The Liberals and Labour have not been so fortunate in their backers: Nonconformists were a dwindling asset for the former, and the trade unions a mixed blessing for the latter. The 1920s and 1980s in particular saw an anti-union vote that helped the Conservatives. Conservative backers in contrast have afforded the party the steady flow of educated and socialized recruits, expertise on a wide variety of subjects from law to finance, and above all have kept the party's coffers consistently fuller than those of other parties.

None of these factors will ensure that the twenty-first century will resemble the twentieth rather than the nineteenth century. The key factor will be which party is able to adapt more convincingly to the new social, economic and technological changes. With Labour moving into the centre ground, stealing many of the clothes and the appeal of the Tories, in a way that neither the New Liberals nor Labour from 1900 to the 1980s ever threatened seriously to do, the Conservative Party faces as big a challenge as during 1846–66 or 1906–24, which is to redefine itself as a party with a distinctive set of policies, effective organization and a defined set of interests to represent. Adaptability, not ideology, is the defining characteristic of the Tory Party. The quicker it adapts to the changed social, economic and technological challenge of the early twenty-first century, the more likely it will continue its natural position of dominance of the British body politic.

William Pitt the Younger
(*Mansell Collection*)

CHAPTER ONE

1783–1806

Jeremy Black

Problems of Definition

Definitions are always a problem, but those set by the sub-title for this book are worse than most. Today it may be clear what is meant by Tory, party and power, but none of those terms is clear for the period 1783–1806. They were not clear to contemporaries and the terms, as used in the period, are not clear today. That they were not clear to contemporaries, that terms such as Tory were controversial and the practice of government, not least issues of party and power, were much debated, reflects the degree to which the very rationale and definitions of political action were far from rigid and the extent to which these in part consti-tuted issues of political contention. This essay will consider the ambivalence of the term 'Tory' and the distinctive mean-ing of the 'Pittite' tradition in the late eighteenth and early nineteenth centuries. It will also assess the combination of influences affecting the formation and end of ministries, especially the strengths and weaknesses of the Crown; and the degree to which both 'government' and 'opposition' operated within a shared political tradition.

An immediate working definition is provided by the notion that William Pitt the Younger's first administration, 1783–1801, the Addington ministry, 1801–4, and Pitt's second administration 1804–6, comprised a period of Tory hegemony spanning the years between the Fox–North ministry of 1783 and the 'Ministry of All the Talents' of 1806–7. The fact that many in these ministries were uncomfortable with the designation 'Tory', however, is important, for the process by which the term ceased to be one of abuse and became, instead, shorthand for a nexus of loyalties and allegiances, and a proud and self-conscious sense of political continuity, was a gradual one. Pitt called himself an independent Whig. Few MPs described themselves as Tories before 1832, the year of the First Reform Act, and a recent discussion of conservative attitudes in this period notes that 'before 1819, few among the right-wing newspapers, journals and periodicals openly avowed themselves "Tory"', and that the process by which the term came to be used as the principal 'descriptive term for the party of the Right' was slow and hesitant.[1] Another problem with the use of the term Tory to describe the government in the later 1780s is that the supporters of Lord North, First Lord of the Treasury 1770–82, who have been described as Tory, had aligned themselves in opposition to the ministry. Even the term 'right-wing' is problematic.

Aside from supporting the influence of the Crown, Toryism as a position had particularly pronounced religious connotations in an age when religion reflected, defined and constituted the prime instance of ideological commitments. As in the early eighteenth century when there had been a coherent Tory Party, Toryism was the party of the Church of England in so far as there was one, and Tories were identified with the defence of the Anglican position. Pitt, like his father, William Pitt the Elder, and the latter's protégé, William, 2nd Earl of Shelburne, had been associated with the Dissenters, but became, perforce, an Anglican champion, defending the Test and Corporation Acts, which enforced Anglican privilege in public life, against Dissenter attempts to repeal them in 1787–90. While forfeiting much support from Dissenters and other reformers, Pitt won considerable Anglican backing. Toryism under Pitt's government was identified with the Church of England and with opposition to Dissent and Catholicism. Anti-Catholic bishops were elevated.

Tory perceptions of the nature of authority drew on Anglican tradition, especially with reference to support for legally constituted authority. This tradition had been confused after 1688 by the crisis over the nature of such authority, in Church and State, that followed the so-called Glorious Revolution of 1688 when the legal monarch, the Catholic James II (1685–88), was replaced. Thereafter, as long as the Jacobite movement for the return of the male line of the Stuarts had been strong, Toryism had been divided. Originally a political tendency that arose in defence of Charles II (1660–85), order and the Church of England in the early 1680s, in response to Whig pressures for the exclusion of the future James II from the succession and for more rights for Dissenters, Toryism found it difficult to cope with the consequences of the Revolution Settlement. Some Tories were prepared to accept that the legally constituted authority was now that of William III (1689–1702), but others regarded him as a latter-day Cromwell and were prepared to conspire for his overthrow.

This tension remained strong until the collapse of the Jacobite option after the defeat of Charles Edward Stuart at Culloden in 1746. It did not, however, prevent the development of a Tory parliamentary politics opposed to the Whigs. This was the basic pattern of national politics in the first half of the century, but it collapsed in 1746–62 as Tory cohesion and identity were seriously compromised: Tory support was wooed first by Whig ministers and then by George III (1760–1820). In the early 1760s the Tories atomized, joining a variety of political groups, including the government establishment in the Commons.

The Power of the Monarch and the Formation of the Pitt Ministry 1783–84

The issue of definition is not an idle one because it relates directly to those of the ideology of the ministries already mentioned, the interests they represented most closely and the reasons for their success and failure. The government was of course the King's government, the ministers appointed by him. Charles James Fox, a Whig stalwart of opposition, felt able to tell his nephew Lord Holland in 1804, 'There is not a power in Europe, no not even [Napoleon] Bonaparte's that is so unlimited', as monarchical authority in Britain.[2] It is certainly possible to answer the points raised in the first sentence of this paragraph by referring to George III, to argue that he was responsible for ministerial changes, most obviously the fall of the Fox–North ministry in 1783 and its replacement by that of Pitt, and, subsequently, the fall of Pitt in 1801 over Catholic Emancipation.[3] It is possible to present the crucial interest and ideology of the Pitt government in terms of the Crown, and indeed to see its rationale in terms of the rallying around Crown, Church and Country that characterized so much of conservative thought in Europe in response to the French Revolution and the subsequent rise of Napoleon.

George greatly distrusted the Fox–North ministry: he saw it as factious and was directly responsible for its replacement in December 1783 by an untried team around the 24-year-old Pitt, who lacked a majority in the House of Commons. George's actions, which were regarded by some as unconstitutional, were countered by a collective resignation of office-holders, similar to the step that had forced George II to abandon his attempt to create a ministry under the unpopular Earl Granville (Lord Carteret) in February 1746. The unsuccessful attempt of the new ministers to reach an agreement with Fox on 21 December 1783 and the resignation the following day of Earl Temple, both Home and Foreign Secretary, in order to lessen the danger of impeach-

28

ment for his crucial role in the fall of the previous government – destabilizing it by conveying the King's opposition
– were evidence of weakness, though it has also been argued
that the resignation was brought about by Pitt's desire to
distance his new administration from the dubious
methods by which it came into existence. On the morning
of 23 December George saw himself as 'on the edge of a
precipice'.[4]

Though a Cabinet had been formed by that evening, the
government was still weak after the Christmas recess. Having lost two Commons divisions on 12 January 1784, Pitt
thought of resigning. Distressed to find the Commons 'much
more willing to enter into any intemperate resolutions of
desperate men than I could have imagined', George III
characteristically reiterated his hostility to 'this faction', his
readiness to struggle against them until the end of his life
and his willingness to abdicate if they gained office. On 23
January Pitt's bill for the government of British India, a
crucial and contentious piece of legislation, was also
defeated. Four days later the ministry was referred to by
Lord George Germain as 'this no government'. There is evidence that Pitt did intend to dissolve Parliament and call a
general election immediately after his appointment in
December 1783, but it was discovered that the necessary
parliamentary timetable did not allow time for a new Parliament to meet and pass the Supplies and Mutiny Bill before
the end of the financial year in March 1784. Therefore Pitt
had to hang on and fight it out despite his weak position
in the Commons.[5]

Despite the King's determination, it was unclear whether
Pitt's tenure of office would be much longer than Temple's.
There was an element of exaggeration in Fox's comment
on the 'unlimited' nature of royal authority. Though George
III could be important in supporting and ending ministries,
not even the support of the Crown could save the Bute
(1762–63), North (1770–82), Shelburne (1782–85) and
Addington (1801–4) governments. In 1784 it was unclear

that the same would not also be true for Pitt's ministry. An unsuccessful attempt by independent MPs to create a broad-based government of national union, a frequently expressed aspiration during the century, gave Pitt breathing space in early February, and his position was further improved by a swelling tide of favourable public opinion, indicated by a large number of addresses from counties and boroughs, with over 50,000 signatures in total, in favour of George III and the free exercise of the royal prerogative in choosing ministers. They also reflected hostility to what was seen as the opportunism of the Fox–North coalition. George's confidence in public support and his view that a Commons majority was not crucial were reflected when he wrote of

> the present strange phenomenon, a majority not exceeding 30 in the House of Commons thinking that justifies the stopping the necessary supplies when the House of Lords by a majority of near two to one and at least that of the People at large approve of my conduct and see as I do that not less is meant than to render the Crown and the Lords perfect cyphers; but it will be seen that I will never submit.

The formation of the Pitt government had not therefore ended the crisis created by the poor relations between George III and the Fox–North political groups, but it had changed its nature, made it more public and united monarch and government. The more public nature of the transformed crisis led to an upsurge in popular interest and this focused on support for George and thus his new ministers. That so many of the latter were little known was very advantageous: they lacked the experience of office that could lead to political charges of opportunism and inconsistency, both of which harmed North. The historian and former MP Edward Gibbon referred to the country as being 'governed by a set of most respectable boys, who were at school half a dozen years ago'.[6]

Pitt was further aided by the active support of many peers, not least their influence with dependants in the Commons; and by the uncertainty of his opponents as to whether they should use Parliament's power to refuse supplies in order to force a change of government. The House of Lords still played a major role in the political system, albeit a lesser one than a century earlier. It posed fewer problems of management than the Commons. The 'Party of the Crown', composed of archbishops, bishops, royal household officers, Scottish representative peers and newly created or promoted peers, provided a consistent basis for the ministerial majority. Thus, a chamber that had posed considerable problems of management during the reign of Anne became the most quiescent of the two Houses of Parliament. Governments took care to ensure that they had effective spokesmen in the Lords, and patronage was applied in a consistent fashion to unite the 'Party of the Crown'.[7]

The backing of the Lords lessened the severity of the political crisis in 1784 and obliged Fox to concentrate his efforts on the Commons. There, Fox's bluff was called over the voting of supplies and he also suffered from a leakage of Northites both before and during the 1784 election. The unstable nature of the Fox–North alignment was revealed in 1784. Not only were there important tensions within it, but it was also weakened by failure and the loss of office and patronage, the last especially serious for the Northites. Pitt's success in gaining the initiative in Parliament helped lead to the turnaround of public opinion in his favour by the time of the election.

By 5 March 1784 Fox's majority in the Commons was down to one, and Pitt felt able to face a general election: Parliament was dissolved on 25 March and the elections, many of which were contested on national political grounds,[8] were very favourable for the ministry. The hostile William Eden referred to a 'frenzy of the people'.[9] The 'popular' aspect of the 1784 elections was clear to contemporaries.

George III and the Pitt Ministry

Secure in the backing of the King and both houses of Parliament, and with clear popular backing, the new government now appeared stable. Even so, ministries that won general elections could fall soon after: the Duke of Newcastle's overwhelming success in the election of 1754 and Lord North's success in 1780 did not prevent their fall from office in the face of adverse military and domestic political circumstances in 1756 and 1782, though Newcastle still had control of both Houses of Parliament when he resigned. Many seats were not contested on national political grounds or at all. An absence or loss of royal favour could also be fatal to ministries, as Godolphin had discovered in 1710, Newcastle in 1762, Grenville in 1765, Rockingham in 1766 and Fox–North in 1783. Yet ministries that had won an election were likely to be longer lasting than those that had not had an opportunity to do so. The normal pattern for governmental formation was appointment and then election, and the creation of the Pitt ministry conformed to this.

Thus the fundamental feature of the Tory, if indeed such it was, ministry of the 1780s was that it was very much a royal creation (as was the Whig ministry of 1714). Its ideology and interest were united in serving a notion of stable, national government. George had realized the role he had sought as a 'patriot king'. His conservative and often moralistic conviction of his crucial constitutional role and preference for stability were, thanks to the signs of popular support for royal policy and the royal position in 1784, married to a greater awareness of the possible popular resonance of the Crown. George felt that the monarch could reach out, beyond antipathy and factional self-interest on the part of politicians, to a wider, responsible, responsive and royalist public opinion.

Much of the politics of the succeeding years can be understood in terms of George's views and changing attitudes. George reflected the stronger emphasis on a monarchical, as opposed to a 'balanced', constitution that characterized the 1790s. George's attitude also made religious issues even more central in the politics of the period than they might otherwise have been. This was true not only in the political sense: he also took theology seriously. George's firmness, not to say rigidity, contrasted with the more flexible attitude of his non-Anglican predecessors, George II, George I, William III and, arguably, Charles II. It also helped to focus the defence of order, hierarchy and continuity in a period of revolutionary and radical threats much more on religion than might otherwise have been the case, though a religious foundation to English electoral behaviour has recently been emphasized, and the rift between Anglican and Dissenter has been regarded as essential both to the continued nature of local political divisions and to the configuration of the national division between the ministry of Pitt the Younger and the Whig opposition. The revival of Toryism as a coherent political position was associated with the defence of the Church of England. Religion has also been seen as playing a central role in political motivation in Ireland and Scotland.[10]

George III opposed the extension of full political rights to Catholics in Ireland or Britain. This helped to precipitate Pitt's resignation in 1801 and the fall of the Grenville ministry in 1807. George was motivated not only by his religious convictions, but also by the argument that the position of the Church of England rested on fundamental parliamentary legislation. Any repeal would also thus challenge the constitutional safeguards that were similarly founded and secured. It was not therefore surprising that Edmund Burke's emphasis, in his *Reflections on the Revolution in France* (1790), on British continuity as contrasted with French discontinuity found favour with George III. He saw his duty as entailing resistance to radicalism at home and French atheism abroad and expected his ministry to further these objectives.

An essential unity of purpose between monarch and ministers characterized politics after the formation of the Pitt ministry, and played a major role in the stabilization of government, though successful policies, such as Pitt's furtherance of commercial growth and fiscal reform, also played an important role. The American War of Independence (1775–83) had more than doubled the national debt, but Pitt's prudent financial management and reforms, and a dramatic growth in trade, not least with America, stabilized the situation. Like Sir Robert Walpole in 1720–42, Henry Pelham and Lord North, Pitt understood the crucial importance of sound finances. The years 1784–90 saw a restoration of confidence in the British system.

There were of course difficulties between monarch and prime minister. George III did not approve of Pitt's support for parliamentary reform in 1785. Pitt proposed to extinguish thirty-six borough seats with small electorates. The electors were to be compensated financially, and the seats transferred to London and the English counties. Pitt also suggested the enfranchisement of copyholders and certain categories of leaseholders, and a system of local polling centres. These were scarcely radical steps. They would not have led to any major increase in the size of the electorate or of the House of Commons. George III, however, was opposed to constitutional change and most parliamentarians shared his views. The proposals were defeated by 248 to 174 on 18 April 1785. Pitt was careful not to push this divisive issue after it had been defeated, and this caution helped to align his ministry with conservative opinion and to create a gulf between Pitt and political and religious reformers.

George III also did not approve of Pitt's opposition to the slave trade in 1804–6. Pitt was suspicious of ministers who were very close to the King and unwilling to follow a lead, especially the Lord Chancellor, Lord Thurlow, whom he forced the King to part with in 1792.[11] Yet, there was fundamental agreement – in the 1780s on the need for national revival after the loss of the American colonies in the recent American War of Independence and the concomitant domestic problems – and subsequently in the 1790s for action to prevent French hegemony in Western Europe and Paineite radicalism at home. There was no rift comparable to that between George II and the Pelhams during the mid-1740s crisis caused by war with France and the Jacobite challenge in Britain.

This was as well because war with France and defeats created major strains. Pitt discovered that leadership in wartime was considerably more difficult than in the period of reform and regeneration he had earlier helped to orchestrate. The cost and economic disruption of the war pressed hard throughout society, leading to inflation, the collapse of the gold standard under which paper currency was met by the Bank of England (1797), the introduction of income tax (1799), the stagnation of average real wages and widespread hardship, especially in the famine years of 1795–6 and 1799–1801. The real wages of Lancashire cotton weavers fell by more than a half in 1792–99. There was a nationalist dimension to radicalism in Ireland, where there was a major, though unsuccessful, rebellion in 1798, and also, to a lesser extent, in Scotland. Radicals found their activities prohibited or limited, while trade unions were hindered, though not disbanded, by the Combination Acts of 1799 and 1800 which made it illegal for employees to combine in seeking for improved pay or conditions.

The Changing Position of the Crown

Although it is possible to think of the years from the outbreak of war with revolutionary France in 1793 as a continuation in political terms of the previous decade, there were important changes, reminders of the extent to which it is mistaken to think of the British *ancien régime* in terms of easy continuity. These changes meant that whereas George III's resistance to Catholic Emancipation had been successful, George IV (1820–30) had, despite bitter hostility, to accept it in 1829. This reflected different political circumstances as well as the contrasting character of the two monarchs, but also a shift in the position of the monarchy. Long-term trends lessened its executive role, despite George III's growing popularity with public opinion from the 1783– 84 crisis on. The growth of business and the increased scope of government lessened the ability of one man, whether monarch or minister, to master the situation. This helped to encourage the development of the Cabinet. The long-lasting ministries of Pitt (1783–1801, 1806–6) and Lord (the 2nd Earl of) Liverpool (1812–27) were especially important in this process, although developments in the conventions of Cabinet were more significant during the Liverpool era than during the Pittite one. The discussions and decisions of the inner core of ministers, the Cabinet council, became more formal and less ad hoc. Collective responsibility – a sense of common identity as a ministry rather than as the individual choices of a monarch – and loyalty to the leading minister increased, and this strengthened the Cabinet's ties with that minister and enhanced his power with reference to the monarch: Cabinet unanimity was a potential weapon against the Crown, and had been employed in 1746 to prevent the appointment of Granville and in 1782 over American independence. Conversely, a lack of Cabinet unity could strengthen the King's position with respect to the Cabinet, as with the clash between George III and Pitt over Catholic Emancipation in 1801. In addition, royal influence and patronage declined with the abolition of sinecures, the diminishing influence of Court favourites, and the growing accountability of ministers to Parliament.

Personal factors were very important to this process: the breakdown of George III's health in 1788 (the basis of the Alan Bennett play and subsequent 1994 film *The Madness of King George*), and the consequent Regency Crisis of 1788– 89, the subsequent slackening of his grasp, and his later illnesses; the weakness and lack of interest displayed by George IV; the impact of Pitt's longevity in office. As a consequence, even with strains evident over policy and patronage after 1794, greater Cabinet cohesion and influence and consistent united Cabinet control of policy-making were more a feature from the 1790s than of the 1780s.

The monarchy, or perhaps the *image* of the monarchy, was reconstructed in important ways in the later years of George III's reign. The patriotism of war and the King's virtual disengagement from day-to-day politics combined fruitfully to facilitate an emphasis less on the reality and more on the ceremony and symbol of monarchy, as with the Jubilee celebrations of 1809. In this sense the precondition of the creation of a popular monarchy was the perceived decline in the Crown's political authority, whereas classic *ancien régime* monarchy had combined the executive role and ceremony. Authority was increasingly very much that of the government, rather than simply the monarch, and within the government the executive role of the monarch, particularly in the initiation of policy, declined. This was an uneven, hesitant process, but it can be seen as beginning under George III. Nevertheless, George III played a crucial role in keeping Fox out of office in 1804.

The Collapse of 'Tory' Dominance in 1806

If the King played a central role in the beginning of Pitt's ministry this was less the case with the ending of 'Tory' dominance in 1806. Pitt died on 23 January 1806 and the ministry collapsed. George III sought to form 'the [new] ministry out of the old remnants' of that of Pitt and to appoint the Home Secretary, Lord Hawkesbury, as Pitt's successor as first lord of the Treasury and head of the ministry. Hawkesbury (1770–1828) was the son of Charles Jenkinson, 1st Earl of Liverpool, long a minister close to the King. Hawkesbury had the necessary experience for high office. An MP from 1790 until raised to the peerage by Addington in 1803, Hawkesbury was an able parliamentary speaker who had supported Pitt until they differed over Catholic Emancipation. He had served as foreign secretary under Addington (1801–4), before being transferred to the Home Office and made leader of the House of Lords in 1804. Hawkesbury had played a major role in bringing Addington into the Pitt ministry. Had he enjoyed the support of leading politicians and the backing of Parliament in 1806, Hawkesbury would have been a good choice as prime minister, and indeed, as 2nd Earl of Liverpool, was subsequently to be a longstanding one.

However, meeting late on the evening of 24 January, the Cabinet decided that it could not undertake the government as George proposed. He was told so on 25 January by Hawkesbury, the Lord Chancellor, Lord Eldon, and the President of the Board of Control, Viscount Castlereagh.[12] The majority of the Cabinet saw little prospect of holding off opposition attacks and the Lord President of the Council, the Duke of Portland, advised George to turn to Lord Grenville and the opposition. Grenville was certain 'that nothing can be done unless with the fullest concurrence of Mr. Fox, and with the abandonment of all idea of exclusion', while Earl Fitzwilliam, heir to the tradition of the Rockinghamite Whigs, welcomed the prospect of a new administration 'founded on principles truly congenial with the spirit of the constitution'. Fox, whom George did not want in the Cabinet, argued that the King 'cannot patch up an Administration', and on 31 January Grenville had an audience with King George and presented him with the plan for a new ministry.[13] The King had to make do with making Hawkesbury Pitt's successor as Warden of the Cinque Ports, a sinecure worth the substantial sum of £3,000 per annum.

This rapid collapse of 'Tory' dominance was not the consequence of any electoral defeat. The 1802 general election had been largely placid and had led to no significant changes. The Foxite opposition remained in a clear minority. Under the Septennial Act, no other election was necessary until 1809. Instead, divisions within the ministerial ranks were crucial in sapping the position of Pitt's ministry prior to his death. Pitt's resignation in 1801 had splintered the Pittite 'party', or the Tories, if such a term is to be used, for, instead of being replaced by an opposition party, the policies of which would maintain Tory unity, in other words a government in which the Foxite Whigs were prominent, Pitt was succeeded by Henry Addington, formerly speaker of the House of Commons, at the head of a weak ministry. Pitt maintained a position of theoretically benevolent neutrality because he did not wish to oppose the King's choice of minister, but in 1804 changed his position and forced his way back into office. George would have liked to keep Addington as prime minister, but he had insufficient support in the Commons. In the meanwhile Grenville, Pitt's former foreign secretary, angered by the terms of Addington's peace with France, terms negotiated by Hawkesbury, had gone into opposition in November 1801. He wrote to Addington the previous month,

> I feel that public duty will compel me to express in Parliament my deep regret at the manner in which both those negotiations have been terminated, and my conviction of the absolute necessity of providing by all possible means of precaution and preparation against the new and imminent dangers to which I fear the country is exposed . . . nothing but a sense of indispensable duty could have led me to this separation from those for whom I entertain sentiments of friendship and regard and whose measures I was most sincerely desirous of supporting.[14]

By the time Pitt replaced Addington, weakening him by parliamentary attacks in the spring of 1804, Grenville and the 'New Opposition' had joined Fox and the 'Old Opposition'. Pitt's promise that he would not raise the issue of Catholic Emancipation ensured that he could not win the support of Grenville, who was firmly in favour of the measure, while George III's determination to exclude from office Fox, whom he saw as an opponent of necessary measures against France, further limited the chances of winning Grenville's support. Grenville rejected Pitt's approach:

> we rest our determination solely on our strong
> sense of the impropriety of our becoming parties to
> a system of government, which is to be formed, at
> such a moment as the present on a principle of
> Exclusion ... An opportunity now offers such as
> this country has seldom seen, for giving to its
> government, in a moment of peculiar difficulty, the
> full benefit of the services of all those who by the
> public voice and sentiment are judged most capable
> of contributing to its prosperity and safety.

Grenville hoped that Pitt would be able to persuade George III to this end,[15] but he was to be disappointed. In addition, Pitt's treatment of Addington left many of the latter's supporters hostile, though others joined the new ministry. On 18 June 1804 the government won a key vote in a full Commons by a majority of only forty-two, a reflection of the consequences of the splintering of the Pittite 'party' of the 1790s.

Pitt had revealed his views on the disadvantage of opposition when, while still out of office, he rejected Grenville's proposal for action in early 1804:

> The immediate effect of an active opposition, will
> be to harass a government not very strong nor vig-
> orous in itself, and in a situation of the country
> the most critical with the constant distraction of
> parliamentary warfare. Such a line though con-
> ducted by the first talents and abilities will, I am
> confident, not be supported by any strength of
> numbers in Parliament nor by public opinion. It will
> therefore have very little chance of accomplishing
> its object of changing the administration, and cer-
> tainly none of doing so in time to afford the country
> the benefit of abler counsels to meet the difficulties
> it will in the mean while certainly aggravate; and

even if sooner or later, it should make a change
necessary, I am afraid that instead of leading to the
establishment of a comprehensive administration
(such as you describe) it will tend to render the
attainment of that object more difficult if not impossible. Whatever unfavourable impression may at any
time have existed in the highest quarter [George III]
towards any of the parties engaged in such a system,
will of course be strengthened and confirmed; and
the natural consequence will be a determination
even in case of a change being found necessary, to
put if possible a negative on them, in forming a new
government.

Having drawn attention to the crucial interplay of royal
choice, ministerial composition and political action, Pitt
added that the situation was very difficult for him, 'as nothing is more probable than that a call might then be made
upon me which I should feel it impossible to decline, and that
I should have no means either of forming that comprehensive
government, which I agree with you in thinking most desirable, or of obtaining the assistance of those with whom from
public and private feelings it has been the greatest happiness
to me, to act during almost the whole of my political life'.[16]

Once in office, Pitt sought to broaden his support by bringing in Addington, promoted to the peerage as Viscount Sidmouth, as Lord President of the Council in January 1805.
However, the new alliance was not a close one, and on 8
April 1805 Sidmouth attacked Pitt over the alleged corruption of his ally and friend Henry Dundas, Lord Melville,
when formerly treasurer of the navy. The Commons
decision for the impeachment of Melville led to his being
driven from office as first lord of the Admiralty. Melville
was forced to resign from the Privy Council in May and an
attempt was then made to impeach him. George, 1st Marquis of Buckingham wrote to his brother Grenville about
the affair:

the pistol put to Mr. Pitt's head by Lord Sidmouth, and nothing could exceed the anxiety or exertions of the latter all yesterday to secure the prosecution by the Attorney General . . . the violence of Pitt's friends against Addington cannot be described . . . the universal conviction that Lord Sidmouth was to have been removed by Pitt if the question of prosecution had been successfully resisted and it is now said that he Pitt means immediately to resign.

The impeachment failed, but Sidmouth's motion for a criminal prosecution won the support of the Foxites and the Grenvillites, and the Pittites were defeated by 238 to 229.[17] This public breach led to Sidmouth's resignation from the ministry and soon after he was cautiously responsive to an approach from Fox. When Pitt died the ministry was still in a weak state, facing an assertive, albeit far from united, opposition in Parliament and with its foreign policy in ruins after Napoleon's victory over Britain's allies, Austria and Russia, at Austerlitz on 2 December. Four days later Austria signed an armistice and on 26 December the Treaty of Pressburg, accepting French hegemony in Germany. George Canning wrote of Pitt on 9 January 1806, 'He is very ill and the Continent worse'.[18]

The Nature of 'Party' in this Period

Pitt suffered because of the nature of 'party' in this period. Parties were essentially connections, held together by shared objectives but not large enough on their own to dominate the Commons. To do so it was necessary for several connections to combine and/or for one connection to impress the independent country gentlemen who composed a fair percentage of the MPs. The government side in the mid-1780s has recently been described as comprising 'Pitt's personal friends and followers, a number of small supporting factions, and the court and administration party, backed by substantial numbers of independents who distrusted Fox and believed that in normal circumstances the king's ministers should receive the necessary support from the Commons'.[19] This alignment had been given a measure of cohesion by long years in office, rather as Walpole and the Pelhams had moulded the 'Old Corps Whigs' in 1720–54, but it lacked the stability of a modern British political party. Such a remark might appear risible in light of the divisions that the latter can be subject to, but in the eighteenth century parties tended to lack an identifiable national leadership, an organized constituent membership and a recognized corpus of policy and principle around which to cohere and which could serve to link local supporters to national activity. It would be mistaken to treat eighteenth-century parties as unsatisfactory anticipations of modern equivalents and, equally, it is foolish to search for modern criteria of political success or failure, such as depleted party finance or organization in disarray, in this period. Some modern criteria, most obviously perceived success in office, can be applied, but others cannot. Instead, connection and personal relationships played major roles in influencing political divisions, far more so than at the close of the twentieth century. Thus, for example, in spite of political uneasiness between them from time to time, Grenville could rely on unquestioning loyalty from his brother and nephew, Buckingham and Temple, respectively. In contrast, a 'preoccupation with personal rivalries hampered Pitt's friends throughout' 1806.[20]

One of the major difficulties of the subject arises from the complex intermingling of personal attachments and rivalries with political beliefs or ideologies. Both governments and oppositions were mixed in their composition and individual attitudes varied greatly, an important aspect of the extent to which the 'unreformed' political system, as that which preceded the First Reform Act of 1832 is somewhat misleadingly described, was far from static or characterized by simple divides. For example, although usually seen as politically opposed, there is a real sense in which both Grenville and Grey were as 'conservative' (Grey hated the radicals) as Liverpool and Canning, especially after 1806 when Fox was no longer there to influence Grey. The division in the ministries after 1806 between those pro- and anti-Catholic Emancipation was such that after 1812 it had to be an 'open' question in the Cabinet. Liverpool was as firm in opposing royal interference in policy and patronage as any 'Whig' would have been. It could be argued that the crisis over parliamentary reform in 1830–32 marked the real beginning of a two-party division based on ideas rather than personalities, though the origins of these party divisions clearly existed before 1806 and in the 1800s there was a political division emerging between conservative Tories, such as Eldon, Sidmouth and Portland, and the Pittite–Grenvillites, including Dundas and Grey. Issues like Catholic Emancipation were obviously important, though it has probably been over-emphasized in Grenville's case. Yet it was also necessary to construct a ministry which could encompass four or five ministers with a significant following in the Commons, to add to the 'natural' Tories. Percival's offer of a place in the Cabinet to Grenville in 1809 was clearly motivated by this.

In addition, it is unclear how far it is appropriate to seek a definition of political alignments and Toryism at the national level and, instead, whether more effort should not be devoted to county, borough, local and university contexts. Alignments at such a level might be framed in national terms, but the picture is less coherent than that presented by an emphasis on parliamentary and ministerial politics. The politics of the period can be understood in terms of a development of earlier eighteenth-century political forms and models. Certainly the Grenvillites, who by 1809 had a Commons following of about fifty to sixty MPs, were as much a connection of family, landowners, bishops and academics as, say, the Whig followers in 1714.

Liverpool's ministry was a crucial period of political transformation: royal incursion into politics was neutralized under the Regency and in George IV's reign; economic and social affairs became polarized and reform of Church and Parliament emerged as 'issues' on which politicians such as Grey could divide from their erstwhile allies.

The failures of the Pittite government contain some important lessons. First, as with other ministries, there is a clear reminder that while success can lead politicians to temper their rivalries and can help in the postponement of problems, it is difficult to overcome the rivalries and they and related problems tend to revive when the general situation becomes more adverse, not least when a sense of confidence in clear leadership and purpose is lost. Thus, there had been important rivalries within Pitt's ministry in the 1780s and 1790s, but they had been contained, whereas the political circumstances of the following decade made them far more serious. The sense of success was gone and the ministry no longer seemed to have much initiative, let alone to be in control of the political agenda.

Foreign Policy and Leadership Factors

It would be inappropriate to treat this issue as a simple function of success and failure. Indeed, the crisis of the late 1790s was far more serious than that of 1805–6. If in 1805 invasion was feared, in 1797 part of the navy had mutinied and in 1798 there had been rebellion in Ireland and French forces had landed there. This offers another suggestion, namely that a decline, or at least tempering, of the apparent threat posed by opponents – France and its supporters in the British Isles – led to a weakening in government cohesion or, at least, an uncertainty of purpose. There had never been complete agreement within government ranks as to how best to deal with revolutionary France and domestic radicals, the major objectives of the ministry in the 1790s, but differences became more serious and fresh occasions for dispute arose, as peace with France became a pressing issue.

The prospect of negotiation of peace had often led to heightened political tension as in 1712–13 with the Peace of Utrecht and to divisions within ministries, as in 1761–63 when first Pitt and then Newcastle fell over the issue of peace and control over negotiations. In 1801–2 there were serious divisions over the possibility of a genuine peace with France and over the terms that should be agreed. Long-standing differences could no longer be concealed or contained. Once war resumed, there were again differences over strategies for war and peace.

The interplay between leadership and party identity also emerges. In the absence of clear party identity it was difficult to bridge the policy divides that did exist among those who had been members of the Pittite group and to provide the leadership that might further unity. Addington himself was not up to the task. He was a political manager, able to reform the finances in 1802, but incapable of preserving the peace or of being an effective war minister. Addington was seen to lack leadership for war; he was seen as a support to the government, not its head. His handling of the armed forces was harshly criticized: army numbers were too low, in part because Addington concentrated on militia and volunteers, and the navy was not kept in a state of preparedness. The renewal of war with France in May 1803 led to pressure for the return of Pitt and for a more broadly based government. Possibly, had Addington been more capable, he would have been able to consolidate his position. He was a favourite with George III who saw him as an ordinary man after his own heart and not, like Pitt, a formidable figure. The King respected Pitt, but never really liked him, and resented his attitude over Catholics in 1801. The reason why Addington kept cropping up in cabinets after 1804 was probably the knowledge of George's favour and the degree to which he was seen as having sensible and safe views: he reassured the backbenchers that the government was safe. Addington was compared to the measles – everyone had to have him once. By 1804 the Addingtonians were a group large enough to form a useful element in any government, whether broadly or narrowly based. Although in 1801 his following in Parliament was small, especially among the capable men of business. Addington's position was strengthened by the trade revival that peace brought, the success of the 1802 election and divisions among the other political groups. The last was reminiscent of the 1760s, a decade of ministerial instability.

In somewhat simplistic terms, the 1800s, like the 1760s, displayed the consequences of a political system where there was no strong political party or, in terms of the language of the period, faction. On his accession in 1760 George III had revealed his support for the ideas and ideals of non-party government that had characterized attempts over the previous thirty-five years to create a united opposition, an attractive alternative to both Old Corps Whiggery and Jacobitism. George III could therefore be seen in a tradition that went back, via Bolingbroke's *Patriot King* and the Leicester House opposition around Frederick Prince of Wales, to 'Country' and 'Patriot' hostility to Walpole. Pitt the Elder had shared these assumptions, but the ministry he headed, as Earl of Chatham, in 1766–67 failed its creator. Chatham hoped to demonstrate that government in the national interest and without a faction was possible, but, instead, he found the first difficult to further, the second impossible to achieve and had compromised his reputation and popularity in the process. Shelburne sought the same ends and also failed. A similar desire to include all the most talented was expressed by politicians in 1806. When Grenville suggested a new Cabinet to George III he added, 'the arrangements for the Board and other offices of less importance, would be formed on a similar principle of comprehending as much as possible those persons of different descriptions who might appear likely to be most useful to the carrying on your Majesty's services'. Fox thought it 'a great satisfaction for us to stand on public ground and not on that of particular arrangement'. Marquis Wellesley, recently returned from his Governor-Generalship of India, pledged his support to Grenville and Sidmouth and wrote, 'no administration can prove equal to the present exigency, which shall exclude any description of persons distinguished by public talents or virtues from His Majesty's Councils – I will not lend my aid to any administration formed upon such a principle of exclusion'. A Scottish office-holder wrote to Grenville, 'The crisis of the country is now too serious for good men to indulge those ideas of party connexion which might have found room in periods of less public difficulty and danger'. Grenville informed his brother that it was crucial not to throw away 'the last chance' of saving the country 'for the gratification of party violence'.[21]

Yet, if ministerial unity could rarely be achieved in the eighteenth and early nineteenth centuries, it still proved possible to create long-lasting ministries based not on sizeable party majorities in Parliament, as the Old Corps Whig government had been, but on royal backing, the support of a number of political groupings and the assent of the bulk of the independent MPs and peers. This was the basis of Lord North's ministry in 1770–82, and later of the Pittite system. Such a system, however, was inherently unstable if the bulk of the independent MPs withdrew their support, as they did from North in early 1782 after Cornwallis's surrender at Yorktown appeared to end the prospect of success in the American War of Independence, or if political groupings within the ministry defined themselves, separated out, and each attracted the backing of some of the independents. This was the fate of the Pittite system. It divided into groups linked to Addington, Grenville and Pitt (and later to Castlereagh, Perceval and Canning), and it then proved impossible to create the government of national unity or 'broadbottom' administration that Pitt had sought and that Spencer Perceval was again to attempt, without success, in 1809.

Many problems were therefore 'structural', but it is also appropriate to ask how far there were deficiencies in leadership. These had certainly affected earlier attempts to govern without, or above, faction. George III had handled the transition to a new reign badly, in part due to inexperience and naivety, but also because the ministers of his grandfather, George II, were unwilling to heed his views while his confidant, the Earl of Bute, to whom he turned in 1762 to form a ministry, proved a broken reed, unable to stand the pressures of politics. Chatham's ministry was disunited and, amidst the complexities of peacetime politics, the sense of national unity that he had been able to benefit from and to foster during the Seven Years War was absent. Chatham was not skilled in political management, and his strong will had become increasingly imperious as a consequence of his successful role in the Seven Years War, while his subsequent political isolation had made him more aloof. The ministry had no 'party' basis around which it could cohere. Chatham's expectation that all good men would come forward to further national interests was shown to be naive, while he was deficient in 'man-management' skills. The ministry was divided over policy, the ministers unsuited to their tasks, Chatham unwilling to extend sufficient patronage to his supporters, and the chances of his creating a stable ministry greatly lessened by his poor physical and mental health. Good health was essential for a leading politician. It was one of the keys to the ministerial longevity of Walpole, Newcastle and North.

The experience of the Chatham ministry is worth stressing because it demonstrated the problem of seeking to create and maintain a ministry without reliance on party, and also because it indicates the importance of the head of the ministry in such a situation. Pitt the Younger inherited from his father and from Shelburne the non-party ethos; hence the problem of calling his ministry Tory.

Pitt the Younger inherited some of his father's health problems; indeed there was a thread of mental instability in the family, although the younger Pitt was not mentally unstable. He had always been under pressure, but by the 1800s the cumulative strain of many years in office was having a greater impact. In particular, Pitt was no war minister, and the defeats and difficulties of the war with revolutionary France would have tested even the most adept statesman in this field. When he resigned in 1801 Pitt was suffering from depression and gout. He appeared to have lost the will to go on, the desire to lead, the killer instinct that is so important in political leadership. An ability to manage or to conciliate was no substitute in the circumstances of the early 1800s.

This slackened drive was possibly as important as any wish not to challenge or be seen to challenge the King's prerogative in choosing ministers, in explaining why Pitt delayed his attack on Addington. He was certainly pressed to mount such an attack by his political friends. Once in office again, Pitt was obviously under great strain. His ability to lead was affected and his judgement can be questioned, as in his willingness to desert Melville and his subsequent refusal to advance Addington's supporters once Melville had fallen. Pitt's neglect to build up a true party can be related to his health and morale as much as to his political views.

Chatham's mental collapse in 1767 and Pitt's state on the eve of his death in 1806 underline a major problem with the political system in this (and other) ages: the difficulty of parting with a leader who was no longer capable of providing the necessary leadership and success. Political groupings organized around an individual politician tend to lack mechanisms for finding a new leader, and this is a particular problem if the grouping, or party, is essentially a vehicle for the leader or becomes such. In the case of a party in office in the late eighteenth century, it was up to the monarch to control or at least influence the leadership by his choice of ministers. George III, however, had no wish to part with Pitt in 1805–6 and this played a part in ensuring that the Pittites had no adequate alternative leader. In opposition the Pittites continued to place considerable weight on royal wishes. In July 1806 Wellesley reported to Grenville a conversation he had had with Canning, who saw himself as Pitt's true heir:

> the greater portion of the present Opposition is personally well disposed towards you and Canning particularly so; that however they are resolved to adhere together as a body, and that the leading individuals would think it injurious to the Public Service, as well as to their own reputations to form any connection without the concurrence of the corps. That if any proposition were to be made to any of them, their first inquiry would be, whether it came from the King without whose direct authority none of them would be disposed to enter into any discussions relative to the acceptance of office. Upon the whole it appeared to me that Canning's opinion is, that it would be difficult to obtain any considerable aid from the opposition without a previous dissolution of the present government.[22]

Crown and party thus acted as two poles of political action.

Conclusion

It would be wrong to blame Pitt alone for the collapse of the Pittite system. The tasks faced by the government were formidable, and the succeeding 'Ministry of All the Talents' was also to fail and be shortlived. There was a general election in the autumn of 1806 designed to strengthen the 'Talents' ministry, but it did so only marginally, perhaps for lack of preparation – the decision to dissolve was very much a 'snap' one. The 'Talents', divided and with uneasy relations with George III over his determined opposition to Catholic reform, fell the following March. Indeed, in 1807 the Pittite system returned in the shape of a ministry led by the Duke of Portland and containing most of the leading

Pittites, including Canning and Hawkesbury, and the Whigs thereafter spent many years in opposition. They were unable to take advantage of the unpopularity and divisions of the Portland ministry in 1809 and it was replaced by a government under Perceval that continued on a Pittite base. It is possible to present the creation and fall of the 'Ministry of All the Talents' in terms of a working through of the consequences of the weaknesses in the Pittite system, but, in noting the revival of the system, to suggest that the basic conservative principles, and policies and personnel that had characterized the system were more successful and appropriate for the government of Britain in the 1800s than those of its rivals.

There was little radicalism even among most of the politicians not seen as Tories. This was partly due to the privileged social context and character of the political system, but also to the extent to which a generally conservative political ideology had become more cautious in response to the radicalism of the French revolutionary period. In May 1810 Grenville wrote from his seat at Dropmore to Henry Brougham, an energetic Whig MP with a commitment to reform:

> This fine weather is not favourable to speculations about Parliamentary Reform and must at all events be my excuse for not having earlier answered the rational and well considered suggestions which you had the goodness to communicate to me. My general view of the situation is this. I continue to object strongly to the vague and undefined notions of reforming merely for the sake of reform. That is determining to make some change without previously considering its extent, its principles or its objects. I hold on the contrary side in equal reprobation the opinions in the other extreme, that on this point alone all change is to be rejected without examination, merely because it is a change. The just

52

sentiment seems to be that in this as in every other matter in which the public interests are concerned the constant and vigilant superintendence of Parliament is required, neither adopting nor rejecting change in the abstract, but weighing each particular proposition in detail by the scale of probable advantage or mischief to the community ... all ideas should be disclaimed of extensive and as you justly call them wholesale plans of reform which are at once to strike out for us a new constitution of government and legislation. The idea of introducing separate bills each containing distinct and limited measures is that which entirely meets with my concurrence.[23]

Thus conservatism in this period was not dependent on politicians termed, then or subsequently, Tory. This accorded with the general situation during the eighteenth century. The stability of the political system was not some God-given national right. It owed much to success in war, especially the avoidance of invasion, to political leadership and to social and economic developments. There was nothing inevitable in the transition that occurred from conspiracy and battlefield to elections and parliamentary government, so that in 1762 the bluestocking Elizabeth Montagu could reflect that 'a virtuoso or a dilettanti may stand as secure in these times behind his Chinese rail as the knight on his battlements in former days'.[24]

The nature, practices and purposes of parliamentary government were not, however, accepted by all. This led to a series of crises in the last quarter of the century, most obviously in the North American colonies in 1775, among British radicals in the 1790s and in Ireland in 1798. However, the authority of the British state was only overthrown in North America. The landed elite and their urban allies remained in control in part because of their shared interests and confidence in their role.

This may appear a far cry from the issue of the fate of 'Tory' ministries, but it is in fact crucial. 'Tory' governments could fall without any sense that the essential continuity and conservatism of social structures and political practices were being compromised. Concern with 'high politics' was far less than at the close of the twentieth century. Just as it would be mistaken to treat eighteenth-century parties as unsatisfactory anticipations of modern equivalents and to appropriate modern criteria of political success and failure, so it is inaccurate to assume that the national context of political activity is a constant.

CHRONOLOGY

1783	DECEMBER 19	Formation of William Pitt's first administration
1784	MARCH 10	House of Commons passes Mutiny Bill
	MARCH 25	Parliament dissolved
	MARCH–MAY	Elections. Victory for Pitt
1785	APRIL 18	Pitt's proposals for parliamentary reform defeated by Commons
1788	NOVEMBER–FEBRUARY 1789	George III ill. The Regency Crisis
1790	OCTOBER 1	Publication of Burke's *Reflections*
1792	APRIL 30	Grey's motion for parliamentary reform defeated
1793	FEBRUARY 1	Revolutionary France declares war on Britain
1794	JULY 11	Duke of Portland, formerly leader of opposition in Lords, becomes home secretary
1795	OCTOBER 29	Mass anti-government demonstration at opening of Parliament
1797	APRIL–MAY	Mutinies in the navy
1798	JUNE	Irish rebellion defeated
1800		Act of Union with Ireland passed
1801	JANUARY 28	George III attacks idea of Catholic Emancipation

	FEBRUARY 3	Pitt offers his resignation
	MARCH 14	Addington forms government
	OCTOBER 1	Peace preliminaries with France concluded
1802	MARCH 27	Peace treaty with France at Amiens
1803	MAY 17	British declare war on France
1804	MARCH 15	Pitt attacks Addington ministry
	MAY 7	Pit forms new government
1805	OCTOBER 21	Battle of Trafalgar
1806	JANUARY 23	Pitt dies

Robert Banks Jenkinson, Second Earl of Liverpool
by Sir Thomas Lawrence
(*The Royal Collection © Her Majesty Queen Elizabeth II*)

CHAPTER TWO

1812–30

Norman Gash

The Political Background

In the history of British parliamentary government the ministry of Lord Liverpool from 1812 to 1827 occupies a unique position. It was the last of the great eighteenth-century-style administrations in its structure and duration, the first of the great nineteenth-century administrations in its outlook and achievements.

The political system which had grown up since the accession of the Hanoverians in 1714 had as its salient features the power of the monarch to appoint his own chief minister, the presence in normal circumstances of a majority in the legislature for any ministry enjoying the confidence of the Crown, and the unimportance of general elections except as a means of confirming changes of government already made. In such a political world a party system in the modern sense could not exist. Lord Liverpool's first and near-contemporary biographer[1] observed that he was the last prime minister who in the strict sense of the word can be said to have governed England. To that extent his administration belonged to a political system so different from our own as to be not merely remote but not easily comprehensible.

The Reform Act of 1832 was the event which conveniently signalled the end of that system; but it was already in decline. Liverpool as prime minister had at his disposal fewer means than his predecessors of attracting support for his ministry. The reaction against corruption and inefficiency, dating back to the American War of Independence, had started a process of 'economical reform' which markedly reduced the number of offices under the Crown that could be used to attract MPs' loyalty. The French Revolution had launched a fierce intellectual debate on the rights of the citizen which led to a sharper scrutiny of the basis of constitutional government. Socially the increasing wealth and intelligence of the expanding British middle classes had produced a desire for a greater share of political power.

One outward sign of these changes was the growth of independent newspapers[2] and magazines which looked to circulation rather than government subsidies for their profits and succeeded commercially by promoting the views and interests of their readers rather than those of ministers. Further down the social scale the 'unstamped' and therefore illegal press, catering for a largely working-class readership, demanded drastic changes in Church and State and ascribed the economic hardships of the time to the corruption and extravagance of government. The bulk of the periodical press, in fact, for the greater part of Liverpool's premiership, was critical of government, some of it violently so. Ministers could neither influence sufficiently the respectable, legal press nor control the unrespectable, illegal press. They had to learn to live in a new political climate in which public opinion was more powerful than ever before and more 'liberal' (to use a new French term increasingly coming into use) than even the House of Commons at its most restive.

In Parliament itself there was no strong party organization to sustain ministers. The historic labels of Whig and Tory were still used but they denoted types and temperaments rather than defined and disciplined groups of politicians. In a loose sense all politicians aspiring to office in the early nineteenth century were Whig because of the traditional

TABLE 2.1 *The Growth of Newspapers*

(A) Comparative Numbers of Newspapers 1790 and 1821

Provincial Newspapers	1790	1821
England	60	135
Scotland	27	31
Ireland	27	56
Islands	0	6
London		
Daily	14	16
Twice weekly	7	8
Weekly	11	32
TOTAL	146	284

SOURCE: Speech of Lord John Russell in House of Commons 29 April 1822.

(B) Newspapers in London

	1801	1821
Daily	16	15
Thrice weekly	0	4
Twice weekly	0	19
Weekly	7	18
TOTAL	23	56

(C) Circulation

	1801	1821
Number of stamps issued for London and Provinces	16.0 million	24.7 million

SOURCE: *Annual Register for 1822*, pp. 350–52. Official Return from Comptroller of Stamp Office.

NOTE: The Stamp Office grouped together newspapers which obtained their stamps collectively. The actual number of different titles was therefore greater than the above figures indicate. This may partially explain the discrepancies between the figures provided by Lord John Russell and the Stamp Office.

proscription of the old Tory Party by the monarchy after their efforts to thwart the Hanoverian succession in 1714. The younger Pitt called himself an independent Whig; and Liverpool, together with his colleagues, regarded themselves as his followers. In so far as Liverpool thought in terms of party, it was in this personal and passing sense. There were other parties of this kind – followers of Lord Grenville,[3] followers of Addington,[4] followers of Canning.[5] The only group which came near to the modern concept of party were the Foxite Whigs who after 1807 were in permanent opposition and in the course of time came to monopolize the generic description of 'Whig'.

In parliamentary terms the support on which the Liverpool government relied was of the traditional heterogeneous kind. In the House of Lords, where the influence of the Court and the executive government was always strong, there were rarely any difficulties. In the Commons the core of the government 'party' was made up of office-holders and their friends, MPs sitting for close boroughs whose patrons supported the ministry, and the bulk of the Scottish and Irish representatives anxious for patronage on behalf of their needy constituents.[6] But this nucleus required the votes of independent members sitting for the counties and large towns to produce a creditable majority. As a body the House of Commons was quite capable of amending or rejecting ministerial proposals and believed it had a right to do so. But it was not often disposed to inflict a deliberate defeat on what was clearly seen to be an issue of confidence or to obstruct routine government business. There was a public tradition of support for the ministers of the Crown and a private reluctance to face the expense and uncertainty of a general election which a significant government defeat might entail. The threat of resignation or dissolution was still a powerful weapon in the hands of ministers, though by its nature it could only be used sparingly.

There was in any case a certain affinity between Lord

Liverpool's ministry and the majority in the Commons which makes the 'Tory' label affixed to that government not altogether meaningless. Respect for the traditional role of the Crown in the constitution, defence of the established Church, vigilance in matters of law and order, rejection of political radicalism, distrust of the Foxite Whigs and their alleged populist tendencies – these formed a common ground. Maintenance of the war against Napoleon, in contrast to the pacifist and Francophile leanings of some prominent Whigs, was in the years between 1810 and 1815 another point of agreement. It was to this underlying community of sentiment that Liverpool was referring when he wrote in 1821 that the county MPs 'if not generally the ablest members in the House [of Commons], are certainly those who have the greatest stake in the country, and may be trusted for the most part in periods of difficulty and danger'.[7]

While, however, there were Tory principles shared by the ministry and most of the gentry in the Commons, this was not enough to furnish a comprehensive policy for a Cabinet facing the daily problems of government. It was in this gap between political principles and administrative decisions, between the Tory outlook of the Commons and the executive minds of the ministers, that differences were apt to show themselves. The government's theoretical majority had a tendency to melt away when it was most needed, that is to say, for unpopular or contentious proposals. It is an indication of the instability of the ministry's parliamentary basis that between March 1815 and the general election of 1818 over a third of the House of Commons at different times voted both for and against the government. In addition absence or abstention from a division by customary government supporters was sometimes a silent form of protest and always a cause for concern. In such circumstances the presence on the front bench of men with talent, prestige and debating skill was of prime importance in the management of the House of Commons.

It was a misfortune also for the Liverpool administration that it served under George IV, the most selfish and inconstant of the Hanoverian kings, whose extravagance and disreputable private life brought discredit not only on himself but on his ministers. Between an indisciplined, critical Parliament and an unreliable and unpopular monarch the Cabinet was often in an uncomfortably isolated position. It thus became a matter of political insurance for the Prime Minister to attach to his administration any outstanding politician who might otherwise become the head of an independent group to which the King could turn for an alternative ministry. This was clearly a consideration in Liverpool's patient handling of Canning and the Grenvillites, in the appointment of the Duke of Wellington to the government in 1818, and in the fears expressed in some ministerial quarters about Peel's influential position in the Commons after his return from Ireland. There was no prospect at any time between 1815 and 1827 that the Whigs would be called upon to form an administration; the danger lay elsewhere. For that reason any politician not a Foxite Whig was eligible for the ministry. The recruitment of talent, besides being an end in itself, was also a method of restricting the King's power to change his government.

The Emergence of Lord Liverpool's Government

Few in 1812 would have predicted that the Liverpool ministry had much of a future. Five ministries in eight years had fragmented the old Pittite party and left a legacy of personal feuds and antipathies among its leading members. The accession of the Prince of Wales as Regent in 1810, necessitated by the mental incapacity of George III, introduced another disturbing element. In earlier days he had been an associate of the Foxite Whigs and was expected to bring some of them into office when he got full Regency powers. Perceval's undistinguished Cabinet of 1809 was only just consolidating when he was assassinated in May 1812. The

Cabinet was ready to carry on even though its late colleagues Canning and Lord Wellesley (Wellington's elder brother) refused to join it. For the House of Commons this seemed unsatisfactory and the same month it passed a less than complimentary motion calling on the Prince Regent to form 'a strong and efficient administration'. The Cabinet tendered their resignations; and only when new negotiations initiated by the Prince with Wellesley, Canning, Grenville and Grey (a leading Foxite Whig) ended in stalemate was Lord Liverpool confirmed in office as prime minister.

As far as the Cabinet was concerned, two significant features emerged in the crisis. In the first place they were determined that if they continued in office, it must be under one of their own number. In particular they refused point blank to accept as their head the Regent's apparent favourite candidate, Lord Wellesley, a difficult and unpopular grandee, of whose vanity and unreliability they had sufficient experience. Secondly, they were agreed that if they stayed in office, they wanted Liverpool to be prime minister. The Regent, wearied by the haughty attitude and exorbitant demands of Grenville and Grey, the only other alternatives, was not averse to this. The fact remained, however, that Liverpool became prime minister not as a result of royal initiative or strong support from the House of Commons, but because his nine Cabinet colleagues thought him the fittest man for the post.

Why they thought so is not difficult to guess. He was one of the small group of politicians who in the previous half dozen years had been periodically mentioned as a possible head of government. He had twice been offered the position by George III. He was a central figure in the mainstream group of Pittites who formed the core of all but one of the early nineteenth-century administrations. He had served in each of the three secretaryships of state – foreign affairs, home department, war and colonies – in the last with notable success. There were other personal qualities to commend him. He had been a consistently conciliatory influence in ministries too often racked by personal rivalries. He was equable and good-natured; he was liked and trusted; he had few enemies; he did not quarrel or intrigue. Not only had he never ostentatiously aimed at power, but he had shown himself ready to withdraw any personal claims to office if it assisted the formation of ministries. Above all, he had a strong sense of the collective nature of government and had been consistently loyal both to his leaders and to his colleagues.

The early decisions he took on policy and the composition of his Cabinet revealed something of his political temperament. Fair offers were made to Canning, an old friend for whose talents he had great admiration. But having deluded himself that he and Wellesley could independently form a government, Canning set too high a price on his services. Liverpool had better luck with Addington, now Viscount Sidmouth, the touchy ex-premier who had only reluctantly and suspiciously joined the Cabinet in the largely ornamental office of President of the Council a month before Perceval's death. Anxious to consolidate the alliance with the Addington party, Liverpool offered him the more attractive and responsible post of home secretary. The reserved and patrician Castlereagh, another of Perceval's recent recruits, was retained as foreign secretary and made leader of the House of Commons. Canning could have had either post but insisted on both: a demand which, in view of the personal enmity between him and Castlereagh (they had even fought a duel) Liverpool could not possibly entertain. It was the greatest mistake of Canning's career and one he never ceased to regret. Even so, Liverpool maintained cordial relations with that brilliant but wayward politician and in 1814 sent him as special envoy to Lisbon. Meanwhile, to consolidate his own position and guard against the Canning–Wellesley alliance (which he regarded as a more serious threat to his ministry than the Whig opposition) he dissolved Parliament in the autumn and obtained a new and slightly more favourable House of Commons.

Before then he lightened the load on his government by disposing of two problems which had been giving concern in the last months of Perceval's life. The unpopular Orders in Council, applying trade sanctions against America in the dispute over rights of search at sea, were revoked in June: too late to avert an American declaration of war but proof of the pacific disposition of the British Cabinet. The well-intentioned but controversial bill sponsored by Sidmouth when out of office to regulate the status of Protestant dissenting ministers was withdrawn. In its place came a new measure, drafted in collaboration with the London Methodists, which not only pacified that body but gave a more generous measure of toleration to Dissenters generally than they had previously enjoyed. On the larger matter of Catholic claims, which had figured prominently in all the 1812 negotiations, there was little the prime minister could do. Ever since 1801 the Pittites, including Liverpool's own Cabinet, had been deeply and evenly divided on the issue. He therefore took immediate steps to disembarrass himself of what was both a contentious and insoluble problem. The day after he took office he announced that the government would not collectively propose or oppose Emancipation (as the Roman Catholic demand for full political and civil equality was called) but leave individual ministers free to take their own line in Parliament whenever the issue came up.

It was a trim and well-prepared, if lightly ballasted, ministry which at the end of 1812 faced the rigours of its first full session of Parliament. But it had already gained one great asset denied to all previous administrations since the outbreak of the French War in 1793. For the first time British attempts to bring pressure to bear against Napoleon through land operations had won a notable success. Wellington's victory at Salamanca in July 1812 was the first tangible vindication of the government's much-criticized

peninsular strategy. From that point on the anti-war sentiment in Parliament lost ground and ministers started to
receive a more cordial response to their mounting requests
to the Commons for money to finance the war effort.

After its uncertain beginning the Liverpool administration
during the next two years rapidly gained in strength and
prestige as the war moved towards a victorious conclusion.
In Wellington ministers had found the successful general
the country had so far lacked; and in turn they reaped
incalculable benefits from his victories. It was no less than
they deserved. They had steadfastly backed him in the early
difficult years against bitter attacks in Parliament and they
had made immense efforts to supply the increasing amounts
of manpower, equipment, and money which he requested.
When the allied sovereigns in all their pomp gathered in
London in the summer of 1814 and Wellington became
commander-in-chief of the Allied Occupation Force in
France, it was clear that for the first time in over a century
Britain was once more among the Great Powers of Europe.

The Aftermath of War

Patriotic gratitude, however, is commonly short-lived. As
Liverpool wrote to Wellington in January 1815, 'the restoration of general peace, though it may relieve the country
from great difficulties, does not make the government more
easy in the House of Commons'.[8] Even under the unreformed system Members of Parliament reflected public
opinion. Since a majority of them were landowners, they
had a strong personal stake in agriculture; but on other
matters they were influenced by feeling in the country, or
at least among what they regarded as the respectable classes
of society. Those with large constituencies (even some with
small) had to consider the views and interest of their
electors.

At the end of years of hostilities peace is welcomed not
only for its own sake but because of the promise it holds of

better things to come. It is the nature of war, unfortunately, to create expectations while removing the means of satisfying them. What the British public wanted in 1815 was relief from wartime taxation, an end to inflation, and a return to cheap goods and prosperity. These were things the government could not easily deliver. In 1815 and 1816 ministers received painful reminders that what seemed reasonable to them would not necessarily be seen as such by the House of Commons. Much of the history of the Liverpool administration can be written in terms of its efforts to recover from the effects of what happened in these two years.

The first setback came at the hands of the powerful agricultural interest. The coming of peace had resulted in a sharp fall in the price of wheat with consequent alarm among farmers. In 1814 a House of Commons committee recommended that eighty shillings per quarter should be taken as the minimum remunerative return to the grower and that all foreign wheat should be prohibited if prices fell below that level. Liverpool, a disciple of Adam Smith and in principle a free-trader, would have preferred a more flexible system. But though ministers tried to obtain control over the resultant legislation by making it a government bill, they were in the end obliged to accept this central provision. The Corn Law of 1815, the first prohibitory measure of its kind in British history, proved a disastrous piece of legislation. The eighty-shilling minimum, though high enough, was not excessively so by wartime standards and there was a case for some temporary measure to ease the transition from wartime monopoly to peacetime competition. But the act failed to provide for postwar deflation; and in any case what decided the price of wheat was not foreign imports but the British climate. The security to farmers which the act seemed to offer proved delusory. In all the years from 1815 to 1828 during which the act was in force, only twice (in 1817 and 1818) did the yearly average price rise above eighty shillings. Most of the time it was appreciably lower, in 1822 falling to 44s 7d. Disgruntled farmers continued to press for more effective protection and the government was saddled with the responsibility for having passed what was widely regarded as an odious piece of class legislation.

The other reverse, more obvious and more painful in its effects, came over the income tax. It had been a wartime innovation, greatly disliked because of its inquisitorial nature; the public believed that the government was pledged to abolish it as soon as peace returned. When ministers proposed in their 1816 budget to continue it, though at half the wartime rate, they were soundly beaten in a House of Commons which on this occasion was undoubtedly speaking for public opinion as a whole. Yet the case for a continuation of the tax was a strong one. Government expenditure was bound to be permanently higher after 1815 than it had been in the last years of peace before 1793. Inflation had reduced the value of the pound by almost 30 per cent. The national debt had almost quadrupled and servicing it absorbed most of the ordinary revenue of the state. Pensions and half-pay for the 332,000 men discharged from the armed forces in 1816–17 amounted to £5 million annually: equivalent to the yield of the income tax proposed in 1816. Seventeen new colonies had been acquired which had to be administered and defended. The income tax (or property tax as it was usually called) was more equitable than most taxes since it was directly related to the wealth of the taxpayer. But the case for it was never adequately presented either to the public or to Parliament. It is possible that ministers had been lulled into a certain financial complacency by the last victorious years of the war. If so, they had much to learn about the arts of peace.

For the next four years they had to struggle with a House of Commons which had tasted power and was supported by a strong if ill-informed public opinion. Left with an ordinary revenue of twelve million pounds to meet an estimated annual expenditure of twenty million, they were forced back on a ruinous policy of short-term expedients, propped up by massive borrowing which in turn increased the crippling proportion of revenue that had to be assigned to debt-repayment. The continued cuts in establishments and government expenditure regularly imposed on the government by the House of Commons did nothing to help the economy. At the same time the rapid demobilization of the armed forces demanded by Parliament swelled the ranks of the unemployed with men accustomed to arms.

Loss of Authority

The period after 1815, as after 1918, was marked by trade depression and unemployment. In the nature of Georgian society this led to frequent popular rioting, outbreaks of machine-breaking, and a rapid growth in radical political societies. Local and sporadic as the violence was, it created an unpleasant catalogue of alternate disorder and repression between 1814 and 1820. Ludditism, food riots in East Anglia, radical 'risings' at Nottingham and Huddersfield, the Spa Fields riots, and 'Peterloo', were met by Special Commissions, occasional suspension of Habeas Corpus, secret committees of enquiry, a Seditious Meetings Act in 1817, and the notorious Six Acts of 1819. It was an unhappy and nervous time. There was a widespread conviction among the governing classes, strengthened by the reports of two secret parliamentary committees set up in 1817 to examine the available evidence, that something like a national conspiracy existed to subvert the constitution. The Cabinet, though it shared this conclusion, did not allow itself to be driven to desperate measures. It knew it could always rely on parliamentary support for any temporary security precautions; and there was no desire on Liverpool's part to ask for more executive powers than seemed necessary. Though this was the era of 'Tory repression', in subsequent liberal and radical tradition, in reality slow communications, the absence of a regular police, the inefficiency of local agencies, the antiquated machinery of the criminal law, and the jealous scrutiny of the House of Commons, made impossible the kind of repressive regime familiar in continental states.

Over the Peterloo 'massacre'[9] Lord Liverpool, while privately critical of the action of the local authorities, felt he could not undermine the morale of the untrained and unpaid magistracy by publicly disowning them. The subsequent Six Acts were provoked less by the incident itself than by Whig attempts to make political capital out of it. Some of the measures were entirely reasonable, such as the prohibition of unauthorized military training; and the two most arbitrary (empowering magistrates in certain districts to search for arms and ban political mass meetings) were only temporary and not renewed when they expired. The Cabinet had no intention of encroaching permanently on the traditional liberties of the subject; and they were sensible enough to draw a distinction between real social hardships and the exploitation of those hardships by political agitators.

Nevertheless, the state of the country in these years gave genuine cause for concern; and the well-to-do classes were uneasy both at the disturbed condition of society and at the apparent inability of the government to offer anything more constructive than repressive legislation. Ministers were less indifferent than appeared. Straitened finances and the prevailing doctrine of *laissez-faire* were not conducive to large-scale government interference. But a small trickle of measures demonstrated that they were not without a social conscience. Lord Liverpool supported the elder Peel's act of 1819 to regulate the employment of children in textile factories. The previous year he had secured a grant of £1 million for church building in towns and industrial areas. In 1816 discharged soldiers were allowed to set up in trade anywhere in the kingdom. In 1817 two truck acts[10] were passed to cover workers in collieries and the iron and steel industries; another encouraged savings banks; a fourth empowered the government to advance loans for public works and fisheries for the purpose of providing employment for the poor. In 1819 an act was passed to assist those early manifestations of self-help among the working classes, the Friendly Societies. It was not much; and much of it was ineffectual. But at least it showed a degree of concern for the poor and a willingness to ignore the teachings of political economy in a social and humanitarian cause.

Confidence in the government, however, continued to ebb. Even in the traditionally more stable rural society the influence of radical ideas, especially those put forward by Cobbett in his *Register*,[11] was beginning to be observable. After the general election of 1818 Huskisson[12] wrote to the prime minister from Sussex that the radical press had done more mischief among farmers than many cared to admit. Though they still despised the Whigs, they 'are no longer what they were ten years ago in their attachment to the old Tory interests and principles'.[13] It was not necessary to believe all Cobbett's propaganda to feel that something was wrong. A large body of moderate, mainly middle-class opinion, while rejecting violence, thought that changes were needed in the antiquated structure of Church and State. It was the gap between the government and these respectable classes which disturbed some ministerial supporters. Peel, returning to England after six strenuous years in Ireland as chief secretary, was particularly struck by this development. He put the question to his friend Croker in March 1820:

> Do not you think that the tone of England ... is more liberal – to use an odious but intelligible phrase – than the policy of the Government? Do not you think that there is a feeling, becoming daily more general and more confirmed ... in favour of some undefined change in the mode of governing the country?[14]

With the freedom of temporary political independence he remarked on the oddity that public opinion, with more influence on government than it had ever had, was never so dissatisfied with the share it possessed. And he went on to speculate whether resistance to parliamentary reform could last another seven years.

Lord Liverpool was painfully aware of the negative, defensive position his ministry had occupied since 1815. The problem was how to break out of it. He was instinctively opposed to any organic changes in the constitution, as were the rest of his colleagues. There were, however, more immediate and practical ways of rescuing the administration from its state of apparent permanent weakness – though it needed political courage to attempt them. By 1819 he had made up his mind that there must be an end to the years of ignominious concession and retreat. The government must stand and fight. Already, in his view, the campaign for administrative retrenchment and tax reduction had gone too far. It had been useless as a means of restoring prosperity and positively harmful in its effects on the administration of public affairs. He believed that the only way to revive the economy was to end inflation, establish a stable currency, and free British trade and industry from the shackles of their mercantilist past. But this could only be achieved if the government first recovered its proper authority.

Resolution and Recovery

A start was made with the currency. The postwar recession, painful as it was, had at least brought inflation down to a more manageable level. The difficulty was not so much to get agreement in principle on the return to the gold standard as to decide on the timing of such an operation after twenty-one years of paper currency. Taught by painful experience, Liverpool (with the backing of the Bank of England) went to work through a parliamentary committee with the membership carefully selected to produce the required result. He used the same tactic with another committee appointed immediately afterwards on national income and expenditure. The reports of these important committees, and of two more on foreign trade set up in 1820, laid the foundation for the revolution in economic policy which was carried out between 1819 and 1824. The first significant step came with the budget of 1819. This, though it involved a degree of financial manipulation in the form of a raid on the Sinking Fund, nevertheless imposed new taxes and resulted for the first time since the war in a small surplus of income over expenditure. It even held out a modest hope of continuing this in future years.

The importance which Liverpool attached to this financially bold and politically risky experiment was shown by his determination to stake the fate of his ministry on the outcome.

> If we cannot carry what has been proposed, [he wrote to his nervous Lord Chancellor in May 1819] it is far, far better for the country that we should cease to be the Government. After the defeats we have already experienced during this Session, our remaining in office is a *positive* evil ... If therefore things are to remain as they are, I am quite clear that there is no advantage, in any way, in our being the persons to carry on the public service. A strong and decisive effort can alone redeem our character and credit, and is as necessary for the country as it is for ourselves.[15]

It was a resolute statement, which also revealed Liverpool's concept of ministerial duty; and, as often happens, the bold policy succeeded. The House of Commons accepted the budget, new taxes and all, despite the furious attacks of the opposition. Even more crucially, it accepted later in the session the recommendation of the committee on finance that the annual surplus of revenue over expenditure should normally be not less than £5 million.

The Cabinet's stand was rewarded with early and remarkable success. The return to the gold standard was completed ahead of its timetable; the budgets continued to show surpluses; and these in turn enabled ministers to begin a systematic operation to reduce tariff barriers. The report of the 1820 committee on trade laid down the principle of the new commercial policy. Restrictions on trade were justifiable only on grounds of political expediency; where no such considerations applied, they should be abolished. In the next half dozen years, notably in the budgets of 1824 and 1825, came the first great instalment of Tariff Reform and Free Trade which was to characterize British policy in the nineteenth century. The surge of industrial and commercial expansion which took place in the mid-1820s earned for the new chancellor of the exchequer the nickname of 'Prosperity' Robinson and for the government unprecedented popularity.

One reason for the success of the tariff legislation of the 1820s was that it did not attempt to do too much in too short a time. Though a free-trader by conviction, Liverpool was not a doctrinaire in practice. He had a strong sense of the limitations of political power and did not try to impose changes at a faster rate than the existing economic structure could reasonably be expected to bear. What resulted from this first great free-trade experiment was not free trade in the absolute sense but a simplified, rational, revenue-producing system of moderate protection. Liverpool thought further advances towards complete freedom of trade (if that was indeed a realizable concept) would depend on the readiness of parliament to sanction more direct taxes, especially (in his private view) the restoration of the income tax. But that was something best left for the future.

What was also noteworthy about the government's new economic policy after 1819 was that it owed almost everything to ministerial initiative, almost nothing to the House of Commons or opinion 'out of doors'. Though the doctrine of free trade laid down by the classical economists found general acceptance with the educated public, individual commercial and manufacturing interests always found special reasons why it should not be applied to their particular case. The famous free-trade petition of the London merchants in 1820, for instance, made little headway until it was taken up by the influential banker Henry Thornton with the active encouragement of the prime minister and his colleagues. The economist Tooke, who had promoted the petition, later asserted that the ministers were 'more sincere and resolute Free Traders than the Merchants of London'.[16] Nevertheless, in its commercial policy after 1820 the Cabinet was clearly heartened by the growing agreement of the public with the principles which inspired government action.

It was a different story with the agriculturalists. The views of their spokesmen in and out of parliament ran completely counter to the economic policy of the ministers. They argued that the current distress among farmers was caused by high taxation, aggravated by deflation and the return to the gold standard. The remedies they put forward included easier credit and higher duties on agricultural imports; and they were prepared to be obstructive in the House of Commons if they did not get their way. The government was in the curious position of having on the one hand to coax the commercial interest into accepting free (or at least freer) trade and, on the other, to rebuff the demands of the landed interest, supposedly their natural supporters, for greater protection. Ministers flatly denied that agricultural distress was caused by high taxation. That, Liverpool told the Lords in 1822, was 'one of the grossest delusions that was ever attempted to be instilled into the minds of the people'. It was the responsibility of government not only to decide economic policy but to ignore the clamour of special interests. Ministers had to aim at the welfare of society as a whole, of all classes and all sections. 'It is the duty of Government and of Parliament', he went on, 'to hold the balance between all the great interests of the country, *as even as possible* . . . the agriculturalist is not the *only* interest in Great Britain . . . It is not even the *most numerous.*' And he reminded the peers that when food prices were low, the mass of the nation benefited.[17]

It was an attitude not much relished by the landed gentry. In the dry, sunny years between 1820 and 1824, when abundant harvests kept prices down and farmers in a ferment, ministers were faced with an agricultural revolt in the House of Commons, led by such influential country gentlemen as Lethbridge of Somerset, Gooch of Suffolk, and Knatchbull of Kent, which was far more dangerous than the official opposition. Two agricultural committees appointed in 1821 and 1822 helped to channel off some of the discontent. Even so, in the 1822 session ministers were driven to the ultimate sanction of threatening to resign if the disgruntled gentry continued to impede the government's financial arrangements. Though often hard pressed, the Cabinet avoided making any concession of substance to the farming lobby. It could count on some cross-bench support; and its arguments, aided by pointed references to the connection between dear food and disorder in the country, gradually prevailed. By the mid-1820s many of the country gentry realized that government retrenchment had reached its limits; that legislation could never guarantee high corn prices; and that lower rents would have to be accepted as part of normal peacetime conditions. By 1824 the government had outflanked its critics not only on the opposition benches but among the discontented of its own party. The ministerial policies were seen to be working; the prosperity of the country was self-evident; popular violence and radical agitation had subsided. The House of Commons had never been so cheerful, or the administration so respected.

Seizing the initiative in the years after 1818 was not just a matter of devising new policies. It also involved firmer and more imaginative tactics when dealing with Parliament. This was evident in the increasingly authoritative tones assumed in debate by Liverpool and Castlereagh, the leaders and principal exponents of government policy in their respective houses. Greater dexterity was displayed in the use of parliamentary committees whose reports, often written by one of the ministers concerned, carried an official weight which it was difficult for the opposition to match. In addition the Cabinet was taking greater pains over press publicity, an area in which it had previously been decidedly inferior to its opponents. Important speeches by Liverpool and Castlereagh were reprinted and put on sale; sympathetic articles circulated to provincial newspaper editors; and specially written pamphlets were prepared under the supervision of the law officers. If Croker's statement in later life is to be trusted, Peel and Palmerston about the years 1818–19 were writing anonymous articles for the *Courier* in an effort to revive the circulation of that not very successful government newspaper.

In 1822 came an interesting innovation in public relations in the shape of a bulky pamphlet entitled *The State of the Nation*, nearly a hundred pages long and costing five shillings. It came out on the eve of the 1822 session in which much agricultural discontent was expected. Though anonymous, it made no attempt to hide its official character. It sold well, going through at least seven editions in its first twelve months, which suggests that it had a measure of success with MPs and members of the educated public for whom it was clearly designed. Despite the title, it was more a kind of primitive White Paper, describing the work of the various government departments and the policies they were following. The standpoint was that of an embattled administration, justifying itself in the face of an unsympathetic and often uncomprehending public. The constant refrain was that ministers were working for the good of the community as a whole and deserved credit for their efforts. If they were given the public support and confidence necessary for effective government in a constitutional state, it was argued, then unrest and sedition would die away and the repressive legislation required in more turbulent times would become a thing of the past. Amateurish as it was in some respects, the pamphlet was both a revelation of the thinking behind

TABLE 2.2 *Analysis of Select List of Divisions in the House of Commons in the 1822 Session*

Constituencies	For government	Against government	Sometimes for and sometimes against	Absent or abstained	TOTALS
English Counties	25	37	10	8	80
Welsh Counties and Boroughs	13	9	1	1	24
Open Boroughs England	59	107	5	11	182
Close Boroughs England	151	41	5	28	225
Universities	3	–	–	1	4
Counties and Burghs Scotland	25	11	–	9	45
Irish Counties	24	14	2	24	64
Irish Boroughs	21	7	–	8	36
TOTALS	321	226	23	90	660

SOURCE: *Annual Register for 1823 (Chronicle)*, p. 16. Abstract of detailed analysis of 14 important and a number of minor divisions in the Commons during the 1822 Session.

NOTE: For a detailed discussion of government support in the House of Commons and more analyses of voting patterns in the 1812–20 period, see R. G. Thorne (ed.), *The House of Commons 1790–1820 (History of Parliament)*, 5 vols (1986). I, pp. 235–77.

ministerial policy and a significant attempt to bridge the gap that still existed between government and the respectable public.[18]

The Reshaping of the Ministry

The State of the Nation appeared little more than a year after the distracting episode of the Queen's divorce bill in 1820 which had strained relations between the King and his ministers almost to breaking point. Caught between two self-willed and unreasonable royal personages, the government was itself humiliated when it first introduced and was then forced by public disapproval and parliamentary defections to withdraw the bill. Angered by the Cabinet's initial reluctance and ultimate inability to meet his wishes, George IV seriously considered changing his government; and would have done so, had there been an acceptable alternative. Even so, the opposition confidently anticipated that Liverpool would not survive the 1821 session. It was only when he allowed it to be known that he would resign rather than let his ministry be dragged further through the mire, that the danger passed and the Commons belatedly realized that they had allowed themselves to be carried too far by sentimental public clamour on behalf of the far from innocent and distinctly unattractive Queen Caroline. With his new economic strategy only just taking shape, the prime minister was more than ever convinced that the ministry needed more speaking talent in the Commons. The need to keep his administration in good repair had never been far from his thoughts. In 1816 Canning was brought back into a less than welcoming Cabinet; though he had to be content with the undistinguished post of President of the India Board. A grander prize was secured in 1818 when Wellington, his continental duties over, consented to join the government as Master-General of the Ordnance. Canning's resignation in 1820, in protest over the treatment of the Queen, made reinforcements for the House of Commons a matter of urgency. Liverpool's main objectives were first to find replacements for the tired and elderly Sidmouth at the Home Office and for Vansittart, a respectable economist but execrable speaker, at the Exchequer; secondly, to make some provision for Canning, if only to prevent him from setting up as an independent critic of government in the House of Commons; thirdly, to bring Peel, who had made a reputation for himself as chief secretary in Ireland, into the Cabinet; and finally to effect a formal alliance with the Grenvillites, whom he had been discreetly courting for some years.

That the plan took some eighteen months, from the spring of 1821 to the start of 1823, to work out was due partly to the difficulty of getting the King's consent for Canning's return to office, partly to the contemporary convention which gave a minister a kind of proprietorial right over his office, to the extent at least of being able to bargain over the terms of its surrender. In the end the King's continuing resentment at Canning's resignation and the presence of a powerful anti-Canning group in the Cabinet, made Liverpool reluctantly agree to send him to India as Governor-General. Castlereagh's suicide in August 1822 transformed the situation. It was accepted even by his Cabinet opponents that Canning alone had the ministerial authority and diplomatic experience to fill the void left in the ministry; but it took another prolonged battle with the King before he was allowed to inherit Castlereagh's double role as foreign secretary and leader of the Commons.[19]

To the public it appeared that the Cabinet was now more talented, more broadly based, and more 'liberal'. Indeed, later historians interpreted the arrival of what they called the 'Liberal Tories' as the real reason for the new policies of the 1820s. This was a misreading of events. Most of the ministers concerned were already in the government. Robinson, the new Chancellor of the Exchequer, had been vice-president of the Board of Trade since 1812 and president since 1818. Huskisson, who succeeded him at the

TABLE 2.3   Changes in the Cabinet 1821–23

Cabinet Members		1821	1823
1st Lord of Treasury		Lord Liverpool	–
Lord Chancellor		Lord Eldon	–
President of the Council		Earl of Harrowby	–
Lord Privy Seal		Earl of Westmorland	–
Secretaries of State	Home	Viscount Sidmouth	R. Peel (Jan. 1822)
	Foreign	Lord Londonderry	G. Canning (Sep. 1822)
	War and Colonies	Earl Bathurst	–
1st Lord of Admiralty		Viscount Melville	–
Master-General of Ordnance		Duke of Wellington	–
Chancellor of Exchequer		N. Vansittart	F. J. Robinson (Jan. 1823)
President of Board of Trade		F. J. Robinson	W. Huskisson[1] (Nov. 1823)
President of Board of Control (India)		C. B. Bathurst	C. W. Wynn[2] (Feb. 1822)
Chancellor of Duchy of Lancaster		C. B. Bathurst	N. Vansittart (cr. Baron Bexley)
Master of the Mint		Lord Maryborough[3]	–
Without Portfolio			Viscount Sidmouth[4]

NOTES: 1. Though appointed President of the Board of Trade in January 1823 he did not immediately enter the Cabinet.

2. Not previously in the government; he was appointed to provide a Cabinet presence for the Grenvillites.

3. The office of Master of the Mint did not normally carry Cabinet rank. This had been accorded exceptionally to Lord Maryborough (formerly known as Wellesley-Pole, elder brother of the Duke of Wellington) at the Duke's request on his return from the Peninsular War in 1814. In June 1823 the death of Lord Cornwallis, Master of the Buckhounds, enabled Lord Liverpool to offer Maryborough that Court appointment and give T. Wallace the Mastership of the Mint. Wallace had resigned as vice-president of the Board of Trade in protest at the appointment of Huskisson to the presidency over his head. In turn the reduction in the size of the Cabinet by one allowed Liverpool to promote Huskisson to the Cabinet later that year.

4. Resigned from the Cabinet in November 1824. Lord Mulgrave had been similarly rewarded on voluntarily giving up his office of Master-General of the Ordnance to accommodate the Duke of Wellington in December 1818. He remained in the Cabinet without office until May 1820.

Board, had been one of Liverpool's closest economic advisers since 1814. Had Vansittart remained at the Exchequer, or Wallace, the energetic vice-president, become president of the Board of Trade, it would have made little difference to policies. Liverpool's primary purpose in reconstructing his ministry was to strengthen the front bench in the Commons where Castlereagh had been left in a dangerously isolated position after 1820. The junction with the Grenvillites reunited the old Pittite party but, more important in Liverpool's view, it denied the King the last vestige of a middle party which he could use as the basis of an alternative ministry without surrendering to the Whigs.

Nevertheless, despite Canning's talents, his oratory, and his popularity in liberal circles, his return to the Cabinet brought discomfort and distrust. The reasons were partly, perhaps mainly, personal. Old memories, old animosities, his restless energy, the ascendancy he seemed to have over the prime minister, all contributed to the uneasy aura which surrounded him. In foreign affairs his arrival did not affect the general lines of policy laid down in Castlereagh's state paper of 1820 which had been approved by the whole Cabinet. But where Castlereagh had been courteous and considerate in his dealings with the great powers of Europe, most of them wartime allies, Canning was outspoken and provocative. As a result there was friction not only with the King but also with Wellington. In 1824 the Duke came close to resignation because he felt so isolated in the Cabinet on the issue.

What was even more disruptive was Canning's desire to do something about Catholic Emancipation. With the mounting success in Ireland of O'Connell's Catholic Association, that stormy topic at the end of 1824 was once more in the forefront of English politics. A crisis came in April 1825 when the House of Commons actually approved Burdett's Emancipation bill. Peel and Liverpool both contemplated resignation: Peel because he thought his position as the sole 'Protestant' Cabinet minister in the Commons was now untenable, Liverpool because he felt he could not go on without Peel's presence there. Canning at this critical juncture proposed that the Cabinet should collectively consider the Emancipation issue. Only when it became clear that an abandonment of the 1812 neutrality rule would bring the ministry to an end, was he induced to give way. In turn Peel and Liverpool put aside their own scruples and consented to stay on.

The internal Cabinet crisis of May 1825, unknown to the public, demonstrated once again Liverpool's indispensability as prime minister. The doubt was how much longer he would be able to sustain the burden of office. During 1826, while the ministry dealt capably with the aftermath of the financial panic of December 1825 (caused by prosperity and over-speculation), a sharp rise in spring-wheat prices, a general election in June, and military intervention to protect Portugal in December, there was growing anxiety behind the scenes over Liverpool's health. The loss of his wife in 1821, followed by the strain of periodic conflicts with the King and in the Cabinet, and recurrent bouts of physical debility only temporarily relieved by visits to Bath, had all taken their toll. While there was much speculation about the true state of his health, what was not in doubt was that his departure would mean the break-up of the ministry. This had long been realized. 'If anything was to induce Lord Liverpool to retire', Croker wrote to the King's former private secretary Bloomfield in May 1824, 'we should have what is vulgarly called a blow-up.'[20] It is clear that Liverpool, already into his fifteenth year as prime minister, would have found it almost impossible to give up his post voluntarily. But a severe stroke in February 1827, the first of a series which eventually brought his life to a close in December 1828, put the matter beyond the control of either himself or his colleagues.

Reflection on Lord Liverpool's Government

At the time of his resignation Liverpool had achieved a higher standing in the country than any of his colleagues. He was respected for his integrity and irreproachable private life, trusted for the prudence and steadiness of his policies. His was the first British administration, in fact, to have an intelligent, coherent, economic philosophy which it tried consistently to apply in practice. Moreover the capacity of his government for reform was far from exhausted. He had used the financial crisis of 1825 to put through a new banking act designed to remedy the weakness implicit in a system of numerous private banks issuing their own notes. Even more importantly he and Huskisson had drawn up a new corn bill for the 1827 session, abolishing prohibition and allowing in foreign wheat under a sliding scale of duties based on a new, much lower, remunerative price of sixty shillings a quarter.

Within the administration Liverpool had always been the central figure, though this was obscured from posterity by his modesty, his position in the Lords, and the presence in his Cabinet of powerful personalities like Canning and Wellington. He was never a mere chairman of committees as sometimes portrayed. He supervised closely the work of all the important departments; he was at the heart of policy-making, and ultimately the deciding voice. Once a decision was arrived at, he was courageous and uncompromising. Nevertheless, he worked by persuasion rather than domination, and was content to allow his reputation to be merged in that of his ministry. By 1822 his Cabinet deserved, more than Lord Grenville's of 1806, to be called one of 'All the Talents'; and he would have been the first to admit that the strength of the government lay in its collective nature. By the mid-1820s its achievements were being recognized by the 'respectable opinion' to which it had always been sensitive. The postwar disorders had passed; taxes had been reduced; inflation curbed; commerce and manufacture encouraged; liberal and enlightened policies pursued not only at the Board of Trade under Huskisson but at the Home Office under Peel. Thirty years earlier Burke had written that 'a disposition to preserve, and an ability to improve, taken together, would be my standard of a statesman'. Liverpool embodied the careful balance implied in that ideal. He was the first great Conservative prime minister in an age when the term 'Conservative' was hardly known, and before an organized Conservative Party had come into existence.

There was, however, one great flaw in the system over which he presided. The neutrality principle on Catholic Emancipation adopted in 1812 was a short-term necessity but a long-term liability. It prevented constructive thinking about the problem within the government and created uncomfortable divisions among ministers whenever the issue came up in Parliament. The inseparable connection between Emancipation and the general problem of governing Ireland ensured that this would happen with increasing frequency. Logically Canning was right when he argued in 1825 that the importance of the issue demanded a response from the government. The practical weakness of his position was that there was no set of politicians available who could persuade the Crown and Parliament to agree on a solution. Yet the longer the problem remained unsolved, the more explosive it became. In his final years Liverpool was convinced that sooner or later Parliament would pass an Emancipation Act and that his ministry would break up on the issue. The House of Lords saved him in 1825 by rejecting Burdett's bill; but whether the peers and the Prime Minister could go on resisting the will of the Commons was a question to which there was only one answer. All he had been able to do, as he recognized himself, was to postpone the inevitable.

Compared with this looming threat, the failure to deal with parliamentary reform was of secondary importance. Nevertheless, though there was no great support among respectable classes for wholesale radical schemes to remodel the electoral system, opinion even in Parliament was beginning to shift. This had been demonstrated in 1821 when Lord John Russell's bill, to give the two seats of the disenfranchised rotten borough of Grampound to the great unrepresented town of Leeds, passed the House of Commons. Liverpool had no objection to penalizing the venal voters of Grampound. What he disliked was strengthening the influence of the urban democratic electorate and its potential demagogue leaders. He therefore secured an amendment in the Lords to assign the seats to Yorkshire.

Liverpool's attitude is understandable. To organic changes in the constitution he was as opposed as any Tory backbencher. In any case there was no great zeal for reform in the Commons, as their quiet acceptance of the Lords' amendment showed. Certainly they would not have passed an even more substantial measure involving the disenfranchisement of a whole group of rotten boroughs and the enfranchisement of an equivalent number of large industrial towns. A parliamentary reform bill based on general principles was not a practical possibility in the 1820s. Even so, a few isolated and specific transfers of seats from such notorious boroughs as Grampound, East Retford and Penryn to towns like Manchester, Leeds and Birmingham would have been perfectly feasible if the government had taken the initiative. Such actions could have been defended on conservative grounds as a prophylactic against a more sweeping measure and would have done much to satisfy moderate reformers. The existing electoral system – illogical, unbalanced, and partially corrupt as it was generally recognized to be – was tolerated by public opinion in the 1820s because the ministry itself was liberal, reforming, and progressive. But if the time ever came when government once more appeared remote or arbitrary, the cry for reform of the legislature would become a clamour.

The Disintegration of the Liverpool System

The three short ministries of the years 1827–30 formed an epilogue to the Liverpool era. Their leadership, their policies and their problems were all an inheritance from the previous fifteen years.

In selecting a successor to Liverpool the King had little choice. Canning, the senior and most talented minister in the Commons, had by common consent an irresistible claim. He had already made his peace with George IV and now gave his assurances that he would uphold the Liverpool principle of neutrality on the Catholic issue. Nevertheless, his appointment was followed by the resignation of half the Cabinet. Some gave as their reason their unwillingness to serve under a 'Catholic' prime minister; probably all in varying degrees were influenced by a fundamental dislike and distrust of the new premier. Even Melville, a 'Catholic', went out with his 'Protestant' colleagues. In those circumstances Canning was forced to make an alliance with those Whigs ready (though not all were) to join his Cabinet without a pledge on Catholic Emancipation and knowing that he was a declared opponent of parliamentary reform. What Canning would have done about those two issues will never be known. He died in August 1827 after only four months in office, having stabilized his rickety coalition but with all his problems ahead of him. His successor, Robinson, now Lord Goderich, though a sound and good-natured man, never looked likely to overcome the internal disagreements of the Cabinet and was eased out of office by the King in January 1828.

George IV then turned to yet another member of Liverpool's Cabinet: one completely different in character and temperament to Canning and Goderich, and one who, he hoped, would be able to construct a rather more durable administration. Self-confident, decisive and authoritarian, the Duke of Wellington represented to the public (and indeed to the King himself) the anti-Canningite, Tory,

Protestant wing of the Liverpool party. This assessment was based on a profound error. It was true that in the last few years of the Liverpool administration the Duke had emerged as the head of the anti-Canning faction. But this did not mean that he disagreed with all Canning's principles. Though it was not widely known, Wellington was as interested in finding a solution to the Catholic problem as any so-called 'Catholic' politician and had clear-cut views on how it could be done. The difference was that for him the resolution of the issue depended on time and circumstance. He had not been prepared to see Liverpool's ministry break up over the question in 1825; and his private opinions did not prevent him from accepting the King's commission in 1828 to form a government with the same neutrality formula agreed to by Canning and Goderich. Perhaps he was confident of his ability to persuade George IV to swallow Emancipation when the time was ripe; a long record of unbroken military success had led him to believe that he was able to deal with any situation he was likely to encounter. Perhaps he did not think that there would be any immediate necessity to consider the question at all. It followed that from the start he was in a false position; and it was this in the end which wrecked his administration.

The first step, however, was to form a respectable ministry; and, as always when the prime minister was in the Lords, the choice of leader of the House of Commons was crucial. Wellington's immediate summons to Peel was natural; he was the ablest politician left in the Commons. But Peel had also become the unofficial head of the 'Protestant' party in the lower house, and his appointment strengthened the image of the new government as a more 'Tory' administration than its predecessors. Peel's own thoughts were centred on the problems of political power rather than religious policy. After the divisions of the previous year his concern was to reunite the old Liverpool party. He regarded this as the only practicable basis for a solid and durable ministry. 'I cannot undertake the business in the House of

Commons', he confided to his wife, 'without more assistance than the mere Tory Party, as it is called, would afford
me.'[21] Consequently, besides the recruitment of two young-
ish liberal peers, Aberdeen and Ellenborough, and the retention of Lyndhurst, Canning's supple and worldly-wise Lord
Chancellor, four of Goderich's colleagues – Huskisson,
Grant, Dudley and Palmerston – found places in the Duke's
Cabinet. Of the old Tory members of Liverpool's last Cabinet
three – Eldon, Bexley[22] and Westmorland – were deliberately omitted. The new administration represented a clear
desire to return to the central, moderate, balanced position
which characterized the Liverpool regime.

Events soon demonstrated, however, that the schism of
1827 had left painful scars on the members of Liverpool's
old administration. Relations within the Cabinet were brittle
from the start. The Canningites had only with difficulty
been persuaded by Peel to serve under Wellington. They
tended to act as a group and their chief spokesmen, Huskisson and Grant, were uncommonly prickly and sensitive
men. For those reasons Wellington's increasing exasper-
ation with the liberal views he encountered among his colleagues on various issues of foreign policy, commercial
regulation, and religion, was chiefly though unfairly
directed against the Canningites. When Huskisson, after his
impulsive vote against the East Retford bill in May 1828,[23]
offered his resignation (the third to emanate from his group
in four months), Wellington accepted it with no attempt to
smooth over what was no more than an emotional lapse
of Cabinet discipline on Huskisson's part. The rest of the
Canningites followed him out of office, thereby confirming,
to Wellington's satisfaction at least, their fundamental unreliability as colleagues. The Duke believed that they had
conspired against him. They for their part distrusted Wellington and thought that their only guarantee lay in keeping
together. Ironically the one who suffered most from their
departure was their frequent ally in the Cabinet, Peel. The
loss was not so much in voting power in the Commons as

in debating strength on the front bench. From then on he had to bear the burden of representing the government in the House of Commons almost unaided. This became a consideration of considerable importance when the greater crisis of Catholic Emancipation arrived the following year.

O'Connell's election for County Clare in July 1828 (though as a Roman Catholic he could not as the law stood take his seat) presented both a challenge to the constitution and a threat to civil order in Ireland. With the House of Commons again on record earlier in the session as in favour of meeting Catholic claims, the government (as Wellington told the King in August) was now effectively paralysed. The time had arrived, in his view, to solve the problem. By the start of the 1829 session he had wrung consent from an unwilling King; and equally important had persuaded Peel to withdraw his proffered resignation since he was the only man who could pilot the necessary legislation through the Commons. By April 1829 the government's Catholic Relief Bill had passed into law. Wellington and Peel had both concluded that political circumstances had made the measure a necessity. The difference between them was that the Duke thought it was right in principle, Peel that it was only the lesser of two evils.

The fact remained that a government which the public had regarded as solidly 'Protestant' had executed a sudden and complete reversal of policy. The revulsion among the Protestant opponents of the bill was profound. It cost Peel his seat for Oxford University and lasting doubts about his integrity as a statesman. It brought upon Wellington wild accusations from the Tory press of military dictatorship and unconstitutional use of government influence to force through the legislature a concession which was against the wishes of the majority of the nation. There were vicious personal attacks on him in some Tory newspapers and in ultra-Tory circles support was voiced for a species of parliamentary reform that would restore the constitutional independence of the House of Commons. The general election of 1830, caused by the death of George IV, did nothing to clarify the confused state of politics. Only about a quarter of the constituencies in England and Wales were contested. There had been no firm majority in the Commons for the government before the election; there was none afterwards. All that had been demonstrated was that the electorate wanted changes of various kinds – abolition of slavery, greater government economy, cheaper bread, reform of the electoral system – and that many of those returned to Westminster had promised to support these objectives.[24] With the economy in the grip of an industrial depression, and a threatened revival of radical violence, the country was clearly in an uneasy mood.

It was an additional handicap for the government that it seemed to be acting entirely on the defensive. The opportunity which briefly presented itself in the spring of 1830 for the economists in the cabinet – Peel, Goulburn (chancellor of the exchequer) and Herries (the veteran wartime administrator) – to launch a new commercial and financial reform programme foundered on Wellington's innate conservatism. In the absence of a ministerial initiative the government appeared to be reverting to the impotent years of 1816–19. There was a string of defeats on minor issues and ministers were increasingly harried on such populist grievances as taxation, government expenditure and departmental establishments.

The only alternative tactic for Wellington and Peel (and that second-best) was to strengthen the Cabinet. Since the Whigs were inadmissible and the ultra-Tories unwelcome, this meant bringing back the Canningite seceders of 1828. The occasion which took Huskisson to the opening of the Manchester–Liverpool railway in September 1830 – and to his fatal accident – was also designed to facilitate a reconciliation between him and the Prime Minister. Despite this hardly auspicious start, overtures continued to be made to the rest of his group right up to the opening of the new parliamentary session in November. They broke down partly on their stipulations for electoral reform, partly on their desire to bring in some of their late Whig colleagues, but most of all (it may be suspected) on their continuing distrust of Wellington.

With no accession of strength the new session was clearly going to be difficult; but the end came more abruptly than anyone could have anticipated. In the debate on the Address Wellington made his celebrated declaration against parliamentary reform. Nine days later the government was defeated on a hostile motion to submit (against all precedent) their Civil List to the scrutiny of a House of Commons committee. The following day the Cabinet resigned. The majority against it had included seventeen of its usually reliable adherents; the greater part of those regarded as generally favourable to it; and, most damning of all, forty-nine of the sixty-six English county members who were present at the division.

Though few, if any, of the Cabinet endorsed Wellington's total rejection of parliamentary reform, and some were ready to give consideration to a moderate measure, there was complete agreement that they themselves could not propose it. One political *volte-face* was enough. After Catholic Emancipation it was psychologically impossible for Wellington's Cabinet to contemplate another great surrender. The defeat on the Civil List, which had not been expected, proved their inability to control the Commons. Since a Whig motion on parliamentary reform was to be debated the next day, it seemed only sensible to quit office and leave everything to their successors. That decision was not as irresponsible as it would have been a year earlier. Certainly the majority against them on the Civil List was both heterogeneous and impermanent. Nevertheless, for the first time for a quarter of a century the Whigs were a possible alternative government. The death of George IV, who had a personal antipathy to Lord Grey, removed one great obstacle. As for their inexperience of government, the alliance with the remaining Canningites gave them a much-needed reinforcement of men who had recently held office.

For all that, there was nothing inevitable about the Whigs' accession to power. Essentially Wellington's ministry destroyed itself. For this the chief immediate cause was the unpolitical character of the Prime Minister. A soldier rather than a politician, Wellington did not possess the flexibility and tact needed in parliamentary life. He was too remote from ordinary men, too confident in his own abilities. To the last moment he believed that his ministry did not lack numbers in the House of Commons, but debating ability on the front bench.[25] What he could not be brought to admit was that he had alienated too many supporters on both the right and the left for his ministry to survive. Accustomed to command and to be obeyed, he never properly appreciated the problems of managing the House of Commons which had been for Liverpool a constant preoccupation. Within the Cabinet he resented criticism and opposition. He had become increasingly frustrated and irritable, ready at one point to throw up his post in favour of Peel. Tired and resentful, he came close to persuading himself that his colleagues were in league against him. They on their side were beginning to despair of the future of the ministry under his leadership. For many of them the decision to resign came as a relief; Peel was positively delighted. The rest were mutely resigned to their fate.[26]

Catholic Emancipation had been a great achievement. Probably only the Duke could have carried it off. But it was an isolated and personal achievement. For the rest the ministry seemed to having nothing left to offer. The image Wellington projected in November 1830 was one of a reactionary, authoritarian minister of the Crown, indifferent to public opinion and the House of Commons, indifferent even to those who were his natural supporters, presiding over an administration that was maladroit, extravagant and corrupt. The image was almost wholly false. Wellington was as constitutional a politician as any liberal; his administration was

upright and parsimonious. Nor was it devoid of useful legislation. In 1828 it had put through a modified version of
Liverpool's 1827 corn bill, the first significant alteration to
the Corn Law of 1815. In 1829, after years of preparation,
Peel at last secured his new Metropolitan Police Act, a landmark in English administrative history. Yet in one sense
public perception was not entirely wrong. The endemic
weaknesses of the political system after 1815 meant that it
needed continuous, skilful, and constructive leadership to
operate efficiently. The Duke was not responsible for those
weaknesses, but of the available politicians he was perhaps
the least fitted to deal with them. His failure completed the
disintegration of the old Liverpool party and the political
support it had received in the country and in Parliament.
More than the legislature, it was the political foundations
of executive government that needed repair and renovation
in 1830. The day of the organized party was close at hand.

In general terms it is clear that the passing of the Liverpool
system was not due to any marked revival of Whig strength,
any perceptible withdrawal of public confidence, any gross
errors of policy or any incompetence in the management
of national finances. It broke up because it was subjected
to strains which it was not adapted to meet. The key to
the pre-1830 government of Britain is to be found in the
limitations of power which attended ministers – any set of
ministers – in their conduct of public affairs. These limitations were inherent in the constitutional and political conventions and practices that had grown up since the
establishment of a limited monarchy in 1688. Only by
operating within these limits could the Liverpool administration, like its predecessors, obtain stability and exercise
influence. The limitations affected not only the pace and
effectiveness of government policy but also the actual range
of problems that ministers could realistically address. For
most purposes, and all important ones, government had to
work through a legislature which prided itself on its independence and whose historic function was to scrutinize and

confine the actions of the executive rather than facilitate them. The King, on the other hand, tended to regard ministers as his personal servants. Once assured of their suitability and competence, he was usually unwilling to incur the fatigues and uncertainties of frequent changes; though this consideration did not prevent him from using his considerable residual powers to inconvenience them in small matters and embarrass them on large ones.

The whole system in fact seemed designed to preserve ministers in office while denying them sufficient power to do all they might think necessary. One particular consequence of this complex apparatus of checks and balances was the difficulty of resolving great controversial issues by a simple process of substituting the existing ministers with their political opponents. General elections were unable to secure this; the monarch was usually unwilling. It was for this reason that Catholic Emancipation proved such a burden for the Liverpool administration. Though not the only issue of its kind, it was the one which between 1801 and 1829 strained the political constitution to breaking-point. The fall of Pitt in 1801, and the resignation of the Grenville administration in 1807, were already examples of its destructive influence. Behind the 'neutrality' principle adopted by Liverpool in self-defence in 1812 was the recognition that it was an issue which lay outside the normal range of Cabinet government. In political terms it was an insoluble problem because the monarch, most of the House of Lords, and a large part of the House of Commons (if not always an absolute majority) were opposed to a solution. No compromise was possible. Yet the state of Ireland ensured that the problem would not go away.

For the Liverpool ministry it was the worst kind of issue that can be faced by a political party. It was not a dispute between government and opposition, but within government and among its own parliamentary supporters. By the early 1820s half the Cabinet and nearly all its members who sat in the Commons were publicly committed to the liberal, pro-Catholic side of the great division in English politics. Against them were ranged a small but influential section of the Cabinet, including the Prime Minister himself, backed by the mass of their traditional following in the Commons. The significance of these last was all the greater because they were spokesmen for the popular instinctive feeling in the country which was untouched by the intellectual liberal principles that were the mark of the urban, educated middle classes of England and Scotland. Disunity in such a form, and on such an issue, was danger enough; the danger became immeasurably greater after 1822 with the emergence inside the government of two strong and determined politicians who, to the public, personified the opposing sides in the dispute, even though their rivalry in reality was more one of temperament than of principle.

What was equally disruptive was the assumption by both Liverpool and his two successors as effective heads of government that the Catholic question would sooner or later have to be solved by the governing set of politicians to which all three belonged. They implicitly accepted, that is to say, that the ultimate responsibility for finding, or refusing, a solution was theirs. It was not a decision which could be passed to the Whig opposition because the formation of a purely Whig ministry was not within the bounds of practical politics. The overwhelming doubt was whether the problem could be solved within the context of the old Liverpool administration without simultaneously destroying it.

The irony of the two years which followed Liverpool's retirement in 1827 was that Canning was forced to go outside the historical framework of the Liverpool system to make his coalition with the Whigs but failed, in the brief period afforded him, to indicate how he could secure the settlement of the Catholic question which would have been the natural outcome of that coalition. Wellington, by contrast, reacting to the crisis in Ireland with a soldier's rather than a politician's instincts, imposed a solution on a political structure which up to that point had shown an almost complete inability to produce one. The price for that successful *coup de main* was the final disintegration of the narrow parliamentary base which constituted what was left of the old Liverpool system. That system, despite its limitations, had served the country well in its time. Indeed, what is surprising is not how little but how much Lord Liverpool's ministry had been able to achieve in its fifteen years of office. But by 1827–30 its divisions had become too open, its resources too restricted, and its political aims too limited to provide an adequate political channel for the forces of change in British and Irish society.

1812	June 8	Lord Liverpool confirmed as prime minister
	July	Wellington's victory at Salamanca
	October	General election
1814	April	General peace in Europe
1815	March–June	Napoleon's Hundred Days
	March	New Corn Law
1816	March	Government defeat on income tax
	June	Canning rejoins Cabinet;
1817		Secret committees; Seditious Meetings Act; suspension of Habeas Corpus
1818	June	General election
	December	Duke of Wellington joins Cabinet
1819	July	Act for Resumption of Cash Payments
	August 16	Peterloo
	December	Six Acts
1820	March	General election
	July–November	Bill of Pains and Penalties against Queen Caroline in Parliament
	December	Canning resigns from Cabinet
1822	January	Peel home secretary

FEBRUARY	Wynn president of Board of Control
AUGUST 12	Suicide of Castlereagh
SEPTEMBER 16	Canning foreign secretary
1823 JANUARY	Robinson chancellor of the exchequer; Huskisson president of Board of Trade
1824 JULY	First free-trade budget
1825 APRIL	Burdett's Catholic Emancipation bill passes House of Commons; Cabinet crisis
1826 JUNE	General election
1827 FEBRUARY 17	Lord Liverpool suffers stroke
APRIL 12	Canning prime minister
AUGUST 8	Death of Canning; Goderich succeeds as prime minister
1828 JANUARY 9	Wellington invited to form government
APRIL	New Corn Law
MAY	Resignation of Huskissonites; Burdett's Catholic relief motion passes Commons
JULY	O'Connell elected for Co. Clare
1829 APRIL	Roman Catholic Emancipation Act
JUNE	Metropolitan Police Act
1830 JUNE 26	Death of George IV; accession of William IV
AUGUST	General election
NOVEMBER	Meeting of Parliament

NOVEMBER 15   Government defeat on Civil List
               motion .
NOVEMBER 16   Resignation of government

Sir Robert Peel by John Linnell
(*Mansell Collection*)

CHAPTER THREE

1841–46

Bruce Coleman

The ministry of 1841–46 stands as a pivotal experience in Conservative Party history. The government's origin in the general election victory of mid-1841 represented the culmination of a remarkable recovery from Toryism's apparently shattering defeat in the post-Reform Act election of December 1832. Reduced to the lowest Commons representation in their history, the Tories would need three general elections within nine years to wear away the Reformers' majority. But the majority of 1841 was decisive and the triumphant opposition had in Robert Peel a leader perhaps better established and recognized than any such figure had been before. His party, increasingly disciplined and cohesive since the mid-1830s, was seen by many contemporaries as the exemplar of a new style of party, effective as an opposition and geared to the reformed political system. The name 'Conservative' had been adopted for most party purposes. The term, first appearing in the late 1820s, had appealed as a label for the opponents of parliamentary reform in 1830–32 and then the developments of 1834–35 had confirmed the need for an identity under which both old Tories and disaffected Whigs could shelter. The talent available to the new ministry of 1841 was formidable and Peel's Cabinets would include two former and three future prime ministers. But the careers of almost all these figures and many others would be reshaped by the experience of 1841–46 and particularly by the disintegration of government and party in 1845–46. The Conservatives would not achieve another Commons majority until 1874. The question of the inevitability of the schism of 1846 and of the long period of minority status which followed it remains an issue for historians. Had Conservative government become incompatible with the dominant mood of early Victorian society or did its breakdown have more immediate and localized causes? Was 1846 the consequence or the cause of a Conservative unfitness to govern?

The historiography of this government, recognized as a remarkable one in its nineteenth-century context, has been dominated by the figure of Peel.[1] The dominant interpretations of the ministry's fate have been sympathetic to a prime minister depicted as a rational, high-minded, almost visionary figure who had fallen victim to the atavism of less enlightened followers.[2] This view appealed to generations of free-traders who viewed Corn Law repeal as a triumph of both sense and morality and also to twentieth-century Conservatives who, beset by democracy and welfarism, needed suitable heroes for their party's pantheon. The provider of 'the poor man's bread' served admirably. Recently historians have become more sceptical about Peel's role and more appreciative of the rationale and strength of early Victorian Conservatism. The question of leadership starts as only one issue in the consideration of a government that began with decisive Conservative victory in the 1841 election and ended in the greatest schism in the party's entire history.

Conservatism and Revival

The 1832 general election had returned at best around 180 opposition MPs against some 480 Reformers. Other estimates, discounting 'waverers', put the figure at 120–150. The English counties, soured by agricultural depression in the 1820s and strong for Reform by 1831, returned only

TABLE 3.1 General Election Results 1832–52

	1832		1835		1837		1841		1847		1852	
	Con	Lib	Con	Lib	Con	Lib	Con	Lib	Con	Lib	Con	Lib
SECTION A												
United Kingdom	179	479	275	383	309	349	368	289	327	329	331	323
England	123	348	205	266	239	232	284	187	247	222	251	216
Wales	13	16	17	12	18	11	19	10	19	10	18	11
Scotland	10	43	15	38	20	33	22	31	19	34	20	33
Ireland	33	72	38	67	32	73	43	62	42	63	42	63
English counties	42	102	74	70	100	44	124	20	108	36	115	29
SECTION B												
South West												
Cornwall	5	9	6	8	7	7	8	6	7(3)	7	8	6
Devon	2	20	5	17	6	16	10	12	10(2)	12	11(1)	11
Somerset	2	11	2	11	8	5	7	6	6(1)	7	7	6
Dorset	5	9	5	9	6	8	8	6	8(3)	6	7	7
Wiltshire	7	11	11	7	13	5	14	4	14(5)	4	13(5)	5
Gloucestershire	3	12	8	7	7	8	7	8	9(2)	6	4	11
Monmouthshire	1	2	1	2	1	2	2	1	2(1)	1	3	0
TOTAL	25	74	38	61	48	51	56	43	56(17)	43	53(6)	46

TABLE 3.1 *Continued*

	1832		1835		1837		1841		1847		1852	
	Con	Lib	Con	Lib	Con	Lib	Con	Lib	Con	Lib	Con	Lib
South												
Hampshire	4	15	9	10	11	8	14	5	11(4)	8	10(1)	9
Sussex	2	16	2	16	7	11	10	8	11(1)	7	13(1)	5
Kent (extra-met)	3	13	8	8	7	9	12	4	7(1)	9	11	5
Surrey (")	2	5	4	3	6	1	5	2	3(2)	4	3	4
Berkshire	4	5	6	3	5	4	8	1	6(1)	3	5	4
Buckinghamshire	5	6	7	4	7	4	8	3	7	4	6	5
Oxfordshire	2	5	4	3	4	3	4	3	4(2)	3	4(1)	3
TOTAL	22	65	40	47	47	40	61	26	49(11)	38	52(3)	35
Eastern Counties												
Essex	6	4	9	1	9	1	10	0	6(1)	4	10	0
Suffolk	4	7	7	4	9	2	6	5	7(1)	2	8	1
Norfolk	4	8	9	3	9	3	8	4	9(2)	3	8(1)	1
Cambridgeshire	1	4	2	3	2	3	5	0	3	2	5	0
Huntingdonshire	3	1	3	1	4	0	4	0	4	0	4	0
Hertfordshire	3	4	4	3	4	3	6	1	4(1)	3	3	2
Bedfordshire	1	3	2	2	3	1	4	0	2	2	2	2
TOTAL	22	31	36	17	40	13	43	10	35(5)	16	40(1)	9

	1832		1835		1837		1841		1847		1852	
	Con	Lib	Con	Lib	Con	Lib	Con	Lib	Con	Lib	Con	Lib
South Midlands												
Northamptonshire	3	5	4	4	4	4	4	4	4	4	4	4
Warwickshire	3	7	4	6	5	5	5	5	5(2)	5	6	4
Worcestershire	2	10	5	7	9	3	9	3	9(2)	3	6(1)	6
Herefordshire	2	5	2	5	3	3	3	4	4(2)	3	4	3
Shropshire	9	3	12	0	9	3	12	0	10(2)	2	11(1)	1
TOTAL	19	30	27	22	30	19	33	16	32(8)	17	31(2)	18
North Midlands												
Derbyshire	0	6	2	4	2	4	2	4	2	4	3	3
Leicestershire	2	4	5	1	4	2	4	2	4	2	4	2
Nottinghamshire	4	6	4	6	6	4	8	2	9(1)	1	9(3)	1
Lincolnshire	4	9	7	6	7	6	10	3	9	4	10	3
Staffordshire	5	12	7	10	9	8	8	9	9(4)	8	5(1)	12
Cheshire	3	7	4	6	4	6	5	5	4(2)	6	5(2)	5
TOTAL	18	44	29	33	32	30	37	25	37(7)	25	36(6)	26

TABLE 3.1 *Continued*

	1832		1835		1837		1841		1847		1852	
	Con	Lib	Con	Lib	Con	Lib	Con	Lib	Con	Lib	Con	Lib
North												
Lancashire	6	20	11	15	13	13	13	13	8(5)	18	7(1)	19
Yorkshire	3	34	13	24	14	23	19	18	13(1)	24	13(2)	24
Durham	0	10	2	8	3	7	3	7	3(1)	7	3(1)	7
Northumberland	2	6	2	6	4	4	3	5	2	6	2(1)	6
Westmorland	2	1	2	1	2	1	2	1	2	1	2	1
Cumberland	3	6	4	5	3	6	3	6	4	5	4	5
TOTAL	16	77	34	59	39	54	43	50	32(7)	61	31(5)	62
SECTION C												
London	1	19	0	13	2	18	4	16	1(1)	19	2	18
Manufacturing towns	6	39	13	32	13	32	13	32	13(7)	32	10(1)	35

NOTES: 1. The figures in Section A are derived from J. Vincent and M. Stenton (eds), *McCalmont's Parliamentary Poll Book. British General Election Results 1832–1918*, 8th edn. (Harvester Press, 1971), pp. xix–xxiii and p. 332B. Those in Section B and the London figures in Section C have been calculated from McCalmont's detailed returns with adjustments for known errors.

2. The Conservative figures include all designated Protectionists and Liberal Conservatives (but see note 3 below): all Whigs, Reformers, Radicals and Chartists are included as Liberals.

3. In Sections B and C Liberal Conservatives (Peelites) are identified within brackets after the Conservative numbers within which they have been included.

4. The figures for London in Section C are made up of the City of London, the metropolitan boroughs and the county of Middlesex. The figures for the thirty-nine manufacturing towns are those calculated by R. Stewart, *The Foundation of the Conservative Party 1830–1867* (Longman, 1978), Appendix 8, pp. 384–5.

forty-two Tories among their 144 members. The opposition's modest survival owed most to the small boroughs spared by the Reform Act. The outcome both reflected and further encouraged Tory demoralization. Some feared that any installation of a Tory ministry would provoke popular insurrection. In the Reform crisis both the Crown and the House of Lords had been humbled. Reform, Tories feared, had brought a new and dangerous relationship between government and opinion 'out of doors'. Shorn of the support of the old Court party – the Treasury's influence on the composition of the Commons, a mainstay of the Pitt regime but declining long before 1832, was now all but eliminated – governments would find it harder to resist 'clamour' and 'agitation'. Tories could hardly view the Reform ministry as a bulwark of stability. Under constituency pressure many ministerial candidates had pledged themselves to further constitutional reforms. Toryism represented constitutional conservatism; after the upheavals of 1829–32 it was no longer clear what that constitution was, let alone what it might become.

How did this party – if the virtually leaderless opposition benches when Parliament convened early in 1833 merited the description – recover to form a secure ministry by 1841? The answer lay partly in the return of more normal politics as the excitement of 1832 cooled and Tory strengths of property, money and influence reasserted themselves. A central organization was created capable of exploiting the good fortune of three general elections between 1835 and 1841. The old Treasury skills of Tory 'men of business' had been evident even in 1832 and the newly founded Carlton Club provided a base for party managers and a social focus for parliamentarians and supporters in Westminster.[3] Self-confidence revived. Many potential candidates had declined to stand in 1832, fearing the hopelessness of contests and the hostility of the popular mood, but soon party managers were finding more candidates with the courage of their convictions. Continued agitation, particularly in Ireland, generated alarm among the propertied. Supporters of the Whigs in modernizing and purifying the electoral system now began to feel themselves threatened in turn and looked to put the genie of radicalism back into the bottle. But the swing of opinion took time. Meanwhile the constitution's corner was fought by three of its central institutions – the Crown, the House of Lords and the established churches.

The first major recasting of post-Reform politics came in 1834. Four members of the Cabinet resigned, virtually en bloc. Ripon (the former Canningite premier Goderich) and Richmond, a pro-Reform Tory, sat in the Lords where Whig weakness was already apparent; more important were the two Commons figures, both moderate Whigs, Edward Stanley and Sir James Graham. O'Connell mocked the dissidents and their followers as the 'Derby Dilly' after the Stanley family's earldom. The resigners objected to government policy towards the established churches, to what they saw as undue truckling to O'Connell in Ireland and to the growing influence of Lord John Russell in the Cabinet. An Irish Church Temporalities Bill to revamp the Church of Ireland and, initially and most controversially, to appropriate 'surplus' revenues for public purposes had brought tensions to breaking-point. The King, himself alarmed, used the opportunity of a ministerial reconstruction in November to force the government's resignation and to install the Tories in office, initially under Wellington while Peel returned from Italy. William's hopes for a Tory–Stanleyite coalition came to nothing, but when the inevitable general election came in January 1835 the Conservatives (as they were now coming to be called) gained over ninety seats, so greatly strengthening their position in the Commons.[4] In December Peel had published an open letter to his constituents, the 'Tamworth Manifesto', defining the stance of his Cabinet. 'Party' was mentioned only once and then pejoratively. The document, ambiguous on some issues and representing an appeal, similar to that of Liverpool's ministry earlier, to an ideal of government above faction, was a *pièce d'occasion* designed to woo disillusioned Reformers like the Stanleyites and to blur the lines of distinction between Toryism and moderate Whiggism. More important electorally were the divisions on the Reform side, the renewed combativeness of the Tories and the reluctance of some Reformers to stand again, so that government gains included a significant number of uncontested seats. (In all 174 seats were uncontested against the 124 of 1832.) The turnover of seats was the largest in the three general elections leading to the 1841 ministry. That reflected the unnaturally low Tory baseline before 1835 but also other factors: the Conservatives were fighting the election as the government; they had the visible support of the Crown; and the Tory-dominated municipal corporations were fighting for their lives against the threat of Whig reform. Most of the gains came in the boroughs but with a proportionate swing in the less numerous county seats. In addition numbers of MPs and candidates were simply changing sides; the election returns were part of a longer-term swing of responsible opinion. But some 290 seats left the Conservatives still short of a majority in a House of 658 members. The Whigs consolidated their position by an agreement, the 'Lichfield House Compact', with O'Connell's Irish party, Peel resigned after the inevitable defeats and the King was humiliated again as Melbourne returned to office and dictated his terms.

Though the restored Whig government was able to dent borough Toryism with the 1835 Municipal Corporations Act (most of the new ratepayer-elected councils were initially Liberal), it continued to have problems with the Lords, who amended that measure and obstructed others. The truculence of the Upper House, where the maverick ex-Chancellor Lyndhurst challenged Wellington's leadership and the Royal Duke of Cumberland was an active Ultra, was a handicap for the Whigs and sometimes to the efforts of the new Conservatism to conciliate Whig waverers. Wellington's personal influence was crucial, though only towards the end of the decade, as the Ultras came to accept party discipline more readily, did he become master in his own House. The prerogative of the Lords had proved itself as an instrument of constitutional defence, particularly in restraining Whig legislation over Ireland and the Church, at a time when Commons Conservatism was still weak. It had also confirmed itself as a constitutional principle dear to Tory hearts. Despite the Upper House's instinct to show loyalty to a Conservative government, as it did for the most part from 1841, it remained a reserve of political grandees capable of a show of independence.

The established churches were one area of constitutional controversy in which the peers had asserted themselves. Relations between Church and State had contributed to the Tory break-up of 1829–30 and in the eyes of many Catholic Emancipation remained a blot upon the leadership's (and particularly Peel's) record. From 1833 the Whig government's measures for the Irish Church and its enquiries into the condition and revenues of the Church of England heightened the political sensitivities of churchmen. The threat of appropriation of ecclesiastical revenues raised the cry of 'the Church in Danger', inspired a High Church re-action in the shape of the Oxford Movement and galvanized the bishops, cowed by their unpopularity in 1831–32, into renewed political activity. Their influence had been a factor in the King's intervention against the Whigs in November 1834. Churchmen feared Whig government as too inclined to a secularizing liberalism and too ready to make concessions to allies amongst English Dissenters and Irish Catholics. The clergy of the establishments remained themselves a significant political force, particularly in the English counties and cathedral cities, and the church interest exerted itself in all three general elections of the Conservative advance. Its recognized spokesman in the Commons was Sir Robert Inglis, member for Oxford University since his celebrated defeat of Peel in the by-election of 1829. Wellington became Chancellor of the University in 1834 and was uplifted by the demonstrations of support at his installation that July. (He commented to Peel that 'there is nothing that people care so much about as the Church, excepting always their own Properties'.) The churches felt themselves to be a species of threatened property too. They were also a central element in the constitution that Conservatism was committed to uphold and in return they contributed generously, in England's Barsetshires and beyond, to its resurgence. This sense of an alliance successfully restored lay behind the young Gladstone's much-noted work of 1838, *The State in its Relations with the Church*. Peel's own relationship with the church interest was more ambiguous. There was unforgiveness on both sides for 1829, he was conscious of the practical problems posed by Dissent and Catholicism, and his relations with Inglis remained distant. In collaboration with Blomfield of London, the leading statesman among the bishops, Peel had worked with the Whig-initiated process of Church reform in the 1830s for ends which he saw as beneficial to the Church itself, but there too he had his critics among churchmen. Important as the church interest and political Conservatism were to each other, there remained uncertainties about the policies of any future Conservative government.

Ireland was an issue not easily separated from religious questions, though it had other dimensions of social order, political control and landlord/tenant relations. If Ireland had been the Achilles heel of Tory government in the late 1820s, so it was again for Whig government in the 1830s. Daniel O'Connell and the popular movement he had created moved on to new targets: the position and privileges of the official church, local government and popular education, the influence to be accorded to the Catholic Church and to the Irish party in the style of government. The 'tithe war' of the early 1830s and the importunity and obstructiveness of O'Connell had helped to produce the Stanleyite secession in 1834 and after the 1835 general election the Whigs and the Irish party were forced into closer alliance in the Commons. Popular hero as 'the Liberator' was to most Irish

Catholics, he was detested in most of Britain and the loathing on the Tory benches was near-pathological. In 1835 the Conservatives spent some £5,000 in pursuing a petition to unseat him as MP for Dublin. Arguably O'Connell contributed more to Conservative unity and revival in the 1830s than anyone else. Irish landownership and the Ascendency interest were well represented at Westminster, both in the Lords (where the Irish representative peers were a Tory fiefdom) and in the Commons. The Stanleys were only one example of a political family with substantial Irish landholdings. Favours to Catholicism in Ireland inflamed the Protestantism of Conservatives; a significant minority of the Commons party had at some time opposed the annual renewal of the parliamentary grant to Maynooth, the Catholic seminary. That issue would produce the first (if minor) backbench revolt after the 1841 victory. Though Conservatives viewed 1841 as a triumph over O'Connell, his Irish party and the Whigs retained a majority of the Irish seats (sixty-three to forty-two for the Conservatives) and, freed of the restraints of Whig government, he intensified his campaign for the repeal of the Union.

Agricultural protectionism had not been prominent in the early stages of Conservative advance, but it was a telling factor in 1841. The Corn Law of 1815 had always been controversial, though the intensity of feelings for and against had fluctuated with agricultural prices and trade cycles. A sliding scale (lower import duties as the domestic price of grain rose) had been introduced in 1828. Aggrieved agriculturalists were a feature of contemporary politics both in the Commons and out in the shires. Peel had often clashed with them. They blamed him for the severe price deflation that followed 'Peel's Act' of 1819 restoring gold convertibility, and then after 1832 he stood out against demands for the repeal or reduction of the malt tax. When Peel formed his minority ministry in 1834, the Marquis of Chandos, established as 'the Farmers' Friend', demanded such a measure as the price of his accepting office; Peel

refused. Yet the reformed political system was more responsive to agricultural opinion than the old one had been. The
Reform Act had distributed sixty-five extra seats to the
counties of England and Wales, almost balancing the sixty-
seven to new boroughs. A Tory amendment (the 'Chandos
clause', though the idea had originated with another Tory,
Sibthorp) had extended the county franchise to fifty-
pound-tenants-at-will alongside other categories of tenants
and the traditional forty-shilling freeholders. The act had
thus reinforced the representation of the agricultural interest to an extent some Whigs later regretted.[5] Though agricultural discontents were not the only factor, the enhanced
county seats produced the most consistent swing to the
Conservatives down to 1841. In the 1837 election following
William IV's death twenty-two gains in the English counties
more than offset minor losses in the boroughs and Ireland.

From that year another factor was present. The Anti-Corn
Law League, a new and politically radical movement for
free trade with a power-base in the Lancashire cotton
industry, was active in many urban constituencies and, in
time, in the Commons. The League combined free-trade
doctrine (not previously a particularly radical trait) with a
class-conscious animus against the supposed privilege
enjoyed by the landed interest. That interest, in its dual
capacity of landownership and the economy's agricultural
sector, reacted to the challenge with an enhanced self-
consciousness. The Whigs were uneasy about the League
and divided about free trade, but agriculturalists were now
less prominent among their Commons support and the League's pressure began to push them towards Corn Law
revision. Their 1841 budget proposal to replace the sliding
scale with a small fixed duty led to defeat in the Commons
and a general election with the fixed duty as the government's platform. The Conservative response, particularly
among candidates in the counties and agricultural boroughs,
was explicit commitment to protection by a sliding scale.
The English and Welsh counties returned 124 Conservatives

among their 144 members in dramatic contrast to the 102 Reformers of 1832. Net gains in the boroughs too, including some conspicuous triumphs in the cities, could not disguise the fact that the Conservatives remained much stronger in the small boroughs than in the large urban constituencies. In the industrial boroughs the party, though performing better than in 1832, remained in a decided minority. The 1841 majority thus represented not just the familiar constitutionalism but also the verdict of agrarian society in favour of significant agricultural protection.

The incoming ministry of September 1841 stood, however, for more than the immediate worries of agriculture. Though shaped by the circumstances of the 1830s and wearing the new Conservative label, the party could trace a much longer pedigree. There was old wine in the new bottles. Important components – the electoral managers trained in the school of Treasury influence, the ministerial elite with its executive mentality, the Country party aspect of the backbench gentry – represented continuity with the coalition gathered around the younger Pitt. Ripon, Peel and Wellington had learned their statecraft in the Liverpool ministry which had preferred to present itself as a national rather than a Tory government. Something of this sense of government above faction now survived among the new ministers. On the other hand the old Court party, the King's Friends, was now gone from the Commons. Party organization and loyalty had to provide the majorities which the Treasury had once delivered. There were other ambiguities. Conservatives saw themselves as upholders of the royal prerogative, yet the throne's occupant was now a Whig partisan who had kept Peel from office in the 'Bedchamber Crisis' of 1839 and virtually campaigned for Melbourne in 1841. The election result had thus been a humiliation for Victoria; for the first time a minority opposition had been returned to power smack against the sovereign's wishes. That lesson would force the Court, notably the Prince Consort, to rethink its political strategy, but the royal couple, though soon reconciled to Peel, would remain potentially troublesome for the Conservatives. On the backbenches formal 'independence' had all but gone. Conservative MPs had stood as party candidates and expected Peel to become premier if a majority were won. The Commons was polarized between two sides and the holding up of the government's majority, despite immense strains, until 1846 would suggest that it was the most cohesive of party majorities to date.[6] At the same time something of the style and culture of 'independence' remained. Most MPs were gentlemen who financed their own politics. They often had personal or family interests in the constituencies they represented and they expected to articulate the local moods and needs. The precedents for severe discipline had been in the old Court party, not among the country gentlemen. The class of 1841 were enthusiastic about ejecting the Whigs from office and installing Peel and Wellington in their places, but they did not expect the maintenance of Conservative government to require servitude to ministers and their whips.

Though politics had become more party-dominated in the 1830s, the new practices were short of precedents, traditions and shared understandings. Parties were, even by later nineteenth-century standards, lacking in representative institutions and ready mechanisms for agreeing general principles and policies, let alone details of legislation. The mutual obligation between leaders and followers remained undefined. Leadership itself might be a matter of royal choice or oligarchic co-option as much as any party decision. Peel, who had refused to serve as party leader until William and Wellington designated him as premier in 1834, could reasonably claim, when in office, to owe his position to more than party choice. Parties were still generally identified with broad principles rather than specific policies or programmes and with men rather than measures. The general stance of Conservatism in 1841 was predictable enough: maintenance of the constitution in Church and State, the upholding of social order and property, resistance to 'agitation' and 'democracy', defence of the union with Ireland and, as with any government, of British interests abroad. On the hot topic of agricultural protection Peel had avoided commitment to any high principle (his economic philosophy had long been broadly *laissez-faire*) but, like other frontbenchers, he had committed himself to the continuation of a sliding scale as a matter of administrative policy. None of this dictated the specifics of a legislative programme.

Meanwhile old scores had been settled, the Whigs were out, O'Connell, Leaguers and radicals had been frustrated, the age of radical reform was surely over, a government of order and constitutional defence had been installed on the back of perhaps the most assured majority since Pitt. (The overall majority was seventy-nine, a larger Conservative lead in England and Wales being cut back by Whig majorities in Scotland and Ireland.) But it was not an Ultra triumph. The Cabinet was broadly based, more so than in 1834. Both Peel and Wellington, now leading the Lords again, had long set themselves to control the Ultras; three members of the Derby Dilly (Stanley, Graham and Ripon) held major offices; Buckingham (the former Chandos) accepted office this time and Knatchbull, seen as a token representative of the gentry, served again. If Inglis remained on the back benches, the young Gladstone, though not initially in the Cabinet, could be seen as representative of the church. No major reforms of the Whig ministries were to be reversed. Soon the once hostile Victoria and Albert were coming to see their new government as the embodiment of stability and responsibility and Peel was becoming the new Court favourite.

No government in the century's second quarter was going to be without problems. Whatever the party complexion, tensions between government and at least some of its followers were inevitable. In this case the initial friction came over the Maynooth renewal and the re-election of the Whig incumbent Shaw Lefevre as Speaker. Peel was much lauded by his followers in the euphoria of victory, and expectations of patronage put the party in good heart, but scars remained from old battles over Catholics and agriculture. Speaking on the motion which brought about the Whig government's defeat, Peel had concluded with a peroration upholding the idea of a minister's 'public duty' as both personal and above party: 'power I will not hold, unless I can hold it consistently with the maintenance of my own opinions'.[7] Peel elaborated the point, again with a hint of resignation if frustrated, in his ministry's first major debate:

> It is right that there should be a distinct understanding as to the terms on which a public man holds office . . . What can be my inducement but the hope of rendering service to my country, and of acquiring honourable fame? Is it likely that I would go through the labour which is daily imposed upon me if I could not claim for myself the liberty of proposing to Parliament those measures which I believe to be conducive to the public weal? I will claim that liberty – I will propose those measures, and I do assure this House that no considerations of mere political support should induce me to hold such an office . . . by a servile tenure which would compel me to be the instrument of carrying other men's opinions into effect.[8]

Government and Party

The ministry of 1841–46 has enjoyed a historical reputation for legislative and administrative achievement. That outcome was not inconsistent with its origin in a mood of constitutional conservatism. The times were disturbed enough to require responses: Ireland, religious tensions, Chartism, the League, sundry agitations 'out of doors', trade depression, all needed some notice from government. The Whigs had left much unfinished business, including a serious running deficit in the public finances. In Ireland the ministry was confronted by O'Connell's repeal movement and a Catholic hierarchy uneasy about Conservative government. In the government's activity there would also be an eager grasping of delayed opportunity. Peel, who came to dominate his government and its legislative programme, had won a reputation in the 1820s as an active administrator and determined legislator. It was a reputation he cultivated and which he set out to enhance after the frustration of eleven years without real legislative opportunity. A merely reactive government was not his intention. That compulsion to tackle problems, to achieve settlements of outstanding issues, would in time unsettle his party to the point of disintegration.

Religion was an obvious area of difficulty. The Church of England, shaken by Catholic Emancipation, had been further affronted by a decade of Whig government. Now it expected more sympathy and support from a Conservative government. In the event the ministry, having raised expectations, dashed most of them. Inglis and the Church lobby had been working for a resumption of parliamentary aid to Anglican church extension – the building of new churches and subdividing of parishes in the cities and populous districts. After some pause Peel and Graham, the Home Secretary, decided not to risk the outcry from Dissenters and radicals which public subvention would have provoked. An Act of 1843 facilitated parochial subdivision and the endowment of livings, but only from the Church's own resources or by voluntary contribution. Despite Peel's private generosity to this cause, the outcome was a grave disappointment to the church's leaders who saw it as signifying a denial of the state's duty to support its church establishment. Also in 1843 Graham introduced clauses into his Factory Bill which would have given the Anglican clergy authority over an enhanced system of schooling for factory children. The sharp reaction from Dissenters forced Graham to retreat. Though a prudent decision politically, again it looked as though the government was concerned less to assist the

Church than to appease its enemies. Almost any piece of religious legislation was bound to affront some interest or other: the 1844 Dissenters' Chapels Act, which settled the right of Unitarians to hold their chapels even if founded for trinitarian worship, was highly unpopular with other varieties of Dissenters and with churchmen. The second reading was opposed by 106 Conservative MPs. The government did achieve a modest concordat with the bishops over the operations of the Committee of the Council on Education and the inspection of grant-assisted National Society schools, an arrangement which left the Church of England to •enjoy the lion's share of the parliamentary subvention to popular education. On the whole, though, the church's expectations had been disappointed by the government's circumspect and largely defensive strategy. Influential churchmen like Blomfield, Inglis and Ashley drifted away from Peel. In effect the ministry had confirmed the Whig legacy and left the church to fend for itself in an ambiguous and semi-voluntarist position. It appeared in sharp contrast to the government's vigorous wooing of the Catholic Church in Ireland which culminated in the Maynooth episode in 1845. But the ministry's relations within the church were irreconcilable only with the Puseyite and ritualist wing, an intractable element for any administration. Most churchmen, however disappointed, preferred Conservative government to a renewal of Whig rule.

In Scotland, however, relations with the Presbyterian establishment turned into one of the government's disasters. A simmering conflict over the right of lay patrons to appoint ministers against the wishes of congregations was handled brusquely and insensitively by the government, in which Peel was strongly for patronage rights, and led to the 'Disruption' of 1843 when over one-third of the ministers of the Church of Scotland seceded to form a free kirk. Thus religious dissent of a voluntarist character had been massively strengthened in Scotland with consequences for that country's political development. Though the worst reckoning lay some decades later, Victorian Conservatism would never again win as many as the twenty-two seats (even then a minority) which it had taken in Scotland in 1841.

In Ireland, where religion was only part of the problem, the ministry showed the same combination of determination and insensitivity. The responsible ministers, de Grey as Viceroy and the more liberal Eliot as chief secretary, were ill-assorted. De Grey's close links with the Ascendency aristocracy made him an inflexible colleague for Peel and Graham, who in time took Irish policy into their own hands. After a period of benign neglect they stamped on O'Connell's repeal agitation in 1843, banned a great meeting planned at Clontarf and prosecuted him for incitement to treason. But with O'Connell convicted and imprisoned (though subsequently acquitted on appeal) Peel and Graham embarked on a policy of conciliating Catholic opinion, particularly the bishops and wealthy laity. De Grey's retirement and replacement by the more liberal and malleable Heytesbury in May 1844 eased the change. Peel's policy – 'of weaning from the cause of Repeal the great body of wealthy and intelligent Catholics, by the steady manifestation of a desire to act with impartiality' – produced an initiative (eventually unsuccessful) over Irish university education and a Charitable Bequests Act in 1844 which gave Catholics parity with Protestants in the body overseeing Irish charities and removed the impediments the law of mortmain put in the way of the Catholic Church's acquisition of property. Little criticized in Parliament, the act succeeded in dividing Irish Catholic opinion sharply and so encouraged Peel, Graham and their confidants to the next step. In 1845 the government proposed to provide a permanent and increased annual grant, together with a capital sum, to the Maynooth seminary. The annual renewal of the grant had always been controversial and Peel was under no illusions about the reaction of his party (he told Gladstone it would 'very probably be fatal to the Government') of whom many saw the measure as not only an undermining of the Irish Church but also an abandonment of the fundamentally Protestant character of the constitution. Gladstone resigned from the Cabinet out of consistency with his published views (though he eventually voted with the ministry) and an extensive revolt on the Conservative benches left the bill to pass only with Whig help. On the third reading 148 Conservatives voted in favour, 149 against, after more than 10,000 petitions had been received opposing the bill. The Ultra peer Winchilsea led a secession from the Carlton to found the National Club 'in support of the Protestant principles of the Constitution'. It was the largest and most passionate of party revolts to date; the pessimistic Graham concluded that government and party were in a final breach. But a revolt which lacked Gladstone's leadership and needed Winchilsea's had clear limitations. The anti-Maynooth movement, which included both Anglicans and Dissenters, was divided between those who wanted to uphold existing establishments against Catholic encroachment and those who opposed establishments altogether. But the damage to party morale and cohesion was serious. 'Everybody knows the Tory party has ceased to exist as a party', wrote the diarist Greville in April. Though tempers were cooling by the session's end, the weakness of a government which survived by grace of the opposition was obvious. By now the recommendations of the Devon commission on Irish land tenure which Peel had appointed earlier were being obstructed fatally in the Lords. The government of Ireland and the contentment of the party were always going to be difficult to combine, but Peel had gone recklessly far in his pursuit of 'impartiality'. *The Times*, usually supportive of Peel, had opposed the Maynooth bill and reflected upon Peel's handling of his party:

> It cannot be consistent that the country was to be saved by creating a party ten years since, and by confounding and smashing all parties, especially that saviour party, now.[9]

Not every area of policy turned out so unfavourably. Britain's economy and social condition looked far stronger by 1845 than in 1841. The government had inherited a severe trade depression which would begin to lift only from 1843. Conservatives had long criticized the Whigs as weak and ineffective in dealing with the unrest which tended to arise from economic depression; the victory of 1841 heralded a tougher enforcement of law and order. Graham at the Home Office accepted the challenge. The year 1842 was critical, with mass unemployment in the industrial districts. The largely lower-class movement for the democratic reforms of the People's Charter reached a new peak of activity and was particularly strong in the depressed textile areas; the League intensified its agitation, blaming trade depression and popular distress upon the Corn Laws. A tense summer culminated in August's dangerous 'Plug Plot' disturbances. Graham and Peel, backed by Wellington, recently restored as commander-in-chief, moved troops and Metropolitan Police to the disturbed areas and mounted a campaign of prosecutions.[10] Though the crisis passed, the experience left Peel and Graham, now close confidants in most areas of government business, seriously alarmed. On social issues like the Poor Law and factory legislation they were both hostile to popular agitation, scornful of the Tory-radical mood among fringe elements of their party, and inclined to a *laissez-faire* view of government's role in the economy. The government renewed the 1834 Poor Law Act and discouraged backbench attempts at factory legislation, denying Ashley and the 'humanity-mongers' of the Ten Hours movement any significant successes. Most social problems and popular agitations would fade, their argument went, as economic prosperity returned. By 1844–45 it had done so, as railway investment and building accelerated. But the experience of 1842 remained a nightmare for the two ministers. The combination of mass distress during a depression, high food prices and League agitation represented a potentially explosive mixture. The fear of popular insurrection affected their thinking on a range of other issues. Graham, who had anyway concluded that continuing population growth would soon necessitate free importation of food, wrote to Peel in the last days of 1842, 'It is a question of *time*. The next change in the Corn Laws must be to an open trade . . .'[11]

Graham's own performance had not helped the government. Initially his toughness had appealed to nervous Tories. On entering office he had appointed over 400 new Tory magistrates to the borough benches, a dramatic alteration of the political balance, while his attempt to help the church over factory schools had at least reflected his party's instincts. But Graham's personal style was unattractive – cold, aloof and uncompromising – and it became clear that the former Whig had little time or sympathy for his new party's backbenchers. His handling of Poor Law and factory reform issues, where there was some significant minority concern within the party, was harsh and insensitive. In dealing with civil disorder his intolerance towards local authorities, including many Tory magistrates, lost friends and won enemies. His attempts to impose stipendiary magistrates on the disturbed areas and to bully or blackmail the localities into adoption of the County Police Act were resented and viewed as doubtfully constitutional. Graham had become a liability to the government's relations with Conservative opinion and the backbench revolt of 1844 over factory reform was in part a rebuff to Graham personally. By 1845 the antagonism he engendered on both sides of the Commons was evident. Yet it was Graham who had become Peel's main confidant in the ministry's policy-making. Each seems to have encouraged the other in common characteristics: the viewing of government as a rational activity above political arts; a black-and-white analysis of complex issues with a distaste for compromise or concession; a refusal to humour or conciliate followers; an intellectual contempt and icy authoritarianism towards critics and dissidents. The sense in late 1845 that Corn Law repeal was a brainchild of Peel and Graham personally, not of the broader leadership, was itself provocation to the back benches.[12]

The government's diplomatic and overseas record, though it still generated strains and tensions, was not a cause of weakness. Much of the wider world was inevitably uncomfortable, whether Brazil's commitment to slavery, the expansionism of the United States, the French pursuit of dynastic ambitions in Spain and colonial ambitions in the Pacific, or the trend among other powers towards protectionist trade policies. Aberdeen, the Foreign Secretary, was pacific and pro-French; Peel, Wellington and Graham were diplomatically tougher and instinctively distrustful of France. These differences caused Aberdeen to seek to resign in 1845. Colonial policy under Stanley and later Gladstone at the Colonial Office was circumspect and non-expansionary, but local circumstances and the ambitions of proconsuls brought a number of significant acquisitions of territory. Ellenborough's expansionism as Governor-General in India alarmed both his Whitehall colleagues and the East India Company which recalled him in 1844. His successor Hardinge was more cautious but even he found himself embroiled in a Sikh war. China and New Zealand gave the government problems it found unwelcome. But despite Wellington's nightmares about military and naval inadequacies, which led to increased spending after years of retrenchment, the ministry could point to peace maintained and a record of diplomatic settlement. France was forced to end its pressure on Morocco, the Treaty of Nanking ended the first Opium War (Hong Kong was ceded by China), British India was secured and extended without major disasters and, most importantly, treaties over Maine in 1842 and Oregon in 1846 ended dangerous territorial disputes with the United States. During its final domestic crisis the ministry was able to lay before the House its latest successes in the Sikh war and the Oregon settlement.

Though the cohesion of the government's support had been weakened by religious and Irish issues, notably

Maynooth, it was the controversy over agricultural protection that finally destroyed the ministry and split the party. Until late 1845 even that issue was kept within bounds. Peel's strategy of handling protection within the framework of a broader budgetary and economic policy had largely succeeded, despite a build-up of backbench and constituency unease. Though not combining the Exchequer with the premiership as in 1834, Peel introduced the major budgets of 1842 and 1845 himself and they were, indeed, of his own making. The 1842 measures remained perhaps his *tour de force*. Inheriting both a major budgetary deficit and the argument over the Corn Laws, Peel, encouraged by Ripon and Graham, pushed through a revision of the sliding scale to a lower level of duties. Despite opposition from both Leaguers and some agriculturalists, the measure passed the Commons overwhelmingly. Next Peel proposed the reintroduction of the income tax which, first adopted as a wartime expedient, had been ended by the Commons in 1816. Set at seven pence in the pound on incomes over £150 per annum, the tax was to be an emergency measure for three years. (Ireland was exempted but bore additional duties elsewhere.) Then Peel introduced a major tariff revision to simplify the scale of import duties by abolishing some, reducing others, ending some prohibitions and generally, he argued, encouraging trade and reducing the cost of living. The most controversial elements were again agricultural. Some eighty-five Conservatives revolted against clauses to permit importation of meat and live cattle.

Although some of the claims made for the measures proved to be misleading (lower duties did not yield more revenue as Peel had predicted and the main generator of extra revenue was the income tax), the programme did amount to a political success. Despite the League's hostility, it was regarded as a settlement by most opinion, both Whig and Conservative. Helped by the trade revival from 1843, the 1842 measures came to be seen as the basis of both economic recovery and public solvency. There had been some rumblings. Buckingham resigned in protest at what he saw as a betrayal of agriculture, but he was no longer an active Farmer's Friend. Vyvyan, one of the *frondeurs* of the 1830s, wrote a critical pamphlet and abandoned politics. But most agriculturalists were willing to accept the revision as a settlement of the Corn Laws. It was, as the protectionist William Miles put it later, 'looked upon as a contract as well as a compromise'. If Peel and Graham were unsettled at the end of 1842, it was by scenes far from those of the House of Commons.

Each subsequent session witnessed clashes between the government and sections of its following, resentments increasing and rebellions growing larger. Despite disappointments over Church matters, 1843 produced only one controversy involving protection, the ministry's proposal (reflecting the needs of colonial government in a troubled Canada) to admit Canadian corn at a nominal duty. Though presented as a measure of colonial preference rather than free trade, it alarmed agriculturalists who had seen 1842 as a final settlement. In the localities agricultural protection societies multiplied. In July Richmond in the Lords promised resistance 'by every constitutional means' to further erosion of protection and so effectively put himself at the head of the agricultural interest. In February 1844 a Central Agricultural Protection Society was formed under his presidency to represent agrarian society's case nationally. Initially it denied itself political activity and may have been 'little more than a pacifier to stop the tenant farmers from crying',[13] but it gave potential for political organization in the future. The lines of later battle were being drawn.

The main issues of 1844 were not agricultural. Sharp clashes between the government and its Commons backbenchers occurred over sugar duties (a sensitive issue involving not only West Indies interests but also the distinction between slave-grown and 'free' sugar) and factory legislation. Historians have disagreed over the significance of these episodes,[14] which ended after Peel had threatened resignation if his backbenchers did not reverse their earlier votes and let the government's proposals through unimpaired. Over sugar he was helped by a rallying speech from Stanley, who retained credit with the back benches, and negatively by a threatening, doctrinaire speech from the Whig Howick, but the main lesson was the lack of mutual sympathy and respect between Peel and a body of his followers. His insistence that relatively minor points of legislation involved issues of confidence seemed pernickety and offensive; it amounted too to a narrowing of his hold over his party to the basic preference for Conservative over Whig government. Though successful, the blackmail raised many questions. *The Times*, generally friendly to Peel, observed that, for all his qualities as a minister, he 'has not identified himself – he has never attempted to identify himself – with the feelings or sympathies of his supporters'. He failed to consult them on his intentions and, when he did eventually announce his policy, told them 'that they must swallow it'.[15] From this point Peel's failings as a manager of his party became a commonplace of political gossip and analysis.

The session produced two less controversial measures which enhanced the administration's reputation for legislative creativity. The Bank Charter Act, Peel's handiwork and a matter of personal pride, provided a tighter regulatory framework for note issue under the superintendence of the Bank of England. Recent historians have questioned its merits and seen it as a crudely bullionist measure which reflected Peel's inability to understand note issue except in terms of gold convertibility. (He was thus still fighting his battle of the 1820s.) Short term, the act was hardly a success and had to be suspended in the financial crisis of 1847, but arguably its long-term psychological impact helped confidence in sterling and in Britain's central financial institutions. The Railway Act was largely the work of Gladstone at the Board of Trade. An interventionist in this matter, Gladstone was seeking to regulate an area where speculative mania was already apparent. The operations of the fast-multiplying companies were causing many practical complications and, as the many railway bills came before Parliament, the relationship between private and public interests was a fraught issue. Gladstone found himself caught between the railway interests and an unsympathetic premier (Peel thought the measure, which allowed opportunity for subsequent state ownership, 'a precedent dangerous to the security of all property') and the act was less stringent than he had wished. The Railway Board created under the act to vet new railway schemes was soon dissolved, partly because of Peel's hostility. Evident here were Peel's readiness to dominate his ministers in their own departmental business, his pronounced *laissez-faire* instincts and his sensitivity to certain kinds of business interest.

Though the 1845 session would be overshadowed by Maynooth, it also saw the second stage of Peel's programme of financial and tariff reforms, now introduced in prosperous times which allowed him to claim success for his earlier measures. Income tax, which had produced an overall budgetary surplus, was extended for a further three years and there was a major reduction in the sugar duties. Import duties were abolished on over half the items previously subject, raw cotton amongst them. The strategy was to use the budgetary surplus to stimulate trade and reduce living costs. Sections of the press hailed it as a free-trade budget and certainly Peel's language had increasingly celebrated free trade as a general principle while permitting exceptions 'to allow for the present state of society'. The agricultural interest, denied direct benefit from the budget, rumbled again. A motion for agricultural relief was the occasion of a notable speech from Disraeli, now working his way back from Young England extravagances, but received fewer than eighty votes; the *Morning Post*, previously loyal to the ministry, declared itself for the landed interest and against Peel whom it accused of betraying 'the principles which he professed when he was raised to office'. Peel's boast to Hardinge, away in India, that he had 'repeated the Coup d'Etat of 1843' with the House of Commons 'taken by surprise' illustrated the almost conspiratorial approach he now had to dealings with his party.[16]

By the end of that year the government had resigned and been reinstated. The cause was neither the budget nor Maynooth and, during the recess, there were no immediate parliamentary problems. The issue was the survival of the Corn Laws. In the late summer it became clear that blight in the European potato harvest was going to affect Ireland severely. Peel and Graham were concerned about Ireland but immediately linked the issue with that of the Corn Laws which, privately, they had already determined should be repealed when opportunity offered. They argued that Ireland's plight necessitated immediate suspension of the sliding scale and that, once suspended, it could not easily be reimposed. But opposition to these conclusions materialized in the Cabinet and at its meeting on 6 November Peel and Graham were supported by only Aberdeen and Herbert. On 22 November Russell, the Whig leader, published his 'Edinburgh Letter' advocating complete repeal of agricultural protection both as a response to the Irish famine and as right and necessary in itself. This challenge intensified the public pressure, the Anti-Corn Law League renewed the agitation that had been in the doldrums since 1844 and on 4 December *The Times*, now converted to repeal, claimed that that was the Cabinet's policy. In fact, despite intense pressure from Peel, two ministers, Stanley and Buccleuch, preferred resignation to such a course.

On 6 December Peel delivered the government's resignation to Victoria. At this stage there was no prospect of an alternative Conservative ministry; Stanley, the only possible leader of one, declared himself against such a role. The Queen invited Russell to attempt to form a Whig ministry. He was, however, in large minorities in both Houses and no leading politician wanted to put an issue which aroused such passions to a general election. There were divisions in

the Whig camp both over protection and between prominent personalities. The Queen and the Prince Consort, hop-
ing Peel might continue in office, were not over-friendly
towards Russell and his problems, while Peel himself
declined to give sufficient assurance of his personal support
for a repeal measure. Eventually Russell declined the royal
commission and returned the poisoned chalice to the Conservatives. On 20 December Peel, urged on by the royal
couple, accepted reinstatement in office without consulting
his Cabinet colleagues, before later 'announcing to them
that he was Her Majesty's Minister, and whether supported
or not, was firmly resolved to meet Parliament as Her
Majesty's Minister, and to propose such measures as the
public exigencies required'. Visibly excited and elated by
the outcome, Peel threw himself into the task of ending the
Corn Laws with the air of a man who had found his destiny.[17] Buccleuch was persuaded to continue; only Stanley
resigned from the Cabinet (though Fremantle, the Irish
Secretary, and various minor office-holders chose to go too)
and he was replaced by Gladstone, atonement for Maynooth
now behind him.

By the time Parliament met on 22 January 1846 political
excitement was intense. The League, revived by the recent
developments, had now mounted a considerable campaign.
Conservative revolt was apparent on a scale not seen before.
The Central Agricultural Protection Society rescinded its no-
politics rule and, under Richmond, began to organize a campaign of resistance.[18] The fiercest rebellion was out in the
counties where the protection societies were virtually
supplanting normal Conservative organization. In many
constituencies the farmers themselves, especially the freeholders independent of landlord influence, were taking the
lead, not the MPs, aristocracy or gentry.[19] A populist 'revolt
of the field' was under way. The Leaguers had presented
their case against the Corn Laws as a middle-class assault
on aristocratic privilege; ironically the most outright rejection of their panacea came from a middle-class agricultural

interest group. Government loyalists argued that the effective choice was now between two free-trade ministries, Conservative or Whig; some of them, including the veteran seer Croker, urged Peel to bring forward a package of measures that balanced Corn Law repeal with substantial compensation to the agricultural interest.[20] But Peel's announcement of his proposals on 27 January dashed that hope. The Corn Laws would not finally disappear for three years but with only a modest sliding scale in the interim, while colonial corn would be admitted almost free immediately. The compensations to agriculture would be few and minor, only a public loans scheme for improvements like drainage being noteworthy. As in 1845, Peel's refusal to recognize agriculture as an interest warranting significant relief was evident. So was the tide of opinion 'out of doors' among Conservatives. Of eight by-elections (some forced by the repeal issue) held in the early weeks of 1846, the protectionists won six and Whig or League opposition two. One of the former was a high-profile victory for a farmers' candidate against the Cabinet minister Lincoln in Nottinghamshire South. Ministerial candidates had almost nowhere to stand or hide. A protectionist party was emerging (Disraeli later identified a meeting of the Central Society on 28 January with the effective establishment of 'a third political party') though it had as yet no real Commons leadership. Disraeli mocked and needled Peel from the backbenches, but it was only the rapid and unexpected emergence of Lord George Bentinck, son of a duke and a previously inarticulate MP, that gave the protectionists a willing leader they could recognize and follow. In the Lords Richmond harried the government but Stanley still refused to serve as leader against Wellington or Peel.

Neither Stanley nor Bentinck was a narrow agriculturalist. Their objections to Peel's course were not the farmers' fears of financial ruin. They saw in the end of agricultural protection a body-blow, part economic, part symbolic, to the landed classes who were the main buttress of the constitution. It would give a triumph to those commercial interests, represented by the League, which were the class enemies of landownership. It would intensify and accelerate the nation's economic transformation and, with it, a political and constitutional transformation of an unacceptable kind. For men who thought this way the defence of the constitution, that central Conservative purpose, was linked with the Corn Laws as firmly as it was in Peel's very different reasoning. They also found the way Peel had treated his party intolerable. His leadership amounted to a betrayal of his followers and their feelings and involved an unabashed surrender to the opposition – one spearheaded by the League with all its offensiveness of language and dubious constitutionality of method. The sense that Peel was now testing his party to breaking point was at the heart of Stanley's refusal to collaborate and Bentinck's determination to resist. Beyond that was the objection that Peel's behaviour, discreditable in itself, was forcing his followers to behave likewise. Many Conservative MPs had pledged themselves to the Corn Laws in 1841 and in subsequent moments of agricultural alarm. The choice was between a breach of faith and, as Bentinck put it, 'Honour – Honesty – and every feeling of a gentleman'. Stanley told the Lords he had resigned rather than 'sacrifice what I conceived to be my own personal consistency and honour'. For many MPs it was their relationship with their constituencies and the pain that 'betrayal' would cause at that level that persuaded them to oppose repeal.[21]

The Corn Importation Bill passed comfortably in the Commons with the aid of Whig votes. The Conservatives supporting the measures consistently numbered 112; those opposing at some stage as many as 250. Peel had lost more than two-thirds of his followers to protectionism. Though the office-holders stood by Peel, the division was otherwise heavily influenced by constituency considerations. Of the party's English county members 86 per cent opposed repeal; among its English borough members the figure was 54 per cent. But many of those boroughs were partly agricultural in character and it was only among Conservatives from the larger non-agricultural boroughs that Peel had majority support. The regional pattern, though not clearcut, was still highly significant. Protectionist feeling was strongest in the main wheat-growing areas – England's southern and eastern counties and the south and east midlands. In 1841 the Conservatives had been most successful in England outside its industrial heartlands and London; that pattern was largely confirmed by 1846 and reflected in the general elections of 1847 and 1852. Social origins of MPs were not the critical determinant in 1846. Peel's loyalists were drawn overwhelmingly from landed families. There was, however, considerable overlap with earlier rebellions. Of 166 Conservatives who had opposed the Maynooth bill at some point, 133 now opposed Corn Law repeal.[22]

These divisions and the emotion they generated meant that there were now enough Conservative critics determined and organized to bring Peel down. He seems to have hoped that his Irish coercion bill would rally the party, but on 25 June (the day the corn bill passed its third reading in a House of Lords heavily pressured by Wellington and Russell) the government was defeated on the measure in the Commons despite the support of nearly half the protectionists. The opposition of some seventy dissidents led by Bentinck and the abstention of some fifty others proved decisive. In a resignation speech badly received in the House but better by the press, Peel condemned his agrarian critics as 'monopolists' and pronounced a startling encomium upon Cobden, the leading League spokesman who throughout that Parliament had harassed and taunted the Conservatives, Peel included. Peel's intention, beyond self-justification, could only have been to humiliate and provoke his former followers.

Though prominent figures on both sides – including Stanley, who accepted the leadership of the protectionists once the ministry had fallen – looked to an early reunification of the party, Peel was unco-operative. He had, once defeated, been determined upon the government's resignation and had thwarted schemes to reconstitute the ministry by dropping himself. Out of office he continued to frustrate prospects of reunion by keeping a body of Liberal Conservatives (soon called Peelites) around him and using them to sustain Russell's Whig government. Many became restive with this policy and by 1850 Peel's original hundred or so supporters had dwindled to about forty-five regulars in Commons divisions.[23] No other deposed Conservative leader has ever renounced and denounced his party so savagely. The nearest equivalent would be Ramsay MacDonald's break with the Labour Party after the formation of the National Government in 1931. Peel's personal role in the 1840s crisis of Conservative government clearly stands out as exceptional.

Peel: Leader as Minister

Peel has been much lionized by posterity. By his death in 1850 the sort of opinion, largely urban, which saw free trade and cheaper food as ideals was already revering him for 'moral heroism'.[24] Mid-twentieth-century historiography found it difficult to overcome its awe of Peel's reputation and the postwar period of welfare democracy and political 'consensus' saw in Peel a style of Conservatism – above partisanship and sectionalism, concerned apparently for the well-being of the masses – of considerable appeal. More recent treatments have, however, been more questioning of Peel's part in the downfall of his own government.

Circumstances have to be taken into account. No ministry in the century's second quarter found the task of government easy. Economic depressions were severe and alarming in their consequences; even after that of the early 1840s had eased, it was not unreasonable to fear a recurrence. Religion and Ireland, separately or together, were immensely difficult areas of policy in which governments were almost bound to lose friends without influencing many people. The Corn Law issue, though variable in intensity, was made more fraught by the interactions of trade cycles and grain prices and was bound to be divisive in national politics, all the more so for the constituency distribution effected by the Reform Act. The spread of free-trade ideology was unsettling and factors of class consciousness and interest-group rivalry were at work. The Corn Laws became an issue of immense symbolism even more than of economic interest.[25] (The main impact of repeal came only with the sharp fall of grain prices in the 1870s.) Peel and Graham had responded to the developments of 1842 in an opposite way to their followers, seeing not a final settlement of tariff policy but evidence that the Corn Laws, so easily depicted as embodying aristocratic disdain for popular suffering, remained a liability for any future industrial crisis that the Anti-Corn Law League chose to exploit. The view that Britain's expanding population would require freer importation of foodstuffs and that, in Peel's later words, 'The worst ground on which we can *now* fight the battle for institutions, for the just privileges of Monarchy and Landed Aristocracy, is on the question of food' was not unreasonable. But the Corn Law repeal on which Peel and Graham became determined was always going to be immensely difficult for their party even when presented as in the interests of social order and constitutional conservatism. An issue which tended to set food producers against food consumers, the agricultural constituencies against the cities and industrial districts, was bound to be difficult for any government to mediate. For a Conservative government the task would be all the harder because 1841 had seen most of the party nail their colours to the mast of protectionism and had confirmed the English county members, the politicians most sensitive to agricultural pressure, as the backbone of their Commons majority. Arguably the ending of protection, as opposed to the gradualism in tariff reform which Peel had practised in 1842 and 1845, was never a sustainable option for such a government. At the very least it required an immense sensitivity and dexterity in handling the ministry's party following.

Peel's strategy had other preoccupations. His response to the apparent dangers exposed by 1842 had been primarily one of fear and the instinctive pessimism of Graham, responsible as home secretary for the maintenance of order, played upon these worries. Such fears were not unusual in a generation for which political folk-memory ran from the Gordon Riots and the French Revolution down to riots over Queen Caroline and parliamentary reform. Peel's establishment in 1829 of the Metropolitan Police, a force under direct Home Office control, had been inspired largely by his fears for the capital's political stability. Now the main threats to order seemed to come from the industrial areas as well as the cities. The response of Peel and Graham was thus not primarily humanitarian (an attitude for which they showed scant sympathy in other policy areas) but prudential. Free food importation, cheap bread and upper-class sacrifice were to neutralize the threatening combination of lower-class distress and middle-class agitation.

Peel's response may also have had a personal dimension. His own nervousness about violence struck many contemporaries. He was held to be easily frightened and short of physical courage. (After his death the *Lancet* carried an article discussing specifically Peel's 'excessive sensibility to pain'.) Certainly two assassination attempts on the Queen in 1842 and the murder in January 1843 of his secretary Drummond, mistaken for himself, had shaken him. In addition Drayton Manor, Peel's seat on the Warwickshire/Staffordshire border, was close to industrial districts. In both 1831–32 and 1842 the house had been fortified and armed to resist expected lower-class assailants and in 1839 the Whig government had provided military protection when rumours of Chartist attack had aroused Peel's fears for family and property. Though the accusation by some critics that Peel had just shown cowardice in the face of the

League's threats was too simple, his personal fears of popular violence may well have encouraged him in the calculation that it was more prudent to abandon agriculture's
interests than to risk future radical revolt. His repeated
insistence that he was, in ending protection, saving propertied interests from a worse fate may have been an argument
with a particular personal appeal.

Peel had anyway had uneasy relations with his party following. Tensions had never been absent within the broad
church of the new Conservatism before or after 1841, but
Peel had courted trouble with the conception of his position
as prime minister which he had articulated at the very start
of his ministry and frequently reiterated. The claim that he
was entitled to be his own man, that he owed no obligation
to followers and would take no instructions from his party,
that he would be his sovereign's minister and would consult
only the 'public interest', that he was entitled to seek
'honourable fame' for himself and would retire from office
if thwarted – all this was remarkable from a party leader in
the moment of triumph and almost without contemporary
parallel. Certainly there were assumptions surviving in the
political culture which gave an element of legitimacy to
such views and, in a period of rapid party development,
theorizing about the position of party in the political system
was tentative and inchoate. Peel, nevertheless, seems to
have been almost obsessed with the issue and he went
beyond the uncertainties of the situation to articulate a view
of himself and by extension his ministry which, if carried
beyond rhetoric, was bound to put party loyalties under
strain.

Peel's historical image has been crafted to show a statesman rational, pragmatic, farsighted, conciliatory, wedded to
compromise – a consensus politician of Baldwinian dimensions whose wisdom had helped the Britain of the 1840s
to surmount dangerous divisions. In fact many of Peel's
performances were ones of high emotional intensity and
even conscious risk-taking. He tended to drive himself and

his colleagues (and in time the political system) to the edge and in 1845–46 he may have been in a state of mental disequilibrium himself. A self-consciously forceful personality, he strove to dominate those around him and tended to resent people and forces he could not control. Despite his frequent complaints to the contrary, he clearly enjoyed the power and celebrity which office brought and he was not inclined to surrender command easily. As a party leader, once he had a secure majority, he was distant, austere (not least in his disinclination to cultivate his followers with a generous use of patronage), authoritarian and contemptuous of dissidents. Confronted by dissent, he became high on a sense of his own rectitude and ability, both moral and intellectual. This arrogance and assertiveness was encapsulated in a favourite metaphor: 'As heads see and tails are blind, I think heads are the best judges as to the course to be taken', a view which denied political rationality and moral legitimacy to the 'tail' of his party. Peel's priggishness towards his followers, especially the country gentlemen, for whom he conceived a particular distaste, verged on the comic. He could not bring himself

> To be the tool of a party – that is to say, to adopt
> the opinions of men who have no access to your
> knowledge, and could not profit by it if they had,
> who spend their time in eating and drinking,
> hunting, shooting, gambling, horseracing, and so
> forth . . .

Fitzroy Kelly, who became Solicitor General during Peel's last months in office, noted 'Peel's contempt for his party was very apparent to all who came into office with him'. A modern reassessment has noted his tendency to intellectual rigidity. His main academic study had been mathematics and he seems to have combined the self-regard of a double first with the conviction of the axiomatic character of truth which mathematics sometimes encourages. Furthermore 'his opinions tended to harden away from a compromise in a crisis', a feature that became evident during the prolonged crisis of 1845–46.[26]

This cast of mind meant Peel tended to be dictatorial with people he regarded as less able than himself. It prevented him from cultivating his followers as their worries required; instead of meeting sympathy and conciliation, they were threatened with the government's resignation unless they obeyed the whips. Peel found it difficult to compromise with opponents and instead looked to beat them. Always a good hater, Peel tended to be unforgiving towards those who had opposed him. Sometimes this amounted to a deliberate humiliation of dissidents. When the final crisis came, Peel was acutely short of personal affection among his back-benchers after years in which he had himself preferred confrontation and friction.

Peel's obsessiveness in driving his own ideas forward showed in the extent of his domination of the work of government. He interfered with departmental business and controlled his ministers to an extent unparalleled among nineteenth-century premiers. His domination of his Cabinet, until Stanley held out, was near total. During the winter of 1845–46, helped by Wellington's loyalty and preference for military-style discipline, he carried most of the Cabinet with him into repeal when the majority were antipathetic to the proposal. As Greville had written in 1845, 'The truth is the government is Peel . . .' Stanley had opted to move to the Lords in 1844 partly because he felt that Peel's personal dominance of Commons business was squeezing out and subordinating other ministers, including himself. It was often noted how much Peel used the first person singular in his Commons speeches. His personal position was emphasized, rather than that of Cabinet, government or party. This egotism left him open to satire from *Punch* and to mockery from Commons critics like Cobden and Disraeli. Historians have noted the egocentricity of the young Disraeli; they might have made more of Peel's obsession with 'honourable fame' and a great name with posterity. (The peroration of his resignation speech reiterated the phrase 'I shall leave a name . . .') The general recognition that the repeal policy was almost entirely personal to Peel (indeed he sought to portray it that way) and had been rejected initially by most of the Cabinet was one of his weaknesses; it legitimized opposition elsewhere in the party and led to a bitter personalization of the argument. *The Times* supported repeal but still concluded that Peel had mishandled his party badly and been driven by a high degree of personal vanity, the 'vindictive treachery of a self-confiding egotism'.[27]

Another consequence of Peel's ubiquity in the business of government was severe personal strain. The burden of toil seems to have induced a degree of paranoia, certainly an increased resentment of 'obstructives' who added to his problems and failed to recognize the extent of his self-sacrifice. (One of Peel's oddities was his conviction of his followers' debt to him and his denial of any reciprocal obligation or gratitude, an attitude resented by men who had given their effort and money to achieve electoral victory.) Peel's appetite for work and for personal control over most areas of government added to what were, by the final year of office, weaknesses both physical and mental.[28] He speculated himself on the possibility of 'failure of the mind' and of the same fate (suicide) as Castlereagh. This may explain both Peel's often emotional state during the concluding phase of government and the extent of his misjudgements – over the attitudes of colleagues, the reactions of his party, by-election results, Commons divisions and his own prospects of continuing in power. Even supportive colleagues like Wellington, Goulburn and Gladstone wondered at the sense of much of Peel's conduct and judgement.

Peel's intolerance of dissent had become a liability to the government. From 1834 he and Wellington had worked to weld a demoralized and divided opposition into a cohesive and effective political force, but from 1841 leadership hardened into a habit of authoritarianism as Peel harnessed his party majority to an intensive legislative programme of a highly personal and often contentious kind. The majority stood up well and did not crumble finally until June 1846; it would probably not have collapsed at all if Peel had not driven it so hard. Heavy whipping of the party's MPs was combined with an insistence on government majorities on even minor matters of legislation, including some left pre-viously to backbench initiative, and with threats of resig-nation if defeated. This denial of reasonable discretion to followers was made more provocative by the refusal of opportunities for consultation before legislative proposals were announced. Peel's secretiveness in preparing his legis-lation until he had the details ready to put before the Com-mons was notorious and seems to have given him an almost conspiratorial pleasure in taking House and party 'by sur-prise'. The law of diminishing returns from these methods of management became more evident session by session. Though Peel's language suggested that the dissentients were just Ultras and *frondeurs*, the reality was that by 1845–46 rebellion embraced not just ancient enemies given renewed vigour but also the solid centre of the party. Stanley, Rich-mond and Bentinck were all former Dilly figures who had earlier helped to pass parliamentary reform. Stanley had stood with Peel on virtually every issue, including May-nooth, until the Corn Law crisis; he and Bentinck (Disraeli too) were notably liberal on religious matters; Richmond was the only ministerial resigner of 1834 who had remained a crossbencher. The agricultural lobby in the Commons, despite the regular jeremiads that irritated Peel so much, had not sought to overthrow the government before. The Conservatives who opposed Peel in 1846 were the great majority of the party (even more so if office-holders were discounted) and represented most of its ballast and com-monsense. Many of those who still supported Peel in order to maintain Conservative government were swallowing profound objections to his policy. By then Peel was the maverick.

One problem was Peel's negativity towards the development of representational politics. Though he has often been depicted as a modernizer who dragged his party into the realities of post-Reform politics, little but his economic liberalism fits that interpretation. If Lancashire in that respect, he was Eton and Christ Church in most others. He remained a largely traditionalistic and anti-liberal figure reluctant to make concessions to opinion 'out of doors'. His commitment to the leading role of a small policy-making elite in government was narrow and restrictive in its implications. Despite his early recognition of the weight of 'public opinion', in effect mainly urban middle-class opinion, it was something he disliked and feared and which he wanted to minimize as an independent political force. 'Agitation' and 'clamour' were to be neutralized, not liberated and encouraged. Peel had resented the way the Whigs had put specific issues before the electorate in 1831 and 1841; he was determined that a general election should not be fought on the Corn Laws not only because he feared the strength of protectionist sentiment but because he held the decision should be Parliament's, not the electorate's. Despite the nature of the 1841 victory won against the personal influence of the Crown, Peel resorted subsequently to a view of himself as first and foremost 'the sovereign's minister', a concept he worked hard in the final crisis, even deploying it against his Cabinet in December 1845 and virtually assuming the role of Court favourite as substitute for the support of his party. Peel's concept of party leadership was thus scarcely 'modern'. His instincts, once he held office, were to revert to the non-partisan rhetoric of Liverpool's ministry and his own Tamworth Manifesto. Compared to government, party became a 'subordinate object'. He was well aware of the arrival of organized party as a phenomenon; as he explained to the Cabinet in June 1846, 'A Government ought to have a natural support. A Conservative government should be supported by a Conservative party'. But he would not concede that party should be much more than support for government or that the relationship between the two involved serious reciprocity. Peel intended to be free of shackles imposed by the fact of party leadership and his personal vanity intensified this dislike of 'subservience to a party'. At the same time he sought to control that party as a tool of his highly personal style of government. When that control eventually broke down and substantial sections of the party resisted, he turned on them as the enemy and, once it was clear he could not continue as leader of a united party, he worked to break it up.

Peel had almost no direct personal experience of representative politics. He had fought only one serious contest himself – the celebrated Oxford University by-election of 1829 when he had lost to Inglis – and had otherwise sat for nomination boroughs. The Catholic Emancipation episode seems to have confirmed a personal distaste for electoral opinion, including that represented within his own party. But the Reform Act, by bringing representation more into line with economic power and by distributing additional seats to both large towns and agrarian counties, made parliamentary politics more keenly representative of the interest groups and opinions of the wider society. Peel seems not to have accepted the implications easily. He had little understanding of county politics and agrarian society and what he saw on the back benches of the agricultural interest (the most important single interest in Britain's society and economy) he distrusted and despised. In the end he was undermined by his own underestimation and misreading, born of both ignorance and dislike, of the representational politics of agrarian society. By refusing to recognize the importance of these politics for his own party, he left the main interest group with little option but to create a new party for itself out of the old and to dispense with his leadership.

The Lessons of 1846

The main reasons for the collapse of Conservative government in 1845–46 stand out clearly. Despite recurrent friction between the ministry and sections of its following, the government and its party support had stood up well to the inevitable strains of office until the Maynooth crisis administered the first major blow. Even Maynooth, the result of government overreaching itself in its policy of conciliating Irish Catholicism, looked to have been weathered, largely because Protestant dissidents still preferred a Conservative ministry to a Whig one. Only during the winter of 1845–46 did the breach between ministry and party become irrevocable. The disintegration of government and party over the Corn Laws followed directly from decisions at leadership level, notably Peel's refusal to accept that past Conservative commitments ruled out any full or early ending of protection and then his unwillingness to handle the issue with sufficient conciliatoriness and compromise once the party crisis had developed around him. In terms of party management this was folly while supporters were still smarting from Maynooth and the agriculturalists still sensitive after the 1845 tariff measures. It was Peel's insistence upon repeal that divided his Cabinet and produced the resignation of December 1845, his reluctance to give Russell sufficient reassurance that helped to deter the Whigs from taking office, and his refusal, when back in office, to offer agriculturalists the safeguards and compensation for which many would by then have settled that ensured government and party would not hold together. During the summer Peel determined that there should not be any reconstitution of Conservative government and that the party should become and remain split between protectionists and his own supporters. His loyalist group retained the party's electoral managers, the central funds, the chief whip and nearly all the frontbench talent in the Commons, resources which, together with the continuing prestige of Peel's own name, were deployed to prevent either a reunion of Conservatism or an assumption of office by the protectionists down to his death in 1850.

The fractured Conservative Party of the late 1840s is little guide to the government's standing before the Corn Law crisis or to what would have happened but for Peel's seizing of the opportunity offered by the Irish potato blight. By 1845 the government had considerable achievements to its credit: the maintenance of social order in Britain and in Ireland, the undermining of O'Connell, the weathering of severe trade depression and the revival of economic prosperity (which would continue until late 1847), the apparent success of budgetary, fiscal and tariff policies, a widely applauded diplomatic and colonial record, and at least a measure of stability in ecclesiastical policy. Despite the continuing agitation of the League and the upheaval in the Scottish Church (the main political consequences of which would take time to develop), Conservative government was probably more broadly acceptable in 1845 than in 1841. The Court had been won over and business opinion, except for elements active in the League, was generally supportive. It was not any sense of general failure that brought down the government; its problems were internal rather than external. One measure of the ministry's position was its continuing success in by-elections, unlike the experience of the Whigs through the 1830s. In July 1844 a protectionist Conservative had even won a seat in Birmingham and as late as October 1845 the government held a seat in the Lancashire industrial town of Wigan with an increased majority. Despite some alarm at the registration activities of the League in some constituencies,[29] the government had had few problems with its electoral performance and prospects down to the end of 1845. Only in the final crisis, when Peel had polarized opinion over agricultural protection, did official candidates suffer a spate of by-election defeats and then more at the hands of protectionist Conservatives than of the opposition. Only then did the party's central manage-

ment and electoral organization prove unavailing in the face
of a revolt in the constituencies paralleling and encouraging
that in the Commons. But even this rebellion reflected no
natural or inevitable division in the party's ranks; the split
was forced upon the party by the leadership's policy
decisions. Though the Whig opposition benefited from this
outcome, it hardly experienced a triumph of its own. The
Conservatives suffered no electoral disaster like that of 1832.
In the general election of 1847, a low-key affair with the
issue of protection muffled by the high agricultural prices
then prevailing and with an unusually high number of
uncontested seats (236 in all), the Conservatives, with both
protectionists and Peelites counted, lost only some forty
seats on the 1841 figure. That Russell's government was
left without a secure majority and dependent upon Peelite
support and that, after Liberal divisions, Stanley's protectionists (in fact he had resumed the Conservative name in
1848) found themselves by 1849 the largest party in the
Commons only underlined the continuing strength of Conservatism. The long period that followed without a parliamentary majority would owe much to the survival of a
balance-holding Peelite residue until 1859 and then to the
long quiescence of Ireland and the immense personal appeal
of Palmerston as Liberal prime minister.

That long exile from effective power could not have been
predicted in 1845 when the Conservatives looked, for all
the Maynooth controversy, to have a high level of public
esteem, a solid electoral position and a record of considerable administrative success. The party revolt against the
government was largely a reluctant one in that most dissidents continued to want a Conservative rather than a Whig
government, but Peel's tactics left the hardline rebels able
to remove him only by removing the ministry as a whole.
Conservatives had found themselves caught between two
ineluctable forces: Peel's determination to repeal the Corn
Laws himself (as Gash has put it, for Peel in those months
'it was the achievement which mattered, not the price

which had to be paid for it'[30]) and the resolve of an embittered agricultural interest to fight back. In the end the sense of loyalty to Conservative government was outweighed by the sense of Peel's own disloyalty to the instincts and commitments of his party.

Nearly thirty years without majority-based tenure of office would be a bitter pill for a large and ambitious party to swallow. Lessons had been learnt about the penalties of major disunity and schism, a fate which the party would set itself to avoid for the rest of the century, and about the dangers of leadership blind or hostile to the attitudes and instincts of its party following in the country. Stanley, not least in his insistence that protectionism be abandoned only slowly and for good reason, Disraeli and Salisbury all recognized Peel's failing and attempted, so far as circumstances permitted, not to repeat them. A party needed reciprocity; loyalty had to operate both ways. Though leaders might seek fame with posterity, that pursuit should normally be based upon the continuing maintenance of party; party cohesion and identity were strengths to be cultivated, not squandered. Constitutional stability and a sense of the general interest would continue to matter to Conservatives, but they would be seen as operating through the medium of party, not on a separate plane over and above it. Strong government would normally require a strong party. Peel's conviction that strong government required the denial of party, except in the narrow sense of a Commons majority to be whipped, proved to have little future, even with successors who came to see that Corn Law repeal might have contributed to mid-Victorian stability. Even political centrism, as the surviving Peelites found, would have to operate within the framework of party-based politics. Parties had come to have a representational character and government would need to consult the social and economic interests represented within its party base. Peel's administration had thus embodied an obsolescent style of constitutional conservatism, not provided the matrix for future political development. It was his rebellious party which, in this sense, looked towards the future. Peel had produced not only an unnecessary breakdown of Conservative government in 1846 but also an example for successors to avoid. The victory of 1841 had, for many contemporaries, been especially associated with the name of Robert Peel. The same has to be concluded about the disaster of 1846.

CHRONOLOGY

1832		Passage of Reform Act
	DECEMBER	General election reduces Tory opposition to perhaps 120–150 seats
1833		Irish Church Temporalities Bill
1834	JUNE	Resignation of four members of the Whig Cabinet ('Derby Dilly')
	NOVEMBER	William IV forces the resignation of the Whig government and installs Wellington as temporary minister while Peel returns from Italy
	DECEMBER	Peel as prime minister issues his 'Tamworth Manifesto'
1835	JANUARY	Conservatives gain some ninety seats but remain in a Commons minority
	APRIL	After defeats in the Commons and the 'Lichfield House Compact' between the Whigs and O'Connell, Peel's government resigns; the Whigs under Melbourne resume office
	SEPTEMBER	Municipal Corporations Act passes after prolonged difficulties in the Lords

1837	JULY/AUGUST	General election follows William's death; the counties provide further modest gains for the Conservatives
1839	MAY	The 'Bedchamber Crisis': Victoria successfully impedes Peel's assumption of office after the Whigs resign; Melbourne's government returns
1841		The Whig budget proposes a fixed duty in place of the Corn Law sliding scale
	JUNE/JULY	General election produces Conservative majority over seventy
	SEPTEMBER	After the Whigs are defeated in the House, Peel forms his ministry
1842	FEBRUARY	Peel's budget proposals: income tax, tariff reductions, modified sliding scale for corn imports; commerical depression, industrial unemployment, mass distress, Anti-Corn Law League agitation, Chartism
	AUGUST	'Plug Plot' disturbances
1843		Canadian corn admitted at nominal duty; agricultural protection societies multiply; Act for Spiritual Care of Populous Parishes; Graham's Factory Bill

	OCTOBER	Clontarf meeting banned and O'Connell prosecuted
1844	FEBRUARY	Central Agricultural Protection Society formed; Bank Charter Act; Railway Act
	MARCH/JUNE	Clashes between government and its supporters in the Commons over factory reform and sugar duties
1845	FEBRUARY	Peel's budget: extension of income tax, further tariff reductions, no relief for agriculture
	APRIL/MAY	Maynooth Bill attracts over 10,000 hostile petitions and passes the Commons only after a major Conservative revolt
	JUNE	The National Club formed; start of worry over Irish potato crop; Peel determines on Corn Law repeal
	NOVEMBER	Cabinet divided over repeal with the majority hostile
	NOVEMBER 22	Russell's 'Edinburgh Letter'
	DECEMBER 6	Cabinet resigns after Stanley and Buccleuch refuse to support repeal
	DECEMBER 20	After Russell's failure to form a government, Peel accepts renewed office in order to repeal

		the Corn Laws; Stanley declines to serve
1846	JANUARY 22	Parliament meets; CAPS has abandoned its no-politics rule and organizes protectionist forces
	JANUARY 27	Peel announces his Corn Law proposals; Bentinck is emerging as Protectionist leader in the Commons
	FEBRUARY 9–27	Main Corn Law debates in the Commons; on second reading Conservatives divide 112–231 against
	JUNE 25	Third reading of the Corn Importation Bill in the Lords; protests entered by ninety-nine peers led by Stanley and Richmond; government is defeated on its Irish Coercion Bill with over seventy Conservatives opposing
	JUNE 29	Peel's resignation speech; government resigns and Russell forms a minority Whig ministry
	JULY	Stanley accepts leadership of the protectionists
1847	JULY/AUGUST	General election returns some 230 protectionists and perhaps 100 Peelites, which leaves no firm Whig majority

1848		Stanley insists the protectionists resume the Conservative name
	SEPTEMBER	Death of Bentinck
1850	JULY	Death of Peel

Benjamin Disraeli, First Earl of Beaconsfield
(*Mansell Collection*)

CHAPTER FOUR

1874–80

John Vincent

The basis of the Conservative victory of 1874, at an electoral level, was clear enough. It arose from an exaggerated dislike, amounting at times to detestation, of Gladstone and all he stood for. It did not arise from a liking for Disraeli and all he stood for. It showed that the landed gentry, if united, could still win general elections, even at this relatively late stage in their decline. It did not show that there were normally more Conservatives than Liberals. The Conservatives by themselves won only four out of twenty elections between 1832 and 1918: the victory of 1874 marked not a new trend but Liberals quarrelling among themselves.

End of the Liberal Ascendancy

The mood of the 1870s was very different from that of the 1860s; rarely have two decades stood in such sharp contrast. The Liberal ascendancy of the 1860s, whether Palmerstonian, Gladstonian, or Radical, embodied a wide range of national feeling, as the elections of 1865 and 1868, with majorities which were larger and firmer[1] than those of previous decades, well showed. What stopped the Liberals continuing to embody these feelings?

The death of Palmerston in October 1865 was one decisive event in the move towards the Conservative consensus of

159

the 1870s. Palmerston's formula of liberalism abroad and reaction at home had suited English public opinion. The general election of July 1865 had given him a much increased majority and, considering that he was nearly eighty-two and beginning to fail, it was a remarkable vote of confidence in the status quo. Disraeli built on Palmerston's achievement, but not immediately and probably not instinctively. The other date in laying the foundations of a Conservative consensus was 1870. The Franco-Prussian War alarmed, the Paris Commune shook all those with anything to lose. By continental standards, England looked too weak to play the part of a great military power. With gunboat diplomacy now behind them, UK politicians had to accept that in the age of Bismarck foreign policy was a matter chiefly of spectacle.

Phases of the Government's Life

If one were to divide the life of the Disraeli government into phases, three would stand out. The first phase was one of quiet and extended to August 1876. By quiet one means not so much the absence of events as freedom from heroic legislation of the Gladstonian type. During this initial period of the three parliamentary sessions of 1874, 1875 and 1876, the government kept well in line with the public mood and probably gained ground while the Liberals weakened. It remained a government of consensus: it did not put the clock back. In 1874 the theme was robust religious legislation in keeping with British Protestant opinion. In 1875, the so-called *annus mirabilis* of social reform, Disraeli allowed some of his more eye-catching slogans to take on reality, though only within the genteel bounds set by another Disraelian slogan, that 'permissive legislation is the characteristic of a free people'. Not many social reforms were actually compulsory and most were remitted to the judgement of the country gentry and the urban magistrates. Consequently, the social reforms of 1875 led to rather few memorable improvements likely to influence voters five years later.

The Artisans Dwellings Act of 1875, described by the Home Secretary as a bill for the suppression of rookeries, produced far fewer dwellings for the poor than already existed as a result of voluntary provisions by charities such as the Peabody Trustees. Far from marking the beginning of modern council housing, the act was in fact a minor piece of Victorian public health legislation; few local authorities had by 1880 availed themselves of the opportunity it gave them to clear their slums. With it went the Act for the Consolidation of the Sanitary Laws, otherwise known as the Public Health Act, which merely consolidated them, without in any solitary particular amending them; and two acts which gave an incautious blessing to whatever trade unions were disposed to attempt in the way of picketing and conspiracy. These Trades Union Laws reflected profound ignorance on the part of the Cabinet, as well as a feeling on Disraeli's part that they would win the Conservatives the affection of the working man for a long time to come. Still, a great mid-Victorian question had been settled for a generation.

The volume of non-party social legislation passed in 1875 was impressively large and various, if not deeply important. The Friendly Societies Act was permissive; but the permission it gave was duly acted upon and gave new statistical accuracy to the Societies' transactions. The Merchant Shipping Act gave powers to the Board of Trade to detain unseaworthy ships, including those with dangerous grain cargoes. Despite all this, Disraeli either forgot to mention, or thought it prudent to omit, all mention of social reform from his 1880 manifesto.

The year 1875 ended dramatically and unexpectedly with the purchase of Suez Canal shares from the Khedive of Egypt, thus giving Britain a minority share in the French company which continued to run the Suez Canal. This stroke of policy, though daring, was popular and did not mark the end of quiet times.

The year 1876 was relatively free of political controversy up to August, while Disraeli himself grew notably frailer. His last important change was the rather unpopular Royal Titles Act, making Queen Victoria Empress of India. In August, however, the excitement that was to lead to the Russo-Turkish War (1877–78) began with the sensational news of the Bulgarian atrocities. Disraeli's ironical comments on these fanned the flames of a vehement popular agitation, which lasted all of two months and ensured Gladstone's return from retirement to prominence. While the excitement lasted the government, after some initial difficulties, was able to carry the country with it, and that well-known ditty of the music halls summed up popular sentiment:

> We don't want to fight but by Jingo! if we do
> We've got the ships, we've got the men, we've got
>   the money too.

Once the excitement died down the government's achievement also began to melt away. Disraeli's government in the summer of 1878 seemed almost to have solved everything there was to solve. It had scared off the Russian Bear, it had acquired Cyprus, it had pacified the Balkans, it had even preserved a credible Turkish Empire. It was on good terms with all the European powers including Bismarck's Germany. As Disraeli said on his return from Berlin, this was 'peace with honour'. But by autumn 1878 it was questioned whether either peace or honour had been brought about. Peace remained uncertain, simply because the vast Russian army took a very long time withdrawing to Russia: war hung in the balance for much of 1879. As for honour, the Russian Bear had not ceased being expansionist at our bidding. He had simply turned his expansionism in the direction of the Caucasus. The British public, which had set its heart on keeping Batum out of Russian hands, found here that Russia had deceived them at the Treaty of Berlin. By 1879 it seemed that peace with honour had a definitely tawdry underside, and the acquisition of Cyprus, which in 1878 had promised much, now looked disappointing.

The commanding position in Europe which Britain seemed to have achieved in summer 1878 melted away in the following years, just as its position in South Africa and Afghanistan received severe and tragic setbacks. The defeat by the Zulus at Isandhlwana in January 1879 marked a terrible beginning to a terrible year and effaced any pretence of British superiority. In September the Afghans massacred the British mission in Kabul. The setbacks of 1879 were all the harder for public opinion to accept because they followed so closely on the heels of the unprecedented imperial success of summer 1878.

In addition the government threw in some fresh mistakes of its own. First, it omitted to express its sympathy for the serious economic hardship people were suffering for all of 1879. Secondly, it made a mess of its own legislative business, for no better reason than that ministers were getting in each other's way in Parliament. In those simple, unplanned times, bills were flung willy-nilly before Parliament without any effective legislative timetable, only to be killed off just as arbitrarily towards the end of the session, thus ensuring a steady flow of bad news in what had hitherto been a mainly favourable press during the preceding period of excitement.

Thirdly, the two main items of government business that did pass in 1879 were both unfortunately chosen, as was the unpopular and costly London Water Bill of 1880. The Army Act of 1879 became notorious for bringing military flogging to the attention of the public just as Tommy Atkins was gaining hard-won success in two distant continents. The only beneficiaries were the Irish and Joseph Chamberlain, both of whom had a field day. The other major act was the Irish University Act, which turned the Queen's University into an examining university, the Royal University. This was rather pointless as a symbol of Anglo-Irish accord, because the Irish did not want a non-sectarian examining body; they wanted regional sectarian colleges, and giving the Irish benefactions they did not seek brought little or no political reward. As a gesture to Irish Catholicism, it fell far short of what was needed. Only a generation later, the Irish Universities Act of 1908 undid Disraeli's handiwork by abolishing his Royal University of 1879 and putting in its place the National University of Ireland, a federal structure based on the University Colleges of Cork, Galway and Dublin.

It was, however, unfortunate that in this pre-election year, the government's most conspicuous activities centred on benefiting Irishmen, punishing soldiers, and even at one point proposing to give a grant to the detested Turks while denying any help to the struggling British – a proposal speedily withdrawn.

Social Factors

The social history of politics certainly does not explain the collapse of Disraeli's majority. All the social factors making for a strong and strengthening Conservatism were little altered in 1880. Conservatism needed commuter suburbs to house the Mr Pooters of *The Diary of a Nobody* (1894) and not only in the south-east, which was rapidly turning into the Home Counties, a Conservative regional bloc which had not existed in 1868 but was unassailably Conservative by 1885.

There were more commuter suburbs, because there were more suburban railway lines, in 1880 than in 1874; many more, indeed, than in 1868. The drink factor, so powerful in 1874, was probably no less so in 1880, because it had as much to fear from the encroachments of the United Kingdom Alliance, the temperance arm of the Liberal Party. There were certainly no fewer pubs and publicans. The church school factor was probably no less in 1880 than in 1874, because the school board elections under the 1870

Education Act had heightened denominational rivalries. Churches, schools, pubs, and suburbs amounted to a large slice of English life, at least as large in 1880 as in 1874. The reason the Conservatives lost in 1880 did not lie in some loss of their social base, or in social history at all. It lay in pure politics, and in freak bad weather.

Economic and Financial Factors

Was the reason for failure a simple matter of economic recession? Had Disraeli gone to the country in 1878 after the Congress of Berlin, there can be little doubt that he would have been re-elected, albeit with a reduced majority. As it was, a slump rapidly set in. Unemployment, as measured by trade union statistics, rose from 4.7 per cent in 1877 to 6.8 per cent in 1878, and then to 11.4 per cent in 1879,[2] and had hardly had time to recover by the April 1880 election. The slump of 1879 was quite short-lived, but undoubtedly went deep – deeper, probably, than any other year between 1842 and 1886.

Of course, governments suffer electorally in slumps, and in more than one way. Disraeli, says his biographer, 'lacked the power to galvanize a tired administration'; he was simply too old. But there was more to it than just tiredness. The Conservatives had run increasingly short of money since 1875. Revenues were declining from their peak in 1874, making it hard for the Conservatives either to finance schemes of social reform, or to engage in electorally attractive projects for cutting taxation or repaying debt. In 1876 Disraeli's Chancellor Sir Stafford Northcote, had introduced progressive taxation on smaller incomes, an idea rather ahead of its time, and one which, together with a plan for painlessly expunging the national debt, might have had enticing electoral possibilities. But, with revenues falling where Gladstone's had effortlessly risen, the whole financial side of politics was out.

The agricultural side of the Great Depression was the most

intractable, and it enhanced urban unrest by sending the rural proletariat in search of work in the cities, thus depressing wages and augmenting unemployment. Conservatism was baffled by this threat to its own rural power base. Whether it was landlords' rent, farm labourers' pay, or farmers' profits, it seemed inconceivable to help such interests at the expense of free-trade, urban Britain. In fact, with a better grip on things, the farmers, if not landlords and labourers, might have been helped. Gladstone, taking over in 1880, provided his own answers: the repeal of the malt tax, and the Hares and Rabbits Bill – small change offered by way of reward to the farmers who had left their normal Conservative allegiance in 1880. Disraeli's government had also offered its own version of small change, by removing certain social costs, such as prisons, from local rates, which were paid chiefly by farmers. But Disraeli's attempts failed to do the trick.

The Liberals, Gladstone and the Imperial Question

The opposition remained weak and divided until the eleventh hour, pulling itself together not over the Eastern Question proper of 1876–78, but only over the 'imperialist' mishaps of the Afghan and Zulu wars of 1879. Disraeli for a short time had the political nation up in arms against him over the Bulgarian Atrocities issue (July–October 1876) but cleverly played the patriotic card and, as in 1867, split the opposition. The vote on Gladstone's resolutions of May 1877 confirmed that the Liberals were a split party. The more Gladstone resumed an entirely unofficial leadership in the course of 1877, with his wooing of the National Liberal Federation and his 'holiday' in Ireland, the more the Liberals appeared an unknown quantity. There was, it is true, little protest or public comment about Gladstone's rather unscrupulous marginalization of his party's elected leadership, perhaps because Lord Hartington's vigour and authority still made it possible to see him as the next

Liberal prime minister. Writing on the period has tended to antedate (and exaggerate) Liberal recovery, Liberal reunion, and the acceptance of Gladstone's renewed leadership.

So far as there was an opposition recovery by 1879, it was a Whig recovery, a recovery of people who were supposed to know what they were talking about when they criticized imperial policy on the basis of the government Blue Books. On Indian questions, the opposition spoke with an aristocratic authority which the Conservatives could not match. On finance, again, there was only one Gladstone, and if he said that 'Beaconsfieldism' had 'aggravated the public distress by continual shocks to confidence', who would dare to disagree? All knew that business confidence was a fragile plant; its collapse in 1879 must have some explanation. Nobody quite knew why 'confidence' was suddenly and painfully replaced by 'distress', but Gladstone's linkage of 'distress' with foreign policy seemed as convincing an explanation as any, and it was one that government ministers themselves used in public addresses in 1879, claiming that prosperity would soon return once war was over.

Competence and success were widely expected even where such expectations were unreasonable or beyond Disraeli's power to fulfil. Imperial disasters such as the Zulu War and the Kabul massacre made criticism not only legitimate but a patriotic duty. Where ministers fell down was in not establishing how much the Zulu and Afghan debacles were the fault of 'prancing proconsuls', disobeying well-conceived instructions, rather than due to their own shortcomings.

Ministers had good reason for keeping quiet, however: Gladstone had two lines of attack, one moral, one financial, and the more the government rebutted his moral claims that the government was a government of massacre with reference to Afghanistan, the more they underlined that its South African policies were indeed highly expensive. Thus the remarkable military successes of General Roberts in

Afghanistan, and the virtual elimination of that country as a separate entity, could not be marked up as a British success.

But did not Disraeli perhaps dream in his Chiltern retreat of some coup which a grateful nation would applaud by re-electing him? Dream he did, but the coups he desired did not come about, while the coups he most feared or wished to prevent arrived and were regarded by a worried public as expensive examples of Disraelian imperialism, or what Gladstone successfully labelled as 'Beaconsfieldism', at work.[3]

Disraeli the private dreamer appears in his letters to Lady Bradford as not without ambition at this time. He had half persuaded himself that he was something of a military genius, that distant war might be his forte. He rested his case on the highly successful Abyssinian expedition of 1868, where a British army had penetrated 400 miles into an unknown and difficult highland country, achieved its objective (the release of European captives) and returned to its port of disembarkation, without the loss of a single life. True, Disraeli agreed, the cost had been twice the original estimate, but 'that will always be the case in any war conducted by me'. Repetition of this distant triumph was not quite out of the question, for China in 1875 seemed on the verge of provoking war by offering a similar affront to British dignity. Disraeli invited Japan, the 'Sardinia of the East', to join in an Anglo-Japanese campaign, with Japanese troops serving in China under British command; a prime ministerial coup, certainly, in the sense that neither Foreign Office nor Cabinet were informed. In the event, nothing came of this initiative, for China prudently gave way. Something so unorthodox as an Anglo-Japanese alliance was not to take place until 1902.

Also in 1875, but in Europe, was the still mysterious 'War in Sight' crisis, one of several episodes which began to persuade Disraeli that he might have diplomatic as well as under-exploited military genius. Even though the inner story of this diplomatic episode, in which England and Russia seemed to combine to preserve the Great Power status of France, can still hardly be unravelled, it may have given Disraeli a sense of personal consequence in handling the affairs of the European balance of power.

Another Disraelian dream which was never to be was his proposal, made several times to senior colleagues in all seriousness, for a British occupation of, or protectorate over, Constantinople, the single most strategic spot in the world. Of conquest there was no mention, but 'protection' can have meant only what elsewhere came to be known as 'painting the map of the world red' – especially as the new semi-colony would have to be held against Russia. The problem with this bright idea (which in itself should dispose of the notion that Disraeli was recklessly pro-Ottoman) was that nobody else in the Establishment supported it. He offered it to the Foreign Office, unimaginative then as now, and received a correct reply by return, pointing out that in time of peace it was not normal to seize the capitals of friendly states. Disraeli hawked the idea of seizing Constantinople around a few times more before giving up without having had a chance to popularize the theme, but it undoubtedly meant something to him, and was perhaps the egg from which the annexation of Cyprus in 1878 was hatched.

Disraeli and the Conservative Party's State

The Conservative collapse cannot be attributed to a negative image of the party leader. Indeed, Disraeli's national standing was probably higher than it had ever been. His authority in Cabinet, party, Parliament, and with the public was almost unchallenged, except by Gladstone and the Irish obstructionists. Murmurs about the betrayal of 1867 had quite died away. Salisbury and the reactionary right had elected to work in partnership with him; yet his partnership with the centrist moderates in the shape of Sir Stafford

Northcote, his House of Commons leader, was in good working order. The opposition leader, Lord Hartington, was often seen as only half opposed to him. There was no more Cabinet disunity after the foreign policy crisis of spring 1878, when Disraeli lost his foreign secretary and recruited a new one who gave the impression of effortless superiority. No rival sought the post of leader, if only because it was obvious that Disraeli could not continue for much longer.

Depleted party finance played only a modest part. The Conservatives were by the nature of things the richer of the parties, as they had been since the 1850s. It was the Liberal rich, not the Conservative rich, who declined to pay up. If money was tight in 1879–80, as no doubt it was, it was because it was tight everywhere in a year when the political class of whichever party was obliged to draw in its horns.

Disraeli, it was true, made no great statements after 1876 to guide opinion, such as his two historic speeches at Crystal Palace and Manchester of 1872. These have rightly passed into Conservative tradition, but at the time and in the context of the 1874 election, they did not have the importance subsequently attributed to them. In tone the 1872 speeches were expansive, but the public mood by 1874 was anything but expansive. Some great utterance by the leader about policy direction in 1880 would also have gone against the grain, for if Disraeli had wished to establish a new Conservative identity based on an alignment with either the masses or the middle classes, he would surely have done it before then. The truth must surely be that he was quite happy with the party identity as he found it, left it, and had always known it – that of the party of the landed gentry. There was, perhaps, not much policy direction as 1880 and defeat approached, but confusion over policy direction there was not.

With no great strategic move in sight, the question of organization became correspondingly more important. Here the Conservatives were not on strong ground. In 1859, Disraeli had set himself to win a general election almost by organization alone, and all but succeeded. By 1880, his attention was elsewhere, and no single strong personality was committed to running the party machine. Probably the Conservatives needed a stronger organization in 1880 than in 1874, if only because of the professionalism and intelligence of their chief opponent, W. P. Adam, the Liberal chief whip. Among the Conservatives there was no one of equivalent stature and single-mindedness, and personal differences between underlings in the party organization played their part. Gorst, whose name was linked to the 1874 victory, had resigned from Central Office in 1877; his role was filled by the chief whip, Sir W. Hart Dyke (inventor of tennis), who then fell ill in the crucial year of 1879. The party thus went into the general election without much guidance from its national organization.[4]

The idea that the 1880 election was widely seen as 'time for a change' is probably an anachronism, based on transplanting post-1918 democratic waywardness to a period where it did not belong. In fact, Gladstone's ministry as it emerged in 1880 was probably best seen as a strengthened version of a Conservative government. 'Time for a change', or simple restlessness, had not previously played a part in Victorian elections, though surges of radicalism had. Indeed, much of Gladstone's Midlothian campaign was based on the argument that he would take the country back to the good old days, and the high standards, of Peel; no 'time for a change' there. Gladstone offered no reformist programme, as in 1868; so obvious was this, especially to himself, that in reaction, those who wanted more activism began the first tentative moves towards British socialism.

Equally, manifest internal disunity was exceedingly limited. The secession of the farmers turned out to be much less than feared, partly because by boldly calling an early election (he need not have called one until 1881) Disraeli nipped it in the bud.[5]

The Irish Spectre

Could Ireland have supplied the basis for a brilliant political and electoral move? In theory, yes. Ireland after all had 105 MPs, most sitting for strongly Catholic constituencies. Yet most Irish MPs tended to an erratic Liberalism; only the Protestants from the North could normally be relied upon for steady Tory votes. Thus it was always the Tories, not the Liberals, who stood to gain most from the enactment of some form of Home Rule which excluded Irish MPs from Westminster. After 1918, this indeed played a part in creating a Tory electoral supremacy. In 1874–80, Disraeli's options were few, and not well handled. Both Disraeli and Isaac Butt, the Irish leader, were old and ill, and nothing requiring great flair and energy could be done. Disraeli himself in autumn 1874 had contemplated a mysterious personal visit to Ireland, for what purpose is unknown; as it turned out, he fell ill, and called it off. Instead, his conscientious and humane Irish administration made a modestly respectable attempt at 'governing Ireland through the [Catholic] bishops' and won a fair amount of support from Irish MPs over foreign policy issues in the Eastern Question, 1876–78. But that speedily evaporated once famine returned in 1879, the year Disraeli's old friend Butt died. By the general election of 1880, Irish politics were at their most radical for a generation, and English parties, issues, and politicians were irrelevant to an Irish election dominated by Parnell and Parnellism. Though Disraeli may be suspected of not being averse to a Tory–Irish alliance (such as fitfully materialized in 1881–86) or even to some discreet version of a socially conservative separatism, he in fact took the opposite tack, and made the main theme of his election manifesto a luridly alarmist appeal to fear of devolution. So far as this had any impact at all, and it certainly had little, it would have been in antagonizing the Irish vote in the British cities.

Bad Weather

Reference has been made to unusually bad weather. Disraeli's letters frequently bemoan this – his peacocks moulted in protest; Tennyson devoted a poem to the black skies of 1879. *The Times Register of Events in 1879* said, in summary, 'last winter [i.e. 1878–79] was remarkable for severe and protracted frosts, followed by bitter east winds, by chilling persistent rain, and dismally clouded skies. The temperature and the duration of sunshine were both far below the average, while the rainfall exceeded the average by one-third'. The weekly rainfall reports showed that there was no summer to speak of. (The year of misery ended memorably with the Tay Bridge railway catastrophe of 28 December 1879, with ninety lives lost in a violent gale.)

Regional Analysis of Results

Turning to the general election itself, we can see with hindsight that it was only in part general,[6] that is the sum of homogeneous nationwide trends (for example, increasing suburban and business conservatism), but was also the product of diverse regional trends which were irreversible and would probably have gone their way even had Gladstone, Disraeli and Midlothian never existed.[7] A general election is a splendid occasion for asserting regional identities and challenging existing social supremacies. The further a region is from metropolitan politics, the more likely it is to use the election in this way: not to change a government, but to challenge the old order locally.

The 1880 election marked an important step in the political modernization of Ireland, Scotland and Wales.[8] All asserted identities based on the idea that they had a special political destiny opposed to the old order in Church and State. All became much more concentrated as a bloc vote. All saw themselves as treading the road away from forms of feudalism towards the emancipation of mankind.

There was a fourth, more shadowy regional identity, that of Ulster. Here the issue was land; the radical reformer inside the Ulster farmer was struggling to get out. The Ulster Liberals returned five MPs in 1868, seven in 1874, and nine in 1880; in 1885, in reaction to the Tory–Irish alliance, even normally illiberal Antrim returned a Liberal briefly. These Ulster Liberals were Protestants, Unionists and tenant righters; their tradition, though going back to 1798, turned out to be one of the dead ends of history.[9]

Scotland had all the stability of the (almost) one-party state; in the landslides of 1874 and 1880, there were few Tory gains or losses.

Indeed, before 1867, and again in 1868 and 1880, it was normal for the Tories to win no urban seats at all in Scotland, so there was in effect not so much a two-party system as a multi-factional Liberal ascendancy. Between 1832 and 1865, the Conservatives never held more than three of the twenty-three to twenty-six burgh seats in Scotland. The hand of Disraeli showed not in the number of Scottish seats won (six county seats won in 1868, rising to fifteen in 1874, only to fall back again to six in 1880) but in the number of seats contested.[10]

TABLE 4.1   *Election Results in Scotland 1868–85*

	Contests	Liberal	Conservative
1868	21	54	6
1874	37	41	19
1880	42	54	6
1885	–	62	10

Wales (without Monmouthshire) stated its national character more clearly than ever before at the 1880 election. This was to be non- or anti-Tory. Wales returned only two Conservatives out of its thirty MPs (increased in 1867 from twenty-nine). Of the twenty-eight Liberals returned in

1880, no less than eight were Dissenters, a breakthrough for the religious majority (over 80 per cent of worshippers in 1851). The 1880 election in Wales was touched with legend. It might, in terms of local supremacies, be called 'the fall of feudalism in Wales', presaging the one-party nation of the 1906 election when Wales returned not a single Tory out of its thirty MPs. What occurred in Wales was part of the long-term evolution of a hitherto submerged society which had acquired its own dynamic from industry and Dissent, not a response to English national politics; and although Palmerston, Disraeli and Gladstone all had Welsh connections (Disraeli knew Tredegar), the outcome would have been not dissimilar had they never existed.

The Feel-bad Factor

From a financial point of view the Mr Pooters of this world did not do badly under the Disraeli government. Certainly they did not do nearly badly enough to explain the landslide defeat of 1880.[11] Taxation was barely raised in the last two budgets before the election, and income tax was not raised at all in 1879 or 1880. The big increase came in the 1878 budget, when income tax went up from threepence to fivepence and thereafter stayed at that level. But fivepence was not an abnormal level by Gladstonian standards.

The rate in 1869–70 was fivepence, falling in April 1870 to fourpence. It was raised again, to sixpence, in 1871 but dropped to fourpence in 1872 and to threepence in 1873. Taking an average one can hardly say there was anything shocking or disturbing in Disraeli's rate of income tax when compared with the standards set by previous Gladstonian finance. In 1874 income tax was reduced, by the Conservatives, from threepence to twopence for a period of two years. In 1876 the rate rose from twopence to threepence, remaining at that level till 1878 when it rose at a bound to fivepence. The Conservative mistake perhaps lay in setting

the rate at a level so low that it could only go in one direction
– upward.

If the rate of income tax itself did not present an obvious
political target, why then was finance a peculiarly vulnerable area for the Conservatives electorally? One obvious
reason was that Gladstone's plan for abolishing income tax
entirely, unveiled in the 1874 election but never carried
out, could be used to make any income tax seem extortion-
ate. The public was also quick to overlook the extraordinary
boom of 1868 to 1873, succeeded by the long-term decline
of the Great Depression. Almost exactly, Gladstone got the
seven fat years and Disraeli the seven lean.

In another respect Mr Pooter had actually done rather
well out of the Conservatives, perhaps because he had voted
for them for the first time in 1874 and there was an election
debt to be paid. The 1876 budget did Mr Pooter proud, with
a redistribution of income by a Conservative government
aimed specifically at the small man in a suburban semi.
Exemption on all incomes large and small was raised from
£100 to £150 per annum, showing that Disraeli not Gladstone was the poor man's friend, while lower-middle-class
incomes of £400 and under, that is, those of the Pooter class
of new Conservative voters, attracted a further exemption of
£125 before any tax was paid. Previously the exemption
had been £80 on incomes of £300 and under. The effect of
all this was that the Pooters who groaned under fivepence
income tax in 1879–80 might actually be paying a smaller
sum than in the decade previously.

But the rate of income tax, though psychologically important, was far from the end of the matter. It could not be
good news that the national outlay rose remorselessly year
in, year out from £70.7 million in 1873 to £84.2 million in
1879. In the 1880 budget it was admitted that the Zulu
War, now all but over, had cost the huge sum of £5,138,000,
leaving a deficit of £3,340,000 for the year 1880. This might
have mattered less had the Conservatives from 1878 not
put off paying their debts until better times should return.

This gamble had not come off: better times did not return either in 1879 or in 1880, and when Disraeli left office it was with a dark cloud of floating debt hanging over the country. Given Victorian attitudes to debt this reckless and irresponsible refusal to pay the nation's bills destroyed any pretensions to competent stewardship.

This was perhaps a pity, because the budget of 1875 had been distinctly creative. It proposed to pay off the national debt by gradually increasing the amount charged for interest. Northcote's Sinking Fund, as this popular measure came to be known, was well received and no doubt prudent; but built into it was the expectation of tranquillity ahead, at least in the three financial years 1875–78. These years in particular were to turn out far from serene, however.

One aspect of Northcote's tax policy which was certainly to most people's taste and which was to prove permanent, was the abolition of the sugar duties in the great giveaway budget of 1874. This proved a landmark in the development of retailing and of various industries connected with confectionery such as jam and chocolate, which mostly date their great expansion from this time. In other respects the Conservatives took up the theme laid down by Disraeli in his abortive 1852 budget of taking from their opponents in the towns in order to give to their supporters in the country. Thus in 1874 they repealed the Race Horse Duty, the Horse Duty, and the Horsedealers' Licence Duty, at a cost of £480,000 per annum, and at the same time they made over £1,010,000 available for the reduction of county rates by taking over the costs of police and lunatic asylums, and a little later the cost of the county jails, and placing the financial burden of these social services on the urban taxpayer.

A different spirit animated the Conservatives in 1878 when it came to Dog Tax, up from five shillings to seven shillings and sixpence, and Tobacco Duty, which rose fourpence a pound: Northcote the chancellor was a Devon man and saw finance and life generally through Devon eyes, the needs and enjoyments of the townsman taking second place.

If Mr Pooter came to the conclusion that the government put the interest of the countryside before that of the towns, his suspicions would have been further aroused by the Contagious Diseases (Animals) Act of 1878. Not content with relieving rural local authorities of the expense of police, lunatics and prisoners, the government now transferred the duty of dealing with the cattle plague from local authorities to the Privy Council and thus to the taxpayer. But not only did the urban taxpayer have to pay for stamping out foot and mouth; he also had to pay more for his butcher's meat in consequence. Foreign animals, ready for the butcher, were to be excluded and slaughtered at the ports of debarkation; store cattle for the farms and fields were to be let in alive after quarantine. Thus the act was open to the charge from free-traders that it was designed more to keep foreign competition from reaching British shops than to shut out contagion from British farms. The butchers declared that meat would soon be as much as two shillings a pound and even Conservative Party discipline could not keep some party members for great towns from rebellion. The question became a party matter and the Liberals struggled long and hard against what they saw as protectionism by the back door.

And yet, for all that Disraeli might appear to be widening the urban–rural divide and putting rural interests first, it was the city voters who convinced Disraeli, in by-elections first at Liverpool, then even more decisively at Southwark, that he could well win. What in modern terms was a 5 per cent swing against the government appears to have occurred after the election was called, if the by-elections are admissible evidence.[12]

Conclusions

In governmental terms, Disraeli's ministry was no worse than other regimes which had run out of money, luck and reasonable weather. The bad news started to arrive as the by-elections began to turn; how far it reinforced an already adverse trend is uncertain.[13] Until 1878 his position was fairly strong, and even in 1879–80 his landslide defeat of 1880 was not foreshadowed by sensational by-election losses (see Table 4.2). Disraeli first deeply divided the public over foreign policy issues, then encountered the 'feel-bad' factor wrapped in Gladstonian oratory, and in diabolical weather, in 1879–80.

TABLE 4.2 *By-Elections 1874–80*

	Conservative Gains	Conservative Losses
1874	3	–
1875	1	4
1876	1	4
1877	1	2
1878	3	3
1879	–	2
1880	1	–
TOTAL	10	15

This brings us to the question of the 1880 election and how far it should be identified with the Midlothian campaigns (for there were two).[14] To whom did the Midlothian campaigns appeal? To whom were they meant to appeal? They were deeply conservative in emphasis; they explicitly looked back to Peel as a model. They had little to say about the political modernization of farming areas likes Wales, Scotland and Ireland. They had little to say about the world of large industry and great cities. If late Victorian elections increasingly turned on victory in Lancashire and London, as the commonplace of the period had it, then Gladstone was not aiming specifically at them. That was left to Lord Hartington, who fought a vigorous campaign in Rossendale, and to Salisbury, who attracted no less than 32,000 people to a rally in Manchester. Gladstone, and Disraeli too, seem to have aimed directly at Middle England, not to the Celtic fringes, nor Lancashire and London (both of which had their own rather volatile long-term trends). Lancashire had gone heavily Tory in 1874; the question remains why Gladstone did not fight a Lancashire seat for his Midlothian campaign.

Disraeli was a sick old man leading an ill Cabinet.[15] At an election this was much harder to conceal than at other times. The Conservatives could not do much campaigning; and when they spoke of their achievements at home or abroad, they could say little without pleading guilty to Gladstone's charge of costliness. They could not reconstruct the government to give a better impression; the additions and alterations of 1878–80 showed how little high talent they had to bring forward. The Conservatives lacked a coup to go to the country on, or a cry to rally opinion with. True, Irishmen were in misery – but though the Dublin administration was competantly humanitarian, this was no basis for a rallying cry. Disraeli had not given, nor had he sought to give, his party either a working-class or a middle-class identity. He left his party in 1880 very much as he found it in 1874, and as he liked to have it, a gentry party; and when the tide of foreign policy and economy ceased to flow his way, this left him stranded and primarily concerned about maintaining farmers' support for the gentry in the counties, an important but secondary issue.

CHRONOLOGY

1872	APRIL 3	Disraeli's speech at the Free Trade Hall, Manchester
	JUNE 24	Disraeli's speech at the Crystal Palace, London
1873	MARCH 13	Gladstone's Liberal government resigns after a defeat in the House of Commons, but Disraeli refuses to form a minority administration; the Liberals resume office on 19 March
1874	JANUARY 24	Dissolution of Parliament suddenly announced, and appearance of Gladstone's election address in the press; polling takes place in early February
	FEBRUARY 17	Disraeli summoned by Queen Victoria and invited to form an administration; his Cabinet includes the 15th Earl of Derby as foreign secretary and R. A. Cross (the only Cabinet member from a middle-class and commercial background) as home secretary
	MARCH 19	Queen's speech sets out the government's legislative programme

AUGUST 5	Public Worship Regulation Act passed, to stop the spread of ritualistic and 'Romanish' practices in the Church of England
AUGUST 7	Patronage Act passed, fails to resolve problems of church appointments in the divided (Presbyterian) Church of Scotland Royal Commission to consider the law on trade unions; Factory Act introduces a maximum 10-hour day for all workers; Intoxicating Liquors Act controversially amends the previous Liberal government's Licensing Act (1872) to the benefit of the drink trade interest
1875	Public Health Act, consolidates and strengthens earlier legislation; Sale of Food and Drugs Act passed, which aimed to set trading standards and prevent adulteration; generally unsuccessful until further powers added in 1879; Conspiracy and Protection of Property Act legalizes peaceful picketing

	JUNE 10	Cross introduces the Employers and Workmen Bill, which frees employees from criminal prosecution for breach of contract
		Artisans' Dwelling Act, enabling legislation intended to encourage local authorities to make improvements in standards and conditions
	JULY	Beginning of the Balkan crisis
	NOVEMBER 9	Disraeli's speech at the Guildhall issues a warning to the other Great Powers not to ignore British interests in the Eastern Question
	NOVEMBER 23	Disraeli moves swiftly to purchase the 44 per cent shareholding in the Suez Canal owned by the Khedive of Eygpt, for £4 million
1876	MAY 13	British Cabinet refuses to agree to the Berlin Memorandum
	JULY 31	Disraeli dismisses reports of Turkish atrocities in Bulgaria as 'coffee-house babble' in a speech in the House of Commons
		Merchant Shipping Act; Rivers Pollution Act passed; Education Act, gives compulsory powers to ensure attendance at

		elementary (primary) schools; Royal Titles Act declares Queen Victoria the Empress of India
	August 12	Disraeli is created the 1st Earl of Beaconsfield, and moves to the House of Lords
	September 6	Publication of Gladstone's pamphlet *The Bulgarian Horrors and the Question of the East*, and beginning of his Bulgarian agitation
	December 8	Bulgarian agitation reaches its peak with a mass meeting at St James's Hall, London, addressed by 32 speakers
1877	April 12	Britain announces annexation of the Boer republic of Transvaal
	April 24	Russia declares war on Turkey
	August 14	W. H. Smith enters the Cabinet as first lord of the Admiralty, becoming its second member with a middle-class background
1878	January 23	Decision of the Cabinet to order the Mediterranean fleet to move to Constantinople results in resignation of the Earl of Derby and Lord Carnarvon from the Cabinet; decision later

	rescinded, and Derby persuaded to stay
MARCH 3	Russia imposes peace terms on Turkey in the Treaty of San Stefano
MARCH 27	Cabinet resolves to call up the reserves and move troops from India to the Mediterranean; Derby finally resigns
APRIL 2	Lord Salisbury appointed foreign secretary
MAY 30	Second Factory Act passed, mainly consolidates earlier measures
	Britain signs a secret convention with Russia, followed by others with Turkey (4 June) and Austria–Hungary (6 June); these pave the way to securing British objectives at the Congress to be held in Berlin
JUNE 13	Congress of Berlin opens, to revise the Treaty of San Stefano and settle the Eastern Question: British delegation led by Disraeli and Salisbury
JULY 13	Treaty of Berlin gives successful outcome to the Eastern crisis, Disraeli returns home in triumph from the Congress

1879	JANUARY 22	British forces defeated by the Zulus at Isandhlwana
	JULY 24	Irish University Bill passed
	SEPTEMBER 3	Massacre of the British legation at Kabul leads to resumption of the Afghan War
	OCTOBER 18	Lord Salisbury addresses rally of 32,000 in Manchester
	OCTOBER 21	Foundation of the Irish National Land League, and start of the 'land war'
	NOVEMBER 25–27	Gladstone's first campaign of speeches in the Midlothian constituency
1880	FEBRUARY 6	Liverpool by-election, held by Conservatives after a campaign dominated by the Irish Home Rule issue
	FEBRUARY 13	Southwark by-election results in a Conservative gain from the Liberals
	MARCH 2	Metropolitan Water Works Purchase Bill introduced in the House of Commons
	MARCH 8	Announcement of the dissolution; at the end of the Parliament there were 351 Conservative, 250 Liberal, and 51 Irish Home Rule MPs
	MARCH 31	First day of polling produces a Liberal net gain of 15 from 69

constituencies; the final result is
349 Liberal, 243 Conservative
and 60 Irish Home Rule MPs

1881 APRIL 19   Death of Disraeli

Robert Salisbury, Third Marquess of Salisbury
(*Reproduced by permission of* Punch)

CHAPTER FIVE

1886–1905

Martin Pugh

'It will be interesting to be the last of the conservatives. I foresee that will be our fate.' Thus wrote a gloomy Lord Salisbury in 1882.[1] His pessimism is understandable. Disraeli's death in the previous year had left the Conservatives bereft of popular statesmen. The Tory revival ushered in by the 1873 general election had been blown away by Gladstone's victory in 1880. Moreover, the terms of the electoral struggle appeared to be tipping further against the party. Gladstone's legislation against corrupt electoral practices in 1883, which curtailed expenditure and effectively obliged the parties to rely more upon unpaid volunteer activists, put the Conservatives under a new disadvantage in relation to the Liberals. Worse was to come when the franchise reform of 1884 granted the vote to manual workers in the counties, thereby increasing the electorate from 3.15 million to 5.7 million and endangering scores of Tory seats. With a view to exploiting this new electorate the Birmingham Radical, Joseph Chamberlain, launched a nationwide campaign in 1885 in which he attacked the wealthy in what, by the standards of the time, was violent language. 'Lord Salisbury', he declared, 'constitutes himself the spokesman of a class – of the class to which he himself belongs – who toil not neither do they spin.'[2] By the mid-1880s it seemed that the famous warning about 'disintegration' issued by Salisbury at the time of the Second Reform Act in 1867 was coming true. An electorate dominated by propertyless men, few of whom even paid income tax, would surely be inveigled sooner or later into backing a programme for the expropriation of the wealth enjoyed by the minority.

In the event British Conservatism had more than a little life still left in it. Though defeated in the 1885 election as expected, the party was returned to power in 1886 after the Liberal split over Irish Home Rule. Thereafter twenty years of power stretched ahead of them, interrupted only by the brief Liberal government from 1892 to 1895.[3] The emphatic Conservative victory of 1895 was followed by another in 1900 – the only occasion since the Second Reform Act when a government succeeded in winning a second term.

Of course these results gave a greatly exaggerated impression of the real Conservative strength in the country. The party's success was conditional on their opponents' failure to mobilize their support as much as on a high level of Toryism. Significantly the party's chief agent, R. W. E. Middleton, believed that Conservatives did best when the proportion of the male population registered as electors was below 60 per cent, an objective which could be achieved as long as the complicated system for registering voters was maintained.[4] Moreover, the lower the turnout of voters, in Middleton's opinion, the better the party's chances of victory. This is why, whenever he was prime minister and thus able to choose the date for an election, Salisbury liked to opt for harvest time, when the agricultural labourers were less likely to cast their votes.[5]

These contemporary assumptions are to some extent corroborated by the election results of the period. Liberal victories between 1885 and 1910 were usually associated with a high turnout, and Conservative victories with a low one. Certainly the combination of a sharp increase in the number of voters and a rise in the turnout – for example between 1880–85, 1886–92 and 1900–06 – heralded a Conservative defeat.

TABLE 5.1 General Election Results 1885–1910

	Conservative		Liberal		Irish Nationalist		Labour	
	% Vote	Seats Won	% Vote	Seats Won	% Vote	Seats Won	% Vote	Seats Won
1885		250		334		86		0
1886		316		191		85		0
		78 (L.U.)*						
1892	47.0	268	45.1	273	7.0	81	0.3	1
		47 (L.U.)*						
1895	49.1	341	45.7	177	4.0	82	1.0	0
		70 (L.U.)*						
1900	51.5	334	44.6	184	2.5	82	1.8	2
		68 (L.U.)*						
1906	43.6	157	49.0	401	0.6	83	5.9	29
1910 (Jan.)	46.9	273	43.2	275	1.0	82	7.7	40
1910 (Dec.)	46.3	272	43.8	272	2.5	84	7.2	42

* Liberal Unionists

This pattern serves as a reminder that when Tory leaders, such as Disraeli in 1867 or Salisbury in 1885, accepted reform in response to Liberal initiatives, they were right to fear the consequences of a wider electorate; their shrewdness lay in perceiving how they might maximize the value of the existing Conservative vote by judicious modifications of the constituency boundaries. Thus, for Salisbury the elections of 1868, 1874 and 1880 underlined the point that while his party could not hope to beat off the advance of democracy in Britain, it could realistically expect to contain its effects by deploying its skill and resources in mobilizing what support it had in the country.

TABLE 5.2   *Electorate and Turnout 1874–1910*

	1874	1880	1885	1886	1892	1895	1900	1906	1910(J)
Voters (millions)	2.75	3.04	5.70	5.70	6.16	6.33	6.73	7.26	6.69
% turnout	66.4	72.2	81.2	74.2	77.4	78.4	74.6	82.6	86.6

The Conservative Electoral Machine

As a popular political organization the British Conservative Party has not been well served by political scientists, whose analyses of political parties have traditionally been influenced by Continental practice.[6] In this perspective traditional, parliamentary-based parties are assumed to be unable or unwilling to mobilize a popular following in contrast to parties which originate outside Parliament, especially in labour movements. The influential study by the late Robert Mackenzie reinforced this assumption by taking a dismissive view of the National Union of Conservative and Constitutional Associations and of the annual party conference.[7] However, the survival of Victorian Conservatism and its emergence as the usual governing party in the twentieth century suggest that scholars have misread British political practice and institutions; recently even the much-derided Conservative conference has begun to be recognized as an influential institution in the party.[8]

Certainly the historical record leaves one in no doubt about the importance Conservatives attached to organization. After the defeat of 1880 activists in the towns blamed Disraeli for neglecting the organization. Although some eight hundred Conservative clubs and local associations had affiliated to the National Union by this time, it was not compulsory to do so, and many parliamentary leaders and local dignitaries regarded them with suspicion. The National Union exercised little power and its resources were controlled by the Central Office which had been established by Disraeli in 1870 so as to be under the patronage of the party leader.

Subsequent claims by Lord Randolph Churchill that the leadership neglected organization were, in fact, taken to heart by Salisbury. It was difficult to deny that the 1883 legislation would force Conservatives to mobilize volunteer workers to carry out the tasks which had traditionally been paid for by a few wealthy local patrons. Salisbury tackled the problem of organization in three main ways. First he defused the immediate row with Churchill in 1884 by making marginal concessions to the National Union and by holding out the offer of a Cabinet post to Churchill himself. From 1885 all Conservative constituency associations automatically affiliated to the National Union whose official functions were to promote new branches, distribute propaganda and organize speaking tours and the annual conference. But, though rapidly deserted by Lord Randolph, the National Union refused to be a mute servant of the party. Throughout the 1880s and 1890s the delegates at conferences felt free to criticize the parliamentary leadership on organizational questions and, more surprisingly perhaps, showed far fewer inhibitions about debating awkward policy issues than twentieth-century commentators have assumed. For example, they took up demands for restrictions on alien immigration, the introduction of votes for women, state help to workingmen to buy their own homes, and, above all, the adoption of protective tariffs.[9] In fact, protectionist resolutions were approved nine times between 1887 and 1902. The conversion of the party's rank and file to tariff reform during the 1890s proved embarrassing for the parliamentary leadership; and though this did not lead to an immediate change in party policy, it ensured that once Joseph Chamberlain had given a lead on the issue in 1903, the majority of Conservatives would swing firmly into the protectionist camp. The party leader, A. J. Balfour, scuttled ignominiously after them.

The second major development within the organization was professionalization. From 1885 onwards the party employed R. W. E. Middleton as chief agent and Hon. Secretary of the National Union. He created a body of professional agents who covered half the constituencies by 1900, in addition to regional organizers. By 1891 they had a professional organization of Conservative agents which set examinations, issued qualifications and published *The Conservative Agent's Journal* to brief members on electoral law and electoral practice. These men undoubtedly played a key role in ensuring that Conservative supporters were actually placed on the register of voters each year, and in trying to remove the names of known opponents. At a time when many constituencies returned an MP on the basis of only a couple of thousand votes the work of a competent agent could make all the difference between victory and defeat.

Naturally this activity called for considerable financial resources. Once, however, the expenditure on elections at the local level became subject to stringent controls, the parties circumvented the law by building up much larger central funds under the management of the chief whip. For the Conservatives this involved supplementing the usual collections from the peers at each general election, by going cap-in-hand to what contemporaries like to call derisively the 'plutocrats'.[10] Increasingly this took the form of an exchange of knighthoods and peerages, or a promise of future honours, in return for direct donations to party funds or subsidies to pro-Conservative newspapers. Significantly, twice as many peerages were being created during the 1880s and 1890s as in the mid-Victorian period, and the proportion awarded to middle-class men rose sharply. 'When I want a peerage', the newspaper proprietor Alfred Harmsworth reputedly said, 'I'll pay for it like an honest man.' Sales were routinely denied; but in 1905 Sir Alexander Acland-Hood, then Tory chief whip, made it abundantly clear that Harmsworth, who became Lord Northcliffe, would have to have his peerage or the party would lose his money.[11] In view of Salisbury's vehement distaste for the corrupting effects of democratic politics one might have expected him to be more scrupulous about honours. Yet, in fact, his brief 1885–86 ministry proved to be a turning-point in terms of the acceleration of the ennoblement of party loyalists. His papers bear eloquent testimony to the amount of time devoted to a careful distribution of rewards by Salisbury, Middleton and the chief whips. He was determined not to repeat the errors of Disraeli who paid the price for upholding the kind of traditional gentlemanly standards which the cynical 3rd Marquis was ruthlessly jettisoning.

The third element in the Conservative strategy for adapting to a more democratic system took the form of the Primrose League, an organization founded in memory of Disraelian principles in November 1883 . It was the League that provided the popular element in the party machine in the late Victorian era. Salisbury himself granted it official recognition when he resolved the dispute with Churchill over the National Union in 1884, and subsequently, if rather improbably, agreed to be Grand Master. Since the Primrose League was not formally part of the party it represented little threat to the parliamentary leadership. But the common personnel ensured that the League reflected the needs and ideology of the Conservative Party. It presented Salisbury with the advantages of a popular organization without the drawbacks.

A crude measure of the significance of the Primrose League for late-Victorian Conservatism is provided by its membership figures which reached one million in 1891. Although these are almost certainly an exaggeration there is little doubt that the party had, by that time, far overtaken the Liberals. This was achieved partly by appealing to the British instinct for social climbing by instituting a hierarchy of knights and dames for the aspiring middle classes. But in addition the League enabled the working class to join their local habitations as associates for as little as threepence a year, in return for which they gained access to an elaborate programme of social events and entertainments.[12] The League succeeded to an unusual degree in crossing the normal social barriers to political participation. For example, it recruited non-voters as well as voters, women as well as men, Catholics as well as Protestants, and even Liberals as well as those already converted to Conservatism.[13] Above all it managed to bring together members of different social classes in support of common causes, thereby giving at least some tangible form to Conservative aspirations to represent the nation as a whole.

However, the most conspicuous single advantage bestowed on the party by the Primrose League was its ability to supply the volunteer workers it now needed. Women were especially in evidence as canvassers and as platform speakers as well as in the quieter work of registering voters and organizing social events. Although best known for social activities, the League assiduously propagated the Conservative message in simple visual forms using magic lanterns and *tableaux vivants* to represent imperial issues or Irish Nationalist atrocities to audiences of people unlikely to gain much information from newspapers. In any case the social side of its work was the key both to attracting large numbers in the first place and to keeping the Conservative membership together during the intervals between elections when the official party organization invariably dwindled or lapsed altogether.

The Alliance of Property

Caught between the bourgeois optimism of the mid-Victorian era and the militant proletarianism of the Edwardian period, late Victorian Britain was, against contemporary expectations, 'an Indian summer for the old order' as one historian has described it.[14] Partly by luck and partly by judgement the Tory leaders discovered during the 1880s that survival in the electoral snake-pit did not necessarily mean abandoning all defence of the status quo or attempting to outflank the Radicals in a bid for the support of the lower classes. Fortunately for them their chief opponent, Gladstone, chose to keep the focus on the traditional constitutional, legal, religious and moral issues rather than develop a novel social or economic programme. Had he surrendered the leadership of Liberalism to Joseph Chamberlain, as seemed likely at one stage, the Conservatives would have faced a far more formidable challenge.[15] Instead they adopted a negative stand against interfering Radical legislation and advocated the maintenance of empire, the glorification of monarchy, the preservation of property, and the defence of religious education and the church establishment.

Yet beneath the public rhetoric of patriotism the fundamental rationale for late Victorian Conservatism lay in the self-interest of the owners of property. Up to the 1880s much of the propertied interests – manufacturing, commercial and even landed – had remained within the Liberal camp, and this continued to some extent to be true right up to 1914. However, the Conservative achievement from the 1880s onwards was to engineer an alliance of traditional landed wealth with that of the towns and suburbs. The catalyst for this realignment of propertied interests was the

Irish Home Rule crisis of 1886 which split the Liberal Party. It not only accelerated the drift of Whig landowners away from Gladstone, but it also brought infusions of middle-class Anglicans more firmly into the Conservative camp. This soon made its mark on the electoral map of Britain; the West Midlands and Scotland moved sharply towards Conservatism after 1886, joining Lancashire which had already done so since 1868 under the influence of Irish immigration into Merseyside.

It is often forgotten that to many Victorians the Irish Question presented itself as much more than a constitutional or strategic matter. At the time it was widely taken to be the first instalment of the class war. Conservatives regarded Gladstone's 1881 Land Act, which used legal tribunals to impose lower rents for the benefit of tenant farmers, as a serious attack on private property rights, and, moreover, one that was capable of extension to the mainland. Legislation to give Scottish crofters security of tenure and fixed rentals, and impose on employers liability for accidents to their workers further underlined their fears. In fact the defection of landed Whig aristocrats such as Lord Lansdowne and the Duke of Argyll from Liberalism predated the Home Rule crisis. They were reacting to the steady adoption of Radicalism by the Liberal rank and file since 1867.

The migration of the landed class was accelerated by the replacement of the traditional two-member constituencies by single-member seats in the redistribution of 1885. This measure also created dozens of new urban and suburban constituencies which were to provide the Conservative Party with a solid electoral base for the next century.[16] The process was most obvious in Liberal-dominated cities such as Leeds which now became five separate constituencies; of these the commercial district (Leeds Central) and the residential area (Leeds North) regularly returned Tory members after 1885.

To a large extent the rightwards shift amongst the middle and especially lower middle class reflected mounting concern about taxation and the costs of educating children. The expansion of local government activities during the last twenty years of the century forced up municipal rates, thereby putting pressure on small property owners especially shopkeepers, clerks and artisans. Gradually the Liberals' role as a party of economy and retrenchment was undermined and the middle classes began to look to Salisbury's governments to contain income tax, relieve the burdens of local authorities and even intervene to check the spending of Radical-controlled bodies such as school boards. Increasingly the Conservatives adopted the arguments of classical liberalism to condemn interventionist measures for undermining business efficiency; a favourite target was the London County Council's use of a direct labour department and public works schemes which were seen as competing with private entrepreneurs. However, in the process the Conservatives began to lose sight of the tradition of One Nation Toryism. Working-class demands for material improvements were apt to be regarded as divisive and sectional. By contrast the subsidization of the land and agriculture was justified in the national interest. This attitude culminated in 1901 when the Salisbury government refused to remedy the trade unions' grievance over the Taff Vale Judgement which made them legally liable for the costs of strike action. The party eventually paid a heavy price in votes for too close an association with the interests of one class.

Ironically, late Victorian Conservatives found it difficult to defend landed interests effectively. The dwindling profitability of most arable farming had triggered a fall in rental values and sales of land at depressed prices. Yet, although this reawakened the traditional demand for agricultural protectionism, Conservatives still shrank from imposing tariffs for fear of raising food prices. Nor was the agricultural community itself always united. For example, the interests of tenant farmers did not entirely coincide with those of the owners, and the Liberals showed some readiness to exploit this gap by means of such measures as the Ground Game Act of 1880. They also won much support amongst agricultural labourers, especially in those counties where Joseph Arch's Agricultural Labourer's Union strengthened the spirit of revolt.

Conservatives did, however, take increasing comfort from the representation of certain religious interests. Vigorous resistance to Radical Liberal campaigns to disestablish the Church of England helped them to recruit middle-class Anglicans especially in the south of the country. Even amongst Nonconformists, however, a perceptible rightwards shift had occurred by the 1890s. This was more pronounced among Wesleyans for whom disestablishment had never been a major concern.[17] In any case, as Liberal governments resolved the many legal grievances of Nonconformists, so the more affluent among them began to behave like their middle-class Anglican counterparts by supporting the Conservatives. Even more strikingly, the Conservatives refurbished their credentials with English Catholics in this period. In view of the militant Protestantism of many local Conservative associations and the obsession of some backbench MPs with the spread of Ritualist practices within the Church, this was a delicate enterprise. On the other hand, the English Catholic community was naturally conservative and felt attracted towards a party increasingly close to the Establishment. Conservative defence of the voluntary schools in school board elections offered a tangible proof of common sympathy. An easy form of participation also appeared in the form of the Primrose League which welcomed Catholics; and the entry of the country's leading Catholic, the Duke of Norfolk, into Salisbury's Cabinet in 1895 placed the seal of respectability on the community after decades of estrangement.[18]

Leadership and Coalitionism

'England does not love coalitions', Disraeli famously declared in 1852. It was one of his less perceptive remarks. For despite regular protestations to the contrary British political parties, of both right and left, have frequently resorted to coalitions throughout the nineteenth and twentieth centuries, and they have underpinned them by resorting to electoral pacts. The post-1886 alliance between the Conservatives and Lord Hartington, Joseph Chamberlain and their Liberal Unionist followers proved to be but the precursor of two later arrangements with Lloyd George and his Liberal supporters during 1916–22, and with Ramsay MacDonald, Sir John Simon and their National Labour and National Liberal parties which kept them in office from 1931 to 1945. Both as an electoral expedient and as a means of sustaining a government the Conservative–Liberal Unionist alliance was an emphatic success. Without it the party would simply not have established or maintained its grip on office until 1905.

Salisbury had always been looking for a coalition, at least in the sense that since 1867 he regarded the position of the Whigs within the Liberal Party as untenable. Consequently when the crisis came to a head in 1886 he seized the opportunity to precipitate the withdrawal of the Whigs by adopting a very negative stance on Home Rule. He did not, however, seek an immediate merger. For some years he was content for the Liberal Unionists to adopt a position similar to that of the Peelites after 1846, that is, as a distinct intermediate group in Parliament which supported the government on all important issues.[19] Salisbury's caution was justified. He rightly feared that the concatenation of Lord Randolph Churchill and Joseph Chamberlain might destabilize his own control of the party and the government. Thus in 1886 his main concern was to achieve electoral cooperation rather than a coalition. To this end the ninety-three rebel Liberal Unionists were largely unopposed by the

Conservatives in the 1886 general election which helped to ensure that seventy-eight of them were re-elected at the expense of the Gladstonians.

However, events between 1886 and 1892 gradually conspired to bring the two parties closer together. With the dramatic resignation of Churchill the internal threat to Salisbury materially diminished, but at the same time it exposed the lack of talent on the Tory front bench. The decision to replace Churchill as Chancellor with a very right-wing former Liberal, G. J. Goschen, was a harbinger of formal coalition. During the lifetime of the 1886–92 administration some of the more radical Liberal Unionists drifted back to their old allegiance which, combined with the Conservatives' defeat at the 1892 election, underlined the need to consolidate the anti-Gladstone alliance. Thus, when Salisbury next formed a government in 1895 he included Hartington (now Duke of Devonshire) and Chamberlain in his Cabinet. Lord Lansdowne, another respected former Liberal, also joined as secretary for war, and, later, foreign secretary. This process culminated in the formal amalgamation of the Liberal Unionists into the Conservative Party in 1912.

Although the alliance undoubtedly boosted the government's popular vote, enhanced its reputation and strengthened its oratorical powers, it suffered from two main drawbacks as seen from the Conservative perspective. First, it forced the Prime Minister to deny jobs to a number of his own party members which inevitably fostered resentment in the long term. Second, Liberal Unionism strengthened the free-trade elements, thereby helping to postpone the adoption of protectionism which was rapidly spreading in the Tory rank and file during the 1890s.

Nonetheless Salisbury's handling of the Liberal Unionist breakaway represented a major triumph. Somewhat against expectations he had proved himself an effective party manager. This had not been at all clear in the early 1880s when the party's leadership was divided between the leaders in the Lords and Commons. In the turmoil of those years Salisbury clearly appeared to be an immensely reassuring figure. He possessed both intellect and administrative competence – rare enough in the ranks of the Victorian Conservative Party. But to find these qualities combined with an aristocratic title and land ownership was irresistibly attractive. Moreover, Salisbury had given proof of his reactionary instincts by his celebrated resignation over Disraeli's reform bill in 1867 and by his robust defence of the rights of the hereditary House of Lords. Here was a leader who could be trusted to uphold the fundamentals of the Conservative faith. The unexpected assets he brought to the leadership were his shrewdness over electoral reform, his readiness to perform the functions of platform speaker in the country and his awareness of the importance of patronage in managing the party organization.

On the other hand, as prime minister Salisbury after 1886 suffered from his membership of the House of Lords and by being burdened with the work of the Foreign Office. Initially he had planned to use Churchill as leader of the Commons and Chancellor to strengthen the front bench. After Churchill's resignation he at first used W. H. Smith as leader of the House, and subsequently elevated his nephew, Arthur Balfour, to this role. He also relied heavily on Balfour and Middleton to keep him in touch with party opinion both at Westminster and in the country.[20] In fact less skill was now required in managing the Commons. Salisbury enjoyed a large majority in three of his four governments. But he also benefited from the marked trend towards party discipline in Parliament during the later 1880s and 1890s. Though developing for some years this had been accelerated by the Home Rule issue which polarized opinion and frightened the upper classes. As a result the traditional crossbench element disappeared from Parliament, especially on the Conservative side. By the 1890s nine out of ten Conservative members voted in the government's lobby in over 90 per cent of all divisions.[21] Thus, by the turn of the century governments suffered only one defeat per session on average in comparison with ten to fifteen during the mid-Victorian era.

In dealing with the Cabinet Salisbury showed some skill, despite his endearing reputation for occasionally failing to recognize his own ministers. Management problems were eased partly by expanding the Cabinet in an attempt to satisfy ambitions and to meet administrative needs. It comprised twenty-two members by 1890 by comparison with twelve to fourteen in mid-Victorian times. In spite of his ostensible hostility to government Salisbury actually created new ministries including the Scottish Office (1885), the Board of Agriculture (1889) and the Board of Education (1899). He showed himself relatively relaxed, if cynical, in handling his ministers, whom he usually left free to run their own departments. He eschewed any attempt to dominate the Cabinet, allowing it to vote and accepting decisions that went against him. Not surprisingly his four governments saw very few resignations on principle; even Chamberlain and Devonshire, whose experience under Gladstone had been marked by continual friction, worked harmoniously.

On the other hand, Cabinet management was no doubt easier under a prime minister whose over-riding aim was to do as little as possible in domestic affairs and be left to manage foreign and imperial matters. Indeed it seems that Salisbury consciously exploited the diffuse nature of his coalition and the size of the Cabinet by allowing it to rehearse at length the difficulties in the way of any course of action in the hope of eventually strangling legislative initiatives.[22]

Conservative Ideology and Programme

In response to the charge of negativism Salisbury was entitled to claim that he had been elected in 1886 for one overwhelming reason: to maintain the Union with Ireland. One step had already been taken to this end by mobilizing

Unionist support among the Protestants of Ulster who returned seventeen MPs to Westminster in 1886. Though a small minority of Ireland's 103 members, they were just enough to demonstrate that the Union was more than purely an English objective.

Beyond that the Chief Secretary, Balfour, combined a policy of repression of agitation in Ireland with a remarkable programme of social and economic concessions. This was, in fact, only a variation on Gladstone's earlier strategy, and it had no more effect in undermining nationalism in the long run. It is, however, of some interest in the context of Conservative ideology in this period. Balfour used state funds to pay for relief work in the most economically distressed areas, to build light railways, and to implement the Congested Districts Bill of 1890 which promoted migration, the amalgamation of uneconomic holdings and the distribution of seed potatoes to the very poor.[23] Most strikingly of all, the Conservatives recognized that the land tribunals established by Gladstone in 1881 had not been as unpopular with Irish landowners as expected. As a result a series of acts in 1885, 1888, 1891 and 1903 empowered the government to buy up big landed estates and resell them as small farms to the tenants on easy terms. In the long run this helped to create a conservative society of small proprietors, and in the process largely emasculated the Anglo-Irish landed class.

Interventionism in Ireland seems inconsistent with the *laissez-faire* philosophy increasingly embraced by Conservative politicians during the last twenty years of the century. 'It is the price we have to pay for the Union', as Salisbury put it. Yet if the Irish case was exceptional, the logic seemed almost as applicable to the social problems of the mainland. In a speech at Manchester, where he represented the Eastern division of the city, Balfour declared that 'the best antidote to Socialism was practical social reform'.[24] Yet such a suggestion created more problems than it solved. Conservatives shrank from implementing their one really distinc-

tive constructive idea – tariff reform – because of its
presumed unpopularity. In any case the party's reputation
for financial probity clashed awkwardly with the demands
of its key supporters for relief from taxation. Disraeli had
already spotted that if farmers and landowners could not
be helped by means of tariffs, then they ought to get some
compensation through grants-in-aid from the Exchequer to
relieve local taxation. The 1886–92 government doubled
central support to local authorities and also reduced income
tax to sixpence halfpenny in the pound. Salisbury's most
blatant attempt to subsidize his own supporters was the
1896 Agricultural Land Rating Act which provided £3.5 million to reduce rates on agricultural land. However, the relief
went directly to owners of land not to farmers, and the
scheme left Conservatives wide open to accusations of using
the urban taxpayers' money to assist the rich. Lloyd George
claimed that ministers themselves stood to benefit greatly,
citing Henry Chaplin, the minister involved, who would
gain £700 per annum.

When seen in the context of Conservative attitudes
towards the working class this policy represented the abandonment of any lingering traditions of 'Disraelianism'. The
leaders reacted to National Union debates on pensions and
housing, for example, merely by setting up royal commissions to investigate; meanwhile they advocated self-help
strategies for the poor as the best means of improving their
lot. Trade union pressure for an eight-hour working day
was rejected on the grounds that such interference with
business would lower efficiency and raise costs as well as
infringing the workers' own freedom to negotiate the conditions of work.[25] Clearly the combination of classical liberal
thinking and Gladstonian finance left little scope for social
welfare reforms. Indeed Goschen, the Chancellor after 1886,
expressed his desire to 'extinguish the cant of Tory
Democracy'.

On the other hand, at the local level Conservatives often
felt it unwise to rely too heavily on a diet of traditional

political issues. Candidates facing an urban, working-class electorate invariably offered a programme of interventionist social policies despite the danger of raising expectations that were unlikely to be fulfilled. Even at the parliamentary level a stance of unrelieved resistance to reform was complicated by the very obvious need to co-operate with Chamberlain who continued to be fertile in generating new social policies. In fact Chamberlain exercised more influence when outside the government between 1886 and 1892 than when in the Cabinet after 1895. In the earlier period Parliament passed an Allotments Act (1887) and a Smallholdings Act (1892), both of which Salisbury disliked because of the powers of compulsory purchase given to local authorities. Elective county councils were established in 1889 and elementary education became free in 1891. All this represented the achievement of at least a part of Chamberlain's programme. But it clearly went against the grain. The instinct was to restrain national and local government where possible. This became very evident in the repeated attempts that were made by legislation and through the law courts to prevent school boards spending funds to improve higher grade education. Eventually they were simply abolished in the 1902 Education Act. 'I fear these social questions are destined to break up our Party', Salisbury complained wearily in 1892, 'but why incur the danger before the necessity has arrived?'[26] Necessity, at least in the form of Joseph Chamberlain, kept announcing its presence. He sketched out a bold programme in 1890 including compensation for industrial accidents, old age pensions, labour exchanges, cheaper train travel for workingmen, an eight-hour day for miners and loans for house purchase. But although several of his ideas were implemented, Salisbury managed to obstruct the broad thrust of the strategy.

In the medium term Salisbury's negative stance justified itself. For the parliamentary leadership did at least have an alternative to the Chamberlainite attempt to outflank the Radicals. This meant concentrating on those issues which united the classes – patriotism, empire, church and monarchy. In the atmosphere of late Victorian Britain this made some sense. The popular imagination was continuously stirred by British exploits in exotic parts of the world; other powers were plainly growing envious of her imperial possessions; the rise of the Prussian military machine and the naval building by several great powers focused thoughts on the prospects of an invasion of the British Isles; and failing businessmen increasingly blamed foreign competitors for taking unfair advantage by means of tariffs and the dumping of goods in Britain. In this xenophobic atmosphere Conservatives surrendered to the temptation to depict their political opponents as, by definition, unpatriotic, determined to break up the empire, and ready to abandon British interests in order to appease the treacherous Irish.

However, though successful as an interim measure, this approach had its limitations. Imperial exploits had a habit of blowing up in the government's face, and in view of their neglect of the army and the navy in the 1890s, the Conservatives were clearly pushing their luck. Also, the public's enthusiasm for empire, though genuine enough, was volatile and apt to collapse when the material advantages of imperialism proved elusive. There is in fact a striking similarity between the overall strategy pursued by late Victorian Conservatives and that adopted under Mrs Thatcher during the 1980s. It comprised two basic elements. First, there was the reversion to classical liberalism and the attempt to restrict government while at the same time appeasing special interest groups with tax concessions. This experiment failed in the most literal sense as Salisbury himself recognized. Whereas in 1870 government expenditure had represented 9 per cent of British gross national product, by 1895 it had expanded to 19 per cent. Second, the leaders tried to distract attention from domestic difficulties by adopting a crude nationalist stance and denouncing their opponents as traitors, something not generally done either by mid-Victorian or by interwar and postwar Conservatives.

This eventually broke down in bitter party divisions arising out of the Boer War and tariff reform. It is to these underlying flaws that we must now turn.

The Intellectual Crisis of Conservatism

By the turn of the century even the continued electoral success of the Conservative Party could scarcely obscure the intellectual dilemmas facing Salisburyian Conservatism. The problem was twofold. In the first place, having linked their fortunes to British expansionism the Conservatives had increasingly to come to terms with the incipient decline of British power in the world. In the second place, they struggled to define the proper role for the state at a time when economic and social deterioration demanded more intervention rather than less.[27] Of course the Conservatives were by no means alone in facing such issues. But whereas the 'New Liberal' writers of the late 1890s and early 1900s offered a coherent revision of their party's traditional creed, Conservatives faced the task of rethinking their ideas while still wrestling with the day-to-day distractions of office. Symptomatic of this dilemma was the appearance of a flock of right-wing pressure groups, including the Liberty and Property Defence League, the Anti-Socialist Union, the Middle-Class Defence League, the National Service League, the Navy League and the Imperial Maritime League.[28] In effect these organizations articulated a Conservative critique of the Conservative Party for its inadequate response to internal and external challenges.

The proximate origins of this discontent lay in the 1870s when mid-Victorian optimism had been rudely deflated by the unwelcome reappearance of a major Continental power in the shape of imperial Germany and by the onset of what contemporaries thought of as the 'Great Depression'. The loss of export markets in the more competitive economies of North America and Europe prompted the creation of the Fair Trade League in 1881. This immediately put the

Conservatives under pressure to live up to both their earlier role as the party of tariffs and their current pretensions as the patriotic party. As cereal farmers in the southern and eastern counties found their prices undercut by imports of wheat, landlords began to reduce rents and sell estates in a weak market. Leading parliamentarians, such as Sir Michael Hicks Beach, resolved their financial embarrassments by abandoning their rural holdings and seeking compensation in company directorships. But what made their situation so galling was the resurgence of Radical attacks upon landed wealth during the last twenty years of the century. These campaigns were founded on the indisputable fact that though many landowners suffered from dwindling agricultural assets, the value of their *urban* holdings was rising rapidly. Stimulated by the visits of the American land reformer, Henry George, Radical Liberals propagated the idea of taxing the 'unearned increment' generated by land and thus forcing the 'idle rich' to contribute to the expenses of the community as a whole. No doubt this was more a rhetorical than a real threat; but Conservatives got an alarming glimpse of the future in Sir William Harcourt's famous budget of 1894 which imposed a scheme of graduated death duties starting at 1 per cent and reaching 8 per cent on estates worth over one million pounds.

Liberal attacks on landed wealth were largely endorsed by the new Socialist organizations of the late Victorian era, the Fabian Society (1884), the Social Democratic Federation (1883) and the Independent Labour Party (1893). As yet, however, Socialism remained a marginal force within the working class, and only the most nervous Tories took the prospect of a British revolution seriously. Yet Socialism posed a much more subtle and effective challenge by virtue of its appeal to the more thoughtful members of the middle classes. The Fabians, for example, argued not so much that capitalism was oppressive and unjust as that it was inefficient, wasteful of scarce economic resources and unable to supply the investment required by British industry and agriculture. This line of thought was complemented by a series of revelations in the late 1880s and 1890s about the extent of poverty and the physical deterioration of the urban population. It now appeared that manufacturing industry could not generate employment for all those fit and able to work as had been confidently assumed in the mid-Victorian era. Fears of long-term decline were corroborated by the mass rejection of men who had volunteered to serve in the war in South Africa (1899–1902) but had failed to meet the army's very modest requirements. Balfour's government gave official recognition to the danger by establishing a Committee on Physical Deterioration whose report in 1904 helped to set the agenda of social reform up to 1914.

Even worse, the defeats suffered by British armies at the hands of the Boers in 1899 and 1900 released a wave of pessimism about British national decadence and the prospect of imperial decline. The immediate targets of criticism were the incompetent, amateur and effete party politicians who, it was claimed, had left Britain exposed militarily and diplomatically and neglected the health and education of the men on whom the future of the empire depended.[29] For a time National Efficiency became the fashionable cry for Conservatives, Fabians and Liberals dissatisfied with the passivity and negativism of the conventional parliamentarians. However, this was inevitably more demoralizing for Conservatives than for Socialists or Liberals as they had been responsible for British policy for most of the previous twenty years. For a radical Conservative such as Sir Alfred Milner, Britain's High Commissioner in South Africa, the achievement of basic Tory objectives abroad now required the adoption of a policy of state-financed social welfare at home. Bismarckian Germany offered a model – and a threat – which influenced a whole generation of politicians. 'Germany is organized not only for war but for peace', as the young Winston Churchill put it a few years later, 'we are organized for nothing but party politics.'[30]

Although the Chamberlainite tariff reform programme

offered a bold response to the problems highlighted by the South African war, it never satisfactorily resolved the Conservative dilemma. This was in part a matter of unfortunate timing. The electoral disaster which overtook the party in 1906 undermined confidence in positive solutions and provoked the critics on the radical right wing to concentrate their attacks upon the traditional parliamentary leadership now symbolized by the unfortunate Balfour. He was, in fact, far more in tune with the constructive ideas of the National Efficiency school than his predecessor, but fell victim to a virulent 'Balfour Must Go' campaign. This left the more liberal Conservatives, who wanted the party to adopt a distinctive social reform policy, in a weak position for the remainder of the Edwardian period. They seemed to want to scuttle ignominiously after the policies of the Liberals at a time when the party urgently sought a reaffirmation of its own traditions. In this way the programme that had characterized Conservatism under Salisbury lost credibility without leading to any agreed alternative.

The Free Trade–Protectionist Schism

As we have already seen the Conservative leaders had contrived to keep the lid on the burgeoning protectionist sentiment among their grassroots supporters since the 1880s. The crucial obstacle to revisionist ideas was the insistence of Sir Michael Hicks Beach, who served as chancellor of the exchequer from 1895 to 1902, on running the economy along orthodox Gladstonian lines. While Hicks Beach's passion for retrenchment and free trade suited the Treasury perfectly, it caused continual friction between him and his ministerial colleagues; he had the habit, in Balfour's words, of 'dropping little grains of sand into the wheels of every department'.[31] The Chancellor felt under constant pressure to pay for naval building and costly colonial campaigns as well as relieving the burden of local taxation. Ironically his task was made easier by the success of the Liberals' system of graduated death duties which yielded more revenue than expected, as well as by the general revival of trade after 1896. As a result he managed to reduce the national debt and restrict income tax to eightpence. Despite this, however, by 1898 Hicks Beach faced a deficit of four million pounds, and the outbreak of war in South Africa in the autumn of 1899 forced the long-standing dilemma over national taxation to a fatal climax.

By stages the increasingly irascible Chancellor increased government borrowing, raised income tax from eightpence to one shilling and twopence, suspended the Sinking Fund and imposed extra duties on beer, spirits, tea, tobacco, coal and corn. By the time the war ended in 1902, Britain's national debt had risen to over £800 million, thereby imposing a new strain upon annual expenditure in the Edwardian period. It was this situation that aroused the slumbering giant within Salisbury's government: Joseph Chamberlain. He concluded that imperial expansionism, for which he had himself been largely responsible, had left the Conservatives in the doldrums; some fresh initiative was therefore required. Chamberlain insisted that Britain could not simply revert to retrenchment or to the level of taxation that had prevailed before the war. The emergency duty placed on corn offered a way out. By retaining the duty for foreign imports but lifting it for the benefit of empire products Britain might begin the process of turning the empire into a coherent economic unit. This vision of an imperial federation had been in currency since the 1880s; it grew out of a feeling that in the long term a power with such limited resources as Britain must utilize her overseas population and assets in order to meet super-states such as the United States on more equal terms.

By contrast Hicks Beach adhered firmly to free trade, retrenchment and the Sinking Fund. However, he had become so isolated within the Cabinet that when Salisbury resigned as prime minister in 1902 he took the opportunity to quit too. Consequently it fell to a new leader, Balfour, to handle the emerging split within the Conservative ranks. As chancellor, Balfour appointed another free-trader, C. T. Ritchie, who soon abandoned the corn duty, thereby helping to precipitate the resignation of Chamberlain. In a famous speech at Birmingham in May 1903 Chamberlain launched a nationwide crusade for tariff reform. At this stage the strength of his policy lay in the appeal it made to several different sections of opinion. It reflected existing concerns about the empire; it reactivated the traditional cause of agricultural protectionism; it addressed the growing fears of German competition amongst some manufacturers; it stimulated chauvinistic instincts by promising to make the foreigners pay; it offered workingmen the prospect of increasing employment by defending the market for their products; and it showed that social reforms could be financed without extra taxation.

In view of the prolonged debates over tariff reform that had been taking place since the 1880s it is scarcely surprising that most of the party in the country rapidly declared in favour of Chamberlain's programme. However, since at least seventy MPs and much of the Cabinet remained loyal to free trade, albeit often under the guise of 'retaliation', the party was doomed to a period of bitter controversy. Some Conservatives argued that tariffs would inevitably alienate an electorate now accustomed to cheap food and rising living standards. Others allowed their judgement to be clouded by personalities. Those such as Lord Hugh Cecil, entrenched within the traditional party elite, denounced Chamberlain as an 'alien immigrant' who aspired to take over the party in the name of a vulgar materialist expedient. Such infighting had not been seen in the Conservative ranks since the ousting of Peel in the 1840s and was to occur only occasionally in the twentieth century.

Up to a point the massive election defeat suffered in 1906 diminished the problem by eliminating most of the free-traders from Parliament. In effect the Edwardian party was committed to tariff reform.[32] However, the protectionists

214

were neatly checkmated by Lloyd George's famous budget of 1909, which demonstrated that the voters could continue to enjoy the benefits of free trade *and* pay for old age pensions and a new navy. When the protectionists in the House of Lords reacted to this by rejecting the budget, the only result was to force the Conservatives into two more unsuccessful elections in 1910 which ensured the passage of legislation curtailing the powers of the upper house in 1911. This in turn opened the way to the enactment of bills for Irish Home Rule and the disestablishment of the Church in Wales between 1912 and 1914. As a result of these setbacks the pragmatic instincts of Tory politicians began to reassert themselves. MPs asked why they had allowed themselves to be led into betraying some of their most cherished principles and institutions by the fanatical pursuit of what was, after all, no more than an economic expedient. Curiously, such a perception largely escaped the Thatcherite enragés of the 1980s as they unwittingly detached their party from its roots in the British Establishment.

Organizational Decline

The Liberal landslide victory in 1906 inevitably increased Conservative dissatisfaction with the state of their party's organization. However, the deterioration of any political party's popular organization is as much a symptom of its loss of popularity as a cause of it.[33] Are there any reasons for thinking that by the turn of the century the Conservative machine was in decline for reasons that had nothing to do with the policies of the party?

Certainly the Primrose League had begun to suffer from the cycle of expansion and contraction to which most mass organizations are prone as one generation of leaders passes its peak and drops out. By 1900 the League's formula, highly successful within its limits, showed signs of breaking down. As a social organization it suffered increasingly from the competition of the commercial entertainment industry.

Politically its heavy reliance on staple propaganda items such as Irish atrocities inevitably wore thin after a prolonged period of comparative calm in the Irish countryside.[34] Above all, the League's use of popular imperialism never really recovered from the setbacks of the Boer War. By 1901 even the *Primrose League Gazette* admitted that in working-class areas 'the idea is there that the war ought to have been over by now'.[35] At a time when real wages were falling back for most workingmen for the first time in twenty years, patriotic sentiment took a back seat. When Milner rashly introduced Chinese indentured labourers into South Africa after 1902 the Chamberlainite claims about new work for British miners swiftly collapsed. Indeed, the Liberals dramatized the point by parading pigtailed 'coolies' in the streets, while Lloyd George mischievously suggested that the Tories might want to employ Chinamen in the Welsh quarries at a shilling a day. Suddenly the Primrose League had lost its best weapons, and seemed to have no new shots in its armoury.

Officially the League claimed no fewer than 1,556,000 'enrolments' in 1901. This, however, was far from being an accurate measure of membership. Provincial tours by its agents revealed that Lancashire, for example, had forty-nine live habitations, thirty dormant ones and thirteen dead ones. By 1906 as many as 115 constituencies in England and Wales no longer possessed any live habitations. In 1912 the total membership was put at 656,000, still substantial, but far below the League's peak. On the eve of the First World War only 950 out of the 2,645 habitations were still alive.[36] Over the years some of the local patrons had allowed the political functions to lapse so that habitations became almost wholly social organizations. And, as the earlier generation of leaders passed away, their successors were not always satisfied with the original League formula. For example, some of the politically aware ladies had become active suffragists, and in the process were diverted from party politics.[37] Even more damaging was the alternative vision of empire offered by the Tariff Reform League (TRL). Officially the Primrose League's Grand Council declined to adopt any view on the subject of protectionism.[38] However, leading figures such as Viscount Ridley became prominent in the TRL, while local habitation members sometimes criticized their MPs for their free-trade views, tried to affiliate to the TRL and even disbanded.[39] This is scarcely surprising. The League's imperialism had always been of a sentimental, Disraelian kind, and it looked increasingly nebulous by comparison with the more coherent economic analysis offered by the protectionists. In the long run the shift of personnel between these two Conservative organizations enabled the party to absorb the majority of the activists and members, both male and female, into its official structure for the first time; but in the short term the effect was to divert much of the effort into internal rivalry and disputes.

Meanwhile the official Conservative organization also suffered from the complacency arising out of years of success. Many associations continued to rely upon a handful of wealthy subscribers, or even the local MP or candidate; this meant that in periods when no election was expected much important work, such as the registration of voters, was neglected. This was especially unwise since the electorate expanded by about a million between 1900 and 1910 while working-class participation in politics was stimulated by the new Labour Representation Committee and the growth of trade union membership. The chief whip still held overall responsibility for these matters; but the management of the parliamentary party as well as Conservative Central Office, fundraising and the party in the country had become an excessive burden. As a result in 1911 the party set up a Unionist Organization Committee against the opposition of Acland-Hood in order to reform the system. In the event the UOC's proposals made little impact. But at least the chief whip's load was lightened by the appointment of a party chairman and a party treasurer; and the National Union was merged with Central Office. Beyond that, however, the party managers could do little more than exhort the constituencies to seek properly trained agents, maintain the register and keep their members active.

The Liberal Revival

Ultimately the Conservative dominance between 1886 and 1905 rested heavily upon the advantages derived from Irish Home Rule which both diverted influential support from the Liberals and distracted them from making an effective appeal to the working-class vote. However, Home Rule was a dwindling asset for the Conservatives. This became clear between 1886 and 1892 when the success of the Salisbury–Balfour policy effectively pushed Ireland down the political agenda, thereby depriving the party of some of the advantage it had enjoyed in 1886. Although the Liberals could do nothing to stop Gladstone making a second Home Rule Bill his priority, many of them regarded it as a liability. Eventually it was repudiated altogether by Lord Rosebery in 1901. Meanwhile the other leading Liberals concentrated on alternative issues, and concluded, not without reason, that they had won the election of 1892 in spite of Home Rule rather than because of it. Though scarcely an overwhelming victory for the Liberals (see Table 5.,1 p. 191) the election served to remind Salisbury of the limitations of his own party's appeal. The revival of trade unionism in 1889–90 after years of economic depression and unemployment should have been a warning against the neglect of working-class interests.

Subsequently, however, the Conservatives again benefited from their opponents' mistakes. Gladstone's last government (1892–94) wasted time on another abortive Home Rule Bill which was rejected by ten to one in the House of Lords. Some constructive legislation was enacted despite obstructionism by the peers, but the Liberals failed to put together a sufficiently popular programme to risk challenging the powers of the peers at an election. After

Gladstone's retirement in 1894 the parliamentary party rapidly disintegrated under the brief premiership of the ineffectual Rosebery. A defeat in the Commons led to a dissolution in unfavourable circumstances in 1895.

As a result the Conservatives won a comfortable victory. But just as in their previous government, so after 1895 they steadily lost momentum, so that by the late 1890s a string of by-elections pointed to a further swing of the pendulum. This time, however, Salisbury was rescued by his own failures in the South African war. By holding an early election in October 1900, at a time when patriotic fervour had reached a peak amid the disasters suffered by British troops and when the Liberals themselves were divided over the merits of the war, Salisbury managed to retain most of the ground won in 1895.

However, the 'khaki' election only disguised the long-term decline in Conservative fortunes. Between 1901 and 1903 the three underlying elements in popular Liberalism were reactivated. The first of these was labour. Until the notorious Taff Vale Judgement in 1901 the newly formed Labour Representation Committee remained weak and short of funds; but the legal ruling immediately led the cautious trade unions to put their resources behind the attempt to strengthen the voice of the workers in Parliament. Meanwhile, Liberal MPs attempted to persuade the House of Commons to amend union law. The government's hostile attitude to this helped to drive Labour and the Liberals into co-operation in the form of an electoral pact between Ramsay MacDonald and the Liberal chief whip, Herbert Gladstone, in 1903. This virtually ensured that areas of traditional Conservative working-class strength such as Lancashire swung decisively against the Conservatives at the 1906 election.

The second element in the recovery of Liberalism was the Nonconformist revival. This was partly fortuitous in that an upsurge of religious fervour in Wales occurred in the early 1900s. More importantly, Balfour's 1902 Education Act revived the long-standing Nonconformist resentments about subsidizing church schools, and antagonized them afresh by abolishing the school boards which were controlled by Radicals in many areas. The results soon manifested themselves in by-election defeats in which middle-class Nonconformists flocked back into the Liberal Party.

The third and most significant cause of the Liberal revival lay in the repercussions of the war. By 1902 Conservative credentials in government finance had been severely dented by increases in both direct and indirect taxation. Consequently the Liberals eagerly reclaimed the cause of retrenchment and balanced budgets and rushed to the defence of free trade when Chamberlain launched his campaign in May 1903. H. H. Asquith, the former Liberal Home Secretary, quickly perceived that free trade offered the perfect means both to unite the parliamentarians who had been embarrassed by their divisions during the war, and to arouse public concern about dearer food. By pursuing Chamberlain around the country Asquith effected his own escape from the factionalism of Liberal imperialism and reworked his passage into the leadership of the party.

Finally, the controversy over tariff reform led to dramatic defections to the Liberal Party. As early as October 1903 the young member for Oldham, Winston Churchill, was contemplating abandoning the Conservatives. In a bitter private letter he wrote:

> I am an English Liberal. I hate the Tory Party, their men, their words and their methods ... I want to take up a clear practical position which masses of people can understand.[40]

By this stage Churchill's constituency party, which shared the general sympathy for tariffs, had shown its dislike over their member's disloyalty to Balfour and had announced their intention of seeking a new candidate. Not surprisingly Churchill dramatically crossed the floor of the House of

Commons in 1904 to sit on the Liberal benches. A number of other free-traders had followed him by 1906, though the scale of the split was not comparable to that of the Liberal Unionists in 1886. However, Churchill alone proved to be an invaluable asset for the Liberals who soon found him a marginal constituency in North-west Manchester and, later, a safe seat at Dundee. The new prime minister, Campbell-Bannerman, immediately gave him junior ministerial office in December 1905, and when Asquith took over as premier in 1908 he recognized Churchill's oratorical and administrative talents by promoting him to a series of major Cabinet posts. In the Edwardian period electoral success was still seen as conditional upon winning the battle on the public platform; and Churchill's formidable energy and eloquence materially assisted the Liberals to their triumph in the controversy caused by the 'People's Budget' in 1909 and House of Lords reform.

Failures of Leadership

By the turn of the century the deficiencies in Salisbury's style of leadership had begun to attract criticism. His penchant for promoting too many of his own relations attracted derisive descriptions of his government as the 'Hotel Cecil'. His tendency to withdraw to Hatfield seemed an increasingly dangerous indulgence, and even his mastery of foreign affairs began to be called in question as Britain continued to drift into a vulnerable diplomatic isolationism. His obvious incapacity as war minister only underlined the point. Under pressure from his family as well as from colleagues, he resigned in 1902.

Unfortunately for the Conservatives, the one figure capable of reinvigorating both the government and the party outside Parliament – Chamberlain – was still too detached and too suspect because of his Radical past to be acceptable as a successor to Salisbury. It was, in fact, almost inevitable that Balfour would inherit his uncle's dubious political legacy. Intellectually he was equal to the task. Indeed, his readiness for such innovations as the creation of the Committee of Imperial Defence as well as the passage of the Education Act in 1902 and the Unemployed Workmen's Act in 1905 suggested that he was much better tuned to the thinking of the National Efficiency school than his predecessor had been.

Beyond that, however, Balfour fell short of the requirements of a modern party leader. Though he had, reluctantly, moved from a traditional patronage borough to a popular working-class constituency in East Manchester, Balfour always shrank from the vulgar side of politics. His nimble and fastidious intelligence proved useful in Parliament, but made him seem detached and aloof outside; he was certainly ill-equipped to respond to the highly charged debate over tariff reform. Initially Balfour attempted to find a neat compromise between free trade and protectionism by opting for 'retaliation', that is, the threat of British tariffs so as to pressurize other states to lower theirs. This ploy simply failed. To the free-traders Balfour appeared to be selling out to the protectionists. This explains Churchill's rather presumptuous complaint to his leader:

> I should like to tell you that an attempt on your part to preserve the Free Trade policy and character of the Tory Party would command my absolute loyalty . . . But if on the other hand you have made up your mind and there is no going back, I must reconsider my position in politics.[41]

His irritation was only increased by a typical Balfourian manoeuvre in September 1903 when both Chamberlain and three leading free-trade ministers were persuaded to leave the Cabinet at the same time. The replacement of a free-trade chancellor of the exchequer by Chamberlain's son, Austen, seemed to indicate a betrayal of free trade. Unfortunately, as Balfour edged his way closer to the protectionists he failed to win their gratitude, for they saw, rightly,

222

that he lacked their convictions and was essentially man-oeuvring to retain control over the competing factions. In this way Balfour lost credibility with both sides.

The leader's stock also fell sharply among Conservative activists in the country. In a much-quoted remark, Balfour declared that he would as soon take advice from his valet as from the Conservative Party conference. But the humiliating truth was that the delegates rejected their leader's officially stated line at the 1904 conference and opted for an unequivocal protectionist policy; and Balfour was obliged to back down.[42] Thereafter it required only the experience of repeated electoral defeat in 1906, January 1910 and December 1910 to make him the first in a long line of twentieth-century Tory leaders to be driven into resignation by their own parliamentary followers. Some eighty years later Balfour's dilemma over the free trade–tariff reform split was repeated under John Major who began as a pro-European but allowed himself to be pushed into adopting an anti-European line which destroyed his credibility with both sides of his party as effectively as Balfour's vacillation had done.

The Strange Death of Conservative England

Although party unity deteriorated fast during 1903 and 1904 Balfour's government remained intact because he enjoyed the large majority won in 1900 and because Parliament still had a seven-year term of office. The Prime Minister's final miscalculation was to deprive himself of this latter advantage by resigning in December 1905. He appears to have believed that this move would catch the Liberals still divided between Liberal imperialists and Gladstonians. However, in the event Sir Henry Campbell-Bannerman took office and promptly incorporated the leading Liberal imperialists into his Cabinet which proved to be an unusually strong one. After so long in the wilderness few Liberals were inclined to throw away the opportunity.

The new prime minister correctly judged that the country had grown disillusioned with the long years of Tory rule, and he held a general election promptly in January 1906. This proved to be a disaster for the Conservatives who returned with only 157 MPs compared to 401 for the Liberals, 29 for Labour and 83 for the Irish Home Rulers. The only region that had withstood the Liberal landslide was Chamberlain's fief around Birmingham. Liberal gains in rural and suburban constituencies across southern England, though dramatic, were not very significant since they could be won back by the Conservatives without much difficulty. The key regions were Lancashire and London, which had been bastions of Conservative strength since 1886 but now moved decisively into the Liberal camp where they remained even in 1910. The Liberal dominance in the other urban-industrial regions – Wales, Scotland, northern England, west Yorkshire and the east midlands – strengthens the view that the Edwardian electorate was becoming polarized along lines of social class. However, the process still had some way to go, for the Liberals' success in south-west England and East Anglia indicates their ability to unite a working-class vote with the support of many middle-class Nonconformists and small farmers.

However, for the Conservatives the scale of this defeat was less significant than its character. After all, the party still won 43.6 per cent of the poll, a performance which was to produce an overall Tory majority of seats on many occasions during the twentieth century. The underlying problem for the party lay in three new developments that were to keep the Conservatives in opposition until 1915. First, despite the appeal of protectionism to workers in such places as Birmingham and Sheffield, where foreign imports damaged the metal industries, the Conservatives had forfeited much of their working-class vote.[43] They had been damned by association with dear food, judges and employers; and they were soon completely outflanked by the Liberals who introduced popular reforms including old age pensions.

The second key change which handicapped the Edwardian Conservatives was the electoral cooperation between the Liberal and Labour parties from 1903 onwards. In 1906 the Liberals would have won even without the pact. But it proved its worth in 1910 when the Conservative poll recovered to 46.9 per cent. However, whereas in 1892 47 per cent of the vote had produced 314 Conservative and Liberal Unionist MPs, in 1910 it left them with only 272–275. The combined Liberal–Labour vote was only 51 per cent, but that sufficed, especially with the support of the Irish members, to ensure that the Conservatives could not recover office. Indeed, the maintenance of what was, in effect, a three-party alliance doomed the Conservatives to an indefinite period in opposition. Every initiative taken by the party during the Edwardian period – rejection of the 1909 budget, the use of the peers' veto, resistance to Home Rule – was almost calculated to keep the pact in place because, in spite of the tensions between the Labour and Liberal grass roots, the parliamentarians were appalled at the prospect of allowing the Conservatives back in power on a minority vote. This situation helps to explain the growing frustration and bitterness in the Edwardian Conservative Party which manifested itself in the ruthless dispatch of Balfour in 1911 and in the reckless backing given by his successor, Andrew Bonar Law, to the Ulster Unionists when they threatened violent resistance to a Dublin Parliament. A weak leader casting around desperately for some means to unite his party, Bonar Law allowed himself to be dragged into extremism by his right wing.

The third underlying flaw in Edwardian Conservatism was that the party was slow to appreciate how far the political agenda had shifted, partly as a result of Chamberlain's own claims about the capacity of the state to influence the level of employment and fund social welfare. Unfortunately for the Conservatives, after Chamberlain suffered a stroke in 1906 no leading figure showed the same imagination or energy in domestic politics, and issues on which the party had relied under Salisbury no longer aroused much popular enthusiasm. Imperialism had not recovered from the setback administered by the Boer War. The cause of private property had been severely discredited by the self-interested intervention of the peers over Lloyd George's 1909 budget, so much so that the Radicals insisted on keeping them in their sights. Lloyd George's Land Campaign in 1913–14 kept the Conservatives firmly on the defensive. As soon as the campaign was launched one leading Tory complained: 'our men are already going in all directions like foxes in a field'.[44] They hesitated to oppose Lloyd George for fear that he would trap them in a repetition of the 1909–10 debate over the budget.

Bonar Law could come up with nothing better than the tried and tested issue of resisting Liberal policy on Ireland. In effect he was conceding that as long as the country remained interested primarily in social and economic questions it would prefer a Liberal government to a Tory one. Though the Ulster cause did help to reunite the party, however, it fell rather flat amongst the electorate. Indeed, by 1914 the imminent establishment of a parliament in Dublin threatened to undermine the essential rationale of what was still officially the Conservative and *Unionist* Party. In this context the famous depiction of the Edwardian era as *The Strange Death of Liberal England* in a book by George Dangerfield in 1934 could hardly have been less apposite. If anything, it was traditional Conservative England that had expired. It was to take nothing less than the Great War to restore the party's declining fortunes.

CHRONOLOGY

1885	DECEMBER 17	The Hawarden 'Kite' announces Gladstone's adoption of Irish Home Rule
1886	JUNE 8	Rejection of the first Home Rule Bill
	JUNE–JULY	Conservatives and Liberal Unionists win general election
	DECEMBER 22	Lord Randolph Churchill resigns as chancellor
1892	JULY	Salisbury loses general election
1894	MARCH 1	Gladstone resigns as prime minister
	APRIL 2	Introduction of graduated death duties
1895	JUNE 25	Chamberlain joins Conservative government as colonial secretary
	JULY	Conservatives win general election
1899	OCTOBER 9	Outbreak of the South African war
1900	SEPTEMBER–OCTOBER	Conservatives win general election
1902	MAY 31	South African war comes to an end
	JULY 12	Balfour becomes prime minister

1903	MAY 15	Chamberlain launches tariff reform campaign at Birmingham
	SEPTEMBER 4–16	Chamberlain, C. T. Ritchie, the Duke of Devonshire, Lord George Hamilton and Lord Balfour of Burleigh resign from the Cabinet
1904	JUNE 8	Winston Churchill joins the Liberal Party
1905	DECEMBER 4	Balfour resigns as prime minister
1906	JANUARY–FEBRUARY	Liberals win landslide election victory
1909	NOVEMBER 30	Conservative peers reject budget
1910	JANUARY–FEBRUARY	Conservatives defeated at general election
	DECEMBER	Conservatives defeated at general election
1911	AUGUST 10	Peers accept the Parliament Act
	NOVEMBER 13	Andrew Bonar Law chosen to replace Balfour as Conservative Party leader

Stanley Baldwin and Neville Chamberlain
(*PA News*)

CHAPTER SIX

1916–29

Stuart Ball

Return to Power 1914–18

The Edwardian era was one of the most troubled times in the history of the Conservative Party, with three consecutive election defeats, organizational chaos, crises over leadership, disputes over policy and bitter factional conflicts. The First World War transformed the fortunes of all four parties in the House of Commons in 1914: it destroyed the Irish Nationalists, set in motion the decline of the Liberals and the rise of the Labour Party, and brought the Conservatives back from the wilderness to become the dominant force in British politics between the two world wars. These effects were not caused by the outbreak of war in 1914, but by the huge and unexpected demands which it made as it continued through the years of stalemate and attrition from 1915 to 1918. At the outset, the Conservatives found themselves in a difficult position. Their role as a 'patriotic opposition' was marginal: they could neither influence government policy, nor openly criticize it. The Shadow Cabinet had already begun to consider the possibility of a coalition when the eruption of two simultaneous crises about the conduct of the war led Asquith to invite them to serve under him in May 1915.[1] The Conservatives had little choice but to accept, and Asquith manoeuvred to keep the key posts as far as possible out of their hands.

The Asquith coalition lasted from May 1915 to December

1916, and was relatively harmonious considering the history of the preceding years and the unequal distribution of offices. The Conservative Party has always been highly pragmatic in any period of national peril, and willing – at least for the duration – to jettison previous assumptions. The party's over-riding aim was the successful prosecution of the war effort, and thus it accepted with few qualms a vastly extended role for the state in regulation and planning, from the provisions of the Defence of the Realm Act to food rationing, increased taxation and anti-profiteering measures. The Conservatives saw the war as a great patriotic endeavour, and their faith in the unity of classes was restored by the scale of voluntary recruitment in 1914 and 1915 and by the continuance of public support for the war effort thereafter. Unlike the Liberals, they had no problem of principle with the compulsory enlistment of manpower for the army, and pressed for this to be introduced as voluntary recruitment began to dry up in 1915. Conscription was eventually implemented in 1916, but only after delays and compromises which debilitated the Asquith coalition. In December 1916 Asquith's dilatory conduct of the war effort led to a further crisis, and with some reluctance the Conservative members of the Cabinet combined with David Lloyd George to oust him.

The creation of the Lloyd George coalition was a turning point in the fortunes of the Conservative Party. With many Liberal ministers refusing to serve under Lloyd George, the balance of power in the government changed. The Conservatives now held most of the key posts, and the party provided around two-thirds of the coalition's support in the House of Commons. The Conservative leader, Andrew Bonar Law, was clearly the second man in the government; his close and effective partnership with Lloyd George was crucial to its viability, and became the guarantee of rank-and-file Conservative confidence. The government passed through dark days in the conduct of the war in 1917 and the spring of 1918, but these stresses forged strong links of mutual understanding amongst its senior figures. When victory arrived with unexpected swiftness in November 1918, the continuation of the coalition into peacetime seemed to be the logical step. There was no need to break up a winning combination on policy grounds: many of the issues which had so bitterly divided the parties before the war had been resolved or were no longer so divisive. They had been displaced by new challenges – the creation of a democratic electorate, the enfranchisement of women, the strains of demobilization, the threat of industrial unrest, and the rise of the Labour Party – which were set against a background of disintegration and revolution in Europe. Conservatives at all level recognized that these problems could be faced better by maintaining the alliance of the 'constitutional' – or anti-socialist – parties. As a result, Lloyd George and Bonar Law had little difficulty in drawing up a coalition programme which matched the contemporary enthusiasm for unity and social reconstruction.[2] It was also acceptable to a wide range of Conservative opinion, although some of the commitments on Ireland, reform of the House of Lords and imperial preference were to lead to problems later.

In the long overdue general election, held soon after the armistice in December 1918, the Prime Minister and the Conservatives were the beneficiaries of public acclaim and gratitude. Lloyd George's prestige was the highest but, being personal, also proved to be more ephemeral. Whilst he was hailed as the 'man who won the war', the Conservatives reaped the credit for their pre-war advocacy of greater military preparedness, their unequivocal commitment to the war effort, and their staunch support of Lloyd George. Of the 523 supporters of the coalition to be returned, 382 were Conservatives; 28 Asquithian Liberals and 63 Labour MPs made up the paltry ranks of the opposition.

TABLE 6.1 *Conservative Performance in General Elections 1918–29*

Date of Election	Candidates Nominated	Unopposed Returns	MPs Elected	Total Votes Received	% Share of Vote
14 Dec. 1918	445	41	382	4,144,192	38.6
15 Nov. 1922	482	42	344	5,502,298	38.5
6 Dec. 1923	536	35	258	5,514,541	38.0
29 Oct. 1924	534	16	412	7,854,523	46.8
30 May 1929	590	4	260	8,656,225	38.1

NOTE: Figures for 1918 are for the Conservative Party, and not for the coalition as a whole.

The Lloyd George Coalition 1918–22

At first the coalition government seemed to be unassailable, enjoying massive popular endorsement and possessing a huge parliamentary majority. Around the Cabinet table sat a glittering array of talent, mixing experienced politicians with men of independent prestige from the worlds of industry and academia. The Prime Minister was astride the world stage at the Paris peace conference, and the domestic programme was in the calm and now authoritative hands of Bonar Law. There was a vigorous and ambitious agenda, ranging from housing to divorce reform at home, and in the empire reconstructing the government of both India and Ireland. The coalition was dominant in the Commons not only in quantity but in quality. The Labour MPs were ineffective, and their party lacked able and experienced leaders. The handful of Liberals made what little running there was, but after his return in a by-election in 1920 Asquith proved to be a damp squib and his party sank further into fraction and decay. Yet despite beginning its life with every advantage, in October 1922 the postwar coalition government was spectacularly overthrown by a revolt from below within the Conservative Party. The leaders were swept out of office, damaging some careers and ending others. However, whatever the fate of individuals, the party as a whole gained rather than lost from this crisis. By this time the coalition had become discredited and unpopular, and it was replaced by a purely Conservative Cabinet which won a majority in the ensuing general election.

All of the nine factors which have been identified as frequent elements in the failure of Conservative governments contributed to the downfall of the coalition, although some were more significant than others.[3] Two provided the background to the events of 1922: problems in the economy, and a shift of public opinion towards the opposition parties. Difficulties began to emerge by the end of 1920, in particular due to the collapse of the postwar economic boom and the consequent rise in unemployment. Together with confrontations with the trade unions and the dropping of much social reform, this tarnished Lloyd George's credentials as the conciliator of labour and the manager of industrial unrest. In this sense, failures of economic management played a part in the fall of the 1918–22 government. The other factor was the ground which the Labour Party gained in local government and in by-elections in 1921 and 1922. This alarming trend called into question the basic purpose of the coalition's existence. Its continuation into peacetime had been accepted as an insurance against the threat of 'Socialism', but during 1921 and 1922 many Conservative backbenchers and constituency executives came to regard the coalition as the problem rather than the solution. The coalition was vulnerable to being portrayed by Labour as hostile to the working class and operating unfairly in the interests of privilege and capital. Whilst Conservatives wished to preserve the existing social hierarchies and distribution of wealth, with the advent of democracy at home and revolution abroad they had no desire to provoke class antagonism. Viewed in this light, the coalition began to seem less of a bulwark against chaos and revolution and more of a likely contributory cause. In this way the growing strength of the Labour Party in the country, rather than in the Commons, indirectly undermined the coalition by changing the perspective of MPs on the government side of the House.[4]

This was crucial, for the coalition was overthrown from within and not from without. The only ballot box to be involved was the one in the tense and crowded room at the Carlton Club on 19 October 1922, where a meeting of Conservative MPs voted by 185 to 88 to reject both their leaders and the continuation of the coalition. To explain why this occurred we must turn to other factors, to be found within the government rather than without. The most important of these was a failure of leadership, both individual and collective. The development of the problems which eventually destroyed the government can easily be seen with hindsight, but to the Cabinet at the time they were separate, manageable – and reasons for preserving the coalition.[5] The leaders' assumption that this was the only rational conclusion was based on over-confidence and complacency, for they had fallen into the trap of regarding themselves as irreplaceable.[6] Lloyd George's position as prime minister was based very much on his personal authority, and hence the failures of initiatives with which he was associated damaged him more than would be the case for a premier with a strong party base. The problem was made greater by Lloyd George's character and methods. His adaptability and adroitness could seem to be a lack of principle verging upon deceit, and there were doubts about the probity of some of his aides and the means by which his personal political fund had been acquired. His development of private sources of advice outside the conventional civil service (the 'garden suburb' at No. 10), his attempts at the management of the press, and his high profile in international conferences gave rise to fears that a 'presidential' style of premiership was emerging, unbalancing the constitution. This was exacerbated by the way in which Lloyd George both charmed and dominated the inner circle of senior Cabinet ministers, who seemed to their followers to have been sapped of their integrity and sense of responsibility to their party and, indeed, country.

The failure of leadership at the top of the coalition was a dual one, for Lloyd George's resignation as prime minister followed directly from the rejection of Austen Chamberlain as leader of the Conservative Party. The latter had been the inevitable choice when illness caused Bonar Law's retirement from the party leadership and ministerial office – but not from the House of Commons – in March 1921. Chamberlain inherited a situation which was already deteriorating, but his own limitations made matters much worse and were to be the most important single factor in the fall of the coalition. Although the confrontation was of his own making, the Carlton Club meeting was to show that he had lost the confidence of the majority of Conservative MPs. More than anything else, this was a matter of personality. Chamberlain was stiff, formal, and remained aloof from his subordinates; he did not take them into his confidence or inspire and enthuse them.[7] His leadership was headmasterly in style, and assumed unquestioning obedience.[8] He lacked imagination and was too inflexible, seeming to be unwilling to contemplate any course other than the continuation of the coalition in its present form. He was unable to establish a strong personal position and the authority necessary to stand up to Lloyd George as Bonar Law had done, and thereby reassure those who feared that the party was losing its independence.[9]

Confusion over the direction of policy also played a large part in the fall of the coalition. There were problems in key areas of external policy, several of which particularly touched upon Conservative sensibilities. In 1921 the government had performed a somersault in its Irish policy, opening negotiations with the 'murder gang' of republican rebels whom Lloyd George had not long before assured the country that the forces of law and order had 'by the throat'. Although the establishment of a separate northern state had secured the position of Ulster, it needed all the authority and prestige of the Conservative leadership to carry the annual conference for the abandonment of southern Ireland in the Anglo-Irish Treaty of 1921. Twists and turns in the government's foreign policy were accompanied by repeated complaints from the foreign secretary, Lord Curzon, about Lloyd George's constant interference in his domain. There was certainly little here to shed lustre upon the government's record, and the other key election slogan of making Germany pay for the war seemed to have been abandoned as cynically as was that of 'homes for heroes'. The peace settlement appeared to produce more problems than it solved, reparations were proving to be of little value, and Europe remained unsettled. Friction with France and Lloyd

George's overtures to Bolshevik Russia alarmed Conservative opinion.[10] Financial strain forced the abandonment of the ambitious imperial policy in the Persian Gulf and Iraq, and Britain's vulnerability in the region led to Conservative despair over Lloyd George's promotion of the Greek cause in Asia Minor.[11] The resulting Anglo-Turkish confrontation at Chanak in September 1922 and the threat of war brought Bonar Law out of retirement, thus providing the rebels with a credible alternative leader and prime minister.

Even more significant were the problems of domestic policy. The onset of the slump in 1920 had thrown into sharp relief the tension between the ambitious plans of social reform on the one hand, and the unprecedented levels of local rates and national taxation on the other. This brought to the fore the instinctive demands of the Tory rank and file that the 'burden' of taxation must be reduced, the 'red-tape' of bureaucracy cast away, and the assumed profligacy of official 'waste' brought to an end. When the government was sluggish to respond, its vulnerability was exploited by a campaign run by the press baron Lord Rothermere. In the summer months of 1921 this 'Anti-Waste League' won by-elections in two Conservative seats and came a respectable second in two more, alarming Central Office and MPs from southern and safe seats. This pressure led to another of the government's humiliating 'U-turns': the establishment of the Geddes committee to 'axe' expenditure, and the abandonment or watering down of policy on health, housing and education. An ironic victim of the need to cut costs was the abandonment of the price controls in the 1920 Agriculture Act. This had proved to be highly expensive but was also – for that reason – popular with farmers; repeal of the act left another sector of the Tory heartland feeling bruised and betrayed by the coalition.

There were other pledges dear to Conservative hearts which the government failed to redeem. Little was done in respect of imperial preference, and nothing at all in the way of curtailing the legal privileges enjoyed by the trade unions or of restoring the powers of the House of Lords.[12] The latter was seen by the Conservative rank and file as a potential barrier against despoliation and dictatorship should the Labour Party ever secure a majority in the Commons. The Cabinet's failure to seize the opportunity to raise the bulwarks of the constitution was regarded with horror and anger by the executive of the National Union and the party chairman, Sir George Younger, and was the reason for their rejection in January 1922 of the idea of an early election.[13] This rebuff publicly humiliated the leadership, although intemperate attacks on Younger as a 'cabin boy' with ideas above his station only consolidated his support and alienated the grass roots. By the early summer of 1922 the National Union was in an unprecedented state of disaffection, attacking the postponement of the promised second chamber reform as 'a breach of the understanding upon which the allegiance of the Party to its leaders depends'.[14]

Two more of the factors common in Conservative defeats were present in 1921–22: internal disunity, and problems in the party organization. The coalition was internally divided in three ways, of which the least significant was the formal party distinction between the Conservative and Liberal wings of the coalition. The failure of the proposal for 'fusion' of the coalition's two wings in 1920 pointed to the existence of fault lines which could be a source of weakness, but the coalition actually fell because of disunity within one of its constituent parties rather than between them. The second area of division was the most public, but not the most damaging. This was the emergence of a group of dissident right-wing Conservative MPs, the 'die-hards', at first only critical of specific measures but later antagonistic to coalition as a concept. However, they were mainly obscure, inarticulate and unimpressive; they attracted no serious leader and had only the distant patronage of Lords Selborne and Salisbury, ex-ministers pursuing the hobby-horse of Lords reform. Limited to around forty MPs, they lacked organization and did not always act together; in view of the coalition's huge majority, they could be dismissed by the Cabinet as no more than an irritant.[15] In fact, they proved to be more significant than this. As the party leaders seemed to drift further and further away from Conservative principles, the 'die-hards' came to represent the heart and soul of the party – sometimes wrong-headed, often simplistic, but nevertheless standing for the pure faith, untarnished by personal ambition. It was in this context that the third and most serious internal division opened up – a horizontal one, uncoupling the Conservative leaders from the party's 'middle management' of junior ministers, whips, Central Office and senior backbenchers.[16] The latter were different from the 'die-hards' and more significant, being established and widely respected figures who were located in the mainstream of Tory opinion. Their disaffection took place below the surface, in stages from the election scare of January 1922 to the meeting called by Sir Samuel Hoare shortly before the Carlton Club meeting. This gathering decisively rejected the coalition, but it was their names rather than their number which influenced Bonar Law in his crucial decision to attend the party meeting at the Carlton and speak against the coalition.[17]

The Conservative Party organization emerged from the First World War in much healthier shape than the Liberals', but there had been considerable strains and the vast new electorate meant that there were many adjustments to be made. At local level the party took some time to recover from the wartime suspension of partisan activities, and some districts were still dormant when the coalition fell in 1922. Those local parties which were more active, mainly in the safer seats, found it difficult to raise enthusiasm for party matters in the atmosphere of 1919–20.[18] During 1921 and 1922 many of these associations became either divided over the continuance of the coalition, or definitely opposed to it. There was a geographical and political basis to their views: support for the coalition remained high in regions where the party was weakest – in particular in Scotland and some parts of north-east England – whilst hostility was greatest in the safer seats in the Midlands and south of England, especially in rural seats and the Home Counties.[19] From the autumn of 1921 onwards many local executives in these areas pressed their MPs to pledge themselves to stand as 'independent' Conservatives at the next election. Some MPs took this initiative for themselves and other displayed little reluctance, but it is clear that some were driven forward by their local associations.[20] Certainly, by October 1922 no Conservative MP could have been unaware of the hostility towards the coalition in the National Union, and the local reaction must have been a factor in the minds of many when they cast their votes at the Carlton Club. Indeed, Chamberlain had summoned the meeting in order to pre-empt the forthcoming party conference – a stratagem which in itself was seen as evidence of the leaders' betrayal of their responsibilities. Chamberlain's personal probity was unchallenged, but his sense of honour seemed to be focused upon his Cabinet colleagues and the Prime Minister rather than the claims and wishes of the party he led. This perception led to the most serious breakdown of trust within the Conservative Party machine between its creation in the age of Disraeli and the present day: in October 1922 Chamberlain found himself openly opposed by the Chief Whip, the Party Chairman, the Principal Agent, and the Executive Committee of the National Union.[21]

The impression that the government was played out became increasingly widespread in the country and amongst MPs during 1922. Confidence was further eroded by a press which was largely hostile, despite Lloyd George's many attempts at management and manipulation. Amongst the group who mattered in the end – the Conservative MPs – there was a growing conviction that it was 'time for a change'. However, most MPs aimed neither to destroy the coalition nor to drive Lloyd George from office. Nearly all of them still considered that a mutual anti-Labour electoral front was essential, although the weakness and unpopularity of the coalition Liberals was beginning to cause alarm. An election could not be many months away; the common expectation was that the massive majority of 1918 would be substantially eroded, with the Liberal wing being the most vulnerable. What the Conservative critics wanted was a change in the government's identity so that it would more closely reflect the balance of forces within the coalition. They wished it to become more distinctively Conservative in its personnel and policies, a development to be symbolized by the appointment of a Conservative as prime minister. On that basis they would have been happy to continue in partnership with the coalition Liberals, and for Lloyd George to hold one of the most senior Cabinet positions.[22] What they did not want was for commitments on these matters to be made before the election which would be binding afterwards and lead to Lloyd George continuing in the same office and in the same manner. Yet this was exactly what Austen Chamberlain and the other leading Conservative Cabinet ministers seemed to be determined to impose.

The reluctance of the leaders even to recognize the legitimacy of these aspirations alienated their supporters. The middle level of the party hierarchy and the rank and file became increasingly distrustful of the motivation and even probity of the coalition's leading lights, considering them to have been bewitched by Lloyd George and to have abandoned their principles for the sake of clinging to office and the exercise of ever more capricious power.[23] Fearing for the very survival of their party, for its continued identity and integrity, the number and resolve of the critics grew swiftly between April and October 1922.[24] Attempts to communicate with the party leaders failed and even made matters worse, with the Earl of Birkenhead treating a deputation of junior ministers to a humiliating harangue on the theme of loyalty to superiors.[25] The crisis which led to the Carlton Club meeting and the destruction of the coalition was not caused by the relatively modest agenda of the critics, but by the arrogance, insensitivity and maladroitness of the Conservative leadership. By the time the latter threw down the gauntlet by summoning the Carlton Club meeting, many of the most respected junior ministers and their friends and allies amongst the senior backbenchers had decided that the only honourable course was rebellion. Most of the dissidents opposed Austen Chamberlain with regret. They regarded him as a decent man fallen amongst thieves, but also as dangerously rigid and blind in giving his loyalty where it was not deserved. Chamberlain failed to make his position clear, and in the end Conservative MPs reacted against what they feared was being planned rather than what their leader actually intended. Even so, they were correct in their diagnosis that he was too much under Lloyd George's influence, and that the unity and identity of the party was in peril.[26] In 1922 the Conservatives avoided defeat by abandoning a charismatic but controversial prime minister and changing the tone of the government, thereby transforming the party's fortunes and paving the way to electoral success. There are many parallels with a later downfall: the overthrow of Margaret Thatcher in 1990.

The Conservative Government of 1922–24

After the result of the Carlton Club meeting was announced, Austen Chamberlain resigned as Conservative leader and Lloyd George retired as prime minister; both positions were assumed by Bonar Law, who then immediately dissolved Parliament. The election was fought largely on the record of the coalition, and the coalition Liberals lost ground heavily. Bonar Law campaigned on the vague platform of an appeal to 'tranquillity' and a return to normality, and he eschewed any controversial proposals. On this occasion the Conservatives benefited from the number of three-cornered contests, and although they received only 38.5 per cent of the vote they won 344 seats. The relatively inexperienced Bonar Law government continued in office whilst the ousted former leadership remained aloof, cocooned by their belief in their superiority and indispensability. This sulking in their tents only further alienated the bulk of the party, and made them more determined than ever to stick to their chosen path of independence, whatever the pitfalls along the way. Although most of the party leaders who were thrown over in 1922 returned to ministerial posts between 1923 and 1925, they were never to recover the power they had formerly held or to regain the trust of the backbenchers and the rank and file. This made them occasionally restless, despite their generally sincere protestations of loyalty to the new regime after reunion in 1924. Suspicion of the Conservative ex-coalitionists and hostility to Lloyd George were to remain a distinctive feature of the Conservative landscape for the next thirteen years. As well as being an important factor in its own right, this distorted the alliances and attitudes which might have developed on other fronts.

This was particularly the case with the policy which played a crucial role in the fortunes of both the 1922–24 and 1924–29 governments, although in rather a different way: tariff reform. This issue dominated Conservative politics from its launch by Joseph Chamberlain in 1903 until its final adoption in 1932; it was also complex, and has often been misunderstood. The tariff programme offered wide-ranging solutions that were intensely attractive to most Conservatives, for they appealed both to their hearts and to their pockets. Its most basic aspect was simple protectionism: the introduction of duties on foreign imports that would shelter British industry in the home market and bring prosperity for employers and workers. This would tackle the problem of unemployment and provide the Conservatives with a positive appeal for social unity with which to counter Socialism. Tariffs would enable social reforms to be financed by indirect taxes rather than further increases in direct taxation, which Conservatives believed had reached its limits. However, for its most fervent supporters the essence of the tariff policy was imperial preference, by which specially reduced tariffs for empire produce would bind the motherland, dominions and colonies more closely together. From economic convergence would follow political co-operation and unity, enabling Britain to survive as a world power in an increasingly competitive environment.

There were three problems with the policy of tariff reform. First, it sought to overturn the orthodoxy of free trade, generally accepted as the foundation of British prosperity since the early nineteenth century, and its radical tone and materialist nature alarmed some of the more traditional and aristocratic Conservatives. Secondly, the tariff policy was not attractive to sectors of the economy whose raw materials or markets lay more outside the empire than within it; this was particularly the case with the Lancashire cotton industry. Finally, and most seriously, imperial preference was unworkable unless it gave the dominions an advantage in their exports to the British home market. As these were primarily agricultural, this meant ending the era of cheap food imports and implied a rise in the cost of living for the industrial working class. The Liberal and Labour parties, united in an instinctive and unquestioning defence of free trade, were swift to pounce on the easy target of 'food taxes'. In the urban constituencies this simple negative factor outweighed the possible attractions, and tariff reform was a heavy liability. This in turn led many Conservatives to oppose it on pragmatic grounds, adding to the confusion and uncertainty within the party. The tariff policy played a large part in the Conservative election defeats of 1906 and January and December 1910; it was to cause further tensions during the 1918–22 and 1924–29 governments, and was the issue upon which the party fought and lost for a fourth time in 1923.

The context of the Conservative defeat of 1923 is the most unusual of modern times, for it took place after only a brief period in office and long before the government needed to face the electorate. The only parallel is with the Heath government in February 1974, which also painted itself into a corner. However, in 1923 the Conservatives had been in power for only just over a year, and their mood was much less beleaguered and exhausted than was the case in 1974. Because of the circumstances under which it came about, the downfall of the 1922–24 Conservative ministry only partly fits the pattern found in those defeats that occurred after longer spells of dominance. Nevertheless, it is striking that seven of the nine common factors mentioned earlier played a role in the election defeat in 1923, although several of them were results rather than causes of the decision to go to the country.

The chain of events which led to defeat began with the sudden and final collapse of Bonar Law's health in May 1923. With most of the former leadership still out in the cold, he was succeeded by the chancellor of the exchequer, Stanley Baldwin, a relatively unknown figure before the fall of the coalition. Within a few months, Baldwin came to the conclusion that a fundamental change in economic policy was necessary. Trade was stagnant, Europe was in turmoil, and the Labour Party – the official opposition since 1922 – was mounting an effective campaign on the issue of rising unemployment. The government seemed to be drifting and its initiatives were having little impact, but its hands were tied by the pledge given by Bonar Law in 1922 that no protectionist measures would be introduced in the next Parliament. Despite having a clear majority in the House, the Conservatives would have to seek a fresh mandate if they wished to introduce tariff reform. It is not possible to be precisely certain of either the timing or the motives of the decision, but by early October 1923 Baldwin had made up his mind to come out publicly for protection.[27] His original plan would seem to have been to educate public opinion over the winter months and prepare the way for a spring election but, whatever his expectations, this soon proved to be impracticable. After Baldwin revealed his intentions in his first address as leader to the Conservative Party annual conference, at Plymouth on 25 October 1923, the situation slipped rapidly out of control. After a fortnight of division and uncertainty, the Cabinet resolved on 9 November that an immediate election was the least of all evils, and polling was fixed for 6 December.

In the circumstances of this election, the public sentiment that it was 'time for a change' – a significant element in Conservative defeats after lengthy spells in office – did not apply. If anything, the reverse was the case. Neither the Conservative Party nor the general public saw the need for another election so soon after the last one, especially when that had been fought on the slogan of 'tranquillity' and the need for a period of quiet and stable government. The upheaval and uncertainty of an election were regarded as nuisances in themselves, especially unwelcome in the pre-Christmas period, and the election was roundly condemned by a range of trade and business organizations.[28] It introduced an element of anxiety into the political and economic situation, for it raised the spectre of a Socialist government coming into power. Conservative MPs were quite unprepared for an election, and there was widespread backbench opposition. This did not come just from MPs whose seats were marginal or located in regions where the party was weak or where there was a strong commitment to free trade, such as Scotland and Lancashire. Cautionary sounds were also heard from the Midlands and the south, and even the leading figure of the 'die-hards', Colonel John Gretton, urged Baldwin to delay going to the country.[29] Some of this opposition was based upon personal circumstances. An unusually high number of Conservative MPs had entered the House of Commons for the first time in 1922, and when the dissolution came Parliament had only sat for 134 days. It seemed as if just at the point when they were beginning to find their feet in the House, they were faced with the prospect of leaving it. In this period most Conservative MPs were responsible for paying their own election expenses, a substantial amount of between £500 and £1,000. The advent of another contest so soon after the last one imposed unpleasant financial burdens which few MPs could face with equanimity, and most acutely resented. For these reasons, it might be said that the feeling that it was *not* 'time for a change' was a factor in the outcome of the 1923 election.

Another of the nine factors linked with Conservative defeats which was absent in 1923 was that of a negative image of the party leader. Baldwin was still enjoying his 'honeymoon' period as prime minister, having only come into the office at the end of May. However, his positive public image was based upon more than just the novelty of his appointment. Since becoming prime minister, Baldwin had shown a felicitous touch in presenting himself to the nation, amongst other things making an early use of the cinema newsreels. Although his prestige was to grow further, especially during the period from 1924 to 1926 in which he articulated his 'New Conservatism' and met the challenge of the General Strike, the foundations for this were already being laid in his period as chancellor of the exchequer from October 1922 to May 1923 and in his first months as prime minister. Baldwin was widely respected and liked; so much so that in many quarters it was assumed that it could not be he who was to blame for the coming of the election, which instead was attributed to shadowy forces behind him or to a misplaced indulgence of young and inexperienced advisers.

However, if the image of the party leader himself was not a problem, there was a consistent undercurrent of doubt over the quality of leadership at Cabinet level. This had been a refrain since the formation of Bonar Law's ministry, and the ousted coalitionists had not been slow to show their scorn and resentment of their usurpers. During the 1922 election Winston Churchill described them as 'the second eleven', and Lord Birkenhead spoke even more insultingly of 'second-class brains'. Whilst their bile exaggerated the position, there were a number of apparent weaknesses. One feature of the new Cabinet to draw adverse comment was the unusual number of peers it contained, with eight of the original eighteen ministers being in the upper house. This caused a problem in two respects. Firstly, it gave an unfortunate impression of hidebound reaction, for the balance resembled the days of Peel or Palmerston. Secondly, it highlighted class divisions in society, for the Labour Party – now the potential alternative government – was almost unrepresented in the Lords. However, Bonar Law had little alternative, for the peers included in the Cabinet possessed the vital ingredient of Cabinet or official experience.

The problems lay mainly where they were most exposed to view – on the depleted front bench in the House of Commons. Even so, only a handful of Cabinet ministers were obviously ineffective, and the proportion was scarcely greater than that found in some of the strongest administrations. Two who ran into difficulties and did not hold Cabinet office again were Sir Clement Barlow, the Minister of Labour, and Sir Robert Sanders, the Minister of Agriculture. Sir Arthur Griffith-Boscawen, the Minister of Health, lost his seat in the 1922 election and was defeated in the Mitcham by-election in March 1923, after which he had to resign. However, the 1922–24 government also saw the entry into the Cabinet of a talented group of Conservative ministers who were to hold high office during the 1920s and 1930s: Neville Chamberlain, Leo Amery, Sir Samuel Hoare, William Bridgeman, Philip Lloyd-Graeme (later Cunliffe-Lister, and Lord Swinton), and Edward Wood (later Lord Irwin, and Earl of Halifax). However, although the ministry did not really lack talent, its conduct during its first few months in particular seemed to give credence to the critics. This led to dismay amongst the government's supporters in the parliamentary party, the constituencies and the press, which in its turn added to a feeling of instability. The government did not seem to know what to do about the worsening economic situation; however well-intentioned it might be, action and imagination were conspicuously lacking. It was the impression of weak leadership which was the damaging factor; once such a perception has become widespread, as was the case in 1903–05 and 1993–95, it is almost impossible to eradicate.

It is also very often linked to one of the other factors which commonly contribute to defeat: disunity within the party, and this was a feature of the life of the 1922–24 government. The most visible aspect of this was the rift within the leadership, and the instability caused by constant rumour and speculation about a reconstruction of the Cabinet and the terms upon which the exiles would return. The process of reunion was a lengthy one, for two reasons. At first, the coalitionists assumed that their successors would prove so inept that they would soon be humbled and repentant; in the process of rescuing the situation, the former elite would resume their natural position at the head of affairs.[30] Later, when there was a recognition that the government would last and some lessening of the ties within the coalitionist group, personal issues complicated the picture. When he became prime minister in May, Baldwin had made overtures for the return of some of the ex-ministers. Unfortunately, he gave offence to Austen Chamberlain, the result of clumsiness on Baldwin's part and Chamberlain's own acute sensitivity and stiffness. A minor Cabinet minister, Laming Worthington-Evans, and some former juniors and whips did rejoin, but Chamberlain himself was the key to any meaningful reunion. It would take time for him to accept – so far as he ever did – that it could only be by his accommodation to the victors of 1922, and not the other way around. Matters were made even more complicated by Chamberlain's assumption of a personal obligation to the former coalition Lord Chancellor, the Earl of Birkenhead. The problem was that Birkenhead was acutely detested by the majority of the parliamentary party for his conduct in 1921–22 and his breaches of the unspoken truce during the 1922 election; his cynicism and ostentatious lifestyle meant that he was regarded as an electoral liability, especially with the new women voters.[31] However, Chamberlain would not return unless Birkenhead also did so. This stumbling block not only complicated contacts through the autumn but also prevented the return of the duo when this was proposed immediately before the dissolution. Baldwin's invitation to them to join the Cabinet had to be finessed and postponed when it became clear that it would provoke several ministers to resign.

Although there was an open rift in the party, it is by no means clear that this played a major part in the downfall of the government. The situation after the 1922 election was static rather than fluid; the movement which did occur was in the direction of greater stability, with the numbers and cohesion of the splinter group dwindling as individuals accepted the status quo and drifted back to the mainstream. At the end of November 1922, forty-nine Conservative MPs had attended a high-profile public dinner in honour of Austen Chamberlain, and during 1923 the existence in the Commons of a core of about twenty-five to thirty supporters of the coalitionists was a source of anxiety. As a result, the government was unable to conduct itself with the confidence that a majority of seventy-seven might suggest. On several occasions the margin in the lobbies fell well below this and once the government suffered the embarrassment of being defeated, on the sensitive issue of employment for ex-servicemen in April 1923. However, the most striking feature of the Conservative disunity of 1922–24 was its moderation and restraint. In sharp contrast with the strife within the Liberal Party, Conservative antagonisms were kept largely out of public sight and – most importantly – out of the constituency associations and away from the ballot box. The few instances of friction to occur are revealing by their very rarity; it is an example of the significance of the dog which did not bark. Nor should too simple a linkage be made between periods of internal dissension and electoral repudiation, especially in the pre-war period. Far more vicious and extensive infighting took place over the coalition in 1921–22, over tariffs in 1929–31, over India in 1933–35, and to a lesser extent over appeasement in 1939–39. None of this prevented election victories in 1922, 1931 and 1935, and both contemporary observers and historians agree that Neville Chamberlain's government looked set for a fairly comfortable victory in a late 1939 or 1940 election. The split at the very top of the party gave no one pleasure, but Austen Chamberlain's conduct was a model of restraint compared to the rifts between Powell and Heath in the 1960s or Heath and Thatcher in the 1970s, neither of which prevented victory in 1970 and 1979.

If there are question marks over the part played on this occasion by staleness in office, unimpressive leadership and internal disunity, then what were the main causes of the party's downfall in 1923? It was almost entirely attributable to two things: the policy itself, and the manner of its presentation. These were the personal responsibility of the Prime Minister, and in this respect a failure of competence in leadership played a key role. In 1923 (and to a lesser extent in 1929) the Conservative Party suffered from the strategic errors of its leader, even though it also benefited from his popularity. The economic situation was gloomy, but it was not yet severe enough to wean the industrial working class, and much of the middle class, away from the orthodoxy of free trade – that was not to happen until the economic slump of 1930–31. In 1923, protection at once raised all the cries of 1906, and was vulnerable to all the old charges against tariff reform. The policy was unpopular, difficult to make attractive to the wider public, too easily identified with the vested interests of the wealthy few, and unsettling and alarming in its implications for the average household. It was almost impossible to show precisely how it would advantage either industries or individuals, and vague promises of prosperity and employment weighed little in the scales against the cry of 'food taxes' raised by the Liberal and Labour parties. Once again, the policy was an easy target for its opponents, who had only to reach for the weapons which had been so effective in 1906 and 1910.[32] Baldwin seemed scarcely to take this into account, and pressed ahead despite counsels of caution and delay. These came from all sides within the Cabinet, and included the leading protectionists.[33]

Almost as much of a problem as the policy itself, was the manner of its launch and the vagueness and lack of definition of what was proposed. After turning the political world on its head at Plymouth on 25 October, Baldwin gave no further details until 2 November, and even then precious few. In a situation such as this, a week was indeed a long time in politics, and it allowed the opposition to seize an advantage which they did not lose. The tariff policy was in fact never to be fully set out, and this shaky foundation undermined the party's confidence. Baldwin's speeches and the manifesto persisted with this broad-brush approach; it may have suited the leader's temperament, but was not what the situation demanded. The gaps and inconsistencies became very apparent under the intense scrutiny of an election campaign. The Conservatives ended up with the worst of both worlds: their programme was open to all the old attacks on a tariff policy, yet much that might have rallied support was left out. There was little for agriculture, and nothing in the way of imperial preference; the policy had swiftly become reduced to the lowest common denominator: simple protection of the domestic market, whether efficient or not. The result of all this was alienation of sections of support acquired since 1918, especially in urban and industrial areas. In the final week of the campaign the Conservative Party seemed unconsciously to realize that the tariff policy was foundering, and turned instead to general evocations of Baldwin's virtues as leader and attacks on the familiar target of the perils of Socialism – but by then it was too late.

Given its inherent problems and the lack of warning before Baldwin dropped his bombshell, it is hardly surprising that once again the tariff policy proved to be disruptive of party unity. Baldwin succeeded in keeping his Cabinet together, partly at the price of avoiding commitments and definitions. However one junior minister resigned, and at constituency level the picture was chaotic. Over twenty Conservative candidates stood openly as free-traders, mainly in Lancashire, Scotland and Wales. Others paid at most lip-service to the official policy – so far as there was one, or that they knew or understood it. In the 1922 election many MPs had given categoric pledges against tariffs which now came back to haunt them. In some cases, their embarrassment or hostility to the policy was too great and they stood down, leaving constituency associations scrambling to find a nominee at the eleventh hour. Many Conservative MPs and local newspapers had only just been extolling the virtues of a period of tranquillity, and were severely wrong-footed by the change of course. As a result, most Conservative candidates started out disconcerted over the policy and apologetic over the timing of the election, and remained unhappily on the defensive for the rest of the campaign. In the absence of detailed guidance from the top, and faced with a mosaic of local interests and commitments, it is hardly surprising that Conservative candidates went their own ways, making up policy to suit themselves as they did so. The result was a tangle of conflicting promises, with candidates in adjacent seats sometimes taking up diametrically different positions.[34] Inconsistency, and even absurdity, were the hallmarks of the Conservative campaign at local level, and their opponents were presented with the easiest of targets. This disunity was more serious than had been the case over the coalition, because it took place during the election rather than before it.

The other factors which played a part in the 1923 defeat followed from these fundamental problems. As well as the divisions it caused and the widespread lack of enthusiasm, the sudden coming of the election found the party organization in disarray. It had been steadily recovering from the torpor of the coalition era, but was still weak in many areas.[35] The new party chairman, Stanley Jackson, possibly over-estimated the improvement, but most of the party's electoral managers were aware of the problems and had advised against an early election.[36] The advantages normally available to the party which is in office and so controls the timing of the election were thrown away; for example, Central Office had no time in which to prepare an effective leaflet or poster campaign. Matters were not helped by the depleted state of the national party funds, due partly to an unexpected election coming so soon after the last one, and partly to problems with the former party treasurer.[37] Lord Farquhar had served in that capacity since 1911 and, as was customary in this era, had kept the money in accounts under his own name. However, due to a mixture of loyalty to the former coalition and advancing senile dementia, he had refused to disgorge a penny for the 1922 campaign. His death in 1923 eased matters a little, but his affairs were in confusion and it was far from clear where the funds had gone.[38]

Internal difficulties and unreadiness meant that the party was all the more vulnerable to external attack. The campaign followed several months of press criticism of the government's performance, and was conducted with little media support. The elite and respectable Conservative press was unenthusiastic about the tariff policy and opposed to an early election. Some journals were sharply critical and others, such as *The Times* and the *Daily Telegraph*, at best lukewarm and dutiful during the contest. More damaging was the active hostility of the mass-circulation newspapers owned by Lords Beaverbrook and Rothermere. This resulted in part from personal hostility to Baldwin, and in part from dislike of his policy – but in this case the objection was that it was too weak, rather than too strong. Beaverbrook was a fervent believer in the ideal of imperial unity through preferential tariffs; because this dimension was lacking in Baldwin's policy, he launched a bitter attack on 18 November and by the end of the campaign was advocating a vote for the Liberals. Rothermere's views were less clear and consistent, but neither press lord had confidence in Baldwin's strategy and both retained links to Lloyd George and were inclining to a revival of the coalition. The dismal picture in the national press was reinforced by an almost complete hostility to the election in the mainly Conservative provincial press, and on the part of many local newspapers.[39]

TABLE 6.2   *The National Press in the Mid-1920s*

Title	Ownership in 1925	Normal Party Affiliation	Circulation in 1925
The Times	Times Association	Conservative	190,000
Morning Post	(syndicate of Conservatives)	Conservative	70,000
Daily Telegraph	Lord Burnham	Conservative	125,000
Daily Express	Lord Beaverbrook	Conservative*	850,000
Daily Mail	Lord Rothermere	Conservative*	1,720,000
Daily Mirror	Lord Rothermere	Conservative/ Independent*	964,000
Daily Sketch	Lord Rothermere	Independent	850,000
Daily Chronicle	D. Lloyd George	Liberal	949,000
Daily News	G. Cadbury	Liberal	570,000
Westminster Gazette	A. Pearson	Liberal	200,000
Daily Herald	Trades Union Congress	Labour	350,000

* nominal affiliation: these titles followed an independent course, directed by their proprietor

The final factor in the Conservative defeat was the revival of the opposition. Despite the end of the coalition, the Liberals were still in disarray at every level. Efforts at reconciliation between the Asquith and Lloyd George wings made little progress until the revival of the tariff issue, which had a transforming effect. The terms of reunion were swiftly agreed; Lloyd George returned to second position under

Asquith's leadership, and promised a vital transfusion from his fund for the cash-starved Liberal organization. The Liberal campaign focused exclusively upon the traditional case against tariffs and defence of free trade.[40] This negativism was a symptom of the Liberal Party's long-term problems, but in the short term it did the Conservatives considerable damage. The Labour Party was equally committed to free trade, and both opposition parties took full advantage of the easy target they had been offered. Even so, at the end of the day there was no landslide. After a difficult campaign, the Conservative share of the vote fell only by 0.5 per cent from 1922, whilst the Liberal and Labour parties gained 0.9 per cent and 1 per cent respectively. However, many of the Conservative victories in 1922 had been finely balanced, and were vulnerable to even this small change. In terms of seats, the outcome certainly seemed to be an emphatic rejection of the tariff policy. The Conservatives suffered a net loss of 88 seats, and were left with only 258 MPs against 191 Labour and 158 Liberal MPs. For tactical reasons, Baldwin decided not to resign immediately but to face Parliament; this would force the Liberals to combine with Labour and eject the government. As the new House did not meet until after the Christmas recess, the Conservatives did not leave office until after defeat on a motion of confidence on 21 January 1924. Their places were taken by the first ever Labour government, with Ramsay MacDonald as prime minister.

The most surprising developments of the early part of 1924 were that the Conservative Party avoided damaging recriminations over the election defeat and that Baldwin survived without serious challenge as Conservative leader. Neither the parliamentary party nor the constituencies would countenance the only alternative, a return to coalitionism. In recognition of this, Austen Chamberlain and Birkenhead accepted Baldwin's leadership and joined the Shadow Cabinet. The existence of a minority Labour government and the fraying of Liberal unity presented the

Conservatives with many opportunities, and the party began to look forward rather than back. By the time the Labour ministry fell in October 1924, the Conservatives had reunited, revitalized their organization and refreshed their policies and appeal. Baldwin abandoned the tariff policy after the debacle of 1923, and in the general election of November 1924 it was explicitly ruled out. With the Liberal Party in disarray and running many fewer candidates, the Conservatives returned to power after winning 46.8 per cent of the votes cast. It was the largest single-party victory in modern British history, with the return of 412 Conservative MPs to 151 Labour and 40 Liberals.

The Basis of Conservative Electoral Success in the 1920s

Whilst this chapter is principally concerned with Conservative downfalls, these failures need to be set in the broader context of the party's striking record of success between the wars. The victory of 1924 was the high point but the Conservatives also won on their own in 1922, and as the main coalition partner they amassed large majorities in 1919, 1931 and 1935. In the absence of modern techniques of social investigation and opinion polling, it is impossible to be precise about the nature of political allegiances or the factors which shaped electoral choices. Nevertheless, it is clear that the Conservative Party was founded upon a wider social and geographical base than either of its opponents. The Conservatives benefited from the expansion of the middle class and from suburbanization, and by the mid-1920s they had largely displaced the Liberals and become the party supported by an overwhelming majority of the middle class, offering an alliance of large and small property owners. In addition, a substantial portion – more than one third – of the various social groups which together form the working class were intermittent or habitual Conservative supporters.

There were several reasons for this attraction across class

259

boundaries.[41] Not least is the fact that social upheaval is as threatening to those who have a little to lose as it is to those who have a lot. There has been a consistent popular tendency to turn to the Conservative Party as the safe option in time of crisis. Despite their traumas in the Edwardian period, the Conservatives retained the aura of competence, experience and authority, and were seen as the 'natural' party of government. In parallel with this, the Conservatives have always done well out of 'wrapping themselves in the flag' and evoking patriotic sentiments. The causes of working-class Conservatism were as varied as the factors which shaped the outlook of any group: it was the product of many different combinations of age, occupation, regional traditions, family influence, personal experience, temperament, relative status, social aspirations and the deferential attitudes ingrained by British education and culture. These influences meant that there was a receptive audience for the political tunes played by Conservative politicians and propaganda: independence, self-reliance, national unity, the rule of law, the security of tradition, confidence in the virtues of the past, patriotism, and pride in the empire. The personality and public image of Stanley Baldwin, leader of the party from 1923 to 1937, also played an important part in Conservative electoral success. Baldwin came to prominence in the overthrow of the Lloyd George coalition and for many he symbolized the victory of honesty and principle over the cynical opportunism they associated with that regime. Baldwin captured the spirit of the age; his 'New Conservatism', established between 1924 and 1926, was principled, distinctive, accessible, moderate and unprovocative.[42] There were many in all classes who responded to its tone and substance: the pursuit of prosperity at home without social upheaval, and the quest for peace abroad without military adventure.

There was a consistent pattern to Conservative electoral support. The party was strongest in the suburbs and the arable farming counties: it was predominant in outer

London and the Home Counties, and in the rural seats and county towns of southern and central England. To this can be added some other farming districts in the north of England, parts of Wales, and Scotland (especially the borders and the eastern counties), and also the coastal resorts around the country. There were safe Conservative seats in the more prosperous residential districts within and around all of the major cities, and the party did notably well in Birmingham, Liverpool and Manchester. Finally, and of pivotal importance, was the party's record of success in the medium-sized industrial boroughs, especially in the west midlands and Lancashire. The number of marginal seats in these last two regions meant that their retention was essential for victory, and the losses here were a key factor in the defeats of 1923 and 1929.

TABLE 6.3 *Regional Patterns of Conservative Support 1922–29*

General Election	Southern England	Midlands	Northern England	Wales	Scotland
1922	173	53	82	6	13
1923	118	45	57	4	14
1924	186	63	98	9	36
1929	135	35	51	1	20

NOTE: The table above does not include the Northern Ireland and the university seats.

The impact of the First World War, and the changes in the party and electoral system which it caused, transformed the Conservatives from the minority position they had occupied in the Edwardian period into a natural majority party. The redistribution of constituency boundaries also helped the Conservatives in 1918, partly because their support was more evenly spread across the country than their opponents' and partly because the new towns and industries which were to draw population to the midlands and south

TABLE 6.4 *Conservative Performance in the Major Cities 1922–29*

	Total No. of Seats	No. won by the Conservative Party			
		1922	1923	1924	1929
Birmingham	12	12	12	11	6
Bradford	4	1	–	2	–
Bristol	5	2	2	2	1
Edinburgh	5	2	1	3	2
Glasgow	15	4	5	7	5
Hull	4	2	2	3	1
Leeds	6	3	3	3	2
Liverpool	11	10	7	8	6
Manchester	10	7	1	6	3
Newcastle	4	1	1	1	1
Nottingham	4	2	1	3	1
Sheffield	7	3	4	4	2

tended to lack established working-class traditions and institutions. There were a larger number of safe Conservative seats with a significant suburban and middle-class element than ever before. These produced a bedrock of 200 constituencies which consistently returned Conservatives, together with a further 100–140 which in varying degrees were frequently winnable; with the House of Commons reduced to 615 MPs after 1921, only 308 seats were now required for a bare majority. Despite the fact that most of the contests between the wars were three-party battles, the Conservative Party's share of the total national vote never fell below 38 per cent. The Conservatives were further advantaged by the survival of two forms of plural voting – both the votes granted for separate business premises and the university seats went heavily in their favour. However, their greatest dividend proved to be the enfranchisement of women. Since 1918 women have provided the largest and hardest-working portion of the local membership, whilst at the ballot box women supported the Conservatives to a larger extent than any other party.

The organizational superiority of the Conservative Party between the wars was another factor in its electoral success. The Conservatives were more truly a national party than either the Liberals or Labour, having an active presence in every part of the country and in all types of constituency. The Conservative Party was financially stronger than its competitors at every level, and this underpinned both the large number of candidates the party fielded in every election and the substantial network of full-time professional agents. For social and political reasons many local associations were able to attract a large membership, especially in the women's branches, and their regular programmes of events gave them a high profile in their own districts. Conservatism appeared in many places to be part of the natural fabric of society, and almost to be non-political. At the national level the Conservatives were able to run a large and elaborate party machine which was a frequent innovator in propaganda and campaigning methods.

Finally, the Conservatives also benefited from the division and weakness of their opponents. The Labour Party had secured its industrial heartlands, but its advance into other areas was slow and fragile. The Liberals were fractious and in terminal decline, although they could still mobilize powerful residual support when their strength and unity enabled them to run a large number of candidates. Even so, the splitting of the hostile vote did not automatically guarantee Conservative success: of the four general elections held during the 1920s, the Conservatives won two and lost two. Defeats occurred when the issues or the public mood did not favour the Conservatives and when they faced a confident Labour Party and a fairly united and effective Liberal Party: this was the case in 1923 and 1929. On the two occasions when the Conservatives won, the Liberal Party was either still badly divided (in 1922) or through internal wrangling unwilling and financially unable to run a large number of candidates (in 1924). The most promising situation for the Conservatives was a Liberal absence from the poll and a large number of straight fights against Labour – of which there were 111 in 1922, a drop to 100 in 1923, and a steep rise to 207 in 1924. Two-cornered contests were a rarity in 1929: with 513 Liberal candidates standing, and the Labour total having risen to 569 (from 427 in 1923 and 514 in 1924), 447 constituencies were contested by three candidates and 98 by only two – by far the lowest number of the period from 1885 to 1970. With rare exceptions, the Conservatives have been pragmatic in opposition and flexible and responsive in government; once ensconced in power it has been very difficult to dislodge them. As this and other chapters demonstrate, their infrequent downfalls have usually been due to internal factors – the failure of their own policies, sometimes exacerbated by an outburst of faction and disunity – rather than to the initiatives of their opponents.

The Baldwin Government of 1924–29

Baldwin became prime minister for the second time on 4 November 1924. He presided over a secure and stable government, which was to remain in office for the next four and a half years. The 1924–29 Conservative administration's major achievements all came within its first two years, including the Locarno agreements and pensions for widows and orphans in 1925; the finest hour was the collapse of the General Strike in May 1926. The Trades Disputes Act of 1927 which followed was in fact a limited and moderate measure, but it aroused a storm of opposition from the Labour Party and the trade unions. This was significant in the recovery of Labour morale, rather than in making any significant inroads into Conservative support. There were no catastrophes or crises during the second half of the government, but an increasing impression of a lack of drive and inspiration. The ministry seemed to be doing no more than plodding dutifully onwards, in the hope that better times would turn up. This was more a matter of presentation than of policies. In fact, the Cabinet gave a good deal of thought to its strategy for the next election during its final eighteen months; the low-key approach was deliberately adopted as a strategic choice, rather than by inertia. The timing of the dissolution was chosen with care, and not forced by any outside circumstance.[43]

The Conservative leadership were confident that they would win the next general election, anticipating the reduction – but not the destruction – of their windfall majority of 1924.[44] Although some MPs with marginal seats were much less sanguine, the optimism of their leaders was only partly the result of complacency.[45] The factors identified as commonly contributing to Conservative downfalls were visible in fewer number and with less force in 1929 than in any other reverse the party has suffered in modern times. Only three of the nine common factors were present in 1929 in any strength, and even so to a smaller degree than in 1906, 1945, 1964 or 1974. There was a mixed record on the economic front, some uncertainty over the direction of policy, and a strengthening of the opposition. Three other factors were present, but to a still lesser extent: there was some popular feeling of 'time for a change', a cool or neutral intellectual and press environment, and a few signs of internal disunity. The remaining three factors played little or not part. The party organization was enjoying the benefits of several years of expansion and elaboration both at the centre and locally, although there were some symptoms of disappointment and apathy amongst the rank and file. There were no financial problems, and the election saw a huge expenditure from national funds. Finally, Baldwin's popular standing was admitted on all sides to be the party's greatest electoral asset.[46]

Although the defeat of 1929 was the Conservative Party's major reverse in the interwar period, its origins are in some ways less complex than the events of 1922 and 1923. The first contributory element was a mixed record on the economy. The government's strategy was founded on the recognition that British prosperity depended upon overseas trade, and hence the priority given to the restoration of international stability. In financial terms, this indicated the restoration of the gold standard, support for European financial institutions in the wake of German hyper-inflation, and the settlement of the onerous war debts and reparations. The last were linked to the political dimension: the promotion of stability in Europe, the recognition of existing borders – exemplified by the Locarno Treaty – and the encouragement of disarmament and the mediatory functions of the League of Nations. The government's principal domestic theme was the recovery of competitiveness through the modernization and rationalization of industries. This could only be achieved without disruption and social conflict if both sides of industry worked together, and hence the constant theme in Baldwin's oratory of the need for harmony and conciliation. The policy of safeguarding, under which an industry suffering unfair foreign competition could make an application for the imposition of specific and restricted protectionist duties, was intended to provide a shelter for schemes of rationalization.

Hopes of a revival of prosperity, and still more of a return to an idealized 'golden age', were to be disappointed. The return to the gold standard in 1925 was made at the prewar rate of exchange for reasons of prestige, but this was unrealistic and imposed economic and financial strains. Industrial relations were still confrontational, and the methods and outlook of management remained hidebound. Taken as a whole, the government's record was not enough to retain support when placed against the rosy appeals of Labour or the promises of Lloyd George. The attacks of the opposition were focused upon one indicator in particular: unemployment, which remained at the level of between one and a quarter and one and a half million.[47] The instinctive Conservative answer to this was tariff reform, but the lesson on 1923 and the pledges given in 1924 ruled this out. The latter also precluded the extension of safeguarding to any major sector of the economy, and the application from the iron and steel industry was therefore refused in 1925.[48] Instead, in 1928 the government took up an alternative and less controversial package, intended to reduce costs, stimulate industry, help agriculture and revive employment.[49] This was the scheme initially devised by the Chancellor of the Exchequer, Winston Churchill, to relieve industries, farms and the railways from the payment of local rates. The plan was adopted as part of a wider programme which also embraced Neville Chamberlain's plans for Poor Law and local government reform, and a series of measures were introduced during 1928. De-rating was to be the positive plank in the government's platform: it would reduce unemployment, assist all sectors of the economy, and benefit every region. It was also intended to demonstrate the vitality of the government, and to overlay the mid-term impression of feebleness and uncertainty with a triumphant finale. In fact, the scheme was a political failure: it was too complex and remote, a long-term policy which was introduced too late to show any effects before the election. It was difficult to get across to the public and failed to enthuse either Conservative candidates or their audiences.[50]

For these reasons, de-rating contributed to the second common cause of Conservative defeat to be present in 1929: uncertainty about the direction and definition of policy. The government's mid-term was characterized by drift and confusion.[51] Baldwin had been tired and unwell in the early part of 1927, and decisions were postponed on topics such as factory legislation, the Poor Law, the equalization of the franchise and the reform of the House of Lords. The ministry recovered from this trough and dealt with the first three of these issues, although its proposals for the second chamber ran into difficulties and were abandoned. By 1929 the government could point to a solid record of achievement. However, some of its most popular and memorable initiatives were now too far in the past to produce much of a dividend in the ballot box. Other measures were worthy but dull; this was especially the case with the most active figure in the Cabinet: Neville Chamberlain, the Minister of Health.[52] Much of his legislation was administratively sound but politically neutral at best, whilst a few of his reforms – especially in the Poor Law and local government – trod on some Conservative and middle-class toes.[53] Ministers appeared to be bound up in their departmental responsibilities, and to have imbibed the cautious outlook of the civil service. The need for the party to have its own research and planning body was recognized, but not yet acted upon.[54] When the election came, the government seemed to be lacking in political instincts and unable to catch the public imagination.

This was not the result of either a lack of proposals or the absence of a theme. Policies were available: as well as de-rating, there were plans to reduce unemployment by encouraging emigration and imperial development, and further social reforms such as slum clearance, maternity benefits and child welfare. Whilst a general tariff had been ruled out on electoral grounds in 1928, the Cabinet had resolved that the manifesto would include promises to simplify the safeguarding procedure and permit applications from any industry, including iron and steel. However, a deliberate decision was made to downplay these policies and campaign instead on the twin slogans of 'Trust Baldwin' and 'Safety First'. The latter of these was chosen on the advice of the advertising agency, Bensons, and echoed a contemporary road safety campaign; it was intended to evoke a reliance upon steadiness and experience. The Cabinet recognized that it could not credibly outbid the schemes Lloyd George was pouring forth, or build more attractive castles in the air than Labour's vague utopia. The Conservative leadership did not consider Lloyd George's schemes to be realistic, but after several by-election defeats they were all too aware of their danger as propaganda. The Conservatives expected to be in power after the election, and so their own programme had to be realistic and attainable. They opted to make a virtue of necessity, by emphasizing the difference in their approach and highlighting the irresponsibility and lack of substance of the alternatives. The Conservative campaign theme of 'Safety First' was chosen from several possible strategies for positive tactical reasons.[55] It would build upon the strengths of the Conservative record and Baldwin's popularity, and counter the threat of the Liberal revival. Instead, it compounded the impression of a government which preferred inaction to innovation and lacked ideas or a sense of direction.

Another of the common factors in Conservative defeats also

TABLE 6.5 *Conservative Performance in By-elections 1919–29*

Period	Total no. of by-election contests*	No. of Conservative seats defended	No. of Conservative seats lost	Average change in Conservative share of the poll
Jan.–Dec. 1919	16	12	5	−16.6%
Jan.–Dec. 1920	21	10	1	−13.3%
Jan.–Dec. 1921	22	11	3	−21.6%
Jan.–Oct. 1922	15	9	3	−16.0%
Dec. 1922– Dec. 1923	16	11	4	−7.9%
Feb.–Aug. 1924	9	5	1	+0.7%
Dec. 1924– Dec. 1925	10	7	1	−7.7%
Jan.–Dec. 1926	13	9	3	−9.2%
Jan.–Dec. 1927	8	6	2	−8.2%
Jan.–Dec. 1928	19	15	6	−13.1%
Jan.–Apr. 1929	9	7	5	−16.4%

* Excluding the university seats, which were contested on a personal rather than party basis.

played a part in this: longevity in office, together with the appearance of exhaustion and staleness, leading to a widespread feeling that it was time for a change. There had been a remarkable degree of stability within the 1924–29 government, with most Cabinet posts being held by the same individual throughout its duration. Apart from the few months of the first Labour government, the Conservatives had been in office since May 1915. Four members of the Cabinet in May 1929 – Earl Balfour, the Earl of Birkenhead, Austen Chamberlain and Winston Churchill – had held Cabinet office through most of these fourteen years, and almost all of the others had served as junior ministers from 1916 to 1922 and as Cabinet ministers since then. There was no doubt that the government possessed a wealth of experience, especially when contrasted to the fledgling Labour Party. However they were also tired, and in some cases their health was breaking down. Their faces had become too familiar to the public, and much of Labour's election propaganda carried an undercurrent of the need for new men and fresh ideas. The Conservatives did their best to make their tenure of office a strength rather than a weakness, and a significant element of the 'Safety First' campaign warned of the danger of allowing novices and cranks to implement their naive, simplistic and even fraudulent policies. However, there remained the handicap of boredom with the government and the perception that many of the senior ministers – though not the Prime Minister – were exhausted or stale.[56] The possible solution to this, a pre-election reshuffle, was considered by Baldwin but rejected as smacking of the very gimmickry with which the Conservatives were charging their opponents.

Two other factors were present in 1929, but only to a minor extent when compared to other Conservative defeats: intellectual and media hostility, and party disunity. The campaign of the right-wing Home Secretary, Sir William Joynson-Hicks, against 'vice' in metropolitan nightclubs had a hidebound Victorian flavour, and the maladroit 'Jix' became something of a figure of fun.[57] Intellectual circles were attracted to the 'idealist' policies of Labour, especially on disarmament. In the later part of the government Austen Chamberlain's foreign policy fell between two stools: too protective of national interests for the left, too oriented to the League of Nations for the right. The Conservatives had no serious problems with the press in 1929. Although it was easy for Conservatives to pin the blame on them afterwards, the mass circulation titles of Rothermere and Beaverbrook varied erratically between lukewarm support and cool indifference, rather than active hostility.[58] Other newspapers followed their normal affiliations, which meant that the Conservatives enjoyed the largest share of press support during the calm and incident-free campaign.

Internal disunity likewise played little part in the 1929 defeat. The only resignation from the Cabinet over policy was that of Lord Cecil in August 1927, but his frustration with the government's record on disarmament mainly reflected his leading position in the League of Nations Union. He was not in tune with Conservative sentiment, and his departure caused barely a ripple. The Cabinet was generally harmonious, although there were two fault-lines which remained sensitive. The first of these concerned any hints of a coalitionist clique; this surfaced during the most potentially serious Cabinet dispute of the period, over naval expenditure in 1925, and occasionally again in 1927–29. The other related to the empire and tariffs, and followed from the tensions caused by Baldwin's appointment of the returning prodigal Winston Churchill as chancellor of the exchequer in 1924. The concern which the presence of a strong free-trader at this key economic post aroused amongst committed protectionists was voiced in Cabinet by the colonial and dominions secretary, Leo Amery. However, Baldwin was adept at smoothing over any problems, and the few instances of embarrassing contradictions in ministerial statements were simple blunders rather than signs of faction or strife.

This was also a period of relative tranquillity in the parliamentary party. A large number of MPs joined the Empire Industries Association, a protectionist group founded in 1925. This pressed for the extension of safeguarding to iron and steel, but by means of deputations to the leaders and the dissemination of propaganda. Neither this, nor the slight restiveness of the 'die-hards' in the later years, were real threats to party unity.[59] Baldwin drew steady support from the many MPs who had won industrial districts in the midlands and north in 1924; the leading lights of this element, nicknamed the 'YMCA', were seen as the rising generation. There were only two instances of open division in the party in the House of Commons. The first resulted in the dropping of the Cabinet's proposals for the reform of the House of Lords in 1927; these were eagerly sought by the right, but regarded as an electoral liability by the centre and left. The second was unexpected, and in any case crossed normal party lines: the controversy over the new Prayer Book in 1927 and 1928.[60] Neither amounted to more than a storm in a teacup; compared to both the Liberals and Labour from 1924 to 1929, the Conservative Party was a model of loyalty and solidarity.

This was equally the case with the party organization in the country. The rank and file accepted the moderate tone of the Baldwin government, although with a diminishing degree of enthusiasm as time passed. The lowering of the voting age for women from thirty to equality with men at twenty-one – the 'flapper vote' – was disliked because it seemed likely to assist the opposition, as well as give a good deal more work to local Conservative associations. However, most of the frustration with the government stemmed from what it did not do, rather than what it did. The loss of the opportunity to strengthen the powers of the House of Lords was one disappointment, although feelings were no longer running as high on this point as they had been in the more unstable atmosphere of the early 1920s.[61] A frequent complaint concerned the failure to cut the level of government expenditure and the size of the civil service; the Cabinet seemed to be tinkering at the margins, lacking the will to deliver the 'drastic economy' for which many MPs and constituencies were clamouring.[62] Policy on the extension of safeguarding and assistance for agriculture were frequently criticized for lack of boldness and vigour.[63] However, the consequences were no worse than some muted grumbling and the apathy which was noted in some areas in early 1929 and during the campaign.[64]

At the same time, the second half of the 1920s saw sustained growth and increased activity in the party organization at every level. This was a period of expanding membership, with many constituencies recruiting several thousand members – many of them women – into a lively and extensive network of branches. There were notable endeavours in the distribution of propaganda, canvassing and fund-raising, whilst the quality and number of full-time trained local agents was rapidly advancing. The chairman of the party from 1926, J.C.C. Davidson, raised and spent large sums on an ever larger, more professional and more elaborate national machine. It is always possible to search out flaws in any large organization, but taken as a whole the Conservative Party was at a peak of strength and effectiveness in the late 1920s.[65] This sound base was also reflected in the party funds. A few of the City businessmen who were approached as potential donors objected to the 'semi-Socialist' record of the government, but Davidson had little difficulty in raising money despite his ambitious targets.[66] There was no shortage of funds, and in May 1929 the Conservative Party fought one of the best resourced and most carefully prepared campaigns in its history.[67] This made possible expensive innovations, such as the mobile cinema vans, as well as the printing of unprecedented quantities of publicity – the 93 million leaflets produced were more than in all four previous elections added together. The content of the message may have been a cause of its failure, but the machinery which delivered it was not.

Nor was the personality of the party leader and prime minister: in 1929, Stanley Baldwin was a popular and trusted figure.[68] His standing was based upon the message he had made his own since 1924: the need for peace and goodwill in industry. Baldwin's sincerity was matched by the simple effectiveness of his oratory, and his skilful evo- cation of images of reassurance and inspiration from a common patriotic heritage struck a chord in all social classes. Although the leader of a great party, he was rarely seen as being a party man; he shone in non-partisan public roles, and his appeal extended across the normal party boundaries. In particular, he was respected and trusted by many in the trade unions and Labour Party, whilst his personal unosten- tatious Christian faith and emphasis upon trust and truth attracted Nonconformist sentiment.[69] The Baldwinian face of Conservatism appealed to many former Liberals; although it was less successful in 1929 than before and after, it played a part in containing the Liberal revival. The appeal once more to trust in Baldwin was the focal point of the Conservative campaign, reinforced in leaflets and posters. His enthusiastic public reception as he toured the country was one of the main reasons why the party managers and Central Office continued to expect a majority of forty to eighty seats until the declaration of the first results – a lesson that had been forgotten by 1945.[70]

In the event, the Conservative majority of 1924 proved as susceptible to erosion as that of the Liberals in 1906 and Labour in 1945. Critically, the Conservatives were unable to retain the breadth of support they had received in 1924. Too much reliance was based upon Baldwin's appeal, which could not overlay a problematic economic, employment and international situation. The advance of the opposition par- ties was the final factor to affect the outcome in 1929. The public was by now familiar with the Labour Party and its leaders, and ironically the defeat of the General Strike removed much of the fear of extremism. Under Ramsay MacDonald the Labour Party was moderate yet idealistic,

274

strong in its working-class industrial base but capable of making inroads into other districts and social strata. However, although Labour was to reap the reward, the most serious damage to Conservative electoral prospects was inflicted by the revival of the Liberal Party.[71] After becoming the leader in 1926, Lloyd George provided it with new energy, a fresh and distinctive programme, and the money to fuel the party organization and subsidize candidates. Only 339 Liberal candidates had stood in 1924, but in 1929 there were 513. The Liberal revival meant that the number of three-cornered contests nearly doubled, from 223 in 1924 to 447 in 1929: it was this that made the Conservatives fear the impact of Lloyd George's stunts upon a credulous electorate. In the end the Liberals gained only a few seats themselves, but in many constituencies the intervention of their candidate took enough votes from the Conservative to let Labour in – a pattern to be echoed in 1974. At 38.1 per cent, the Conservative share of the poll returned to the level of 1922 and 1923; the party lost 159 seats, and for the only time between the wars ceased to be the largest party in the House of Commons. Labour took office as a minority government for the second time, with 287 seats to 260 Conservatives; the Liberals with 59 MPs held the balance.

Conclusion
The Forces that Shape Conservative Defeats

The Conservatives were in office for almost the whole of the period from 1916 to 1929, and were the largest party in the House of Commons from the general election of 1918 to that of 1929. The three governments in which the Conservative Party was involved during these years were each of a different nature, and each came to an end for different reasons. The first government was a coalition, whilst the other two were purely Conservative in composition. The latter two also differed: the 1922–24 administration was formed during a period of party disunity, whilst that of

1924–29 was based upon a reunited party. One ministry took its own life by calling a general election on an unpopular platform after only a year in office, one was unexpectedly overthrown by an internal revolt, and the other lasted a full term. At first sight, there may seem to be little in common between the circumstances of the downfall of these three ministries. However, although the differences cannot be ignored, there are several connecting themes.

Most of the factors commonly found in Conservative defeats were present in 1922, 1923 and 1929, but only three played a significant part on every occasion. First was a failure of leadership, although this was more a matter of errors in strategic command than a negative public image. Second was the economic situation and the level of public confidence in the government's competence; all three ministries suffered from a context of pessimism, stagnation and relatively high unemployment. Third was confusion or lack of definition over policy direction. This played a part in the fall of the coalition in 1922, although it was an asset in the ensuing general election. In 1923 it was forced on the leadership by blunders of haste and adopted as the lesser evil, but still did much damage; in 1929 it was more clearly a positive choice, but again the tactic failed. The other factors played intermittent roles of varying effect. The feeling of stagnation, or 'time for a change', played a part in 1922 and 1929 – but not in 1923. Internal disunity was manifest in 1923, but negligible in 1929. In 1922 the Cabinet fell even though all its major figures were united, whilst the party was victorious in the resulting general election despite its divisions. There were problems in the party organization in 1922 and 1923, but the period from 1924 to 1929 was marked by an unparalleled expansion in the scale, complexity and wealth of the machine at both national and local level. Although there was a lack of national party funds in 1922, there was no real shortage in 1923. The Conservatives were always better placed than their opponents and, despite grumbles from some sectors of business, were able to raise an ample war chest for the 1929 campaign. The coalition certainly suffered from a hostile media and intellectual climate in 1922, and the tariff campaign of 1923 was met with considerable press antagonism – but in 1929 the Conservative campaign had little difficulty and the 'press lords' were at least neutral, although certainly not as supportive as they had been in the elections of 1922 and 1924. The strength and credibility of the opposition parties was a minor factor in 1922, and in the case of the Liberals was an eleventh-hour and paper-thin affair in 1923. However, in 1929 the combination of Labour's growing prestige and the financing of over 500 Liberal candidates were the twin rocks upon which the Conservative vessel foundered.

None of the nine factors is critical in itself: the Conservatives won in 1922 despite the economic situation and the extreme vagueness of their manifesto, although it is true to say that it was clear what they stood for in general terms, by definition of their rejection of the coalition. Victory in 1970 and 1979 was achieved despite having a less popular and attractive leader than their opponents, whilst riding on the coat-tails of a heroic leader did not work in 1945. That the feeling of staleness and 'time for a change' is not enough on its own is shown by the narrowness of defeat in 1964, and by the winning of a fourth term in 1992. Disunity within the governing party may cause some disquiet, but internal strife did not prevent the Conservative victories of 1922, 1931, 1935, 1959, 1970 and 1992. A hostile media and intellectual environment is a problem, but one that can be overcome; the Conservatives enjoyed only partial support in 1874, 1951 and 1970. An increased challenge from the opposition is normally a result of the decline of public confidence in a ministry, rather than a cause of it. A capable and effective opposition can exploit a government's problems and accelerate the downwards trend, as was the case in 1906 and 1964. However, whilst a credible and united opposition is always a tougher prospect than a weak or divided one, it is not enough on its own to cause defeat.

Dwindling public support also leads to the final two factors, which are usually found together: problems in the party organization, and lack of funds. These have often played a part in piling up the sorrows, but have never been critical on their own. In 1951 the best funded and most efficient organization the party has ever had only just scraped home to victory, whilst in 1992 the Conservatives held on despite a long-term organizational decay which the impact of recession was swiftly accelerating.

The record of the coalition and Conservative ministries of 1916–1929 demonstrates clearly that it is the combination of factors which is crucial. Their cumulative range and severity is the explanation of defeat, and the measure of the problems which the Conservatives have to absorb or overcome if they are to return to office. It is indicative of the adaptability and resilience of the party that, until now, they have always done so – and often with surprising swiftness.[72]

CHRONOLOGY

1915 MAY 19   H. H. Asquith (Liberal prime minister) and Andrew Bonar Law (Conservative Party leader) announce that a coalition ministry will be formed

1916 DECEMBER 6   Conservative leaders agree to join a new coalition, with David Lloyd George as prime minister

1918 NOVEMBER 12   The coalition manifesto agreed between Bonar Law and Lloyd George is endorsed by a meeting of the parliamentary Conservative Party

      DECEMBER 14   Polling day (but votes not counted until 28 December): 523 supporters of the coalition elected (382 Conservative MPs), 28 Asquithian Liberals, 63 Labour MPs

1921 MARCH 21   Bonar Law retires from the party leadership due to ill-health

      NOVEMBER 17   Conservative annual conference at Liverpool endorses the Anglo-Irish settlement

1922 JANUARY 11   The Party Chairman, Sir George Younger, makes public a

	circular to local associations opposing the holding of a general election before the redeeming of pledges on House of Lords reform
AUGUST 3	Junior ministers meet with party leaders to express their concern over the future of the coalition, but are enraged by a humiliating lecture from Lord Birkenhead
OCTOBER 19	Meeting of Conservative MPs at the Carlton Club rejects the advice of Austen Chamberlain by 185 to 88; Chamberlain resigns as party leader, and Lloyd George as prime minister, later the same day
OCTOBER 23	After forming Cabinet, Bonar Law announces a general election
NOVEMBER 15	Polling day: 344 Conservative MPs elected, 53 National (Lloyd George) Liberals, 62 Asquithian Liberals, 142 Labour MPs
1923 MAY 20	Bonar Law tenders his resignation as prime minister to the King; after some uncertainty, he is succeeded by Stanley Baldwin on 28 May

	OCTOBER 5–7	Baldwin decides to adopt a tariff policy to tackle the problem of unemployment
	OCTOBER 25	Baldwin declares for protection in his speech to the annual party conference at Plymouth
	NOVEMBER 13	Announcement of general election; Parliament dissolved on 16 November
	DECEMBER 6	Polling day: 258 Conservative MPs elected, 191 Labour MPs, 158 Liberals
1924	JANUARY 21	Conservative ministry resigns after defeat in the House of Commons by a combined Liberal and Labour vote, by 256 to 328
	FEBRUARY 11	Conservative Party meeting at the Hotel Cecil endorses the dropping of the tariff policy and confirms Baldwin's leadership
	OCTOBER 29	Polling day: 412 Conservative MPs elected, 151 Labour MPs, 40 Liberals
1925	JULY 18	'Cruiser crisis': W. Bridgeman, First Lord of the Admiralty, threatens to resign; fears aroused of a coalitionist attempt to take over the Cabinet
	DECEMBER 12	Baldwin announces that the

		application of the steel industry for safeguarding duties will be refused
1926	MAY 8	Baldwin broadcasts to the nation by radio, portraying the General Strike as an attack on constitutional democracy
1927	MARCH 27	Publication of the Trade Disputes Bill
	APRIL 13	Announcement of the bill to equalize the franchise for both sexes at age 21
1928	FEBRUARY 9	Lancaster by-election lost to Liberals, followed by St Ives on 6 March, leads to concern about impact of a Liberal revival
	JULY 23	Deputation of Conservative MPs urges Baldwin to extend safeguarding duties to iron and steel
	AUGUST 4	Publication of open letter from Baldwin to the chief whip, repeating for the next election the 1924 pledge not to introduce a general tariff or any duties on food
1929	MARCH 20	Eddisbury by-election lost to Liberals; the next day Holland (Lincolnshire) also lost on a large swing

APRIL 18   Baldwin unveils the election
                  platform at a party meeting held
                  at Drury Lane

MAY 30   Polling day: 260 Conservative
                  MPs elected, 287 Labour MPs, 59
                  Liberals

Winston Churchill
(*Hulton Getty Collection*)

CHAPTER SEVEN

1931–45

Michael Bentley

Power without Office:
The National Government and Churchill
Coalition

The Meaning of 'National' Government

To a far greater extent than the nineteenth, the twentieth
century has witnessed a remarkable grip on government by
the Conservative Party. The paradox is rather piquant.
Before 1918 Britain had no universal manhood suffrage;
before 1894 no one paid death duties; before 1872 the very
act of voting was done in public and under surveillance.
Yet through the middle quarters of the nineteenth century
the Tory Party struggled for power against a formidable
Liberal opponent at the time when structurally its fortunes
ought to have been at their highest. Come the annihilation
of Balfour's government in 1906 those structures altered.
A growing notion of welfarism, the levelling effects of the
Great War, the rise of a worrying Socialist alternative in
politics, above all the arrival of a democratic franchise, ought
to have spelt the end for Toryism. What happened, on the
contrary, was that Baldwin's party entrenched itself with
one of the modern age's great parliamentary majorities in
1924 and has dominated British government in various

ways until the present. In the unravelling of this odd
narrative, the National Government of 1931 to 1940 and
Winston Churchill's wartime coalition that succeeded it play
a very important part; but historians feel uneasy about what
part to accord them. This disquiet arises not least because
the Tory Party during these years reversed its frustrating
experiences of the 1850s and 1860s: it was in power without
in any simple or exclusive sense behaving as though it were
in office. It participated in government without formally
possessing it. It shared the Cabinet table yet hoarded most
forms of hegemony. The history of the party during these
years loses, therefore, the hard edges of previous histories,
apart from the confusions of 1916–22. We know how it
went into the new constellation of 1931; we know how it
emerged in the frozen Attlee winters after 1945. But these
seem junctions whose direct entry and exit mask a chaos
of tracks between.

Questions aimed at other periods and configurations
sometimes miss their target here. How did the Tory Party
achieve power? Not by popularity nor even by stealth, but
by invitation (rather like Hitler). The economic crisis of 1931
brought about a situation in which the Prime Minister,
Ramsay MacDonald, felt driven into bringing in other parties to sustain him when his own party split over the means
of coping with the problem. How did it sustain that power?
By pretending that it had none. It argued that its power lay
only in the goodwill of the people – the general public –
whose crucial interests it had been formed to protect. What
were its policies? To avoid policy through language that
made it sound like a form of unworthy calculation. Why did
it fall from power? Because of a cumulative disenchantment
(probably) whose elements, like those of 1906, ran back ten
or fifteen years. Beggaring enquiry at every point we have
the Second World War which one cannot lift out of the
puzzle to see how the world would have looked without it,
for the war shaped and interfered with so many other
pieces. Would the Tory Party have lost an election in 1940,

assuming no war and assuming that it fought as a single party? It is impossible to say. Had the Labour 'revival' already occurred by 1939, as a few by-election results might suggest? Or did it take the events of 1940 to provoke it? Would Labour have swept to power in a pre-Beveridge election in 1942? All is conjecture. Should we see Baldwin as *de facto* premier from October 1931 or only from 1935? Should we see Churchill as a Tory in 1940 or, since he had recently completed a biography of his most famous ancestor, as a displaced Marlborough seeking his Blenheim?

What is certain is that this period turns Tory history on a silent hinge. In the early 1930s the political culture of Britain had a preponderance of Tory characteristics redolent of Bonar Law and Balfour. For all the vulgarity of press lords such as Beaverbrook and Rothermere, great houses survived, salons flourished, 'influence' – the oil in so many Tory mechanisms – continued to matter. A dinner at a dining club such as Grillions, conversation over cocktails in Mayfair, thoughts tossed across a Pullman table, a walk among unemployed blackspots,[1] could go further in their effects, still, than a speech in the Commons or a letter to the ministry. Political conversation might mention India quite as readily as it did in the hearing of Joseph Chamberlain or Rudyard Kipling. People read John Buchan without giggling. 'Labour', meanwhile, could virtually be forgotten as a serious enemy until at least 1937. In 1945, by contrast, the electorate had become a strange, alienated, educated force that had come to think its voice overwhelming. It was the first ungullible audience in the history of modern politics. And politicians brought up on the gentle art of gulling found themselves quite as dated as those used to declaiming lines on the silent screen now felt among 'talkies'. They became quaint and their party with them. The Tories were to keep Churchill as their popular mascot; but the Tories behind him after 1945 were not the men who had wept over or for Neville Chamberlain. They would stand for the mixed economy, just-right-of-centre 'common sense' and an accommodation with the powerful Labour movement that would have struck Baldwin and his circle of 1931 as a dismal denial of Conservative identity.

Standing back from these shifts in mood and stance, we may be able to see some prominent features in a few of them, though we do not yet have anything resembling an overview of the period.[2] It would not be profitable to attempt a detailed narrative of events within government when a single facet of them – the foreign policy of the National Government, for example – might already have given rise to many dense volumes of analysis. More promising may be an outline of a few aspects of the story. The electoral history of the Conservative Party during the period obviously merits some comment, as does the character of Tory leadership, for we need a map of when it changed and why. Policy is harder to reduce to an essay's proportions but it will become important to think about domestic management in an era of overwhelming economic difficulty; of foreign policy in the age of the dictators even if facing them often amounted, as A.J.P. Taylor once said, to making faces at them; and the direction of the war effort which was to propel Churchill back into government and create the context in which the political environment underwent fundamental change.

Elections

Ostensibly, the electoral performance of the National Government suggested a pattern of consistent success. It won massively in 1931, persuasively in 1935 and when it lost in 1945 the defeat, for all its momentous consequences in ushering in the first majority Labour government, did not amount to an electoral debacle. The strength acquired in English urban, and particularly northern industrial seats after 1918 offered a good working base; the performance of the party in Wales seems to have improved slightly because of the favour that a 'national' appeal won with the

Nonconformist churches there;[3] and in Scotland, though the party had traditionally been weak in the face of an overwhelming Liberal or Liberal Unionist presence, the Conservatives strengthened through the interwar period to become a serious force by 1945.[4]

In October 1931 the administration formed out of the August crisis presented itself to the country and, on the largest turnout of the interwar period, attracted 67 per cent of the total vote, which produced 554 seats out of the 615 then available. Conservative candidates fared particularly well: the 260 returned in 1929 now stood at 473, much the best result for any political party in the twentieth century.[5] If this figure is set beside the 52 seats won by Labour, the extent of Tory dominance becomes clear. For those who had once thought themselves Labour people, it was a cruel moment. 'I sat in Downing Street until three this morning,' Thomas Jones wrote, 'watching the tape ticking the monotonous Conservative gains from North and South and East and West . . . I voted Conservative for the first time in my life and so did Rene [Jones]. We had to do it. "Labour" had to be thrashed, but it cannot be destroyed. We could not trust them with the Bank of England – just yet.'[6] The winning side also managed only two cheers – ominously – because there were those who found the entire spectacle of associating with MacDonald's Labour Party uncomfortable and unprofitable in the long run. '[I]f you will indulge in "National Governments",' the sour Cuthbert Headlam mused on the eve of victory, ' – by which is implied a union of totally divergent points of view – what is to be expected? How much better it would have been to have had a straight fight between Conservatives and Socialists and to have had the benefit of the inevitable split among the Liberals.'[7]

Acquiring the Liberal vote became an important part of Conservative strategy in the early 1930s. Not that the parliamentary Liberals mattered much any more: 1931 had decimated even the sad returns of 1929.[8] But over five million men and women had voted Liberal in 1929 and attaching them to the cause of the Tory or Labour party had an obvious urgency, which is one explanation for the National Government's solicitous behaviour over 'liberal' issues after 1931, especially the future of the League of Nations and the ideal of international disarmament. This urgency deepened after October 1933 when the remarkable Labour win at East Fulham persuaded Baldwin that the electors had punished the Conservative candidate for supporting a government that had allowed Hitler to leave the Geneva Disarmament Conference, thereby bringing the prospect of an arms race and war distinctly closer. Subsequent analysis has shown Baldwin's reading of the result an implausible one: the central issues at the by-election had turned on unemployment and domestic social concerns rather than internationalist anxieties.[9] No matter: the belief strengthened Conservative intentions to play the international card electorally and in a way that would most mortify Labour during its period of intense internal embarrassment about armaments over which the pacifist George Lansbury had presided since the split of 1931.[10] Opportunity struck in the autumn of 1935 as Mussolini eyed Abyssinia and Lansbury fell in flames at the Brighton Labour Party conference of September. Baldwin, who had succeeded MacDonald as prime minister in June, called a general election and rested the National Government's appeal on a League-based firmness about aggression, amplified by a speech of impeccable orthodoxy which his foreign secretary, Sir Samuel Hoare, delivered in Geneva.

The ruse worked so well that the results proved almost embarrassing when the constituencies declared in mid-November 1935. For all the impact of unemployment, which peaked in the winter of 1932–33, and the criticisms that had been mounted of the 'means test' when it was introduced in 1934, the Tory presence in the House of Commons reduced only to 432, against which Labour's 154 could still be seen as the recession of a flood tide to 'normal' proportions.[11] But the impression remained a superficial one. Labour had been made to fight under peculiar conditions of extreme difficulty. The possibility of compelling this situation to occur again receded once the Hoare–Laval pact of December sullied the stance taken by Baldwin for the election and ruined Hoare's career in the process. Germany's developing strength and the tactical finesse displayed by Hitler in his militarization of the Rhineland in March 1936 suggested that a 'national' government would have to move towards rearmament in a serious way without the cosmetic help of the League of Nations (a dead letter after the Abyssinian crisis). And it would have to do so in the face of a Labour Party that had become a party of aggressive foreign policy in the context of the opening of the Spanish Civil War in July 1936 and the emerging power within the party and trade union movement respectively of Dalton and Bevin. A good by-election record from Labour in 1938–39 sharpens the evidence in favour of Tory difficulty in the hypothetical general election of 1940.[12]

Because that election never took place, the durability of the National Government in electoral terms at the outset of the Second World War raises unanswerable questions. One way of framing the argument lies in rejecting the view that 1931 annihilated Labour at all by stressing the Labour vote (over six and a half million) rather than its seats and then going on to see 1935 as a qualified success on the same criterion (the Labour vote went up to nearly eight and a half million, its share of the vote up to 37.9 per cent).[13] The counter-view can enjoy other facets of the same data. The British system requires parties to concentrate their supporters in clumps rather than disperse them too thinly – the Liberal problem – or so cluster them that vast numbers vote redundantly to return a candidate whose success would be assured with a half or a third of such a number. On this basis Labour showed little sign of breaking out of the prison into which 1931 had led it. True, the by-election record for 1935–39 shows a Labour tendency; but the evidence from by-elections may realistically be taken to be worthless in this decade as in every other and written off as a protest vote against government rather than a potential vote for Labour in the next election. If it is not clear that the National Government would have won in 1940, it is not clear that it would have lost, especially if Chamberlain could have pulled off a Polish 'Munich' and revived some popular credibility. Seen in whatever light, the electoral evidence suffers from simple dearth. We have no systematic test of opinion after 1935, apart from primitive 'Gallup' information compiled in conditions quite unlike those of modern psephological practice and the results of a general election held in postwar euphoria and in conditions quite unlike those of 1935–39. What can be said in safety is that Conservative members of the National Government had no overwhelming reason to concern themselves over opposition threats and every reason to consider their grip on power secure in the wake of the August crisis of 1931.

Personnel

As the party had discovered to its benefit when Asquith had formed his coalition government in 1915, indispensability brings its own power that need not find a reflection in offices and status to retain its potency. Baldwin himself chose to lie low and take nothing more elevated than the Lord Presidency of the Council: his lesser men would need advancement to prevent them from 'kicking'.[14] Some got it. Neville Chamberlain's replacement of Snowden at the Exchequer perhaps signalled the greatest forward move by a Conservative and Hoare's securing of the India Office – a crucial location of policy in the wake of the Irwin Declaration of 1929 – not much less so. But, taken as a whole, the Tory occupation of power amounted to only eleven ministerial positions out of twenty, though one has to remember Gilmour's move to the Home Office that made way for Walter Elliot's very successful tenancy of Agriculture from the autumn of 1932 and Kingsley Wood's arrival as post-master-general (first step in a rapid rise) at the end of the following year. Self-abnegation mattered little since Conservatives could bide their time and wait for the world to come to them. Everyone knew of the 'National' Liberals' sense of unease within a government that teetered on the edge of economic protection. And when the Imperial Conference went in that direction at Ottowa in 1932, the resignation of Samuel's little group (and Snowden for whom free trade remained totemic), plus the non-appearance of Lloyd George's even smaller one, left the Tory presence undiluted apart from persistent 'National Labour' individuals such as J.H. Thomas, who failed to understand the Dominions with all the acuity he had brought to failing to understand unemployment, and Lord Sankey who held on to the Woolsack until 1935.

In many ways, indeed, 1935 proved pivotal in recasting the National Government into a more Tory form. That Baldwin would ultimately replace the distant and ill MacDonald had seemed clear at the inception. The problems faced by 'SB' had turned far more on his own party colleagues during the fight to displace him in 1930 – 'the year they tried to get rid of me' – and Chamberlain's premature thrust in the spring of 1931 that had left him in no doubt that he would remain number two until Baldwin went.[15] With MacDonald's resignation in June 1935, Baldwin was therefore free to construct his own Cabinet and since he no longer had to worry about Liberal interference, as in 1931, he constructed one closer to the Tory ideal with fifteen Tories of one kind or another out of a total Cabinet of twenty-two. There is a case for seeing the period from June 1935 to May 1937 as the peak of Tory ascendancy in ministerial politics throughout the period under review here. Before then the claims of Labour and Liberals made assertion impolitic; after then Chamberlain's inability to control the party, admittedly in the face of greater foreign difficulty than either MacDonald or Baldwin had faced, led to a degree of volatility within key positions – it was a good government from which to resign. When the war came, the return to power of Churchill via the Admiralty in 1939/40 heralded a certain degree of bulldogism in government; but Churchill knew as well as anyone that a national crisis made party prescriptions unwise. He had to settle for an increased role for the Labour Party without which there would be no government at all. This no more made him a creature of Labour than 1931 had made Baldwin a creature of MacDonald: one senses a certain implausibility in accounts that make Churchill sound like a follower of Attlee.[16] But total war demanded a total politics and Toryism was hardly that.

These shifts of weight inside what were in fact three working coalitions from 1931 to 1945 carried with them implications for party leadership, for all that they suffered mediation, as always, from the effects of personality and ambition. Of the three leaders, Baldwin exercised the most skill in holding colleagues together through a difficult and (for some) repellent experiment. He was already a veteran: case-hardened by the attacks on him in 1930–31 and long used, from his dealings with the pro-coalition faction in the party after 1918, to compromising over anything but strategy. His defeatist desire of just a couple of years earlier – to turn the country over to a protectionist basis and then clear out – had eased by the sheer pressure of circumstance that had made him man of the moment again. The rhetorical basis of the National Government, regeneration through wholesomeness, suited him perfectly because of his stress on 'service' as a virtue and informed the speeches sprinkled with morning dew and bursting with spring flowers, for

> one would not be a true son of the soil if one did not carry at the back of one's mind a hope that the day might come, some time, when one might be spared for a few peaceful years of life once more in that country in which one was brought up, to look out once more upon those hills, and ultimately to lay one's bones in that red soil from which one was

made, in the full confidence that whatever may happen to England, ... at any rate in that one corner of England the apple blossom will always blow in the spring; and that there whatsoever is lovely and of good report will be born and will flourish to the world's end.[17]

It suited, too, the granite that could only be seen in close-up. The editor of the *Guardian* (who had never met Baldwin) had the chance of an interview at the House of Commons in 1934. He felt at once the distance between language and persona once he entered the presence. 'Baldwin's face,' he wrote in his diary, 'seen close to, was most interesting':

> His face is rugged and nobbly; his right eye is either going wrong or has some sort of a cast in it and was mostly half-shut. But the characteristic of his face is its determination and shrewdness – or rather, because it is much more than shrewdness, a sort of deep rustic craftiness. More than any other politician he reminded me of Lloyd George in this, but while LG is gleefully and maliciously cunning, Baldwin seemed to me to look shrewd and crafty in a rather grim and hard way. I got quite a new idea of him and for the first time understood how he had come to be leader of the Tory party and Prime Minister.[18]

It was not an inapposite analogy. Lloyd George had faced the difficulty of holding together a coalition from a position of weakness. Baldwin did it from a far stronger one but the task required coolness and political 'touch'. In fact he faced little that was alarming when he lurked behind the scenes as Lord President. Trouble began when he became prime minister in 1935 – first with the embarrassment of Hoare's over-enthusiastic commitment to acting complicitly with the French in letting Mussolini have his way, or most of his way, in Abyssinia, then with the appalling constitutional mess surrounding the abdication of Edward VIII. Yet neither of these contingencies caused major problems of a party nature. Hoare had to be allowed (and then told) to resign the Foreign Office, 'a little inclined to bitterness', as Chamberlain obtusely observed;[19] but Baldwin smuggled him back again into the Admiralty within six months. Over the King, on the other hand, Baldwin panicked privately but kept up an impressive public facade of resolution and direction, supported by popular opinion and criticized only by romantic ranters of whom Churchill had latterly assumed the lead. The latter presented a third problem that undoubtedly did have a party flavour: Churchill loathed most of the current hierarchy for having flirted with protection, winked at state socialism and given away India. But his judgement had appeared so wild that he hardly represented an opposition of the kind his father had presented to Salisbury in the 1880s. By the time Churchill discovered Hitler (and that was far later than his memoirs would imply), Baldwin had retired and Chamberlain, nature's number two, had become a disturbing number one.

What did Chamberlain's arrival as prime minister in May 1937 do to Tory conduct of power? He brought to it a certain self-belief, a serious political intelligence and a history of bad luck – none of which need have brought him down. But power meant responsibility and, in one incapable of delegation, a consuming sense of personal intervention put politics on a knife-edge. Colleagues felt excluded and marginalized unless they were part of the inner circle: Lord Halifax, Horace Wilson, Alexander Cadogan. Those who counted increasingly helped with the construction of attitudes towards Europe. Baldwin's gentle urges towards a policy of realistic rearmament[20] combined with a basic pro-French position found little echo in Chamberlain's situation or his beliefs. A background in business and an ignorance of both France and Germany conspired to darken political horizons which Churchill in his most rampant phase of warning did nothing to lighten. For some Conservatives,

Chamberlain seemed little less than the new messiah as he prepared to make his first ever flight in order to negotiate with Hitler. Sir Henry Channon could hardly hold back the tears when he thought of all this bravery.

> Towards the end of the Banquet came the news, the great world stirring news, that Neville, on his own initiative, seeing war coming closer and closer, had telegraphed to Hitler that he wanted to see him, and asked him to name an immediate rendezvous . . . [S]o Neville, at the age of 69, for the first time in his life, gets into an aeroplane tomorrow morning and flies to Berchtesgarten [*sic*]! It is one of the finest, most inspiring acts of all history . . . I am staggered.[21]

For others the drift of policy and the personalization of power became insupportable as first Eden went over Italian policy (February 1938), then Duff Cooper over Munich. But one can overstress their significance and begin a process of 'joining up the dots' that will propel an historical narrative in the direction of May 1940 and Churchill's seeming deposition of a despised leader. In fact, had Chamberlain pulled something out of the hat in 1939, or had Hitler suffered more domestic difficulty, the story could have ended very differently. The end came not over the entry into war – indeed it is noticeable in the Gallup ratings how popular Chamberlain remained until at least January 1940[22] – but over the twin challenges of military failure in Norway and the increasing success of anti-Chamberlain groupings inside the party. The debates of 8–10 May brought these strands famously together when words were uttered that several generations of textbook have felt obliged to quote, partly for their drama but also because they supply evidence for a mood of Churchillian 'emergence' as a great national leader. It requires stress all the same the Churchill's immersion in 'Narvik' was potentially quite as damaging as his role in the 'Dardanelles' had been in the First World War;

and that when Chamberlain went he did so undefeated with only thirty-three Conservatives actually voting against him.[23] The reduction of the government's majority to eighty-one was accomplished mostly by abstention.

Churchill's history since 1935 had been characterized by public inflammation over German rearmament and the abdication, during which he supported the King. It had shown touches of prophecy; it had shown a good deal of flexibility. There had been as much effort to get into the government as there had been to terminate it. His fury when Inskip was preferred to him as Minister for the Co-ordination of Defence in 1936 is well known.[24] He saw virtue as a poor companion for impotence and probed ways to rediscover some political force within a party that he had grossly offended since his resignation from the Shadow Cabinet at the beginning of 1931. The events of August and September 1939 presented that opportunity; but in responding to them with his usual vigour and single-mindedness at the Admiralty he did not forget the existence of the Conservative Party and knew perfectly well that it held whatever future he had. Criticism of Chamberlain he studiously avoided. And when the crisis came nine months later he acted, as Sheila Lawlor shows in her recent monograph on the subject, with considerable sensitivity to the senior Conservatives around him and avoided deployments, when Chamberlain retired in the autumn, that might have antagonized orthodox Tories.[25] He reduced the size of the War Cabinet, out of strategic necessity, but ensured that the Conservative presence within what remained would fend off allegations that undesirable elements had been allowed to triumph and the prospects for the postwar party compromised. He misjudged, however, the nature and the force of public expectation, as we shall see. He reflected a 1930s confidence that policy could be insulated from public pressure, a view that the experience of the war had led others to modify.

Policy

Policy perhaps presents a more searching problem to the historians of the National Government than to its inventors. They groped their way forward. We try to find elusive (and possibly illusory) patterns in their groping. Tories had an ideology for national crisis drawn from the economic downturn of the 1870s, the threats from aggressors abroad in the age of imperialism and the experience of the First World War when they emerged as champions of British identity. They also had an emerging commitment, some of them, to an ideal of state involvement in the ills of society, plus a willingness to tweak economic controls when doing so seemed necessary in order to preserve an organic sense of social well-being. Together, these two forms of ammunition would give the National Government a version of Tory idealism for its speeches and policy pronouncements. Neither of them, on the other hand, predicted what ought to be done – a pressing matter once the election of 1931 had been safely surmounted. Two extreme views seem unpersuasive. One is that the National Government did nothing at all beyond mouth platitudes and allow the unemployed and the poor to rot. The other sees the coalition as an agency of mission, bringing a new urgency and shape of policy that would have important implications for the future, possibly laying the foundation of the centrism and welfare state of the later 1940s.

The latter view is the more recent and it echoes a sympathetic historiography that now traverses the twentieth century in finding something substantial in the claims of 'centre parties' to have adopted a genuinely innovative or creative stance rather than simply to have radiated compromise and muddle.[26] Seen in this light, the National Government appears to transcend party politics and move towards policy initiatives that no single party would have been able to attempt. We are to take seriously Neville Chamberlain's claim 'that this Government ... might fairly be described as revolutionary' and to reject '[a]ny accusation against the National Government that it had no mind, no policy, no spirit of adventure . . .'[27] And beyond rhetoric we are directed to concrete achievements – the importance of the agricultural marketing boards and Elliot's success in developing them; the willingness to do something for 'special areas'; the move towards state involvement culminating in what would have been the country's first nationalized industry (BOAC) had not the war interfered and deferred the measure. Yet the problems with this view do not easily evaporate in the face of enthusiasm. If Chamberlain sounded committed on the platform, he sometimes sounded far less so in private. If government interfered, it often did so to minimize its commitments, through the means test for example, and its measures had the same atmosphere of 'permissiveness' that has been pointed out in criticism of Disraeli's social measures.[28] Above all, those governed by the National Government frequently felt that its vision, where it had one, was bifocal: one law for the south and east and another for the hard-hit periphery. Even in the periphery we find a thoughtful and energetic MP like Robert Boothby (East Aberdeenshire) going to his constituents in 1931 armed with a poster saying only 'Vote Boothby. The Friend of All'. When it was suggested that the message sounded a little thin, he is said to have replied: 'Well, I don't have any policies.'[29]

Politics, as well as beliefs and commitments, has much to say about policy; and the peculiar structure of political power after 1931 did not make policy necessary even if it remained desirable. In the areas within which the National Government had swept the board, it sufficed to stand for responsibility, service, soundness. Excitement was at a discount and excitability implied danger. In those areas where unemployment and hardship called for a more radical response – South Wales, the industrial north of England, Tyneside and Clydeside – the population voted Labour anyway and would continue to do so whatever the Tories did, a point not lost on strategic minds in the Conservative Party. Of course the younger and more active wings of the party thought in different terms, especially if, like Boothby and Macmillan, they sat for constituencies that were socially deprived. But their responses took the form of agitation via the printed word or the speech or the private letter, such as this one from Boothby to Baldwin at the beginning of 1934:

> I don't share the views of some regarding the neces-
> sity for state 'planning' of industry, although I think
> that some guiding principles have to be laid down to
> enable us to deal with certain industries of national
> importance along modern scientific lines.
> But I do jib at starving the unemployed.
> And that is what it amounts to in some districts
> at the present time.
> If the Government is to prosper, the people must
> be given something in which to believe.[30]

Macmillan helped develop the Next Five Years group to apply pressure in this direction; indeed he went so far as to renounce the Tory whip for a time.[31] But none of this activity looked likely to sway senior politicians obsessed with India or foreign policy, who saw no great reward for making the effort and who in any case lacked an economic theory that would legitimate departing from time-honoured Gladstonian fiscal methods.

Of course one can argue that the economic theories of Keynes and those associated with him (or those advocated by Oswald Mosley) provided an alternative model on which the National Government could have acted.[32] But recent work warns stridently against treating the period before the final appearance of Keynes's connected ideas in *The General Theory of Employment, Interest and Money* (1936) as one in which the theory existed in all but name: we have to acknowledge a slow and painful evolution.[33] In Mosley's case, the appeal of a Tory defector, Labour minister and latter-day fascist was bound to be limited whether he had interesting ideas or not. Neville Chamberlain, chancellor of the exchequer from November 1931 until his accession to the premiership in May 1937, brought to his task all the orthodoxies of which the Treasury approved and his much-vaunted 'business experience' besides. He was hardly the man to inaugurate a revolution in economic policy. It followed that the combination of political and theoretical restraints would compel politicians to seek a way forward in palliatives to meet immediate difficulties. Tories compromised by, on the one hand, offering the Labour and Liberal elements of the coalition measures to help locate industry in 'special' (that is, depressed) areas and restoring cuts in unemployment benefit and salaries made in the emergency of 1931, while on the other hand means-testing benefits from 1934 and devoting what income they had to the escalating requirements of defence.

From 1934 onwards the centrality of this commitment made itself felt in all aspects of government. Following successive reports of the Defence Requirements Committee of the Cabinet, expenditure on defence reached 11 per cent of the whole by 1935, 30 per cent by 1938.[34] This aspect of politicians' activity bore a direct relation, moreover, to the opinions and proclivities of the (Tory and Liberal) electorate, unlike the question of deficit financing or unemployment insurance. Evidence mounted after the League of Nations, failure to eject the Japanese from Manchuria in 1931 that voters worried urgently about a future war. East Fulham became part, as we have seen, of that 'evidence'; but there was more. The Peace Ballot – an extraordinary canvass of public opinion about issues of collective security that reported in the summer of 1935 – reinforced the feeling that an overwhelming majority of the British public shared concerns about avoiding isolation and the risks of a new arms race, reinforced by the language of 1934 which among both politicians and journalists suggested a new tone of anxiety about the consequences of a possible air war.[35]

Politicians as divergent in their instincts as Baldwin and Chamberlain picked up this ball and ran with it: the former out of a fear that the party would be annihilated if it missed the groundswell of 'pacificist' opinion;[36] the latter because he understood better than most that inadvertent rearmament on behalf of a dead League of Nations was the worst possible outcome – either the country should head for determined and expensive armament production or it should explore the possibility of bilateral or regional pacts to reduce its dependence on building an army and airforce. Partly because of this clear-headedness, Chamberlain's role in defining how Conservatives ought to react to the threat posed by the Third Reich in league, potentially, with both fascist Italy and Japan would prove crucial between 1934 and 1938.

Until 1937 that contribution concerned cutting the army estimates proposed by the Defence Requirements Committee in order to focus on the question of fighter production which Chamberlain rightly took to be the first defensive priority. He toyed in the run-up to the 1935 election with a programme of rearmament that would go beyond anything that the National Government had so far attempted, partly to help the regionally depressed economy but mainly to turn 'the Labour party's dishonest weapon into a boomerang'.[37] This proved unsaleable and he slowly moved towards seeing the issue as one of accelerating the air plan so far as he deemed consistent with economic stability while simultaneously devising ways to renegotiate the Versailles settlement, which German conscription and the announcement of the existence of the Luftwaffe in 1935 had in any case abrogated, in such a way as to buy off the Germans with kindness, at least until the air defences in Britain reached better levels. From May 1937 contemporaries noticed a personality shift. Like many excellent subordinates who are too promising to be junior and too peculiar to be promoted, Chamberlain discovered as prime minister first charisma and then historic mission. He knew that he could save

Britain and that only he could. Politically this was interesting: it turned Tory leadership into something like a Gladstonian rapport with 'the people'. Chamberlain entered into a dialogue with his public over the heads of Cabinet colleagues, backbenchers, newspaper proprietors, carrying the masses with him in the cramped monoplane that took him on his visits to see Hitler at the Berghof, Bad Godesberg and eventually Munich, bringing home his piece of paper signed by the German Chancellor and making a public pact with his audience behind the cameras at the aerodrome.

Between 1938 and Chamberlain's fall in 1940 foreign policy acted as the medium through which Tory power and perception were mediated. The trying on of gas masks during 'Godesberg week' and the digging of trenches focused popular thoughts on the imminence of another war and reinforced the feeling that to countenance one would be disastrous. If Chamberlain had gone to the country in the aftermath of Munich it seems likely that, for all the discomfort produced in Britain by the Nazi *Kristallnacht*, the Tory Party would have been returned by acclamation. But the high-point proved short lived and once it became clear that Hitler had designs on Rumania and Poland and that his piece of paper was worthless – a judgement made long before the Nazi invasion of the rump of Czechoslovakia in March 1939 – then Conservative Party policy appeared hard to construct in face of an election that could not be delayed beyond 1940. On the one hand policy had to sound firm in replying to Hitler's provocations; on the other it had to reflect a perceived weakness in air defences and the prejudices of Tory 'society' in London. Of course there is some distortion in surviving evidence: we know more about wealthy and leisured people who frequented clubland, the corridors of Whitehall and Westminster than we do about provincial voters and what they wanted. But one does not have to read far in the diaries of Sir Henry 'Chips' Channon to realize how well entrenched the *ancien régime*, as he called it, remained. From his viewpoint Tory politics in the

National Government had become a Chamberlain question and nothing more, 'a one man show'. 'Should Neville collapse or die or resign,' he had written in his diary precisely one year before Chamberlain's departure, 'the whole National Government would cave in, for, excepting Edward Halifax, it is composed of comparative nonentities.'[38] This was nonsense, reinforced by the diarist's having fallen rather painfully in love with the Prime Minister, but it was influential nonsense which humanized the political world to make it look like the personal one reflected in Mayfair. Just one year later, as Churchill came into power, his future private secretary, John Colville, caught the same mood in a single sentence that could have been written in the Napoleonic Wars as easily as 1940. 'Rode at Richmond in summer heat. As I dismounted the groom told me that Holland and Belgium had been invaded.'[39]

Left to such people and underpinned by such outlooks, Chamberlain might have survived for a considerable period. He seemed to them in many ways an excellent leader: unemotional, steady, dependable. The growing opposition to Chamberlain inside the Conservative Party appeared by contrast furtive, backstabbing and unEnglish. Nor had any convincing alternative come to light before the outbreak of war. Churchill struck most observers as wild and self-obsessed; 'Shakes' Morrison, once a runner, had turned out a ministerial flop; Hore-Belisha[40] attracted anti-semitic attitudes but also intelligent criticism of his ability and stature; Samuel Hoare struck some as a runner of the other kind – one who would run for cover if the war-scares materialized.[41] Nonetheless it is possible to discern growing unease among Tory backbench groups in the spring and summer of 1939, both in the so-called Eden group (or Glamour Boys to their critics) and in the circles of Lord Salisbury and Leo Amery. The latter had his comical aspect: he behaved as though he wielded supreme power while in fact having none. But he voiced a significant Tory position during the Chamberlain government by emphasizing its 'national' or cross-party origins as a form of allegation. From the start in 1937 all Chamberlain had achieved (in leaving out Amery, of course) was

> a mere reshuffle dominated by no other consider-
> ation apparently than of giving the appropriate
> number of places to the representatives of the so-
> called parties ... That Neville should not only put
> a Liberal at the Exchequer [Simon] but a very par-
> tially converted free trader at the Board of Trade
> [Oliver Stanley] at a time like this shows a complete
> disregard not only of the feelings of the party but
> an even more complete lack of any real interest or
> understanding in his father's [Joseph Chamber-
> lain's] policy.[42]

The imperial critique came to little after the failure of appeasing Hitler by offering him colonies. But the 'party' resentment endured, especially when Salisbury, eldest son of the great prime minister, added his weight to the wide-spread anxieties over Chamberlain's leadership.

That form of Tory leadership and the conception of power on which it rested fell to the ground in the spring of 1940. One can stress personal incapacity as a wartime leader as an explanation for Chamberlain's fall. 'How I do hate and loathe this war,' he had written on the declaration of hostil-ities. 'I was never meant to be a war leader and the thought of all those homes wrecked ... makes me want to hand over my responsibilities to someone else.'[43] One can stress the Labour Party's indispensability to the changed condition of war and its insistence that it might consent to serve under an alternative leader – Halifax, perhaps, or more likely Churchill[44] – but never under Chamberlain. One can stress the ill-fortunes of war, leading to the humiliation of the Narvik expedition as the occasion for the final crisis. There is force in all these contentions. Yet ultimately Tory power suffered a gravitational collapse from within itself. Neither personal defeatism nor Labour pressure pushed Chamberlain into resignation so much as the sight of his own followers trooping into the opposition lobby and the recognition that he had against him not one kind of dissident faction but several. It was exactly as Beaverbrook, with his experience of crumbling Liberal power in 1916 behind him, had prophesied. Replying to a private call to 'come forth from your tent and put an end to the drifting, muddle and tom foolery of the present crowd', Beaverbrook pointed out the lesson of Lloyd George and Asquith and of Lloyd George's downfall in 1922. 'You will note that in every case the revolt that broke the Government came from within. The same applies this time.'[45]

The Churchill Government

From both a party standpoint and a national one, Churchill came to power not at the worst time but the best. The very severity of the situation he faced (and the vibrant language of reconciliation and cohesion that he developed in order to meet it) moved political argument to a new domain and closed the door on a kitchen full of unsavoury smells and broken crockery. It opened the possibility of doing three things. First, the Tory Party need not talk about politics at all: the priority was national survival. Second, if and when the war became more manageable, which meant after the United States came into it, the Tories could talk about the future rather than the past and attempt a reconstruction strategy *à la* Lloyd George which might give them a sustained period of postwar power. Third, they ought to be able to find an appropriate moment to stage a khaki election and capitalize on their tenure of power on the way to victory.

In fact only the first of these possibilities came about. The year from May 1940 to Hitler's invasion of Russia in the summer of 1941 proved the most perilous of the war. The Dunkirk 'miracle', the fall of France, the threatened invasion from Operation Sealion, the Battle of Britain, the

London and provincial blitz through the winter – all these life-threatening events focused the mind on national solidarity, apart from that of 'Cato', the pseudonymous authors of *Guilty Men* which reviled the memory of the National Government and blamed the Toryism of Baldwin and Chamberlain for the present crisis.[46] This was worrying for the future of Tory argument, but for the moment a pattern established itself of opposition remaining token and Churchill's personal popularity, which *News Chronicle* polls suggested remained very high throughout the war,[47] carrying the government through its minor tremors.The emergence of a new party, Common Wealth, led by a member of the Liberal Acland family, caused a popular stir in the later years of the war and won by-elections at Eddisbury, Skipton and Chelmsford.[48] Inside Parliament, however, Churchill faced only two votes of confidence and won both with enormous majorities. He concentrated almost entirely on the war effort, once he had settled the political regime during his first year, and left Labour colleagues, particularly Attlee and Bevin, to run domestic administration unless he deemed it to raise party difficulties.[49]

The second opportunity concerned reconstruction. In 1941–42 the combination of Barbarossa, El Alamein and Pearl Harbor put much writing on the wall about an ultimate victory for the allies. So when William Beveridge's report on future plans for social security appeared in December 1942 it did so against a background of real promise – throwing the document not only into newspaper headlines but into the bestseller lists. The party that made most noise about it was Common Wealth; but it achieved its platform largely by default because Tories failed to grasp their chance to look impressive. Churchill had once seen himself as a New Liberal, committed to state intervention for the purposes of social reform. Chamberlain at the Ministry of Health from 1924 to 1929 had shown how reformist a modern Tory might appear. Yet all that the Conservative Party could come up with after 1942 was the Butler Education Act of 1944, and then probably as a way of distracting attention from their unwillingness to come up with anything else.[50] Certainly some Tories wanted to go further in the tradition that Macmillan and Boothby had pressed before the war: the appointment of Lord Woolton, with his executive business background in John Lewis's, commented on a felt need.[51] The need to radicalize policy nevertheless failed to match the opportunity and the failure itself comments on a modern disposition to see the war as a time of emerging 'consensus'.[52] It seems striking in retrospect how little the Tory Party moved into the centre when beckoned there in 1943–44. And by hanging back it confirmed the bad memories among electors that the war had temporarily suppressed. It was a mistake and one that Lloyd George had shown them how to avoid in 1917–18.

He had won his khaki election. Churchill's Conservatives were crushed in theirs. Need it have been so? In order for a different result to have become plausible, the Conservative Party would have needed to appreciate more fully than it did that patriotism would not be enough and that Churchill would not be able to play the mascot as successfully as Lloyd George had proved able to do. Churchill held his popularity to the end; but the electors seemingly distinguished between him and his party. Circumstances, as well as temperament, conspired to keep Churchill out of domestic political leadership. He and Eden had little alternative from the autumn of 1943 but to concern themselves with the diplomacy of victory as much as the fighting. They were taken away from the centre of the domestic scene in the crucial meetings at Casablanca, Teheran and Yalta, so that when Eden, for example, turned to face the general election after the end of the European war he did so in a mood of depression and bewilderment rather than zest.[53] Nor could the Churchill coalition plunge straight into a vote-catching plebiscite: the realities of organizing an election and the determination of the Labour Party to prevent a khaki ramp meant that a 'caretaker government' had to be endured between May and the beginning of July which would give time for any nationalistic euphoria to subside and for the army vote to come into play. 1945 reversed 1935: this time the Labour Party determined when the election would take place and on what ground. If the results did not reverse the 1935 figures, they said all too clearly that a new political formation had emerged. The Tories' 213 MPs gave them their weakest return since the Liberals annihilated them in 1906. Labour's 393 rivalled the Liberals' total in that momentous year. The Liberal Party became a football team. Common Wealth and the Communists all but disappeared. Thomas Jones found his mind running back to 1886 for a perspective on the profundity of the shift as he counted seven coalminers in the Cabinet.[54]

The news of seats lost seemed unbearable through that black Friday in July. 'I felt that my entrails had been pulled right out of me,' groaned the Chief Whip;[55] and it was hard to see grounds for comfort in the short term. From our greater distance the question, why did they lose so heavily, continues to attract discussion and disagreement. It is possible to treat the Tory Party as a neutral backdrop and see the Labour Party as coming through on its own merits with a vision for the future that Conservatives lacked. But one can also accuse the Conservative Party of having lost to a lacklustre opponent through its own tiredness, through the effect of Churchill's war leadership and through the structural problems facing the party both in organization and policy. The scale of the loss can, in the first place, be overstressed. A swing of something like 13 per cent cannot be wished away; but the Tory share of the poll held at 40 per cent, which gave the party a firm platform on which to rebuild. And the fact that the party was to form governments continuously for thirteen years from 1951 to 1964 itself argues that reports of the death of Toryism may have been exaggerated.

Certainly much had gone wrong. Local organization had largely collapsed (to a degree that Labour's had not) and by 1941 many local associations had discontinued political meetings. Equally, we can see in retrospect that the constituencies struggled against a dearth of agents when the election came round in 1945. The much-vaunted supremacy of the Tory machine – silence but omnipresent in the twentieth century – did not operate on this occasion.[56] Churchill's view of wartime leadership hardly helped. It was not simply that he avoided party matters unless they threatened the stability of the administration, but that he failed to delegate dealing with them to someone with more time to think about Conservative difficulties. This fundamental problem spilled over into policy at a number of points, not only because Churchill arrogated to himself the right to make announcements of breathtaking shortsightedness, as in the infamous 'Gestapo speech' when he envisaged a future Labour administration operating a secret police, but for a more general reason that was to do with how the Tory Party was run and the place of the leader in formulating policy. As John Ramsden explains:

> The problem was that in the Conservative party there was no way of identifying party policy except through the pronouncements of its Leader; between 1940 and 1945 Churchill authorized no policy statements except those of his government. For Labour, with a constitution that defined party policy and how it was made by Conference the party could continue to develop party policy outside government.[57]

When we ask why the Tory-controlled governments of 1931–45 came to an end, therefore, we face a long list of possibilities from which the psychological cannot be excluded. As Ramsden suggests, the evidence supports a picture of the Tory electorate as one that wanted to be generous to Churchill, even after the election defeat, while feeling less so about his party.[58] Some voters appear not even to have appreciated that voting for the Labour Party would mean that Churchill could no longer be prime minister. The party, too, had shown lapses of realism, consistently failing to grasp the significance of electoral evidence that pointed to trouble after 1942, doubtless believing that the great war leader would somehow see them through as Lloyd George had done in 1918. Over 80 per cent of the electorate had made up their minds about how they were going to vote before the election campaign of 1945 got under way:[59] important evidence not merely for the unimportance of the campaign itself but also an indictment of Tory indifference during the war years. Labour reacted to events after 1940 with more flexibility than their opponents and in a more focused anticipation of the election that must come at the end of the war. Their success did not imply that they had conquered power for a generation; the Conservative vote and its standing in the Commons after the election hardly implied that. But it undoubtedly signalled the demise of a particular style of Conservative assumption that the National Government had embodied and in which the Churchill coalition had persisted, a style that future Tory governments would need to address and transcend.

CHRONOLOGY

1931	AUGUST 24	Formation of National Government
	OCTOBER 27	General Election
1932	SEPTEMBER 28	Reconstruction of National Government following resignation of Samuelite Liberals
1933	OCTOBER 25	East Fulham by-election
1934	FEBRUARY 28	Report of Defence Requirements Committee
1935	FEBRUARY 11	Second Reading of Government of India Bill
	NOVEMBER 14	General Election
	DECEMBER 18	Sir Samuel Hoare resigns as foreign secretary
1936	DECEMBER 7	Parliamentary debate on abdication crisis
1938	FEBRUARY 22	Anthony Eden resigns as foreign secretary
	OCTOBER 6	Parliamentary debate on Munich settlement
1939	SEPTEMBER 3	Declaration of war with Germany
1940	MAY 10	Resignation of Neville Chamberlain as prime minister
1942	JULY 2	Censure motion against government fails by 476–25

1943	MARCH 18	Parliamentary debate on Beveridge Report of December 1942
1945	JUNE 4	Churchill's 'Gestapo' speech on radio
	JULY 5	General Election

NOTE: This information is drawn mostly from Anthony Seldon and Stuart Ball (eds.), *Conservative Century* (Oxford, 1994), appendix 5.

Harold Macmillan and Lord Home
(*PA News*)

CHAPTER EIGHT

1951–64

John Turner

The Conservative governments of 1951 to 1964 were disparate in character, purpose and leadership. Characterized in 1964 by a soon to be triumphant opposition as 'thirteen wasted years', their period of office in fact saw a revolution in society at home and in the balance of power abroad. The party accommodated to these changes with reasonable competence and grace. By the time they were defeated in 1964 the Conservatives had succeeded in giving away an empire, very significantly expanding the welfare state, loosening the bonds of financial orthodoxy, and increasing the role of government in society while liberalizing in a variety of ways the social conventions that had held that society together before 1951. They had also begun a deliberate journey away from Great Power status and towards co-operation in Europe. Although little of this was what Conservatives at large had expected or intended in 1951, it had been enough to win two elections and almost win a third. It had also prepared the way for a Conservative electoral hegemony in the latter part of the century by nurturing a property-owning democracy in which materialist and individualist values were widely disseminated. Considered as an exercise in party government it must be regarded as a remarkable achievement in stacking the odds in favour of Conservative political survival.[1]

A New Start

The Conservatives returned to office in 1951 by an electoral technicality (Table 8.1). Their Labour opponents, despite an uncomfortable and demoralizing period in office after the 1950 election, had won a larger share of the popular vote than in 1945 or 1950, and a larger share than the Conservatives and their allies. Conservative advantage in seats had come about because of the first-past-the-post system, abetted by the collapse of the Liberal Party, which could no longer afford to put up candidates in sufficient numbers to split the anti-Conservative vote, and by the dominance of Unionists in Northern Ireland.[2] Although Conservative electoral revival in opposition after 1945 had been dramatic, there was no sign that Labour's support had been eroded by six years of government.

The Conservatives therefore had a governing objective in 1951. In opposition they had issued a number of policy papers which deliberately distanced them from their pre-war record. The *Industrial Charter*, by far the most ambitious of these, seemed to commit them to maintaining full employment policies, and being prepared to intervene in industry in the interests of prosperity and progress. Leading Conservatives believed that they had won the election because of an electoral rebound from the Labour governments, but Labour's shortcomings were expressed, even in party literature, in rather general terms. The party had, in effect, accepted the verdict of the 1945 electorate on Beveridge and the idea of a welfare state. It had little enthusiasm for the structure Labour had erected, but it had no intention of dismantling it either. A good deal of its rhetorical effort had gone to proving how it could deliver a better welfare state by using Tory methods. The target of building 300,000 houses a year, invented by Lord Woolton, the party chairman, on the hoof at the 1951 party conference and handed to Harold Macmillan to achieve after the election victory, was a good example. On the economy, much of the ground

TABLE 8.1 *United Kingdom Aggregate Election Results 1951–64*

	1951			1955			1959			1964		
	Votes	%	Seats	Votes	%	Seats	Votes	%	Seats	Votes	%	Seats
Conservative	13,718,199	48.0	321	13,310,891	49.7	345	13,750,875	49.3	365	12,002,642	43.4	304
Labour	13,948,883	48.8	295	12,405,254	46.4	277	12,216,172	43.9	258	12,205,808	44.1	317
Liberal	730,456	2.6	6	722,402	2.7	6	1,640,760	5.9	6	3,099,283	11.2	9
Other	198,966	0.6	3	321,182	1.2	2	254,845	0.9	1	349,915	1.3	0
Total	28,596,594		625	26,759,729		630	27,862,652		630	27,657,148		630

SOURCE: F. W. S. Craig, *British Electoral Facts 1885–1975*, Parliamentary Research Services (1976–1st Ed.)

had been cut from under the new government's feet by the recent flight from economic controls undertaken by Harold Wilson at the Board of Trade, and by Gaitskell's economical habits at the Treasury. The Conservatives were even unwilling to contemplate any but the most peripheral denationalization of public assets. Road Haulage was despatched back to the private sector, and then steel, about which the Labour Party itself had never been very convinced.[3] This left the party anxious to prove that it would not rock the boat and that it would be a better manager of the economy than the 'socialists'.

But the political fortunes of the Conservative Party were transformed by the experience of government, and their opponents in the 1950s were to be fragmented and demoralized by the experience of opposition. Just as the 1945 election had persuaded politicians that the electorate wanted much of what the Labour Party promised, so the election of 1951 confirmed in the minds of the new government the political importance of holding on to the middle ground. This was especially so if the Liberals threatened a revival. Churchill's government, in his 'Indian Summer', concentrated on maintaining a prosperity which at first seemed to be assured. The economy grew fast. Wage claims were a problem, 'solved' by the disposition of the new Minister of Labour, Walter Monckton, to settle disputes with concessions. Harold Macmillan as Minister of Housing and Local Government fulfilled the housing pledge. Physical controls were rapidly removed from the economy. The rest of the economic innovations of the Labour governments were left untouched. Butler even took over the Keynesian demand-management tools that his predecessors had used, and proceeded to deliver a series of budgets which progressively reduced the tax burden on the individual. His high point was the April 1955 budget which preceded the general election of that year; but within five months there was a balance of payments crisis which had to be remedied by emergency measures in the autumn.

The history of Conservative behaviour in government in the 1950s goes to the heart of the debate among historians about the postwar consensus. In the first phase, under Churchill, there was a clear political analysis, to which all leading ministers subscribed but many party activists clearly did not. This took the form of a rational calculation of electoral advantage. So many voters wanted the social if not the economic regime that Labour had left behind that any party which destroyed it would be defeated at the polls. At the same time, many voters, who liked the welfare state and believed that some nationalization was economically necessary, nevertheless responded to Conservative appeals to the values of liberty and enterprise. Moreover the party could always outflank Labour by appealing to patriotism and Cold War values. Conservative rhetoric, mostly for the benefit of the activists, was therefore directed to old-fashioned economic liberalism, while substantial Conservative policy, for the voters, was governed by the need to seem to be better than Labour at running the welfare state. This self-contradictory stance was easy to maintain in the good years of the early 1950s.

Leadership Troubles

Churchill's senior colleagues had been trying to get rid of him since 1946, but he had proved resistant: 'the strong wolf will retain his lead if his fangs are still firmly bedded in his jaws.'[4] His principal strength was an enormous public reputation. On domestic policy and electioneering his grip was weak, and he provided little effective leadership to the party in the final years of the Attlee administration: 'Mr Churchill believes that his own popularity and the mistakes of the Socialists are sufficient to win the Election, and that it is unwise to produce a policy in such difficult times.'[5] Eden was the heir apparent, and it was widely expected that within a year or two of the party's return to office in 1951 Churchill would retire in his favour. In June 1952 a group of colleagues pressed the leader to go, but without success.[6] The effort was repeated in December by Eden himself, again to no avail. In June 1953 Churchill had a major stroke, but Eden was in hospital at the same time. Churchill's position and Eden's succession were protected by arranging for Butler to conduct the government's business without the right of reversion, and Churchill was back at work in October. In June 1954 Eden was once again pressing him to set a date, but Churchill, remarking that 'I like the work', once more declined; Macmillan complained that 'All of us, who really have loved as well as admired him, are slowly being driven into something like hatred.' In the end it was Macmillan who led the campaign of attrition which overcame Churchill's resistance in the spring of 1955. He finally resigned in April 1955, though as late as February Butler was convinced that he still intended to 'run out of his engagement with Anthony'.[7] He left office in his eighty-first year.

Churchill's resignation was important to the party because it was essential to fight the next election with Eden as a secure leader. The election was planned for the autumn but brought forward to 26 May, because of the weakness of sterling and the threat to the balance of payments, together with the perennial difficulty of containing wage-claims. The Conservative share of the vote went up to almost 50 per cent, Labour's share went down, and the Liberals stayed at 2.7 per cent. Eden's style on the hustings was admired, even though an aide complained of his tendency to make 'speeches and even policies on the hoof'.[8] Not long after his triumphant return to office, though, it became apparent that in his style of leadership he was the least effective Conservative prime minister of this century and that the party he led was in danger of serious internal dissension for the first time since Munich. The most irritated colleague was Macmillan, who became foreign secretary and irked his master by perversely insisting on taking a major role in the conduct of external relations. In December 1955, after a protracted negotiation, the Cabinet was reshuffled and Macmillan sent to the Treasury, with Butler established as leader of the House and the tamer Selwyn Lloyd at the Foreign Office. The reshuffle did not satisfy critics in the party or in the press; nor did it result in a more harmonious or effective Cabinet.

Leaders and Followers

Lower down in the party, there were signs of discontent. Over lesser foreign policy questions, such as the handling of the nationalist movement in Cyprus or the withdrawal from the military base in Egypt, some activists condemned the leadership for weakness and lack of resolution. The dismissal of General Glubb from the Arab Legion in March 1956 was seen from the same viewpoint as a national humiliation. Over the death penalty, which was debated on a private member's bill in June 1956, it was clear that the rank and file did not share the generally liberal sentiments of the front bench. The immigration of non-white Commonwealth citizens had alarmed Churchill and Salisbury for its effect on 'the racial character of the English people', and many candidates had been challenged about it during the 1955 election. It was referred to a Cabinet Committee under Kilmuir, which decided that it was not a problem; and although most of the Cabinet and the party probably shared this view, the minority which did not was outraged by Cabinet complacency.[9] A much larger problem, because it concerned more people, was the loss of confidence by the rank and file in the party's ability to defend the interests of the middle classes. After the Tonbridge by-election of June 1956, in which Conservative voters had abstained in large numbers and reduced the majority from more than 10,000 to 1,602, an angry letter to *The Times* made clear that abstention

> is a wonderfully encouraging gesture from a class
> which, after all, refuses to be exterminated. For –

and let the Conservative headquarters be under no misapprehension about this – if we refuse to vote and thereby admit the Socialists to power, we allow a period of Socialist legislation which can later be revoked. If we permit the Conservatives to frame Socialist measures in their ill-considered bid for left-wing support, we are saddled with such measures for ever. Which is the greater evil?[10]

Many who thought along the same lines were persuaded to join one of two recently created groups, the People's League for the Defence of Freedom or the Middle Class Alliance. The appearance of these two groups disturbed Conservative Party managers, not so much because they represented any direct electoral threat as because their sympathizers were discovered to be 'good, solid, reasonable folk, with average middle class backgrounds', a category of elector on which the party had come to rely.[11]

The Fall of Eden

In the short term the government had yet greater evils to face in the Cabinet's handling of the Suez affair. The crisis itself is beyond the scope of this chapter, but its handling raises important questions about the rhetoric of Conservative politics in the aftermath of the Second World War. The crisis arose because Colonel Nasser in Egypt, already distrusted by British and American policy-makers, was denied Western financial support to build a dam at Aswan. He then 'nationalized' the Suez Canal and put it under military control in July 1956. Eden and most of his Cabinet looked back to the 1930s; they saw Nasser as the 'Asiatic Mussolini', and many of the failings and misjudgements of later policy flowed from this interpretation. Not only Eden, but also his colleagues were afflicted by the temptation to make policy by historical analogy. This error, compounded by the conviction that the United States would support the use of force against Egypt, dragged Eden's Cabinet to disaster. Collaboration with France and Israel was allowed to develop into a full-scale invasion scheme. In the end, reality broke in. The land attack on the Canal Zone was aborted when it became clear that America would withhold support for the British economy. Between then and the final withdrawal, announced on 3 December, the Conservative Party tore itself apart. On 9 January 1957 Eden, whose health and political credibility had both been broken, resigned.[12]

One must distinguish between the ensuing leadership crisis, which pivoted on the competition between Butler and Macmillan, and the collapse of confidence within a party suddenly forced to confront its illusions. At the top, the question was fairly simple. Eden's health, which had never fully recovered from the major operations of 1953, genuinely broke down under the stress of the crisis. He went for a convalescent holiday in Jamaica on 23 November, leaving Butler to chair the Cabinet and answer to the House of Commons while the government extricated itself from Suez. A particularly hard decision was to accept American demands for unconditional withdrawal before financial and economic support would be forthcoming. In Cabinet the leading advocate of withdrawal and submission was Macmillan, who had been at the forefront of the hawks until the ceasefire. In public, Butler took the blame from angry and humiliated backbenchers. Eden's absence was itself a source of embarrassment, and both Macmillan and Butler were convinced that he could not survive long as prime minister. Even so, they and their colleagues feared for the unity of the party if Eden resigned too soon under pressure from the right-wing backbenchers who were condemning his policy.

When Eden's doctors finally told him that he must go there was still no clear successor. Eden preferred Butler, though this was neither relevant nor widely known. When Lords Kilmuir and Salisbury polled their Cabinet colleagues with the famous question, 'Well, which is it, Wab or

Hawold?',[13] the answer was unequivocal, though not unanimous. Macmillan had made his mark with the back benches, in large measure by a deft speech on 22 November in which he had presented himself as a courageous and stalwart leader and allowed the contrast with Butler's circumspection to be seen by everyone. Butler was convinced that he had been plotting for some time, with Peter Thorneycroft among other members of the Cabinet, to seize the leadership. Cabinet colleagues, in their later recollections, said they simply thought of him as a man who could give a clear lead.[14]

Within the party Macmillan's accession was generally welcomed, but the crisis had opened wounds it was essential to heal. A few MPs had stood out against the use of force before the invasion, and were attacked in their constituency parties for disloyalty. A few others, centred on the right-wing backbench 'Suez Group', had long criticized the government for its weakness in relinquishing control over British bases in Egypt, and found further evidence of incompetent wickedness in the crisis itself. Within this strand of opinion there was nostalgia for an empire under threat, but also a strain of anti-Americanism which grumbled away as Macmillan tried desperately to repair relations with President Eisenhower. This all too open quarrel between the party's activists and their leaders in Cabinet spilled over into domestic policy; and a great deal of attention was paid in the following years to cultivating afresh the traditional Conservative voter whose interested had allegedly been overlooked in the rush to the middle ground.

Macmillan Abroad

The new Prime Minister had an active devotion to foreign affairs. Among his many memorable phrases were his appeal to the 'wind of change' in Africa and his constant allusions to 'the British as Greeks in the Roman Empire of the Americans'.[15] He was an enthusiastic traveller and a keen exponent of summit meetings between the superpowers. He also had a Grand Design for the world, in which Britain would act as a broker between the superpowers, lead the Commonwealth, and also take a leading part in a western European bloc. This occupied his mind (and his memoirs), but not all of it was of vital interest to the voter or the party activist. During the Macmillan premiership the main political issues to emerge from his overseas interests were the run-down of the African empire and the belated attempt to join the European Economic Community, both of which caused anguish within the party and at times threatened his control of the party and the House of Commons.

The 'special relationship' with the United States caused further party problems over foreign and defence policy. In general, Macmillan's governments were keen to cut defence expenditure. This process, which began with the 1957 Defence White Paper, attracted the hostility of the right, led after his resignation by Lord Salisbury.[16] Economizing on military expenditure led to a reduction of overseas garrisons, and thus to an imperial retreat which was itself divisive, and to an increasing reliance on nuclear technology that inevitably was American. By 1961 the British 'independent nuclear deterrent' was a warhead manufactured with borrowed technology, to be delivered by a wholly American missile system known as Skybolt. When the American government cancelled the Skybolt project at the end of 1962 Britain's embarrassing and even humiliating dependence was made clear. This further convinced the right wing of the party that Macmillan's pro-American stance was culpably unpatriotic, even though he was able to negotiate in return the British purchase of the submarine-launched Polaris system. On the other hand Macmillan's 'Wind of Change' speech in Cape Town, his vigorous defence of British interests at the United Nations, his efforts to negotiate a test-ban treaty, his intimacy with American presidents, his path-breaking visit to Russia and his commitment to summit meetings were all exploited in party literature and other propaganda. But it was evident all the time that successes abroad did not make up for perceived failure at home.

Macmillan at Home

The domestic policy of the Macmillan government has been vilified by the right for its failure to challenge the welfarist and interventionist consensus of 1945, and by the left for its failure to modernize the economy. But as one historian has put it, 'it made a better fist of delivering a combination of economic growth, cuts in taxation, full employment and low inflation than any of its successors'.[17] Moreover, it did so with an overtly political purpose, marrying economic policy to social objectives and aiming all the time to buttress the position of the Conservative Party. In this period the party organization was closely integrated in the governing process. As a result, Macmillan and his ministers were able to undo some of the damage to the government's relations with its committed supporters, and at the same time confirm to voters in the middle of the political spectrum that the Conservatives had far more to offer than Labour. An election victory in 1959, with 49.3 per cent of the popular vote giving a parliamentary majority of over a hundred seats, stood witness to Macmillan's success in 'bringing his Party back from the dead'.[18]

Macmillan launched his premiership with a radical review of public expenditure, implemented by the new Chancellor, Peter Thorneycroft, and justified with the blunt observation that 'the defence and social services, however desirable they might be in themselves, would be of no avail if the attempt to sustain them at unrealistic levels resulted in the collapse of the economy'.[19] After that, there was remarkably little disagreement about the direction of policy. Although the immediate financial context was the Suez crisis, ministers were also concerned about inflation in the long run. It was nevertheless not immediately obvious what should be done.

The reaction to Thorneycroft's initial proposals for expenditure cuts included the complaint that they 'would involve a complete reversal of the policy and philosophy followed by the Government since 1951'.[20] In a way they did. Macmillan had issued his notorious question to Michael Fraser of the Research Department:

> I am always hearing about the Middle Classes. What is it they really want? Can you put it down on a sheet of notepaper, and then I will see whether we can give it to them?[21]

The answer had been that the people who needed most help were those on fixed incomes: consequently the 1957 budget was generous in surtax remissions and much less generous to public expenditure, especially transfer payments to poorer members of society.

During a summer in which worries about inflation were capped by a sterling crisis, Macmillan and Thorneycroft brooded. The Chancellor's draft proposals for supporting sterling were drenched in political pessimism. He observed that the Tory Party might lose the next election anyway, and preferred to be remembered for 'being too tough in defence of what we conceived to be our national and imperial interests . . . The essence of my proposal is that we take steps and be seen to take steps which will limit the level of money available in the economy.'[22] This was not in fact monetarism in the modern sense, merely a firm commitment to protect the sterling reserves and limit public borrowing by controlling expenditure rather than raising taxes. Its logic led Thorneycroft to press his case on the 1958 Estimates so hard that his colleagues finally lost patience, and Macmillan had no alternative but to accept his resignation in January 1958, along with that of Enoch Powell and Nigel Birch. His disappearance from the scene made very little difference either to economic policy, which carried on much as before under Derick Heathcoat Amory, or to the political focus of ministers, who were ever more preoccupied with the long-term electoral consequences of their policy.

To sharpen their aim on the electorate at the end of 1957, Macmillan and Butler created the Steering Group, 'in effect an inner Cabinet group which met without the Cabinet Office staff in order to think out its strategy in a consciously party frame of mind'.[23] There was a constant tension in the group between proposals designed to improve industrial performance and proposals aimed at taxpayers and consumers. During 1958, after a budget which had been almost as deflationary as Thorneycroft had wanted, the condition of the economy was difficult to predict. The Treasury expected expansion to continue; the Prime Minister detected signs of a slump; the party organization was anxious about the morale of the middle classes. There were consequently at least three policy strands in conflict. In the end, it was possible to reconcile all three in the party's stance in 1959, but only just.[24] The policy adopted in the budget of 1959 was directed to short-term economic considerations: it was a compromise between Macmillan's expansionism and Heathcoat Amory's Treasury-induced caution, and Macmillan had the better of the argument. The government had begun to increase public investment in late 1958, and the budget itself cut purchase tax and income tax. The effect was to boost an economy which, as it turned out, was about to expand anyway, and during the autumn of 1959 there was a palpable feeling of well-being which helped to win the election for the Conservatives.

Longer-term political calculations were also being made during Macmillan's first administration. Michael Fraser advised that the first step would be to woo the 'hard core' of middle-class support for the party, and concentrate later on the 'margins' such as the newly affluent working class, in order to re-establish a favourable 'pattern in the public mind'.[25] This pointed to a more active government, with Macmillan himself anxious to assure supporters that the 'Middle Way' of combining freedom of enterprise with strategic control by the government was the essence of modern Conservatism. He also harked back often to unemployment in interwar Teesside and declared his determination 'never to allow this shadow to fall again upon our country. Even the social injustices suffered by a minority in the post-war period – and they are very real – are more tolerable than this major injustice'.[26] This was reflected in the tone taken by Butler, who noted at the very beginning of the process that 'We have to find a theme, which I feel should *not* be the "Property-Owning Democracy" but rather that of "Personal responsibility" '.[27] One interpretation of these developments, which is to some extent borne out by the evolution of policy later in the ministry, is that the defeat of Thorneycroft's bid to hold down public expenditure represented a turning-point in Conservative thinking, so that from this point onwards the party's leaders broadly accepted the proposition that the only way to make the country modern and prosperous was to invest in public services and industry.[28] Meanwhile party officials were worrying more about a middle-class backlash against various aspects of 1950s life, including taxation, immigration, and the consequences of inflation. The Cabinet had already noticed that their traditional supporters might abandon the government at the next election.[29]

In 1958 and 1959 it was clear that the government's policy was successfully wooing Fraser's 'margins' but doing rather less for the core. Party officers therefore spent a remarkable amount of time on tax, on pensions, and on the embarrassing decline in the value of the War Loan, into which many loyal and now ageing Conservatives had put their savings. These two matters dominated all other issues in the party's postbag during the 1959 election campaign, and figured strongly among voters' concerns in the Gallup polls.[30] However, this emphasis partly reflected the fact that the government felt it could do something about the problems, and was therefore prepared to talk about them in election broadcasts. Other concerns of the hard core were more difficult to meet. Many Conservatives were disquieted about the immigration of non-white people from the Commonwealth, a concern brought to a head by the Notting Hill race-riots of August 1958. For the moment this was fairly localized as a political problem, and the late 1950s in fact saw a slackening of immigration from the Caribbean. In 1959 Oswald Mosley fought Hammersmith on an overtly racist platform and took enough votes to suggest that his intervention saved the seat for Labour; it was a warning for the Conservatives.

In the 1959 election Macmillan's government achieved the near miracle about which he had been so pessimistic two years before. Much of the explanation undoubtedly lay in the sense of well-being created by the 1959 budget. Party enquiries also suggested that Macmillan's foreign expeditions, especially his attempts to broker a test-ban treaty, helped him in the public estimation. This was largely because they added to his stature, not because the electorate had strong views on the minutiae of foreign affairs. The voters seem to have been convinced that the Conservatives were maintaining Britain's position as a world power. Suez, if not forgotten, was forgiven. Much of this was fragile, because there were economic troubles ahead and some major embarrassments in foreign affairs, but at the moment of election all seemed to be going well. The government seemed just to satisfy the middle-class 'hard core', and the campaign was helped by disarray in the ranks of Labour and a particularly clumsy attempt by Gaitskell to promise improvements to the social services without tax increases to pay for them. The quality of campaigning was also changed by the use of television, on which neither party shone but on which the Conservatives had more money to spend. The party's political advertising was much improved, and its poster campaign – based on 'Life's Better with the Conservatives' and 'Don't Let Labour Ruin It' – was a model for future campaigns. The Conservatives were returned, having increased their majority for the third successive election – an unprecedented result in itself – and having done so from a very weak position in public estimation in 1957. It is likely that one factor in this increasing share of the vote was that the Conservatives were beneficiaries of a long-term shift in the class structure and class alignments of British society which had begun under their government and partly as a result of their policies. While this could not completely cushion the impact of an adverse swing such as eventually took place in 1964, it put the Conservatives at an advantage which they were not to lose for many years.

Nemesis

The pre-election boom proved too much for industries which had not increased their productivity to the same degree as their foreign competitors, and the result was over-full employment, pressure on wages, and the near evaporation of the balance of payments surplus. The bank rate went up. Consumer credit restrictions were imposed in April 1960. By the middle of that year the balance of payments, always a sensitive political indicator, slipped into the red. Heathcoat Amory introduced his budget in March but retired in July, disenchanted with politics and with his ebullient Prime Minister. He was succeeded by Selwyn Lloyd. For the next four years Lloyd and his successor Reginald Maudling struggled with the central dilemma of the Conservative government in the early 1960s. It had set itself up as the party of economic competence, but now found itself unable to prolong the nation's good fortune.

The government responded with three policies which, had they succeeded, might have been regarded in retrospect as bold, coherent and imaginative. Ministers and officials began to look at French methods of 'indicative planning', which Macmillan described delicately as 'a switch over to more direction'.[31] This became a keynote of the 1961 party conference, and the eventual result was the establishment of the National Economic Development Council (NEDC or

'Neddy') in 1962 with representation from government, employers and trade unions and the aim of drawing up a growth plan for British industry. The second strand of policy, parallel to but regrettably not connected with these discussions, was Lloyd's increasingly direct intervention in certain key economic areas. He increased the number of tools available for demand management by inventing the 'Regulators': powers to change tax levels between budgets. Scarcely were they invented, in the April 1961 budget, when Lloyd had to use them to curb a run on sterling in July. In the July 'Little Budget' he introduced the 'Pay Pause', a temporary restriction on the size of pay rises in the public sector. Although these interventions were not philosophically very different from the demand management of the 1950s, Lloyd was more obviously febrile in their use than his predecessors had been. The government appeared to be on the run in a hostile economic environment.

The third innovation in policy reflected the view that exposure to European competition would force British firms to become more efficient and competitive. Since the first meeting of future Common Market countries at Messina in 1955 it had been the government's policy to achieve this without joining the Common Market itself and without permitting the Market to dominate the European economy. Through the European Free Trade Area (EFTA), Britain would operate in a large free-trading community without losing the advantage of cheap food imports from the Commonwealth or the 'special relationship' with the United States. Soon after the formal establishment of EFTA by seven non-Common Market states in November 1959, it became obvious that this policy was not working. Britain's trade with the Common Market grew much faster than trade with EFTA, and still there was no sign that the six founder members of the Common Market would slow down their journey towards an exclusive economic integration. During 1960 the government tried to set up a special relationship between EFTA and the Six, without success. After eighteen months of futile negotiation, the Cabinet decided in June 1961 to make a formal application for entry to the European Common Market. In this step they were encouraged by the United States, which regarded the Common Market not only as an instrument of economic stabilization but also as a political bulwark against the expansion of Communism; and it is one of the ironies of British policy towards Europe that the American view of the cherished 'special relationship' was so relaxed. In 1961, indeed, the decision to apply for entry to the Six was concerned at least as much with a geopolitical strategy to contain Soviet Russia as it was with an economic strategy for structural renewal.

Economic Difficulties

Both in the short and the long term the government's attempts to repair the economy by domestic intervention proved futile and ultimately embarrassing. Lloyd's first budget, in April 1961 created a budget surplus, but was not tough enough or timely enough to curb a rapid growth in employment, prices and imports. The emergency budget on 25 July raised both purchase tax and bank rate, and foreshadowed a reduction in government spending, without increasing income tax or imposing a capital gains tax. Almost in the same breath Lloyd announced a Pay Pause, a standstill in wage increases to last until the end of March 1962.

The Pay Pause had a disproportionate effect on the government's fortunes. Economically it was of no great significance; politically, it was a major muddle. There were no powers of enforcement, so private sector employers ignored it. The electricity industry, though nationalized, agreed a settlement twice as high as expected in November 1961; and the only workers whose pay was genuinely held static were government employees such as nurses and teachers with whom the general public had considerable sympathy. The TUC and its member unions refused to have anything to do with it. By the end of the year there was a backlash in public opinion which led to by-election defeats, most famously in Orpington in March 1962. Lloyd's reputation was further diminished, and voters began to lose confidence in the government's understanding of the economy.

Another consequence of the Pay Pause was that the National Economic Development Council was tainted by its unpopularity. The establishment of the council was announced in the same speech as the Pay Pause, but the TUC, in protest against the latter, refused to participate until February 1962. Thereafter it moved at a snail's pace. The unions had joined on condition that they would not support any form of wage restraint, and this limited the policy options. The NEDC's first report, published in February 1963, became famous for declaring that a 4 per cent annual growth rate could be achieved between 1961 and 1966, without explaining how this could be done. No policy resulted, and what little there was of substance was hijacked by the Labour Party for its equally empty National Plan of 1964.

In any case the hope of sustained growth in an international market was thwarted by General de Gaulle's veto on Britain's entry to the Common Market, declared in January 1963. This setback was the culmination of a period of damaging internal debate for the Conservative Party. By embarking formally on negotiations for entry the party leadership had broken the crust on a seething pot of sentiment and commitment. The price of food alone presented three deadly traps. First, the party's commitment to subsidizing British agriculture was based in part on the realistic assumption that a subsidized rural society would return a lot of Conservatives to Westminster. Second, to move from a cheap food policy to a system which kept food prices higher than world prices would strike at the heart of the party's implicit bargain with consumers. Third, the terms demanded by the Six threatened agricultural imports from Australia and New Zealand. The Commonwealth problem led directly to another minefield for Conservative leaders. Disadvantaged New Zealand farmers were 'kith and kin' to some loyal Conservative voters and activists. A move that would damage their interests further inflamed the anxieties of those who regretted the loss of empire in Africa. Disquiet at the European policy was very widespread at constituency level as well as in some quarters at Westminster, even though the general public, especially Conservative voters, were consistently in favour of the application to join.[32] It hardly helped to explain that the move towards Europe was consistent with American policy, since that merely conjured up a latent anti-Americanism in the party. The result was that opposition to European involvement became a persistent theme of correspondence from the party in the country to Central Office from 1962 onwards. The fact that the government embarked on a policy of major importance relying on its own good judgement rather than the whole-hearted support of the party illustrates how easy it is for a government which has been in office for so long to retreat into the bunker. This was in many ways more surprising because the party had by now developed, through the Conservative Political Centre, a regular and efficient way of discovering what its members thought.

When the policy was associated, in timing and in logic, with other failing or controversial efforts such as the NEDC or the Pay Pause, it could only damage the government's credibility and power. That credibility came under further strain with the Orpington by-election of March 1962. The electors in this Outer London seat overturned a huge Conservative majority to return a Liberal, Eric Lubbock, with a majority of nearly 8,000.[33] Postmortem analysis within the government focused on two types of explanation. The first, short-term explanation was that the Pay Pause and the rest of the government's economic management policy were unpopular and had to be changed. This led in due course to the notorious Night of the Long Knives of 12–13 July 1962, in which not only Lloyd but also Lord Kilmuir (the lord chancellor), David Eccles (the education minister), Harold Watkinson (the defence minister) and a number of lesser figures lost their jobs and others, including R. A. Butler, were reshuffled. Reginald Maudling became Chancellor.[34]

The long-term explanation for Orpington rested on the realization that the social change which the party had itself engendered could not be taken for granted. Policies leading to fast growth, owner-occupation of houses, the expectation of increases in the standard of living, and a welfare state which claimed to shelter all citizens against most misfortunes, had interacted with socio-economic changes. The manual working class was smaller, two-earner families were more common, new jobs in new industries had created new skills, and new affluence had given many more people the experience of consumption and leisure that had hitherto been confined to the traditional middle class (and thus, for the most part, to Conservative voters). This had produced, in place of a traditionally understood two-class structure upon which political allegiance was grounded directly, a more critical electorate whose allegiance to the two main parties was less predictable. This had been noted as early as 1958, when a Conservative Research Department paper noted that the party was weakest among the age groups under thirty-five, both in the 'New Middle Class' and the 'New Working Class'. At that time particular emphasis was placed on making sure that the new middle class, specifically the lower middle class, did not slip away to Labour, and it was observed that in this group 'the Conservatives are generally regarded as the better technicians of the two Parties in the craft of Government, and whenever this view of the Party has been shaken we have suffered'.[35] The Conservatives' traditional emphasis on their own competence cut little ice when their economic management was clearly failing, as it had begun to do by 1962, especially for the more recently affluent. As a Conservative Research Department official noted in 1963 about the political consequences of 'the *embourgeoisement* of the proletariat', 'They . . . show an understandable dissatisfaction if the gains which they have made in recent years appear to be threatened or to be tailing off.'[36] Although the danger to traditional Labour allegiances was probably more profound, the main immediate effect was to expose Conservative governments to truculent discontent. 'The working classes will never submit to a return to the conditions of the twenties and thirties,' observed a junior minister in the autumn of 1962. 'They are different people now.'[37]

The Conservatives had begun to respond to these changes before the general election by launching such initiatives as the Housing and House Purchase Act of 1959, whose provisions for 100 per cent mortgages helped to 'manufacture Conservatives'.[38] Yet there was always a tension between such efforts to bring in the new political classes and the more traditional need to keep the existing middle classes happy by maintaining low taxation. In the aftermath of Orpington Macmillan tried to resolve this tension by radical measures, urging his colleagues to 'leap forward in the same kind of way and in the same kind of spirit that we should have done had we been now in Opposition instead of in power for eleven years'.[39] He believed that economic expansion was the only way to give the electorate what it wanted, but feared inflation as much as any minister. He therefore wanted the Cabinet to set up a coherent incomes policy with the theoretical justification and institutional underpinning which the Pay Pause had lacked, and 'a realization of the spiritual and moral issues at stake'.[40] This led to the National Incomes Commission (NIC), which was to rule on the acceptability of wage settlements falling outside the guidelines that were to be established by the formal incomes policy. The Commission, predictably dubbed 'Nicky' to go with 'Neddy', was boycotted by the trade union movement, and came to nothing.

Downhill All the Way

The political failure of the NIC coincided with a period of unusually uncertain and divided policy-making. Reginald Maudling, the new Chancellor, made cautious use of the regulators and finally announced a significant but rather slow-acting expansion in the 1963 budget. He ignored the NEDC until he wanted trade union agreement to incomes restriction as an anti-inflationary hedge. Meanwhile Macmillan, without taking very much interest in Maudling's policy, busied himself with speculation about a 'New Approach' to the longer-term future, calling for a transformation of industrial relations, a redistribution of economic activity from rich to poor areas, and steps to increase labour productivity. All this, and Neddy too, was played out against the background of the Common Market negotiations, a 'new direction for the country and for our Party', which Macleod and Macmillan hoped would help the Conservatives recapture the initiative after Orpington.[41] In fact there were yet further distractions at the end of 1962 in the shape of the Skybolt affair.[42]

The sheer number of simultaneous and inter-related failures towards the end of 1962 explains why the French veto on British entry to the Common Market, announced in January 1963, seemed such a major blow to the government. Indeed from then until Macmillan's forced retirement in October 1963 there was one convincing success, which was the signature of the nuclear Test-ban Treaty in July 1963. For the rest, the year was dominated by the Profumo scandal, which led to the resignation of Jack Profumo, the minister for war, but not, as even some Conservatives hopes, to the fall of the prime minister or even the government.[43] The affair, which seemed to reveal Macmillan's complete loss of grip on the political significance of his colleagues' real or alleged behaviour, aggravated this concern. Conservatives began to talk in July about the need for Macmillan to step down, and by the end of September he was almost ready to go. Just before the party conference which opened on 8 October he decided, with the qualified support of his Cabinet, to stay on. Between that decision and the time of the leader's speech to the conference on 10 October he was struck down by a prostate illness; he decided on 8 October to step down before the election, told the Queen of his decision on the 9th, and had his prostate gland removed on the 10th. Within hours of his resignation announcement being read to the conference by Lord Home on the afternoon of the 10th, the Conservative leadership had begun a self-destructive pantomime which discredited not only a number of the most prominent contenders but also the process of selection itself.

Macmillan's main concern from the beginning seems to have been to prevent Butler from succeeding him. Probably his own first choice was Hailsham, then the Party Chairman, who was soon to be able to set aside his peerage under legislation forced through by Anthony Wedgwood Benn.[44] Hailsham destroyed his own chances by showing himself off at the conference in a blatant bid for office. By his own account he was out of consideration within twenty-four hours, though the campaign by his supporters actually went on much longer and made considerable headway against Butler, who was at first regarded as the principal contender. The other known serious candidates were Maudling, Macleod and perhaps Heath. Macmillan insisted on a four-part straw poll being taken before he would make a recommendation to the Queen, and it was therefore among the parliamentary party, the Conservative peers, the Cabinet, and the Executive of the National Union (about 150 people representing the party in the constituencies), that the battle for favour was fought. Until 16 October it was not known that Home regarded himself as a candidate, and his Cabinet colleagues thought that he had eliminated himself from consideration on the Tuesday before Macmillan's announcement by declaring that 'in no circumstances am I a candidate'.[45] The intervention of Selwyn Lloyd and others, not apparently at Macmillan's instigation, convinced Home to offer himself as a candidate, and when this was known the effect on the straw polls was remarkable. Largely because both Butler and Hailsham had passionate enemies as well as staunch friends, Home emerged as the favourite of all the polls except that of the constituency associations, who were barely aware that he was a candidate. Macmillan, greatly relieved, resigned peacefully and recommended Home to the Queen.[46]

The backlash severely damaged Cabinet morale. Although most of the Cabinet and all the former contenders agreed to serve under Home, Ian Macleod and Enoch Powell, who had both in the end been strong supporters of Butler, declined his approaches. Macleod, who became editor of the *Spectator*, eventually published his account of the affair in its pages, and the subsequent row led to the preparation by Humphry Berkeley of a method for the open election of the Conservative leaders which was intended to avoid the accusations of a corrupt deal by the 'Magic Circle' of grandees. In the shorter term it left the Conservative Party to be led by a man who was relatively unfamiliar to the general public, whose capacities in domestic policy were completely unknown, and who had never held a frontbench position in the House of Commons.

Twilight and RPM

One of the justifiable complaints against Macmillan's final year as premier was that he was hanging on too long to enable a successor to be chosen in time for the next election, which had to be held before the autumn of 1964. The manner of his going could not alter the onward march of the calendar: Sir Alec Douglas-Home would have to go to the country within twelve months. There was, in fact, little for him to do except set about fighting an election. At home the administration had few notable legislative measures ready to bring forward. Abroad the Test-ban Treaty had already been accomplished. The final months of the government were therefore dominated by a protracted election pseudo-campaign in which Douglas-Home was pitted against Harold Wilson. In this he was doubly unfortunate. The Labour challenge in the 1950s had been distinctly weakened by Gaitskll's personality and the leadership style which had divided the opposition between a right-wing leadership and a motley of more left-wing backbench and out-of-doors groups. Harold Wilson, who won the leadership after Gaitskell's sudden death in January 1963, was everything that the Conservatives had feared in a Labour leader: he was young and witty, and he was able to unite the party temporarily and present it to the voters as a modern organization. Macmillan, who had contrived to make the best of invidious comparisons between his age and President Kennedy's youth, might have managed him; Douglas-Home, in the last resort, could not. Nevertheless the new leader's lowest Gallup poll ratings were higher than the highest Macmillan had enjoyed since 1961.

The last months of the government were dominated by a single policy issue which illustrated the tension between short-term political management and Conservative concerns about the economic health of the country. The issue was Resale Price Maintenance, the set of contractual arrangements which enabled manufacturers to fix the price at which their products were sold to consumers. Resale Price Maintenance had first been targeted by Harold Wilson as President of the Board of Trade in the last Labour government. Nothing had been done about it in the intervening period, though the government had made tentative moves in other areas of competition policy. The reason for hesitation was clear: the principal sufferers from reform would be small manufacturers and small shopkeepers, whom Conservative party managers believed to be very influential in local associations. The issue had been popular among progressive Conservatives throughout the 1950s, and the outline of legislation had been prepared by the Board of Trade.

The new president, Edward Heath, took it up when a private member's bill from Labour forced it on to the agenda in January 1964. Resale Price Maintenance began to cause trouble before it even reached the Commons. In Cabinet both the Chief Whip, Martin Redmayne, and the Party Chairman, Lord Blakenham, opposed it passionately. So did Butler, Selwyn Lloyd and some lesser lights. Heath simply refused to give in, and was supported by Douglas-Home, who understandably regarded him as the minister most likely to deliver a modernization policy. When the issue reached the Commons there was a furious response from the Conservative back benches against what they perceived as attacks on 'the little man'. In one critical division (the 'Chemists' amendment' on 24 March 1964) the government won by only one vote. In some measure this was a consequence of Heath's personal rigidity as well as the unpopularity of the policy among Conservatives, but it reflected the huge difficulty faced by a man whose principal mission was to modernize the party.

With the election campaign proper the party was finally plunged into the debate about 'modernizing Britain' which Macmillan had seen coming in 1962. The terms of debate set by the opposition enabled Labour to take advantage not only of the faltering economic position, in which the effects of Maudling's expansionist 1963 budget were being seen in the balance of payments and in share prices, but of the absence of action on key areas of change which the Conservatives had identified after Orpington but not, in the event, done much about. The party was trailing in the opinion polls and had suffered even in the friendly press, partly because of the wobbles in economic management and partly because the leadership contest had divided the normally Conservative newspapers. The Beaverbrook papers (led by the *Daily Express*) were hostile because of their proprietor's antagonism towards the Common Market policy; Rothermere's papers (led by the *Daily Mail*) had been urging that it was 'time for a change' since 1962. Nevertheless, it would be quite wrong to over-explain the ultimate defeat of the party in 1964, simply because the margin of Labour's victory was so narrow. At the end of an exceptionally fierce campaign which both sides tried to portray as a critical election for Britain's emergence into the modern world, Labour polled 12.2 million votes to the Conservatives' 12 million, and returned to office with a majority of nineteen over the Conservatives and their allies but only four over all parties combined. In a poll which was 200,000 less than that of 1959, the Conservatives had lost one and three-quarter million votes, almost exactly as many as the Liberals gained; and Labour had lost eleven thousand. If not quite the sort of electoral technicality which had brought the Conservatives in, this was hardly a catastrophic defeat.

The Reckoning

In with a whimper, out with a whimper, the Conservatives had achieved much in their years of office, even if they had failed in much of what they had set out to do. Their success was based firmly on their ability to govern, but this was not limited to short-term economic management. They had seen the effects of affluence and the new class structure and structure of aspirations which it created. At the centre of the party, for most of the time, this knowledge was used to shape policy. It was a Conservative aspiration to create a society whose values would support the return of Conservative governments, and by emphasizing prosperity and property ownership to ensure that those values were embedded in the very fabric of society.

This insight was not vouchsafed to all Conservatives all of the time. From 1951 to 1955 there was little concern for the long-term consequences of policy, and Butler's handling of the economy was insouciantly directed at putting more money in the housewife's purse. After the crisis of September 1955 there was always a contest between advocates of expansion and advocates of a balanced budget, with victory generally going to the side adopted at any given time by the Prime Minister. Politically the objective was to protect the interests of established Conservative voters and add to their number wherever opportunity presented itself. There were, however, two other strands of policy. One reflected both an acceptance of the implications of the welfare state and a willingness to use public expenditure, whether in social services, transfer payments, or public investment, to modernize the country and thus escape from a cycle of relative decline. This policy was linked, both in logic and in personnel, to the approach to the European Common Market, coupled with a willingness to accept (albeit without enthusiasm) some diminution of Britain's imperial possessions and global status. This combination was the policy of Macmillan and, to an extent, of Home. Churchill or Eden, significantly, rejected the European element and would have been uncomfortable with the pace of decolonization. Throughout the Macmillan and Home premierships, various elements of it were opposed by different factions of the party, and there was thus always some measure of Conservative disunity; but the direction taken by the leadership was rarely in doubt. It was largely driven by the belief that for a growing proportion of the electorate economic policy, specifically the impact of that policy on personal and family prosperity, was, in the words of Iain Macleod, 'probably more important than all other subjects put together'.[47] At the end of its period of office it was discussing a programme of social welfare and economic reform which might have rivalled European Christian Democrat programmes in the later 1960s.[48] Macmillan was a radical leader who sometimes had difficulty in persuading his Cabinet, let alone the rest of the party, that considerations such as these were more important than the protection of the empire, the church, family life or the privileges of the old middle classes, all of which were of critical importance to one section or another. He tended to get his way by persuading the party and some of the electorate that he was in fact preserving the empire and British greatness, but by the end the Conservative Party under his leadership was conserving very little except the nation's illusions. In this way he began a tradition of Conservative leadership which was continued (with different illusions) by Heath and Thatcher.

The party itself had changed during the period of government, but more in central organization than at Cabinet level or at the grass roots. Conservative activists were still very largely the 'good, solid, reasonable folk, with average middle class backgrounds' who had once been regarded as the backbone of the Conservative vote. They had not changed much since the 1930s, though the voters had. In fact the most significant steps towards modernization of the party organization had taken place in the period of opposition from 1945 to 1951. On the one hand the Maxwell-Fyfe reforms adopted in 1948 had 'democratized' candidate selection procedures to the very limited extent that candidates were no longer allowed to contribute more than £25 to local party funds, and that local associations were required to collect subscriptions from local supporters. The new candidate selection methods did not immediately change the social background of candidates selected, though they probably allowed a few of the more able but impoverished members of the professional classes to get into Parliament. The process of selection remained with the local associations. Despite the effect of Central Office's list of approved candidates, the associations remained markedly reluctant to select women, trade unionists or non-Anglicans.[49] On the other hand Lord Woolton, as party chairman from 1946 to 1955, built upon the requirement to get funds from individual subscriptions to launch a drive for membership which saw national party membership at its peak in the early 1950s.[50]

Members brought funds through constituency quota payments to the central organization, but the greater part of the party's income was raised from individual wealthy supporters through a Central Board of Finance and from business, both through the organization known as British United Industrialists and by direct requests from senior party officers to major companies.[51] The party was thus enabled to spend on organization, with help given to poorer constituencies, on exploitation of television, and on advertising.[52] Much of this effort was directed to the sectors of the electorate that were considered volatile, such as the newly affluent skilled working class, and in this way the central party organization was able to communicate with an audience which traditional organization simply did not reach. The importance of mass organization had thus shifted somewhat from that prevailing at the turn of the century: the purpose of the Conservative Party in the country was largely to raise funds, and to a lesser extent to give the leadership information, through the work of the Conservative Political Centre, about grassroots opinion; the party itself was less concerned with raising political consciousness through its own agency.

The Conservative Party's period of dominance was temporarily interrupted in 1964. It did not come to an end, because most of the conditions which had established it were still in place, and it had, after all, retained 43.4 per cent of the vote to Labour's 44.1 per cent. The proximate reason for the temporary interruption was a loss of votes to a resurgent Liberal Party. The explanation given for this by Conservatives, especially by the party managers who had been following the issue avidly since the mid-1950s, was that the party was not completely succeeding in its appeal to new classes of voter who were expecting the pace of change and material improvement to be maintained. These voters – the 'Orpingtonians', as Macmillan called them – were not automatic converts to Labour, and the intervention of the Liberals as a third party of protest, rather than as inheritor of any distinctive political traditions of its own, enabled them to find a voice which in the event unseated the Conservative government.[53] The Conservatives' policy direction was somewhat inchoate, but scarcely more so than that of its principal opponents. The image of the leader was also a mixed indicator. Since Kennedy entered the White House Conservative leaders had been obsessed with the contrast between opposition youth and Conservative age. The succession of Home, who was just as closely associated with the grouse moor as Macmillan but lacked his predecessor's obvious intelligence and sense of irony, might have been expected to damn them forever in comparison with Harold Wilson. In the event, though, the electoral contrast between 'Smart Alec and Dull Alec' did not redound exclusively to Wilson's credit.

Other factors purporting to explain Conservative defeat are harder to pin down. The party had been visibly disunited in Macmillan's last year, and was further riven by Resale Price Maintenance; but disunity is a relative term, and the party was far worse afflicted by Suez, by the India question under the National Government in the 1930s, or by tariff reform before and after the First World War. With this disunity came press calls for a change of leadership and a change of government. The party was not in favour with the journalists of the new media, or with the intellectual leaders of the early 1960s: it was unmistakably associated with the 'Establishment' (Anthony Sampson's *Anatomy of Britain*, which elaborated the idea, was first published in 1962); it was lampooned on the television programme *That Was The Week That Was* by David Frost in the now unfamiliar role of iconoclast; and the government made itself ridiculous in the eyes of the literate classes by prosecuting the publishers of *Lady Chatterley's Lover* for obscenity in 1962. The party was so nervous of its reputation in the universities that after defeat it sent some of its leaders on a series of dinner raids on senior common rooms across the land.[54] Local organization in the early 1960s was feebler than in the early 1950s, but not completely ruined, and in any case had partly been superseded by new forms of communication. The party was not drastically limited in its activities by severe shortage of money, though it could always have

TABLE 8.2   *Gallup Poll Reports on Voting Intentions,*
1951–64

'If there were a General Election tomorrow,
how would you vote?'

		Cons	Labour	Liberal	Other	Don't Know
1951	March	43½	33½	7½	1	14½
	June	42	36	9	1	12
	September	49	39	10½	1½	–[1]
	December	43	41½	6	½	9
1952	March	37½	43½	9	1	9
	June	38	45½	9	1	6½
	August[2]	37	44	6	5	8
	December	39	40	8½	1	11½
1953	March	44	41½	2½	–[3]	12
	June	43½	42	2	–[3]	12½
	September	39	42	6	1	12
	December	42	43	2	–[3]	13
1954	March	41	40	6½	½	12
	June	39½	41½	6	½	12½
	September	38	43	7	1	11
1955	January[4]	40	39	6	1	14
	April[5]	40½	38	7	½	13
	July	42	38½	8	½	11
	October	40	39	7	1	13
1956	January	40	41	6½	½	12
	April	35½	39½	6½	1	17½
	July	36	41½	7	1	14½
	October	36	40	8	1	15
1957	January	39	43½	6	1	10½
	April	34½	42	6	1	16½
	July	35	41½	6½	1	16
	October	31	41	11	½	16½[6]
1958	January	35	40	8	1	16
	March[7]	29½	41	16	–[8]	13½
	July	34½	37½	14½	½	13
	October	36½	35½	11	–[8]	17

		Cons	Labour	Liberal	Other	Don't Know
1959	January	37	36½	7	½	19
	April	38	38	8½	1½	14
	July	38½	35	10½	½	15½
1960	January[9]	39	35	8	1	17
	April	39	35	8½	½	17
	July	39	36½	9	1	14½
	October	40	34	9	1	16
1961	January	36½	33½	10	1	19
	April	35½	33	12½	1	18
	July	36	34	11½	½	18
	October	37	37	10½	1	14½
1962	January	34½	34½	12	½	18½
	April	29½	36	21½	1	12
	July	30½	34	19	1	15½
	October	34	36	16	1	13
1963	January	30	44	17	1	8
	April	30½	44½	14½	½	10
	July	29½	45	11½	1	13
	October	31	42	14½	1½	11
1964	January	35	45½	9½	½	9½
	April	34½	44½	11	½	9½
	July	37	46½	8	½	8
	September/ October	40	45	8	½	6½

SOURCE: George H. Gallup (ed.), *The Gallup International Public Opinion Polls: Great Britain, 1937–1975* (Random House, 1977).

NOTES:
[1] Don't knows excluded from this survey
[2] No election question in September survey
[3] 'Liberal & other' was the choice presented.
[4] No survey in December 1954
[5] No election question in March survey
[6] 'Wouldn't vote' included in this category in this survey
[7] No election question in April survey
[8] Not shown in this survey
[9]The September and October surveys included daily fieldwork during the election, and no election questions were asked in November or December so those months have been omitted.

used more. One must, however, question whether any of this was a cause of their defeat. Indeed, as Table 8.2 suggests, the party was in fact getting *more* popular as the election approached.

Perhaps the historian should turn to a more holistic, or perhaps ecological explanation of the fate of the Conservatives in 1964 after their years of supremacy in the 1950s. The party existed in a political environment which was constantly changing, and in order to survive it had to change itself. This process of adaptation was the mark of its political success. Often it was able to change the external environment in order to protect its own interests, and the Macmillan government was particularly successful in this endeavour. But sometimes external change was too fast, and the party's response slightly too slow or indecisive to bring complete success. The year 1964 was one of these occasions, but it was not by any means the end of the party's dominance of postwar British politics.

CHRONOLOGY

1951	OCTOBER 23	Conservative victory with 321 seats to Labour's 295
1952	JANUARY 29	R. A. Butler announces further NHS cuts
	OCTOBER 10	Butler warns party conference not to call for unnecessary spending cuts
1953	MARCH 17	Iron and Steel Denationalization Bill passes the Commons
	JUNE	Churchill suffers a stroke (concealed from the public)
	NOVEMBER	White Paper on Commercial Television published
1954	FEBRUARY 25	Nasser seizes power in Egypt
	JUNE 29	'Potomac Charter' reiterates special relationship between USA and Great Britain
	JULY	'Suez Group' forms in the party to resist withdrawal from Egyptian bases
	OCTOBER 7–9	Butler at party conference prophesies that living standards will double in the next 25 years
1955	APRIL 5	Churchill retires, succeeded by Eden
	MAY 26	General election: 345

		Conservative, 277 Labour, 6 Liberals, 2 Sinn Fein
	OCTOBER 26	'Pots and pans' supplementary budget increases purchase tax by one fifth
	DECEMBER 20	Cabinet reshuffle: Butler becomes Lord Privy Seal, Macmillan to Treasury, Selwyn Lloyd to Foreign Office
1956	MARCH 2	Glubb Pasha dismissed from command of Arab Legion in Jordan
	APRIL 17	Macmillan introduces Premium Bonds in budget
	JUNE 7	Tonbridge by-election: Cons. majority reduced from 10,196 to 1,602
	JULY 26	Nasser nationalizes the Suez Canal
	NOVEMBER 5	Invasion of Egypt begins
	NOVEMBER 7	Ceasefire in Egypt
1957	JANUARY 9	Eden resigns: Macmillan succeeds as prime minister
	MARCH 6	Ghanaian independence inaugurates decolonization in Africa
	APRIL 4	Defence White Paper
1958	JANUARY 6	Thorneycroft, Birch and Powell resign over Estimates crisis

	AUGUST 30– SEPTEMBER 7	Race riots at Notting Hill
	OCTOBER 8–11	Party conference attacks front bench for laxity about immigration
1959	APRIL 7	Budget cuts taxes by £350m
	MAY 7	Conservative gains in local elections
	OCTOBER 8	General election: 365 Conservative, 258 Labour, 6 Liberal, 1 Independent Conservative
	NOVEMBER 20	European Free Trade Area formally established
1960	FEBRUARY 3	Macmillan's 'Wind of Change' speech in Cape Town
	APRIL 13	'Blue Streak' missile abandoned in favour of Skybolt
	MAY 12	Large Conservative gains in local elections
	JUNE 23	Bank rate rises to 6 per cent; credit restricted
	JULY 27	Amory succeeded as chancellor by Selwyn Lloyd
1961	MARCH 7	Lord Salisbury criticizes pace of decolonization
	JULY 25	Pay Pause announced
	JULY 31	Application to EEC announced in Commons

	NOVEMBER 1	Commonwealth Immigrants Bill introduced
1962	FEBRUARY 8	National Economic Development Commission (NEDC) established
	MARCH 14	At Orpington, Eric Lubbock turns 14,760 Conservative majority into 7,885 Liberal majority
	MAY 10	Heavy Conservative losses to Liberals in local elections
	JULY 13	'Night of the Long Knives' Cabinet reshuffle
	JULY 26	National Incomes Commission announced
	DECEMBER 21	Skybolt cancelled, replaced by Polaris
1963	JANUARY 14	De Gaulle announces French veto on Britain's EEC application
	JANUARY 24	NEDC announces 4 per cent growth rate target
	MARCH 22	Profumo denies 'impropriety' in relationship with Christine Keeler
	APRIL 3	Maudling announces expansionary budget
	JUNE 21	Denning enquiry set up after Profumo admits lying to the House

	August 5	Test-ban Treaty signed
	October 10	Macmillan's intention to resign announced
1964	March 10	Resale Price Maintenance Bill only passed because of Labour abstention
	April 9	Home announces that the election will be held in the autumn
	October 15	General election: Conservative 304, Labour 317, Liberal 9

Edward Heath, Margaret Thatcher, Geoffrey Howe
(*PA News*)

CHAPTER NINE

1970–74

Dennis Kavanagh

The literature on government failure is much larger than that on government success. In part this is because there are more failures to analyse. Enoch Powell's observation that all political lives end in failure is probably also true of most political ventures.[1] It is emphatically so for the 1970–74 Conservative government led by Ted Heath. The Heath government's record has posed a problem to students of postwar British politics and of the Conservative Party. The record has spawned only a slight literature of defence and been buried under the weight of ideological onslaught from the Thatcherites and centre-left commentators. The attacks started with the public *mea culpa* of Sir Keith Joseph in 1974 and continued more recently in Mrs Thatcher's memoirs.[2] Their view is that Heath's failure stemmed from ministers' lack of political resolve, which caused the 'correct' initial strategy to be abandoned. Political scientists, without a political axe to grind, regard the 1970–74 experience as a stark example of the limits on governments whose policies are only one input to the process and have to compete with other forces.[3]

In the last two decades the new political right in much of the West has countered the political left's traditional critique of why markets fail with their own analysis of the shortcomings of governments. In Britain, the experience of the 1970s, particularly of the Heath government, was crucial in underlining for the free market right the failure of the

Keynesian welfare state and encouraging the neo-liberal backlash of the Thatcher governments in the 1980s. The political right claimed that there was a crisis of social democracy, as governments had come to spend and tax too much, and interest groups, particularly trade unions, had become too powerful.

Postwar Britain has become a case study of decline. The 1970–74 government has joined the long roll-call of administrations which have failed to reverse the cycle of relative economic decline. On a number of macro-economic indicators, notably unemployment, inflation and living standards, most postwar British governments have failed to do better than their predecessors. Notwithstanding the formidable resources a British government normally possesses, in the shape of a sovereign Parliament and a majority in the House of Commons, the persisting failures of economic management point to its weakness *vis-à-vis* other actors and forces.[4]

Popular memories of the 1970–74 government are of the record number of work days lost due to strikes, some of which severely dislocated life for millions of ordinary people, states of emergency, double digit inflation, a three-day working week, blank television screens, lawlessness and vandalism and, at the end, a crisis general election which the government lost. The government appeared to be struggling against seemingly overwhelming odds. Many of these features continued under the successor Labour governments led by Harold Wilson and James Callaghan. The spectre of ungovernable Britain was conveyed by contemporary academic books and articles on the themes of *Bankruptcy, Political Overload, Disease of Government* and *Decline* and *Crisis*. Governments seem to be weighed down with too many commitments which they could not deliver and locked into cycles of interdependence, both domestically and externally. By the end of the 1970s the sense of economic decline and political failure in Britain was acute.

All governments and organizations face problems in

implementing their policies, and there is now a large literature explaining why governments fail to meet their objectives. Essentially, the chances of failure have increased because of growing complexity or the greater dependence of government on favourable circumstances. Of a number of constraints suggested by the political scientist Sabatier, three seem to have been particularly relevant in the case of the Heath government.[5] They are:

- *Inadequate causal theory*, particularly about the role of money supply as a cause of inflation (between 1971 and 1973 there was a 20 per cent expansion of M3, the broad measure of money supply). Yet at the time, apart from the Institute of Economic Affairs and some followers of Enoch Powell, there was little interest in monetarist explanations of inflation.

- *Lack of support or cooperation from key groups*, particularly from trade unions for incomes policy. The unions had already rendered the Industrial Relations Act (1971) unworkable simply by not registering.

- *An unstable socio-economic context*, including adverse international economic trends, particularly the rise in commodity prices and then Arab oil prices, and the ending of the Bretton Woods system of fixed exchange rates. These undermined the postwar economic policy goals of full employment and stable prices. The new conditions reduced the effectiveness of Keynesian economics and established tools of economic management, in the form of the Bretton Woods system of fixed exchange rates.

What is Failure, What is Success?

We can point to a number of criteria of success for government. They include:

- *Winning re-election*. Gaining office is a necessary if not

361

sufficient condition for political power. Ministers may claim that they need at least two full terms of office to carry out their strategy and that re-election demonstrates popular support for their programme. But it has shortcomings as a criterion of success. A government may win an election by neglecting the long-term interests of the country (economists, for example, have often criticized the vote-seeking pre-election budget sprees and the economic harm they cause) or by default, largely because the political opposition is feeble or divided. But even on this inadequate indicator the Heath government did badly. It lost the February 1974 general election, is the only postwar government which lasted for a single term, and suffered the biggest fall in its share of the vote of any postwar government – 8.6 per cent.

- *Fulfilling manifesto promises.* British governments with a party majority in the Commons are well placed to carry out specific commitments. The Heath government delivered many of its promises which could be cast in a legislative form, for example, ending mandatory comprehensive education, reforming industrial relations, entering the EEC, reforming taxes and housing finance and reorganizing central government.

- *Introducing legislation or policies, which survive the lifetime of government.* The Heath government performed poorly on this criterion. Legislation on industrial relations, housing finance, secondary education and statutory controls on incomes was quickly scrapped by the succeeding Labour government. Reforms of central government machinery as well as the reorganization of the health service and local government also proved to be short-lived. Apart from membership of the EEC, which was thrown into question until the 1975 referendum, the government left the fewest policy legacies of any postwar administration.[6]

- *Achieving intended outcomes.* Party manifestos rarely state objectives in a form which can be tested empirically. They do not provide clear, unambiguous indicators for pledges, for example, to improve Britain's international standing, promote honest government, increase educational opportunity, improve living standards, and make the streets safer. Ministers may explain breaches of explicit promises by changes in circumstances, the priority accorded to competing goals, or the need to adopt a longer term perspective. Where we can reasonably assess the Heath record on this criterion, the performance is also bleak. Contrary to its 1970 manifesto the government at the end of its term presided over record levels of inflation and balance of payments deficits, public spending had increased by nearly 50 per cent in real terms, inefficient firms were propped up and a record number of days had been lost due to strikes.

Of the four suggested criteria of success, the Heath government therefore fails on three and its success in delivering legislation may not be considered the most important criterion. Legislation, after all, is often an input to the policy process, designed to achieve broader goals. A reasonable conclusion is that if any postwar government failed, the 1970–74 one clearly did. This chapter considers the strengths and weaknesses of the government's position at the onset in June 1970, its record in office, the reasons for its failure and, finally, the lessons which may be drawn from the record.

A Flawed Victory

The Conservative Party that won the general election in 1970 was much changed from that which had dominated British politics between 1951 and 1964. Edward Heath was elected as leader by Conservative MPs, under new rules drawn up in 1965. His predecessor, Sir Alec Douglas-Home, had 'emerged' in 1963 amid controversy, indeed acrimony, and under arrangements which were not democratic. In contrast to the aristocratic and wealthy Sir Alec, Mr Heath was self-made, a grammar school boy of modest background. Many of his close political colleagues were also 'new' men, sometimes called 'Heathmen'. They came from grammar school or minor public school backgrounds and were meritocrats. They included Robert Carr, Peter Walker, Reginald Maudling and Anthony Barber. Older style Conservatives, like Sir Alec, William Whitelaw and Lord Carrington, remained but the social balance at the top of the party was changing.

Loss of office, by however narrow a margin, in the October 1964 general election came as a shock to a Conservative Party which had been in power for so long. This sense of shock was reinforced when Labour, eighteen months later, called an election and increased its majority over the Conservatives to 110 seats. After the decisive election defeat in 1966 the party could concentrate afresh on rethinking its strategy. In government between 1951 and 1964 the party had accepted the main policy innovations of the 1945–51 Labour government. These included public ownership, full employment, the retreat from empire, a national health service and the welfare state. Accepting these policies had paid rich electoral dividends for the Conservatives. But by the early 1960s there was a growing awareness that Britain was economically falling behind her West European neighbours. Labour seemed to be more in tune with the climate of opinion and its charge of 'thirteen wasted years' resonated with many voters. A study of the 1966 general election commented that voters regarded Labour as the party of ideas, youthful leadership and modernization. It continued, 'the Conservatives in the early 1960s came to be regarded in the eyes of many voters as antipathetic: tired, out of touch with ordinary people, too much dominated by the upper classes'.[7] This disheartening message was confirmed by the party's private polls.

No Conservative politician was more strongly associated with the new thinking about policy than Edward Heath. Indeed Sir Alec had made him chairman of the Advisory Committee on Policy soon after the 1964 election defeat. The policies resulting from this revision were already evident in the 1966 manifesto; they included trade union reform, changes in taxation, concentrating welfare provision on those most in need, as well as entry into Europe.

As opposition leader Edward Heath had a difficult time. His lack of public appeal was a continuing concern to party managers. While opinion polls from the beginning of 1967 until early 1970 reported substantial Conservative leads over Labour, often by margins of more than 20 per cent, they also showed Mr Heath lagging behind Mr Wilson. As leader of the opposition (1965–70) his mean opinion poll approval rating was 34 per cent, the lowest figure of any opposition leader till then (subsequently, the only opposition leader to score lower has been Labour's Michael Foot [1980–83] with 17 per cent). Heath also had problems in keeping the party together over incomes policy, Rhodesia's seizure of independence, and immigration in the wake of Enoch Powell's speech on the subject in April 1968. When Wilson called a general election in 1970, against a background of decisive public opinion leads, he was widely expected to be successful again. Labour appeared to be the natural party of government.

The Conservative general election success in 1970 still remains the most unexpected in the postwar period. It was won in defiance of the forecasts of virtually all the opinion polls and judgements of political commentators. Before polling day many Conservative candidates and organizers were reconciled to the prospect of the party's defeat. Yet the victory was a decisive one: the party had a majority over Labour of forty-two seats and one of thirty overall. Its share of the vote, at 46.4 per cent, was the party's highest since 1959 and has not been exceeded since.

There were, however, flaws in the victory. For one thing it seems to have been won in spite of the climate of opinion. If the record and personalities of the Wilson government were discredited, the broad thrust of its policies – interventionist, anti-market and egalitarian – was not. Douglas Hurd, who had a ringside seat of events as Heath's political secretary in these years, later reflected that the election was won 'against and not with the tide of intellectual opinion'.[8] The election result was more a rejection of Labour than an endorsement of the Conservative Party, reflected perhaps in the lowest electoral turnout (72 per cent) in the postwar period and the small proportion who 'cared very much' which party won.[9] Another cause for concern in Conservative Central Office was the information conveyed by the party's private polling. In 1968 and 1969, when the Conservatives enjoyed massive leads on voting intentions, more people still regarded themselves as Labour than Conservative supporters. Wise Central Office officials knew that the opinion poll leads were quite unrealistic; Conservatives were no longer the natural majority party, as the long-term effects of social class and party identification were working against them.[10] The Conservatives were preferred to Labour as the party best able to stem rising prices and were seen as more competent in government, but the support was conditional.[11] The government's honeymoon with the electorate was short. Within four months of the election success in June 1970, Gallup reported that Labour had overtaken the Conservatives on voting intention.

The Heath government began with a clear set of policy objectives. First and foremost Britain must enter the European Community. (Heath has to date been the only consistently pro-European British prime minister.) Yet to make entry work economically, Britain had to become more competitive, more efficient. Hence the importance of a reformed system of industrial relations, government disengagement from industry, and encouraging the free market by reductions in income tax and cuts in public spending. Government had become too involved in propping up inefficient firms and influencing wage and price levels. It had to stand aside and allow the market to operate and enterprise to flourish. It is a matter of dispute as to whether Heath was in 1970 what was later to be termed a 'Thatcherite'. His many right-wing critics now complain, variously, that he did not believe in the 1970 prospectus, that he did not understand its implications or that he simply lacked the will to persist with it. A side of Heath certainly stressed the need for more individualism, greater self-reliance, lower taxes and a smaller government and he believed that trade unions had to operate in a more disciplined framework. Yet Heath was also a child of the postwar consensus and saw himself as an heir of Macmillan and R. A. Butler.[12] He never doubted that full employment and the welfare state were responsibilities of government. His record, not least at the Board of Trade (1963–64), showed that he was prepared to use government as a lever to improve economic competition and promote economic growth. Much of his 1970 image as a Thatcherite stemmed from the rhetoric he used as leader of a party in opposition to Labour's interventionist economic policies.

Ted Heath was not an ideologue. In this, he resembles most postwar prime ministers and it is Mrs Thatcher who is the exception. He had been elected as party leader in 1965 as a counter to Harold Wilson at a time when the Conservative Party was seeking a pragmatic, modern, efficient, classless leader – the virtues associated at the time with Wilson. He prided himself on pursuing 'rational' or 'reasonable' policies. Heath was consistent about ends, flexible about means: he was a pragmatist, concerned with pursuing the best means to achieving economic growth and greater personal freedom.

The Record

Mr Heath was impatient to deliver on the promises of the party's manifesto and to catch up on what he regarded as years of missed opportunities. Addressing the 1970 party conference he warned of the challenges that faced his government:

> If we are to achieve this task we will have to embark on a journey so radical, so quiet and yet so total, that it will go far beyond the programme ... to which we are committed and which we have already embarked; far beyond this decade and into the 1980s.

At the heart of the revolution was British entry to the European Community. Negotiations over membership had started in the last weeks of the Labour government, continued under the Heath government and were completed in July 1971. A year later a European Communities Bill received its third reading in the House of Commons.The issue was divisive for both parties but entry was achieved and the manifesto fulfilled.

For much of the time inflation was the main concern of the public and of party strategists. Party leaders were convinced that public concern over rising prices had, more than any other single issue, decided the 1970 general election. Yet, apart from a promise to cut taxes and halt price rises in the nationalized industries, the government started out with few concrete proposals. Its task was made more difficult by the steady rises in world interest rates and prices. At home mortgage rates increased from 8.5 per cent in June 1970, to 11 per cent by the end of 1973 and house prices rose by nearly 75 per cent over two years. Food prices rose by 19 per cent and international commodity prices by over 25 per cent in 1973 alone.

From the outset, the government operated an incomes policy in all but name for the public sector. In public, ministers claimed that wage settlements were to be settled by free collective bargaining, although the government favoured 'responsible' settlements and, as an employer in the public sector, would act accordingly. This policy met with some success until it was smashed in early 1972 by a coal-miners' strike which was ended only when a government-appointed court of inquiry awarded the miners an increase of 32 per cent. The settlement not only ruined the government's counter-inflation strategy but also damaged its authority. There was no disguising that it had surrendered to industrial muscle and there was disillusion among supporters. Ministers came under increasing pressure to take action on rising prices. On 26 September the government announced plans for a prices and incomes policy and began meetings with the CBI and TUC to see if agreement could be reached on a voluntary basis. The experiment in 'partnership' was a clear breach of manifesto promises which abjured income policy. The talks failed to reach agreement and on 6 November ministers announced a compulsory three-month standstill on pay and prices. For many Conservatives, worried by previous U-turns on industry (see below), maintenance of the new policy became a decisive test of the government's credibility.

The sectarian violence in Northern Ireland was a continuing source of concern to ministers. In August 1970 Reginald Maudling, the Home Secretary, authorized the Stormont government to intern (imprison without trial) suspected terrorists. This step served only to alienate Catholics further and violence, including bombings in Northern Ireland and on the mainland, increased. In March 1972 the government suspended the Stormont Parliament and placed Northern Ireland under direct rule from Whitehall. In June 1973 elections were held for a new assembly and a non-sectarian executive took office in 1974. The suspension of Stormont led to a loosening of the traditional Conservative links with the Ulster Unionist MPs – no longer could the latter be relied upon to support the Conservative Party at Westminster.

Another pledge was honoured when the Industrial Relations Act became law in August 1971. This provided a legal framework for industrial relations and, according to opinion polls, had strong public support. Crucially, however, most of the trade unions opposed the measure and the TUC expelled unions which registered under it. The Labour Party announced that it would repeal the legislation, if and when it was returned to office. Several unions refused to recognize the new Industrial Relations Court and the number of working days lost due to strikes soared dramatically. By the closing months of the administration the act was virtually inoperable.

On industry, concern over rising unemployment soon forced the government to reverse its policy of disengagement. The Rolls-Royce company went bankrupt and was nationalized in February 1971 to preserve jobs. A few months later a rescue package was provided for the Upper Clyde Shipyards, although this was associated with a work-in organized by the unions and the government had originally refused to become involved. The rescue of Upper Clyde caused much unease among government backbenchers and the contrast between words and action was commented on by supporters and political opponents. This was followed by the Industry Act which provided scope for massive state intervention. Ministers felt that they had to take steps to strengthen industrial capacity if Britain was to benefit from entry to the European Community. By 1972, Heath was disappointed at the investment record of industry and the City. According to his biographer, Heath did not betray private enterprise, 'rather it was private enterprise which had disappointed him'.[13]

Another radical measure was the reform of local council housing finance in the Housing Finance Act. The government believed that rents for a number of the well-off households were too low and should not be subsidized. The new scheme was designed to reduce total subsidies and provide rent rebates for those in need. The number of households paying higher rents outnumbered those receiving rebates and the measure did not gain votes; it prompted bitter opposition from the Labour Party and the refusal of a number of Labour councils to implement the act only added to the general impression of lawlessness and weak government.

It is difficult to discern any period when the government was dominant. It is true that there was a new kind of Conservatism, and rhetoric to match – an impression encouraged by both Heath and the Labour opposition. The former talked about the challenge of change and opportunity, the latter about the government break with the postwar consensus. At the outset, there was certainly some discontinuity with the policies of the outgoing Labour government, particularly over taxation and the balance between individualism and state authority, between free enterprise and public ownership. But there were also continuities, notably on entry into Europe and the reform of industrial relations. The fact that Labour, once it moved into opposition, changed its mind on both policies brought much discredit upon it. The Heath government enjoyed the briefest of political honeymoons with the electorate, according to the opinion polls (see Table 9.1). Surveys also showed that the popular mood turned against entry into Europe and there was a 3:1 majority against entry by early 1971. Public support for some of the policies such as the Industrial Relations Act and for resisting wage claims in the public sector were fragile, given the opposition of powerful groups to those policies. The Heath government also lacked good working relations with major interest groups. Relations with the trade unions for most of the time were poor, soured by the Industrial Relations Act, but also because the unions were becoming more political.

Reasons for Failure

There seems little doubt that Mr Heath was the dominant figure in government, and Cabinet colleagues, with the notable exception of Mrs Thatcher, have generally expressed admiration for his leadership. It is a tribute to his management of Cabinet, or perhaps to its like-mindedness, that no ministers resigned because of policy disagreement. Heath's self-confidence had been greatly boosted by success in the 1970 election, when so many in his party were prepared for defeat. The government's initial economic strategy was clearly his, and he was closely involved with the subsequent policy modifications and U-turns. He also had a special interest in the European negotiations, the counter-inflation policy, particularly its latter stages, and the imposition of direct rule in Northern Ireland. As Heath gradually lost confidence in the Treasury, economic policy seems to have been made in No. 10 by Heath in conjunction with Sir William Armstrong, then head of the civil service.[14] Had Iain Macleod, the Chancellor of the Exchequer, not died so suddenly in 1970 things might have been different. His replacement, Anthony Barber, lacked both the political weight and expertise to provide an alternative economic overview.

As we have seen, Heath was never a popular figure, according to the opinion polls. Even in the 1970 election he was not an electoral asset to the party.[15] Heath's approval rating as prime minister averaged 37 per cent, the lowest figure of any postwar prime minister until John Major.[16] One should not, however, make too much of the electoral impact of a leader's popularity. After all, Heath in 1970 and Mrs Thatcher in 1979 trailed the Labour leaders in the opinion polls but this did not prevent them leading their parties to victory in the general elections.

There was certainly confusion over the direction of government policy. One might state this more accurately by saying that policy was clear until it was reversed and then the new line became clear. The term 'U-turn' was coined with reference to the government's spectacular economic policy reversals. Even if one allows for policy learning and adaptation, the abrupt shifts in economic policy were striking and were disquieting for supporters. The government began by announcing cuts in public spending, income

tax and corporation tax in budgets in October 1970 and
March 1971. It declared that it would reduce assistance to
industry, not rescue 'lame duck' companies, and scrap the
Labour government's Industrial Reorganization Board and
Ministry of Technology. Faced, however, with an increase
in the jobless total (the figure at the beginning of 1972 was
the highest postwar number since the exceptional winter
of 1947) the government changed tack. Between July 1971
and the budget in March 1973 it reflated in classic
Keynesian style, boosting public spending and cutting taxes.
The November 1971 White Paper on Public Expenditure
announced big increases in spending totals for the following
four years. It also abandoned disengagement and its 1972
Industry Act allowed extensive state assistance for industry.
This restored the regional investment grants to areas of high
unemployment and provided financial incentives for investment in new plant and machinery. The reflation in 1971
was stimulated in part by an offer from the CBI to use its
good offices to limit price increases among member firms
to 5 per cent or less per annum, if the government took
steps to reflate the economy and limited price increases in
the nationalized industries to the same figure. The government had the prospect of economic growth with a reduced
risk of inflation. In late 1973, faced with the inflationary
consequences of the rise in oil prices, it changed tack again
and cut back on public spending, as part of its battle against
inflation.

An even more dramatic reversal was the resort in November 1972 to a far-reaching statutory prices and incomes
policy. The 1970 manifesto had expressed the party's utter
opposition to the philosophy of incomes policy and one of
the government's first actions was to scrap the Prices and
Incomes Board of the previous Labour government. This
U-turn led Enoch Powell to ask Heath in the House of Commons on 6 November 1972 if he had taken leave of his
senses, to pursue policies so flatly in contradiction to the
manifesto on which he had been elected.

It is worth noting that the government's plans for expansion and incomes policy had few contemporary critics. During 1972 the Treasury, Central Policy Review Staff ('Think Tank') and Bank of England were urging the adoption of a prices and incomes policy. Much of the press was also supportive. Public opinion was worried over the rise in unemployment, held the government responsible, and supported the pay policy. Significantly, ministers themselves accepted responsibility for the level of unemployment. They still subscribed to the objective of full employment, as propounded in the 1944 Employment White Paper. As Peter Hall comments: 'the British policy community was virtually united on the appropriateness of Keynesian approaches to economic problems'.[17]

What is intriguing about these policy reversals is that they were made by a government which took pride in its preparation for office and in having a clear strategy. Two-thirds of the original Cabinet ministers had shadowed their posts in opposition, often for lengthy periods, and engaged in elaborate policy-making exercises, even to the point of drafting legislation. Detailed advance planning had been done on tax changes, industrial relations and reform of the machinery of government. This did not always deliver the promised benefits. The industrial relations legislation, for example, had been drawn up without the benefit of advice from the then Ministry of Labour or consultation with the trade unions. Ministers were aware of the opposition of the trade unions but they expected them to come round in time. The impact of the legislation was nullified by the simple expedient of unions refusing to register.

The most striking failure in opposition was the lack of an effective anti-inflation policy. In policy discussions inflation seems to have been relegated to a side issue. Brendon Sewill, the Conservative Director of Research until the 1970 election and then a special adviser to the Chancellor of the Exchequer, reflected, 'We went into the 1970 election totally unprepared on what was going to be the crucial issue.'[18] The manifesto promised that a Conservative government would eschew an incomes policy, bear down on public sector wage settlements, exhort private sector employers to follow suit and appeal for restraint. This was not sufficient to cope with the inflationary pressures.

— The research of Philip Norton, the foremost authority on parliamentary dissent, shows that the Heath government experienced the highest level of revolt until that point of any postwar government.[19] Backbench rebellions nearly wrecked the European Communities Bill on its second reading and led to defeat for proposed changes to the immigration rules in 1972. Norton squarely blames Heath's leadership – particularly the controversial nature of some of the legislation, his failure to cultivate backbenchers and his ungenerous use of political patronage and honours – for the scale of dissent. The suggestions of colleagues that he make himself more accessible to backbenchers and listen to their views did not have much success. He appeared to take his party's support for granted and failed, as Campbell notes, to give Conservative MPs the sense that they were all part of a shared enterprise.[20] Concern over the U-turns was one thing, but the manner in which the changes were made added to dissatisfaction.[21] As Stuart Ball notes, 'Too often an unheralded somersault on policy was followed by lack of consultation on the legislation, unresponsiveness to backbench opinion, and grudgingly few concessions to objections raised in debate.'[22]

Warning signs of the disquiet and resentment of backbenchers were shown in the election in 1972 of Edward Du Cann as Chairman of the 1922 Committee (Du Cann and Heath had long had a frosty relationship) and the election of John Biffen and Nicholas Ridley, both free-marketeers, as chairmen of the party's backbench Industry and Finance Committees respectively. Over time the sense of distance between the Cabinet and backbenchers increased, a division that became apparent in the leadership election when backbenchers rallied to Mrs Thatcher to defeat Heath in February 1975.

During the late 1960s a coherent right wing had been emerging on the Conservative back benches. In the 1970 Parliament a small but recognizable core group of MPs called for tougher measures against immigration, and objected to direct rule in Northern Ireland, a statutory prices and incomes policy and Britain's membership of the European Community. This wing was to flourish more under Heath's successor as leader, Margaret Thatcher, and even more when she became prime minister. But between 1970 and 1974 Heath was probably helped by the comprehensive opposition of Enoch Powell – on Europe, Ulster, economic policy and incomes policy. Few doubters of the government's line wished to be tarred with the charge of being a supporter of Powell.

Heath's neglect of his backbenchers is surprising in view of his earlier experiences as chief whip. In that position between 1957 and 1959, he had seen Macmillan almost daily. By contrast, his own chief whip, Francis Pym, saw him only weekly. Yet it is remarkable that the government with a majority of less than thirty, passed so much controversial legislation. Much credit is due to this to the skill of Pym. His flexible and conciliatory style did much to compensate for his leader's stiff and aloof manner.

Heath had little trouble from the activists' grass roots and conferences were loyal. Yet he did little to hide his disdain for grassroots leaders. It did not help that his chairman from 1972 was Lord Carrington, based in the House of Lords and a busy secretary of state for defence. Carrington's patrician manner and dislike of gladhanding party workers did not compensate for the party leader's distance.

The Parliament was no happier for the Labour opposition. It might be thought that the troubles of the government meant that support for Labour grew and that it was able to shape the political agenda. This was not so. Labour's ability to profit electorally from the Conservative unpopularity was

TABLE 9.1 *Party Support 1970–73 (Gallup)*

	Quarter	Cons. % lead
1970	III	2½
	IV	−1
1971	I	−6
	II	−9
	III	−14½
	IV	−6
1972	I	−7
	II	−2
	III	−12
	IV	−7
1973	I	−4
	II	−2
	III	−6
	IV	−4

dented by the Liberal revival and indeed its by-election record was the worst of any opposition party since the 1945 Parliament. Labour led the Conservatives by some 20 per cent in the polls twelve months into the Parliament but over the next two years the growth of Liberal support cut this lead (Table 9.1). At by-elections, the Liberals gained four seats from the Conservatives and one from Labour although voters expressed themselves dissatisfied with the government's record – during 1973 an average of only a third claimed to be satisfied (Table 9.2).

None of this helped the official opposition. Voters wished a plague on both Labour and Conservative houses. Within the Labour Party the left and the trade unions emerged stronger and conference reasserted its authority after the

TABLE 9.2   *Responses to the Question: 'Are you satisfied or dissatisfied with the way the government is running the country?'*

	Satisfied %	Dissatisfied %	Don't Know %
July 1970	40	15	45
January 1971	39	46	15
January 1972	33	56	11
January 1973	39	49	12
January 1974	32	60	8

SOURCE: National Opinion Polls

election defeat in 1970. The party swung sharply to the left and new policies included a wealth tax, extension of nationalization, creation of a National Enterprise Board with powers to intervene in private manufacturing and repeal of the Industrial Relations Act. Most of the parliamentary leadership were unhappy with this programme and surveys showed little public support for more nationalization or for increasing the power of trade unions.

Europe caused more divisions in Labour than in any other party and the leadership was humiliated when nearly a third of its MPs defied a three-line whip to support the key vote on entry in October 1971. Roy Jenkins, the deputy leader, resigned in April 1972 when the Shadow Cabinet decided to support a referendum on EC membership. Caught between Labour pro-Europeans, who supported the terms of entry and those, mainly on the left, who were opposed, Wilson resorted to a typical fudge. The agreed line was to call for a renegotiation of terms, with the results to be submitted to the British people either through a referendum or a general election. The press gave the compromise a broadly hostile treatment.

If Labour failed to provide a credible alternative government, its own policy switches from its time in office contributed to a political polarization and undermined the prospects for the acceptability of some government measures. In bitterly opposing the terms of entry to the European Community, the Industrial Relations Act and the statutory incomes policy, Labour was gainsaying three major policies it had pursued when in government. But before 1970 the Conservative opposition had also opposed the Labour government's incomes policies, trade union reforms and intervention in industry. This was adversary politics at its most irresponsible.

It is not surprising that many of the principal government actors showed growing signs of fatigue. John Campbell's biography of Heath refers *en passant* to the illness or exhaustion of Whitelaw, Barber, Heath, William Armstrong and Rothschild.[23] The sense of pressure and strain is also conveyed in Hurd's memoir. The government's ambitious – perhaps over-ambitious – programme meant that ministers had been involved in long and hard parliamentary battles over Europe and industrial relations legislation as well as lengthy negotiations with trade unions and the CBI in pursuit of a voluntary prices and incomes agreement, and again on averting the miners' strike during the winter of 1973.

Communication was not a strong point for Heath or indeed most of his Cabinet colleagues. He failed to project to the public his vision – whether on Europe, free enterprise or the battle against inflation. He was suspicious of discussion of presentation or public relations, associating it with Wilsonian 'slickness'. Douglas Hurd regretted Heath's tendency to 'speak at' rather than to people, his liking for jargon and belief that the facts should be allowed to speak for themselves. After a few months in office, Hurd warned Heath of the widespread impression that his government was 'less politically conscious than its Conservative predecessors'.[24] Campbell adds, 'The problem was that Heath seemed to like it that way.'[25] Colleagues found it difficult to interest the leader in preparations for television interviews, broadcasts and conference speeches. Like most prime ministers, Heath complained about the press. Resolutions from constituency associations and tactical papers from party officers regularly complained of ministers' failing to get their message across. Private polling confirmed that Heath was seen as lacking warmth and the party as remote from people and uncaring.[26] Anthony King expresses it well: 'His goals were Anthony Eden's and Harold Macmillan's: his rhetoric sometimes bordered on Lenin's.'[27]

Yet it can be argued that all of the above factors pale into insignificance when compared with the changing international context. The abandonment by the United States of the Bretton Woods system of fixed but adjustable exchange rates added to economic uncertainty. In June 1972 the pound was floated and during the next eighteen months its value against a basket of international currencies depreciated by 20 per cent. The government's anti-inflation policy was challenged increasingly by the steady rise in international commodity prices. By October 1973 the government's dash for growth had contributed to both a public sector borrowing and balance of payments crisis. A weak economy was in no position to cope with the outbreak of the Yom Kippur War between Israel and Arab states on 6 October 1973, which led to the quadrupling of oil prices by OPEC countries. This had a major deflationary impact on Western economies. The government's dash for economic growth would have to be abandoned and ministers would have to take tough measures to deal with inflationary pressures and balance of payments deficits in the next few years. As Douglas Hurd prophesied, ministers would require a new vocabulary for the harsher times ahead; there would have to be 'an end to promises'. On 13 December a White Paper announced public spending increases for 1974–75; two days later the Chancellor announced reductions in the planned spending levels. The dash for growth had been abandoned. The miners' imposition of an overtime ban in November 1973 and eventually a strike in support of a pay claim which exceeded Phase III of the government's pay policy only added to the energy shortfall. In the short term the bargaining position of the National Union of Mineworkers was immensely strengthened and that threatened the government's anti-inflation policy.

The events and calculations that led Mr Heath to call a crisis election in February 1974 have been described elsewhere.[28] As with so much of the administration's economic policy, the handling of the election was shrouded in confusion. It was never clear why the election was called, or how a Conservative victory would produce a solution to the problem which forced the election in the first place. Until late 1973, ministers had planned a general election in October 1974, or even later, on the back of economic prosperity. But when the miners voted to go on strike, most ministers were convinced that they had no option but to call an election. They calculated that an election would allow the people to decide who governs – the government or the unions – and they were confident of the outcome. Heath was more interested in persuading people of the consequences of the energy crisis and the need to share sacrifices. It was hoped that a new government, backed by the authority of an election success, would be able to take tough decisions. But on the immediate issue, it was never clear whether it would be strong enough to deny the National Union of Miners, or would have sufficient authority to give in and then draw up a new incomes policy. In the event, a large number of voters decided that the government's economic record was weak, particularly on prices, and voted for other parties.

The result was indeterminate, in the sense that no one party gained a clear majority of seats in the new Parliament. Under the new minority Labour government, the pay policy was abandoned and the miners were bought off. For Heath himself, the result was a disaster. Another failure followed in the October 1974 general election, when the Conservative Party scored its lowest vote in the twentieth century.

There followed a passionate debate about the failures of the Heath government. It was damned by the free-marketeers for becoming involved in the statutory incomes policy and confrontation with the unions. Mr Heath fared no better at the hands of supporters of one-nation Conservatism. Indeed, surveys showed that in the February election, voters regarded the Conservatives as a divisive, class party. There is a cruel irony in the Heath government calling an election in defence of a statutory incomes policy, the very policy which its 1970 election manifesto had repudiated.

Drawing Lessons

In the short term, the circumstances in which the Heath government fell and Labour came to office only underscored the power of the trade unions and demonstrated the fallibility of statutory incomes policies. When powerful groups successfully challenged the law – or made it unworkable – they put at risk the authority of government. The key question in British politics seemed to be not so much who governed but who could best get on with the trade unions. Labour ministers in 1974 abandoned statutory incomes policies and any industrial relations legislation to which the TUC objected; they decided that stable government required that they rule with the cooperation of the trade unions and largely on their terms, as expressed in the social contract.[29] Labour ministers regularly warned voters that a Conservative vote risked a return to darkened streets, blank television screens and a three-day week. The lessons appeared to be reinforced by the failure of Labour's social contract and pay policy in 1979.

Conservatives differed in their reactions. For the Thatcherites, the policies of the Heath government represented much that they abhorred – U-turns, corporatism, government intervention in the economy, distrust of the free market and a lack of conviction among political leaders.

382

Mr Heath's supporters claimed that the policies had been correct but failed because of bad luck. The government's experience showed both the influence which the Keynesian paradigm exercised over ministers and the limits of that policy. Middlemas fairly describes the Heath government as 'the last loyal signatory of the 1944 pact' of full employment and the social partners approach between government and the major interests.[30] In fact the Wilson and Callaghan governments were signatories also, and Labour's social contract ended in ruins, in the winter of discontent. It can be argued that it was 1979 rather than 1974 which witnessed the end of the postwar settlement. Middlemas also claims that the Heath (and Callaghan) experience pointed to a number of other lessons:

1. Domestic policy objectives had to take account of broader international economic forces. The failures demonstrated the limits on the autonomy of the nation state.

2. The social partners approach would not work if the members of the key interest groups were not convinced that the policies operated in their own self-interest.

3. Political decision-makers, commentators and international markets had to take account of economic indicators other than rates of unemployment and inflation – particularly those for money supply and the public sector borrowing requirement.

4. The decline in political deference and rise of a more assertive media reduced the scope for government exhortation to shape economic behaviour.

There is nothing special about Tory governments failing. Indeed, historically Labour governments may have been less successful. Richard Rose has argued that the failure of most postwar British governments to reverse the trend of secular economic decline shows that there is 'something stronger

How Tory Governments Fall

than party'. The larger question, perhaps, is why most governments fail.

One obvious reason for failure is that a government's initial strategy might be misconceived. Correlli Barnett, for example, argues that the 1945 Labour government misdirected economic resources to welfare and consumption rather than investing in industry and damaged the country's long-term economic prospects.[31] It can be argued that the crucial mistake of Wilson's 1964 government was not to devalue the pound much earlier than it did in 1967. Investment in industry and social programmes was sacrificed to maintain sterling at a level which proved unsustainable. John Major and the country paid a heavy price in bankruptcies, lost jobs and high interest rates for taking Britain into the ERM in 1990 at a rate which was unsustainable. The Heath government's crucial failure was to try and maintain the postwar economic settlement, particularly the objective of full employment, at a time when changed conditions had made it well-nigh impossible. Ministers and advisers clung to a Keynesian paradigm which was out of date, but no credible alternative was available in the early 1970s.

The alleged economic successes of Mrs Thatcher's government of 1979 have led some to argue that Heath could have succeeded had he shown a similar resolve in carrying out the original strategy. Two points are relevant here. The Heath government's U-turns in economic policy were significant and disheartening for supporters, but elsewhere the government achieved a good deal of its manifesto. In three and a half years it achieved nine of its major pledges and reversed itself on four.[32] By contrast, in six years the 1964 Labour government fulfilled only four of its major pledges and reversed itself on three. The second point to emphasize is that the Thatcher government held more cards than Mr Heath did in 1970. The trade unions and the left wing of the Labour Party were more powerful and obstructive between 1970 and 1974 than they were after 1979. The Labour government's resort to the IMF in 1976, the subsequent winter of discontent and collapse of the social contract, and the economic record of the Callaghan government had all discredited Labour and the unions by 1979. The rise in unemployment in 1971–72, although much more modest than was to occur in the 1980s, had more impact on public opinion. In the first six months of the Heath government unemployment was 2.6 per cent and was falling slightly at the end of the government. But in the first quarter of 1972, when it rose to 4 per cent, or nearly one million, the government felt compelled to take action, because the tolerance of voters and politicians was then much lower than was to be the case a decade later. Mrs Thatcher could win re-election in 1983 with unemployment at a 'real' level of over three million and not be blamed for it. In 1970 incomes policies were not widely regarded as a failure and there was no comprehensive monetarist analysis available at the time.[33] As one key figure recalled, the party's thinking was handicapped by its attachment to the goal of full employment and a refusal to realize that reducing the power of the unions and tackling inflation actually required an increase in unemployment: 'Nobody was prepared to take that mental leap away from the total Keynesian tradition in which everyone had grown up during the 1940s, 1950s and 1960s.'[34]

Apologists for Mr Heath say that he was ahead of his time. His administration did anticipate many of the post-1979 reforms which a decade later the Thatcher government was to implement more successfully. These included council house sales, trade union reforms, measures to improve efficiency in Whitehall and disengaging from industry. Yet this is a backhanded defence. A sense of correct timing involves the appropriate reading of circumstances, including the balance of support for and forces ranged against reform. The government attempted many policies too quickly; for example, contrast the sweeping nature of the reform of industrial relations with the incremental approach of the Thatcher government.

The most important handicap the Heath government faced was that it required cooperation or support from unpredictable or unreliable sources – namely, the trade unions and international economic forces. It transpired that both operated to undermine the dash for growth and the anti-inflation strategy. The unions had become more politicized and had already shown their power in forcing the Labour government to abandon its proposed reform of industrial relations in 1969. The ending of US economic hegemony and the growing importance of the Arab oil states added new uncertainties. As the pro-Conservative journalist Ronald Butt commented shortly after the February 1974 election: 'The Conservative Government came to disaster through sheer lack of political instinct about what are and what are not workable policies . . . The greatest weakness was its wishful thinking that if its will was strong enough, it would prevail.'[35]

CHRONOLOGY

1970   JUNE 18   General election: Conservatives, 330 seats; Labour, 287; Liberals, 6; others, 7

JUNE 30   EEC entry negotiations start

JULY 20   Iain Macleod dies. Succeeded as chancellor of the exchequer by Anthony Barber

DECEMBER 3   Electricity work-to-rule with blackouts

1971   FEBRUARY 5   First British soldier killed in Belfast

FEBRUARY 15   Decimal currency introduced

FEBRUARY 25   Rolls-Royce nationalized following bankruptcy

MARCH 30   First Conservative budget makes major tax changes and foreshadows value added tax

MAY 27   Labour win Bromsgrove by-election

JUNE 8   Upper Clyde Shipbuilders liquidation followed by work-in

JUNE 23   EEC negotiations concluded

AUGUST 5   Royal assent to Industrial Relations Act

AUGUST 20   First auction of North Sea oil concessions

AUGUST 23	Pound floated (within limits)
OCTOBER 28	Commons votes in favour of EEC entry 356–244 (69 Labour MPs vote for)
1972 JANUARY	Unemployment exceeds 1 million
JANUARY 30	13 killed in Londonderry ('Bloody Sunday')
FEBRUARY 18	Wilberforce Report to settle 6-week miners' strike
MARCH 29	First National Industrial Relations Court fines of unions
MARCH 30	Stormont suspended; William Whitelaw appointed Secretary of State for Northern Ireland
APRIL 7	After Cabinet reshuffle Lord Carrington succeeds Peter Thomas as chairman of the Conservative Party
APRIL 10	Roy Jenkins resigns as deputy leader of the Labour Party
APRIL 17	British Rail work-to-rule (settled on 12 June)
JUNE 23	Pound floated freely
JULY 18	Reginald Maudling resigns as home secretary
JULY 21	Dock strike (till 16 August)
	Housing Finance Act passed
AUGUST 4	Expulsion of Asians from

		Uganda begins
	SEPTEMBER 4	TUC confirms the suspension of unions registering under the Industrial Relations Act
	SEPTEMBER 26	Government proposes prices and incomes policy. Abortive tripartite talks follow
	OCTOBER 26	Liberals win Rochdale (followed by Sutton and Cheam on 7 December)
	NOVEMBER 6	90-day wages and prices standstill following failure of tripartite talks on a voluntary policy (Stage I)
1873	JANUARY 1	Britain joins the EEC
	MARCH 1	Dick Taverne re-elected at Lincoln as an independent (having resigned as sitting Labour MP)
	MARCH 16	'Neutral' budget
	APRIL 1	Stage II of prices and incomes policy
	APRIL 12	First elections to new county authorities under Local Government Act 1972
	MAY	Unemployment falls to less than the 600,000 inherited from the Labour Party
	MAY 12	Lord Lambton and (24 May) Earl Jellicoe resign from

	government
JULY 26	Liberals win Isle of Ely and Ripon by-elections
SEPTEMBER 4	Len Murray succeeds Vic Feather as general secretary of the TUC
OCTOBER 6–22	Middle East War and consequent oil crisis
OCTOBER 31	Kilbrandon Report on devolution to Scotland and Wales
NOVEMBER 8	Scottish Nationalists win Govan by-election; Liberals win Berwick-upon-Tweed
NOVEMBER 12	Miners start overtime ban
DECEMBER 6	Sunningdale talks on Northern Ireland
DECEMBER 12	ASLEF (the Associated Society of Locomotive Engineers and Firemen) starts work-to-rule
DECEMBER 13	3-day week announced, to save electricity
DECEMBER 17	Big cuts in public expenditure announced
1974 JANUARY 10–17	Abortive speculation about election on 7 February
FEBRUARY 5	Miners decide to strike
FEBRUARY 7	General election announced for 28 February

Margaret Thatcher and John Major
(*PA News*)

CHAPTER TEN

1979–96

Ivor Crewe

No period in modern Britain has been as dominated by a single party as the eighteen continuous years of Conservative government from 1979 to 1996.[1] The Conservatives won four elections in succession, an unprecedented feat for any party since the arrival of the mass franchise (see Table 10.1). The victories of 1979, 1983 and 1987 gave the Conservatives, under Margaret Thatcher's leadership, comfortable parliamentary majorities which enabled her to govern confident in the knowledge that her measures would be passed relatively unscathed by opposition or backbench amendment. In 1992, however, the Conservatives under John Major were returned with a relatively slender majority of twenty-one, which defections and by-election losses whittled down to nothing by the summer of 1996. The post-1992 Major administration found itself increasingly at the mercy of small dissident Conservative backbenchers and problems of party management absorbed more and more of its energy.

Conservative supremacy in the Commons owed more to the electoral system than to popularity with the electorate. The Conservatives won between 42 and 44 per cent of the vote, considerably less than the 48 to 50 per cent share they took in their election victories of 1951, 1955 and 1959, or their 46 per cent share when they won under Edward Heath in 1970. In 1979 the Conservatives took 44 per cent of the

How Tory Governments Fall

TABLE 10.1   *General Election Results 1979–92*

| | % of vote (UK) | | | | | Seats | | | |
	1979	1983	1987	1992		1979	1983	1987	1992
Con	44	42	42	42		339	397	376	336
Lab	37	28	31	34		269	209	229	271
Lib	14	25	23	18		11	23	22	20
Other	5	5	4	6		16	21	23	24
Con. maj.	7	14	11	8		43	144	102	21

SOURCE: David Butler and Gareth Butler, *British Political Facts 1900–1994* 7th edition (Macmillan, 1994), pp. 218–19.

vote and won 339 seats, an overall majority of 43. In 1983 the Conservative vote ebbed to 42 per cent, yet as a result of the slump in the Labour vote they won 397 seats and a landslide majority of 144. In 1987 the Conservative vote remained at 42 per cent but because the Labour vote recovered somewhat Conservative strength in the Commons fell to 376, a still handsome majority of 102. In 1992 the Conservative vote remained at 42 per cent but its majority fell to a precarious 21, because of the vagaries of constituency size, turnout and swing.[2]

The Thatcher–Major years were not a period of uninterrupted political dominance. They can be usefully divided into three periods: the Thatcher Supremacy from 1979 to 1990, the Major Honeymoon in 1991–92 and the Disintegration from 1993 to 1996. The Thatcher Supremacy was marked by short periods of intense electoral unpopularity and divisions in the parliamentary party, notably 1980–82 as unemployment soared and the government persisted with a monetarist strategy and a strong pound, the early spring of 1986 at the time of the Westland crisis, and 1989–90 when the poll tax, divisions over Europe and mismanagement of Cabinet relations combined to topple Margaret

Thatcher from the leadership. But, the last apart, Margaret Thatcher weathered these storms without serious difficulty. Her personality, policies and political project dominated the 1980s.

The Conservative dominance from 1979 amounted to much more than longevity in office, important though such continuity was for consolidating Conservative power. Previous periods of continuous Conservative government, such as the 1930s and the 1950s, did not involve as radical a break with the past or as systematic an attempt to implement a programme of reform. The Thatcher Supremacy in particular was a distinctive political era, constituted by three elements. The first was the overwhelming dominance of Margaret Thatcher over Cabinet, party and public imagination from 1979 to her sudden downfall in 1990. The second was her mission to change the political culture, a mission that succeeded with the political classes but failed with the general public. The third was the implementation of social and economic measures shaped by an ideology, which altered the balance of interests that won and lost under the Thatcher governments. Each of these elements of Conservative dominance will be analysed in turn. Many commentators assumed they contributed to the Conservatives' election victories, but, as we shall see, they were the consequence more than the cause of the Conservatives' electoral success.

The Conservative Victory in May 1979

The Conservatives' victory in May 1979 is commonly portrayed as a watershed in British politics, akin to 1906 and 1945, when the British people recognized the need for a fundamental change of political direction. The win was certainly decisive. The Conservative percentage lead over Labour in the popular vote was the largest since 1945 and the national swing of 5.2 per cent was the most emphatic turnaround of party fortunes since the war. Yet the result owed more to the voters' rejection of Labour than their embrace of the Conservatives. By historic standards the Labour vote was exceptionally low but the Conservative vote was not especially high. Margaret Thatcher consistently trailed behind James Callaghan, the Labour leader, in polls of preference for prime minister. The Conservatives won by default.

Overwhelmingly the most important reason for the popular swing against Labour was the 'Winter of Discontent' – the rash of strikes, often accompanied by aggressive picketing, that broke out in pursuit of wage claims above the government's 5 per cent 'norm' in December 1978 and January 1979. Three unusual features marked the strikes. First, the coincidence of so many strikes badly disrupted almost everybody's day-to-day existence: buses and trains did not run; shops ran out of basic items; and schools, petrol stations and even cemeteries closed. Secondly, much of the picketing was vehement, and sometimes violent, with what appeared to be a malicious disregard for the safety and health of the ordinary public. Thirdly, this unusual fierceness and nastiness was vividly communicated to the public day after day in the newspapers and on television: shortages in the supermarkets, piling rubbish on the streets, and the turning away of ambulances were gifts for the media – and the Conservative opposition.

The Winter of Discontent destroyed the Labour government's credibility as the party that could handle the unions, the boast it had consistently made since it ended the miners' strike on winning the February 1974 election, and its most potent appeal when compared with the Conservatives. For many voters, however, it also represented the bankruptcy of the postwar social democratic and corporatist tradition of the Labour Party. It was time for something new.

Personal Dominance? Thatcher's Leadership

Margaret Thatcher was prime minister from May 1979 to November 1990, the longest continuous period for one person to hold the office since the Earl of Liverpool (1812–27). She gave her name to the 1980s – the 'Thatcher decade' – and to the policies of her governments – 'Thatcherism'. Until her final year she dominated her party in the constituencies, Parliament and the Cabinet. Whether the Conservatives owed their dominance of the country to Thatcher, however, is more doubtful.

THATCHER'S DOMINANCE OF THE CABINET

Thatcher held an austerely centralist conception of the role of government: it should rule untrammelled by organized interests, or by other governments, whether local or European; and within government the prime minister should be unimpeded by doubting ministers or officials. 'It must be a conviction government. I could not waste time having any internal arguments,' she told a journalist.[3] This view sprang partly from a wilful and crusading personality; but it also reflected her contempt, shared by most Conservative politicians, for the way preceding governments (including the 1970–74 Heath administration) had kowtowed to trade unions and bankrupt companies and lost control of public expenditure. It would not be allowed to happen while she was in charge.

Her preferred way of dealing with obstructive institutions was not to reform them but to abolish or by-pass them, unless they were so weak that she could ignore them. In Downing Street the structure stayed intact, but the style changed. Decision-making steadily became less collegial and more concentrated in the person of the Prime Minister or her private office. The Cabinet met less frequently and for shorter periods. The number of Cabinet committees was reduced and on some key issues and crises – such as the Falklands War and the 1984 miners' strike – she by-passed the Cabinet committee system and worked through informal groups of trusted officials, politicians and outsiders.[4] Over the years she came to rely increasingly on a small number of personal staff, notably one of her private secretaries, Charles Powell, her press secretary Bernard Ingham and her economic adviser Professor Alan Walters. The breakdown of her relations with some senior Cabinet ministers in 1989 and 1990 precipitated her own downfall in November 1990. It was not until June 1982, when British forces recaptured the Falkland Islands from Argentinian occupation, that Thatcher secured total command of the Cabinet. She began as an outsider, a free-market doctrinaire pitched against corporatist pragmatists, a provincially minded bourgeois among wealthy metropolitans, a woman surrounded by men. Only a minority of her first Cabinet had voted for her in the Conservative leadership election of 1975; her Cabinet colleagues were 'them'. She established her authority by force of personality and conviction, leading rather than chairing the Cabinet, by stating her views from the outset rather than sitting back and inviting discussion; by brooking no contradictions, and belittling dissenters. She consolidated her authority by systematically dismissing 'wets' as soon as she felt safe to do so and replacing them with ideological allies in the key economic ministries.

The most serious challenge to her leadership in this period came in March 1981. Already disconcerted by the Cabinet dismissal two months earlier of the liberal and independent-minded leader of the House, Norman St John Stevas, the wets were appalled by the budget. It cut public expenditure savagely at a time of spiralling unemployment; worse, none of them had been consulted. James Prior, the secretary of state for employment, led the protests but his bluff was called and he settled for the sop of a place on the Economic Cabinet Committee. It was a turning-point in the Prime Minister's relations with the Cabinet. In September Thatcher dismissed three wets – Gilmour, Soames and Carlisle (and Maude) – brought the 'dry' Tebbit and Lawson into the Cabinet and moved Prior to the Northern Ireland Office. Unhappy backbenchers looked to Gilmour to raise the standard of revolt but were disappointed.

The Falklands War was a military and political gamble,

taken by Thatcher alone, which paid off. It secured her total dominance of Cabinet and party, which was renewed by resounding election victories in 1983 and 1987, until the year of disintegration in 1990. Her only moment of vulnerability was in January–February 1986 during the Westland affair, an inter-departmental row which got out of control. An American company, Sikorski, was set to take over Westland, Britain's last remaining helicopter company; the Department of Trade and Industry accepted the financial logic of the takeover whereas Michael Heseltine, as minister for defence, vehemently opposed it as detrimental to Britain's long-term defence and industrial interests. Seeking to settle the issue in the DTI's favour, Thatcher prohibited discussion in Cabinet, precipitating a flamboyant resignation by Heseltine. It soon emerged that her private office had condoned the illegal leaking of documents to blacken Heseltine's name. Her resignation might have been forced by abstentions from backbenchers in the Commons debate on the issue but she was saved by the limp speech and maladroit tactics of the Labour leader, Neil Kinnock.

THATCHER'S DOWNFALL

However, Thatcher paid a heavy price for her cavalier treatment of Heseltine and for her growing carelessness in relations with senior colleagues which it signified. Insecure during her first year of office she became emboldened by her popularity in the party at large and the ease with which she was able to dispatch senior ministers – not only the wets in September 1981, but the foreign secretary Francis Pym immediately after the 1983 election and his successor, Sir Geoffrey Howe, in June 1989, both on grounds of little more than personal dislike. In October 1989 Nigel Lawson, Chancellor of the Exchequer, resigned in frustration at Thatcher's increasing, and very public, reliance on her private economic adviser, Alan Walters, which was her way of signalling disagreement with Lawson's policy on sterling. In November 1989, an obscure pro-European backbencher,

Sir Anthony Meyer, exploited the laxity of the party's rules to challenge her for the leadership, attracting thirty-three votes and provoking twenty-seven abstentions. Thus she began the year 1990 having lost the support of a fifth of her backbenchers and having bitterly alienated her two most senior ministers. In November 1990, she was again challenged for the leadership, this time by her old adversary Heseltine, publicly supported by Howe and Lawson. Heseltine won 152 votes to Thatcher's 204 (there were 16 abstentions), enough under the rules to force a second ballot. Immediately it became clear that she had lost the confidence of almost half her backbenchers, she lost the confidence of her ministers and resigned.

Policy differences over European integration and the poll tax, as well as personal resentments, played a part in turning the parliamentary party against Thatcher. But the decisive factor was MPs' conclusion that Mrs Thatcher had become a serious and irreversible electoral liability. Under her leadership, they believed, the Conservatives would lose office at the next election. Even worse, under her leadership many of them would lose their seats.

This pessimism arose from a variety of poll findings over the course of 1990. Three are worth highlighting. First, Thatcher ceased to outshine her party. For the first six years of her premiership, irrespective of Conservative fortunes, her popularity consistently ran about 5 per cent ahead of her party's. She was therefore a potential vote-puller in an election campaign. Between the Westland affair in early 1986 and Lawson's resignation in October 1989 she ran equally with her party. But thereafter she was running 3 or 4 per cent behind and in that sense had become an electoral burden. Secondly, by 1990 her 'satisfaction rating' as prime minister had dropped very low. In April 1990, when people received their poll tax demands, it fell to 23 per cent, a record low for any prime minister. Over the entire year (up to her resignation in November) it averaged 29 per cent, the lowest recorded annual mean. Finally,

Thatcher's continuation in office became a damaging electoral issue in itself. In March 1990 the government lost the hitherto ultra-safe Conservative seat of mid-Staffordshire in a by-election. The Conservative-to-Labour swing was the largest for over fifty years. According to the ITN/Harris exit poll 90 per cent of Conservative defectors said she had 'gone too far in her policies and lost touch with ordinary people' and 77 per cent said she should 'not remain as leader at the next election'. Among loyalists the proportions were 41 and 27 per cent respectively.[5] No other issue divided defectors from loyalists so sharply. Another by-election poll suggested that Mrs Thatcher's departure would produce a 'resignation bonus' of up to 14 percentage points: 15 per cent were 'more likely' to vote Conservative, and only 1 per cent 'less likely', if Mrs Thatcher were to resign as prime minister.[6]

By mid-November, Conservative MPs contemplating for whom to vote in the leadership contest were saturated with polls suggesting that she was a vote loser while Michael Heseltine was a vote winner. The 'resignation bonus' had increased to 21 percentage points: 28 per cent said they were more likely to vote Conservative if Mrs Thatcher resigned, 7 per cent less likely.[7] In the week before the leadership contest seven polling organizations conducted 'trial runs' of the next general election: with Thatcher as leader the Conservatives trailed Labour by an average of 10 per cent; with Heseltine as leader they led Labour by an average of 5 per cent. Two-thirds of the electorate thought that Mrs Thatcher should resign immediately or 'if a significant number of MPs vote against her or abstain'.[8] Not surprisingly many Conservative MPs thought so too.

THATCHER'S DOMINANCE OF THE ELECTORATE:
MYTH AND REALITY
In the 1980s the Conservative Party dominated the country and Mrs Thatcher dominated the Conservative Party. But it would be mistaken to infer that the Conservatives owed their dominance primarily to Thatcher. They won the three

elections of 1979, 1983 and 1987 under her leadership – but not solely or primarily *because* of her leadership. In 1979 the Conservatives won – or, rather, Labour lost – despite her: voters preferred Callaghan to Thatcher as prime minister.[9] In 1983, her post-Falklands popularity did add a few percentage points to the Conservatives' margin of victory, but even under a different leader, and without the Falklands campaign, the Conservatives would have been re-elected on the back of a credit-led economic recovery and the implausibility of Labour's leader, Michael Foot. In 1987 her net impact was neutral.

Thatcher was frequently depicted by contemporary commentators as an exceptionally popular prime minister with a special relationship to the British electorate. But the satisfaction ratings in the monthly Gallup poll show that Mrs Thatcher was the second *least* popular prime minister since the war, surpassed only (and just) by Edward Heath (see Table 10.2). The 'dissatisfied' outnumbered the 'satisfied' in 120 of her 138 months at No. 10. Her mean satisfaction score was 39 per cent during her 1979–83 administration, 39 per cent again in her second government of 1983–87 and 38 per cent in the three and a half years she presided over her third administration. There was no sudden deterioration from an earlier period of adulation. There was a consistent lack of adulation.

Of course, the mean figures incorporate fluctuations. In her first government her score topped 50 per cent immediately after the Falklands victory in June 1982, having been at 25 per cent only six months earlier, when unemployment was rising rapidly. In her second government she again exceeded 50 per cent, in summer 1983 soon after her election victory, but fell to under 30 per cent at the time of the Westland affair. In her third government she exceeded 50 per cent just once, again shortly after her election victory, but plummeted to below 25 per cent when the poll tax came into operation in March/April 1990.

Yet there was never a love affair between the electorate

TABLE 10.2   *The Popularity of Postwar Prime Ministers*

Question: 'Are you satisfied or dissatisfied with ... as prime minister?

Period	Prime Minister	Mean	% satisfied Low	High
1945–51	Attlee (Lab.)	47	37	66
1951–55	Churchill (Con.)	52	48	56
1955–57	Eden (Con.)	55	41	70
1957–63	Macmillan (Con.)	51	30	79
1963–64	Douglas-Home (Con.)	45	41	48
1964–66	Wilson (Lab.)	59	48	66
1966–70	Wilson (Lab.)	41	27	69
1970–74	Heath (Con.)	37	31	45
1974–76	Wilson (Lab.)	46	40	53
1976–79	Callaghan (Lab.)	46	33	59
1979–82	Thatcher (pre-Falklands)	36	25	46
1982–83	Thatcher (post-Falklands)	47	44	52
1983–87	Thatcher (Con.)	39	28	53
1987–90	Thatcher (Con.)	38	23	52
1990–92	Major (Con.)	51	46	59
1992–95	Major (Con.)	25	18	54

SOURCE: *Gallup Political Index*

and Mrs Thatcher. Her peaks of popularity did not approach Callaghan's in the 1970s, Wilson's in the 1960s, Eden's and Macmillan's in the 1950s or Attlee's after the war. Her troughs, however, sank lower than those of any other prime minister. Despite the force of her personality, a personality that stamped the decade, she rarely won the hearts of British voters – and their minds only sometimes.

Ideological Dominance? Thatcher's Cultural Crusade

Myths about Thatcher's electoral dominance arise from the kind of prime minister she was. Most peacetime prime ministers in Britain this century have been healers, not warriors

– consensus politicians without strong opinions on most issues, but anxious to ensure unity in their party and co-operation in the country. Mrs Thatcher, by contrast, was a 'warrior': 'I am a conviction politician,' she claimed in the 1979 election campaign. 'The Old Testament prophets did not say "Brothers I want consensus." They said, "This is my faith and vision. This is what I passionately believe. If you believe it, too, then come with me."' She was the most evangelical and opinionated prime minister since Gladstone, the most combative and radical since Lloyd George.[10]

Thatcher's objective was nothing less than a cultural revolution. The public had to be persuaded to lower its expectations of, and dependence upon, the state; the social democratic consensus had to be replaced by a new neo-liberal consensus.

The 1980s provided almost perfect conditions for creating such a new consensus. Thatcher was granted considerably more time and greater powers than most elected leaders are to reshape the public consciousness. Few party leaders are elected to the helm of a centralized, unitary state for an unbroken eleven years, with no serious institutional opposition and with the following wind of an enthusiastically partisan press. The only parallel abroad, dictatorships excluded, was de Gaulle's eleven years as president of the fledgling Fifth Republic.

Thatcher's cultural crusade half succeeded. Among opinion formers the social democratic consensus crumbled. Intellectual vitality was conspicuously greater on the right than the left. Intellectuals of the right were confident: history was on their side and left-wing ideas were in retreat both in Britain and throughout the world. Intellectuals of the left, by contrast, were defensive and in the case of many Marxists half-admiring of the New Right's radicalism and theoretical muscle. Right-wing think tanks, such as the Institute for Economic Affairs, the Adam Smith Institute and the Centre for Policy Studies, expanded their influence, while their only counterpart on the left, the Fabian Society, made little impact on informed opinion. Magazines on the centre-left declined: in 1987 *New Society* had to merge with the *New Statesman*, and in 1991 *The Listener* and *Marxism Today*, the liveliest of them all, closed down. On the right, by contrast, the neo-liberal *Economist* and high Tory *Spectator* flourished.

Even more tellingly, the opposition parties shifted decisively and steadily to the right. In 1974 Sir Keith Joseph had complained of a 'socialist ratchet' in British party politics. In the 1980s the ratchet was capitalist.

The brief life and times of the Social Democratic Party (SDP) are instructive. It began in 1981 as a Labour Party Mark II, with the nasty socialist bits left out, but a party of the social and economic left for all that. It believed in spending Britain's way out of the recession, in a statutory incomes policy, in a high tax/welfare economy and, on defence, in scrapping the Trident submarine programme. Six years later, under David Owen, it stood for a low tax/low expenditure economy, had abandoned incomes policy as a counter-inflationary instrument, proposed internal markets within the public sector, accepted the advantages of privatization (while insisting on more competition and regulation) and had done an about-turn on Trident. It ended up as a Conservative Party Mark II, without the nastier Thatcherite bits.

The progression of Labour Party policy followed the same path, but a few steps behind. Its 1989 policy review[11] amounted to a wholesale abandonment of its 1983 and 1987 programmes and was the least socialist policy statement published in the history of the party. It included a 180-degree reversal on most major policy areas, including the discarding of price and import controls; the dropping of the wealth tax; the commitment not to return to penal rates of personal taxation; the refusal to restore the trade unions' former legal immunities; and, most spectacular of all, the rejection of unilateral nuclear disarmament. But it went further: it adopted Thatcher's language of markets and individualism, referring to the 'strengths' and 'vital role' of free markets and to 'consumers' and 'users' rather than 'the working class'. In effect the Labour Party jettisoned socialism in all but name and turned itself into a party of private enterprise and the free market.

The Labour Party's policy transformation was of course brought about by electoral and practical considerations: only a clean break from the party's ideological past would make it electable, Labour leaders believed, and much of the Thatcher governments' record was irreversible anyway. Nor was there much stomach for reversing it. They had sincerely opposed the privatization programme and trade union reforms but their success seemed undeniable: higher profits, better service, improved industrial relations. They could hardly admit it, even to themselves, but most of the Labour leadership had been converted. Thatcher had won the political argument.

Yet she did not win the political argument with ordinary voters, let alone change their cultural values. Asked in March 1989, ten years after Thatcher came to power, to choose between a 'Thatcherite' and a 'socialist' society, respondents in a MORI opinion poll opted for the Thatcherite model on only two out of five dimensions, and then by slender majorities. They preferred a free but unequal society to an egalitarian one, and an efficient economy to one that subsidized jobs. Yet a small majority preferred 'a mainly socialist society in which public interests and a more controlled economy are most important' (49 per cent) to a 'mainly capitalist society' (43 per cent), and a larger majority opted for a society 'which emphasizes the social and collective provision of welfare' (55 per cent) over one in which 'the individual is encouraged to look after himself' (40 per cent). And by a massive five to one ratio the respondents preferred a society in which 'caring for others' (79 per cent) is more highly rewarded than 'the creation of wealth' (16 per cent).[12] In other words, efficiency is necessary and the inequalities that accompany it are acceptable; but untrammelled free enterprise and individual acquisitiveness are not. After a decade of Thatcherism, the public remained wedded to the collectivist, welfare ethic of social democracy – or so they said.

Nor was there evidence that the ethic of self-reliance, Thatcher's favourite 'Victorian virtue', grew during the Thatcher years. In 1984 Gallup asked voters whether they thought the government's most important job was to provide good opportunities for everyone to get ahead or whether its job was to guarantee everybody steady employment and a decent standard of living. At that time only 30 per cent said they were content with good opportunities; 65 per cent wanted a government guarantee. The proportion believing in self-reliance had actually been higher when the identical question was put, after six years of war, under Attlee's government in 1945.[13] Asked in 1987 whether the unemployed have usually themselves to blame for their condition, only 13 per cent agreed; 87 per cent disagreed. Thatcher's self-help doctrines seemingly fell on deaf ears.

This refusal to embrace broad Thatcherite values was paralleled by a growing rejection of more specific Thatcherite positions. For example, in May 1979 equal numbers of Gallup poll respondents opted for tax cuts – even at the cost of some reduction in government services such as health, education and welfare – as for the extension of these services even if this meant some tax increases. By 1983 there were twice as many service-extenders as tax-cutters; by 1987 six times as many; by October 1989 seven times as many.[14]

The public overwhelmingly supported the Employment Acts of the 1980s, which stripped trade unions of many of their traditional immunities and disruptive powers, but Thatcherism failed in its more ambitious aim of persuading the electorate that trade unions are undesirable or unnecessary institutions. Throughout the decade a majority thought that 'generally speaking, and thinking of Britain as a while, trade unions are a good thing', despite the sharp decline in trade union membership, and that majority increased after

1985.[15] Thus the electorate's response to Thatcherite policies on trade unions was entirely pragmatic. It welcomed the elimination of obvious abuses without embracing any principled objection to the collectivism of trade unions.

Privatization provides a third example. The Thatcher governments spent large sums of public money and much political energy trying to persuade the public of the virtues of privatization; but to little avail. Thatcher came to power when the public was already firmly in favour of it; between 1979 and 1983 the majority preferring privatization to nationalization hovered around 20 per cent. By 1987, the majority was a mere 4 per cent, and the proportion believing that nationalized industries were less efficient than private companies steadily declined during the Thatcher decade.[16] Thus the Thatcher governments failed to alter public attitudes: if anything, British people edged further away from Thatcherite positions as the decade progressed. Thatcher transformed the political economy, reshaped the social structure and overturned the political debate; but this was done without a cultural counter-revolution in the thinking of ordinary people.

The New Balance of Interests: Thatcher's Social Project

The Thatcher administration was far more determined than previous Conservative governments to reshape the social structure. The government's first priority was to spread individual property-ownership more widely than before, in the name of individual 'self-sufficiency' and 'responsibility'. The motive was mainly ideological, but the anticipated economic and partisan side-benefits played an important part too. The two main means of extending property were the sales of shares in the newly privatized utilities and industries such as British Telecom and British Gas and the sale of council houses (that is, houses rented from local authorities) to long-standing tenants at a discount on their market value.

Privatization was not part of the original Thatcherite project. It rated barely a mention in the Conservative Party's 1979 manifesto and played little part during Thatcher's first term. The 1983–87 government stumbled across privatization as an effective, quick means of cutting the public sector borrowing requirement and packaged it as 'popular capitalism' – a means of spreading wealth and the ownership of industry. Before the 1980s share-ownership was confined to small numbers of the monied middle classes and was the opposite of 'user-friendly'. The privatization share issues were therefore specially tailored for the modest investor and backed up by a massive advertising campaign.

The campaign was effective. Over a fifth of the public (22 per cent) bought shares in at least one of the privatization issues, and the total number of shareholders more than trebled from 7 per cent in 1979 to 25 per cent in 1991.[17] If indirect owners of shares through private pension schemes are added, at least a third of the electorate by 1991 had a personal stake in share values. First-time share-buyers, moreover, were drawn fairly evenly from across the entire social spectrum. Exactly half were in the skilled manual and semi- and unskilled manual classes.[18] When Thatcher became prime minister trade unionists outnumbered shareholders in the electorate by four to one; when she left Downing Street shareholders outnumbered trade unionists by five to four.

The electoral significance of the privatization issues, however, turned out to be small. First-time share-buyers were drawn disproportionately from Conservative ranks in the first place and swung to Labour between 1983 and 1987 in line with the national average.[19] This was hardly surprising. Most of them bought small quantities of shares which made up only a tiny part of their assets (and many quickly sold them for a windfall gain). But the bare voting figures probably underestimate the political importance of the growing numbers of share-owners, for they might have voted differently had the Labour Party threatened the value of their holdings. The Labour manifesto carefully assured voters that the 'special new securities' to which British Telecom and British Gas shares would be converted 'would be bought and sold in the market in the usual way'.[20] The Labour Party could no longer risk any hint of renationalizing the industries that had been privatised. The privatization programme of the 1980s permanently scuppered the Labour Party's historic commitment, still enshrined in its constitution, to the public ownership of industry.

Housing, of course, represents a much larger investment for most people. In the 1930s Herbert Morrison, the Labour leader of London, promised to 'build the Tories out of London' by planning large council estates in the London suburbs. Thatcher's aim was to march the Conservatives back in again by selling the estates to their tenants at a substantial discount on their market value.

Between 1980 and 1990 over 1.2 million council houses were sold. Nothing more perfectly encapsulated Thatcherism's appeal to the aspiring, modestly affluent working class, and it yielded electoral dividends for the Conservatives. As in the case of shares, the tenants who bought were more likely to be Conservative than those who did not; but, in the early years especially, the Labour tenants who bought were much more likely to have stopped voting Labour by the time of the next election than those who continued to rent. In 1987 the impact of council house purchases was weaker than in 1983 but was nonetheless to the disadvantage of Labour: buyers swung by 2 per cent from Labour to Conservative (against the national trend) whereas the continuing renters swung by 5.5 per cent from Conservative to Labour.[21] To this extent, the Conservative government legislated away part of Labour's electoral base. But one should not exaggerate the overall impact. Sales affected only 7 per cent of the whole electorate and about 8 per cent of manual workers. Their political significance was symbolic as much as substantive.

Council house sales merely accelerated a steady, long-term growth of house-ownership in Britain. The mid to late

1980s in particular witnessed a new housing boom, fuelled by the entry of the high street banks into the home loans market (following the deregulation of the financial services industry) and by relatively low interest rates. People borrowed to the hilt to step on to the housing ladder or up to a higher rung. New housing estates and DIY superstores sprouted up on the outskirts of every city. In 1979 just over half (52 per cent) of all households owned their homes, either outright or through a loan ('mortgage'); by 1989 two-thirds (66 per cent) did, including the majority (56 per cent) of manual workers. Over the same period the proportion renting from a local authority fell from a third (34 per cent) to a quarter (24 per cent).[22]

The spread of home-ownership in the 1980s undoubtedly helped the Conservatives: at a rough estimate, it produced a 2 to 3 per cent swing from Labour to the Conservatives between 1979 and 1991[23] – the equivalent of twenty to thirty seats. The Conservatives benefited from being histori-cally associated with low rates and mortgage tax relief while Labour was associated with high rates and an ambivalent attitude to mortgage tax relief. Labour may have suffered from the fragmentation of formerly homogeneous council housing estates into buyers and non-buyers. The departure of the more affluent and skilled manual workers to private housing estates deprived the Labour Party of the elite of neighbourhood activists who had mobilized the Labour vote in the past: as council estates became increasingly occupied by a residual 'underclass' of welfare dependants, their elec-toral turnout declined.

It would nevertheless be misleading to say that the private housing boom in the Thatcher years gave the Conservatives an electoral advantage that was permanent and automatic, for that would depend on home-owners continuing to regard the Conservative Party as their friend and the Labour Party as their enemy. By the late 1980s they no longer did. Their gratitude quickly wore thin in the 1989–92 recession, as home loan interest rates soared, the housing market collapsed and building societies and banks increasingly resorted to the repossession of loan defaulters' homes. The opinion polls showed that by 1990 Labour was the preferred party both of mortgagees and outright owners.[24]

The mortgage rate problems in the late 1980s represented the electoral downside of Thatcher's social engineering – and then only part of it. Between 1981 and 1990 outstanding debt *excluding* mortgages more than doubled both in real terms and as a proportion of household expenditure.[25] The credit booms of 1982–83 and 1986–88, fuelled by lowering interest rates and the wealth illusion of rising house prices, swung more voters to the Conservatives than share issues or house buying. The real symbol of social change in the Thatcher years – and the source of its electoral dominance – was not the share certificate or property title deed but the credit card.

The New Electoral Geography 1979–92

A leading sociologist of Britain summarized the social and economic trends of the Thatcher years as follows:

> A pattern has emerged of a more unequal society with a majority securely attached to a still prosperous country and a minority in a marginal economic and social position, the former moving into the suburbs of the new economy of a 'green and pleasant land', the latter tending to be trapped in the old provincial industrial cities and their displaced fragments of peripheral council housing estates.[26]

These inequalities were reflected in the electoral geography of the Thatcher years. Until the 1980s the whole of the country moved in the same direction at elections: it responded as one nation. But both the 1983 and 1987 elections were 'two nations' elections: the Conservatives advanced where there was prosperity and growth but retreated where there was deprivation and decline. Broadly speaking the economy was most dynamic in the southern and eastern regions, most sluggish in the northern and western regions. As the geographical axis of economic growth tilted, so did that of party support. The country as a whole swung by a mere 0.3 per cent from Labour to the Conservatives between 1979 and 1992. But, as Table 10.3 shows, there was a pronounced swing to the Conservatives in high growth regions of the south-east (2.8 per cent) and East Anglia (2.5 per cent), whereas voters swung to Labour in the depressed regions of the north-west (by 4.1 per cent), and north (3.6 per cent), Wales (2.3 per cent) and Scotland (1.6 per cent). Within the regions the Conservatives gained most in the suburbs, small towns and countryside and least in the large towns, inner-city and outer-fringe council estates.

TABLE 10.3 *Britain's Changing Electoral Geography 1979–92*

Region	% Change in vote				Change in seats			
	Con.	Lab.	Lib.	Swing	Con.	Lab.	Lib.	Nat.
Great Britain	−2.1	−2.6	+4.2	+0.3	−3	+3	+9	+3
Scotland	−5.7	−2.5	+4.4	−1.6	−11	+5	+6	+1
North-west	−5.9	+2.3	+2.8	−4.1	−4	−1	−	
North	−4.4	+2.8	+2.6	−3.6	−3	−	−	
Yorkshire & Humberside	−0.9	−0.6	+1.4	−0.2	+1	−	−1	
Wales	−3.6	+0.9	+1.8	−2.3	−5	+6	−	+2
West Midlands	−2.3	−1.3	+3.5	−0.5	−2	+4	−	
East Midlands	0.0	−2.2	+2.5	+1.1	+8	−2	−	
East Anglia	+0.3	−4.6	+3.5	+2.5	+4	−	−1	
South-west	−3.7	−5.6	+8.7	+1.0	+1	−1	+5	
London	−0.7	−2.6	+3.3	+1.0	−2	−7	+1	
South-east	−0.4	−5.9	+5.9	+2.8	+10	−1	−	

SOURCE: *Gallup Political Index*

This geographical pattern rapidly accelerated a long-term trend that went back to 1959, with two important consequences for the party system. The first was that in the 1980s the Conservative and Labour parties ceased to be national parties in the sense of representing the full range of Britain's social and geographical spectrum. In the 1960s and 1970s most conservative MPs came from the shires, suburbs and seaside resorts, but a sufficient minority were elected from the big cities of the north to keep their party in touch with the realities of industrial decline. In 1959 the northern cities of Glasgow, Edinburgh, Liverpool, Manchester, Newcastle, Bradford, Leeds, Sheffield and Hull elected twenty-eight Conservative MPs; in 1979 they elected twelve; but in 1987 they elected a mere five. Old industrial Britain was one world, the Conservative Party another. There was a parallel in the Labour Party. It had always represented the inner-city, smokestack towns and council estates, but in the 1960s and 1970s a sufficient minority was elected from the New Towns and other parts of the urban south to keep the party in touch with the changing expectations of the more affluent working class. In 1959 nineteen Labour MPs were elected from the south-eastern third of Britain (excluding London); in 1979 the number was fourteen, by 1987 only three. Prosperous Britain was one world, the Labour Party quite another. Each party had become the almost exclusive representative of only one of the historic two 'nations'.

John Major's Long Honeymoon
November 1990 to March 1992

A measure of the electoral liability Margaret Thatcher had become by late 1990 is the overnight transformation of the Conservative Party's electoral position after John Major succeeded her as leader and prime minister.[27] Although the party did poorly (but not disastrously) in the 1991 local elections and lost four by-elections – Ribble Valley, Monmouth, Kincardine & Deeside and Langbaugh – its standing in the polls recovered dramatically, from a 12 per cent deficit in the Gallup 9000 in October 1990 to a 6 per cent lead in December 1990 – a 9 per cent swing from Labour to Conservative. Thereafter Conservative support was remarkably stable, rising slightly during the Gulf War in early 1991, ebbing back in the summer and autumn. It stayed ahead of Labour in ten of the fifteen months, the parties' average standing being Con. 40, Lab. 38. In the fifteen months prior to Mrs Thatcher's downfall, Labour had led the Conservatives throughout, and the average was Con. 34, Lab. 46. Thus voters continued to use by-elections and local elections to protest against the government's performance, but their attitude to a fourth term of Conservative government was open-minded. The electoral atmosphere was completely different.

The shift of electoral mood owed far more to Thatcher's departure than to Major's arrival. Major was an obscure figure to the voters, an unexceptionable politician who had risen without trace, but with the important virtue of not being Thatcher.

Once Major was prime minister, his popularity soared. His 'satisfaction rating' ('Are you satisfied or dissatisfied with Mr Major as prime minister?') averaged 52 per cent in 1991, a level never reached by Mrs Thatcher, even in the Falklands year of 1983. His satisfaction ratings ran well ahead of the government's – and by a much wider margin than Mrs Thatcher's did. What voters liked about Major was the change in prime ministerial style, in particular the end of macho leadership. He got only moderate scores on 'decisiveness' (54 per cent), strength of personality (49 per cent) and being 'firmly in charge' (50 per cent) (Gallup, September 1991). But the overwhelming majority of people regarded him as 'concerned for the country as a whole' (67 per cent), trustworthy (70 per cent), competent (75 per cent), caring (77 per cent) and, above all, plain likable (86 per cent). He was Honest John, a decent and reasonable man doing his best for the country; and he had a wonderfully disarming smile.

The specific difference made by John Major rather than Douglas Hurd or Michael Heseltine becoming prime minister was probably modest. He undoubtedly won back disaffected Conservatives by abolishing the poll tax, and his emollient and engaging manner gave Conservatism a softer and more pragmatic face, but Hurd or Heseltine would probably have moved the party in a similar direction. Major's most distinctive electoral strength was his capacity to unite the party. He belonged to no faction, bore no ideological label and had made few enemies. He was an instinctive healer and party broker (he had, after all, been a whip). Most crucially, as the contender favoured by Thatcher, his election helped to reconcile Thatcher's supporters to her downfall.

Conservative support would almost certainly have recovered under any of the contenders to replace Thatcher. When Thatcher was prime minister voters thought in terms of 'Mrs Thatcher's government' as much as 'the Conservative government'. By changing the prime minister, the Conservative Party could present itself to the electorate as a wholly new government. At the general election sixteen months later, when Gallup asked people 'who or what is more to blame for the recession' 48 per cent replied 'the worldwide economic recession', 43 per cent 'the Thatcher government' and only 4 per cent 'the Major government' (6 per cent said 'don't know'). By changing their leader – albeit for the former Chancellor of the Exchequer – the Conservative Party was absolved of past sins and given a new period of grace.

The 1992 Election: More Continuity than Change

Favourable comparisons of Major to Kinnock played a prominent part in the media's coverage of the 1992 election campaign. Major's sincere, unflashy style of campaigning, it was argued, eventually got through to ordinary voters. But although voters decidedly preferred Major to Kinnock as prospective prime minister – and by a much larger margin than they preferred Thatcher to Kinnock in 1987 – detailed analysis suggests that his personal boost to the Conservative vote was probably minuscule.[28] Detailed accounts of the 1992 election result can be found elsewhere.[29] The main explanations look very similar to those for the 1987 election and can be summarized as follows:

1. The baseline vote continued its glacial shift to the right. Social demography, notably the contraction of the working class, council housing and trade unionism, and the ageing of society, continued to benefit the Conservatives.

2. The four-week campaign made very little difference, except for a small tactical shift from Labour to the Liberal Democrats in the last few days.

3. The main factor behind both the late swing to the Conservatives and the Conservatives' recovery prior to the campaign was the broad sense that the Conservatives were more capable than Labour of managing the economy at a time of recession. This overrode recriminations against the government for the recession, concern about unemployment and the public services, and the belief that, other things being equal, a Labour government would be better for jobs, the health service, education and pensions.

4. The greater confidence in the Conservatives' economic competence was helped by the gradual reduction of interest and inflation rates in the nine months prior to the election. Personal economic optimism – a crucial factor among uncommitted voters – increased sharply in March and April 1992.

5. Voters did not trust the Conservatives so much as distrust Labour. A lack of confidence in Kinnock, the

belief that a Labour government would raise income tax, and the anti-Labour campaign of the Conservative tabloid press all contributed to this distrust of the Labour Party. The Conservatives did not win the election: Labour lost it – and had lost it before the campaign began.

6. The Liberal Democrat vote declined from 1987 because of the electoral damage inflicted by the botched merger of the SDP and the Liberals. The belief that a vote for the Liberal Democrats was wasted and that it would 'let Labour in', reinforced perhaps by talk of a Labour–Liberal Democrat coalition in the final week of the campaign, helped the Conservatives.

Most of these explanations applied equally to the Conservative victory in 1987 and reflected enduring features of British electoral behaviour whose origins went back to the Thatcher era – or beyond. Social demography had been undermining Labour's base for two decades. Perceptions of the government's economic competence, judged by trends in the economy, were always important, and usually decisive. The centre party suffers from the 'wasted vote' argument at every election.

An exceptional feature of the election, however, was that for the first time since the 1950s Labour's national vote was more efficiently distributed than the Conservatives'. Two of the regions with above average swings to Labour – London and the east midlands – contained a disproportionate concentration of Conservative-held marginals. Moreover, tactical voting by Liberal Democrats pushed the Labour vote up by more than average in Conservative marginals. As a result Labour's gain in seats was disproportionate to its gain in the popular vote: hence the Conservatives' overall majority was reduced to 21 even though they were fully eight percentage points ahead of Labour in the national vote.

Disintegration: 1993–96

Within months of the 1992 election the deepest and longest electoral slump in modern British politics began. Every indicator of public confidence in the government – vote intention, approval of the government's record, preference for prime minister, perceived economic competence – sank to unprecedented depths (see Table 10.4). Previous Conservative administrations had had crises of public confidence: the 1963 Profumo scandal, the 1973–74 miners' strike and three-day week, the 1981–82 recession, the 1990 poll tax furore. None was as severe or prolonged as 1993–96.

The slump occurred in three stages: after the government's undignified scuttle from the Exchange Rate Mechanism on 'Black Wednesday'; after its by-election and local election humiliations in the summer of 1993; and after the election of Tony Blair as Labour leader in July 1994.

Black Wednesday was, in effect, a devaluation of the pound, symbolizing national humiliation and a failure both of macro-economic strategy and of short-term currency management. It contradicted the traditional basis of Conservative claims to superiority over other parties: the defence of sterling, financial discipline, an understanding of the City, a safe pair of hands. As Thatcher's chancellor John Major had propelled Britain into the ERM; in the election he had repeatedly insisted on the long-term necessity of ERM currency discipline; in the summer, he mocked the policy of withdrawal as 'fool's gold'. Who were the fools now?

The electoral impact of Black Wednesday was dramatic. In the three months from June to August 1992, the average standing of the parties was Con. 39 per cent, Lab. 42 per cent, a Labour lead of 3 per cent. In the three months from October to December 1992, the figures were Con. 32 per cent, Lab. 49 per cent, a Labour lead of 17 per cent. Confidence in John Major, the government's overall record and the future of the economy collapsed in tandem (see Table 10.5).

TABLE 10.4 *Public Confidence in the Government and Prime Minister: Comparison of 1993–5 with Three Previous Worst Postwar Years*

	(mean)			
	1993	1994	1995	Lowest previous years
% intending to vote Conservative	27%	23%	24%	1981: 31% 1985: 34% 1986: 34%
% who 'approve of the government's record to date	14%	12%	13%	1968 (Lab.) 21% 1981 (Con.) 25% 1992 (Con.) 26%
% who believe that the government 'is handling the economic situation properly'*	14%	15%	15%	1990 (Con.) 19% 1992 (Con.) 22% 1981 (Con.) 22%
% who are 'satisfied with _____ as Prime Minister'	23%	21%	23%	1990 (Thatcher) 29%** 1981 (Thatcher) 31% 1968 (Wilson) 32%

* This question was asked only from 1980 onwards
** December 1990 is excluded.

SOURCE: Gallup Polls

QUESTIONS: 'If there were a general election tomorrow, which party would you support?'
'Do you approve or disapprove of the government's record to date?'
'Do the government's plans for tackling the economic situation give you the feeling that they are or are not handling the situation properly?'
'Are you satisfied or dissatisfied with _____ as prime minister?'

COLLAPSE IN THE COUNTIES, NEMESIS AT NEWBURY

The depths of public dissatisfaction suggested by the polls was put to its first nationwide test at the county council elections in May 1993. The Conservatives were routed,

TABLE 10.5 *The Impact of 'Black Wednesday' on Public Confidence in John Major, the Government's Record and the Future of the Economy*

	June– Aug. 1992	Oct.– Dec. 1992	Change	Jan.– Dec. 1993
% 'satisfied' with prime minister	49%	25%	−24	23%
% saying Major would make best prime minister	41%	23%	−18	20%
% who 'approve of the government's record to date'	30%	15%	−15	14%
optimism index about 'general economic situation'*	−3	−27	−24	−4
optimism index about 'financial situation of your household'*	0	−13	−13	−8

* per cent replying will get 'a lot better' or 'a little better' *minus* per cent replying will get 'a little worse' or 'a lot worse'.

SOURCE: Gallup Polls

losing control of every county council except Buckingham-shire, including impregnable Conservative shires such as Dorset, Kent and Norfolk, which had been Conservative-run throughout their 105-year history. The Conservatives' vote crumbled to the national (Great Britain) equivalent of 31 per cent, its lowest level in any nationwide election in modern history. The primary gainers were the Liberal Democrats, the Conservatives' main challengers in rural and small town England (see Table 10.6).

On local election day a by-election was held in Newbury, a prosperous market town and rural seat in Berkshire. It was a lucky break for the Liberal Democrats, who were strong locally: they had nearly won the seat back in 1974,

TABLE 10.6 *Conservative Collapse in Local Elections 1993–95*

	1993	1994	1995
Conservative wards			
Con. wards being defended	1,444	1,317	4,087
Number retained	966	888	2,069
Net loss	−478	−429	−2,018
% loss	−33%	−33%	−49%
Conservative-controlled councils			
Number defended	17	33	70
Number retained	1	15	9
Net loss	−16	−18	−61
% loss	−94%	−55	−87%
vote share (national equivalent)			
	%	%	%
Con.	31	27	25
Lab.	41	41	46
Lib-Dem.	24	27	24
Other	4	5	5

SOURCES: Colin Rallings and Michael Thrasher, *Local Elections Handbook* (Local Government Chronicle Elections Centre, 1993, 1994 and 1995); BBC Political Research Unit.

had progressively squeezed the Labour vote, and ran the local council. They campaigned on the recession, which had hit the town badly. The result was even more dramatic than the local elections (see Table 10.7): the Conservative majority of 12,357 was turned into a Liberal Democrat majority of 22,055. The Conservative vote plunged from 56 to 27 per cent, the largest by-election drop in a Conservative seat since the war.

A second by-election was held in July at Christchurch,

TABLE 10.7 *The Collapse of the Conservative Vote in By-elections 1993–96*

	Date	Anti-Con. swing**	Fall in Con. share of vote	Con. vote loss since general election* (% points)	Result
Conservative seats					
Newbury	6 May 93	28.4% (to Lib. D.)	−27.8%	59%	Lib. D. gain
Christchurch	29 Jul. 93	35.4% (to Lib. D.)	−32.1%	54%	Lib. D. gain
Eastleigh	9 Jun. 94	21.5% (to Lib. D.)	−26.6%	65%	Lib. D. gain. Con. 3rd
Dudley West	17 Dec. 94	29.3% (to Lab.)	−30.4%	78%	Lab. gain. Con. 3rd
Perth & Kinross	25 May 95	14.7% (to Lab.)	−18.8%	55%	SNP gain. Con. 3rd
Littleborough & Saddleworth	27 Jul. 95	17.3% (to Lab.)	−20.9%	58%	Lib. D. gain. Con. 3rd
Staffs SE	11 Apr. 96	22.1% (to Lab.)	−22.2%	58%	Lab. gain
Labour seats					
Rotherham	5 May 94	15.6% (to Lib. D.)	−13.8%	74%	Lab. hold
Barking	9 Jun. 94	22.0% (to Lab.)	−23.5%	84%	Lab. hold
Bradford South	9 Jun. 94	14.2% (to Lab.)	−20.6%	73%	Lab. hold
Dagenham	9 Jun. 94	23.1% (to Lab.)	−26.4%	86%	Lab. hold
Newham NE	9 Jun. 94	16.3% (to Lab.)	−15.9%	74%	Lab. hold
Monklands E	30 Jun. 94	20.3% (to SNP)	−13.7%	86%	Lab. hold
Islwyn	16 Feb. 95	9.9% (to Plaid C.)	−11.0%	85%	Lab. hold
Hemsworth	1 Feb. 96	5.5% (to Lab.)	−9.8%	75%	Lab. hold

* i.e. the fall in the Conservative vote as a proportion of the Conservatives' vote at the 1992 general election.
** The largest of the swings from Con to another party is given, irrespective of which party won the seat.

an affluent retirement area on the south coast. It was the Conservative Party's fifteenth safest seat at the general election, with a majority of over 23,000. Unlike Newbury, the local Liberals had always been weak, yet the result was even more spectacular than in Newbury. On an unprecedented swing of 35.4 per cent, the Liberal Democrats won with a majority of over 16,000. The Conservative vote collapsed from 64 to 32 per cent. Once again the Labour vote was squeezed to almost nothing (2.7 per cent) by ruthlessly tactical anti-Conservative voting. Christchurch confirmed that the government's unpopularity had penetrated deep into Conservative territory. Following the county council elections and by-elections the Liberal Democrats surged in the polls primarily at the expense of the Conservatives. Between February–April 1993 and June–August 1993 Conservative support in the Gallup 9000 polls fell from 31 to 24 per cent while Liberal Democrat support increased from 16 to 26 per cent.

THE 1994 LOCAL AND EUROPEAN ELECTIONS:
FURTHER HUMILIATION

In the year following the Conservatives' local election debacle public opinion barely moved. The series of sexual incidents that embarrassed the government in early 1994 and the wide-ranging tax rises that came into effect in April prevented the growing evidence of economic recovery from translating into political recovery. The 1994 local elections proved to be even more humiliating for the Conservatives than the previous year's (see Table 10.6). Their estimated share of the national vote was 27 per cent, four points down on the previous year. In terms of councils and seats the Conservatives came third in England and fourth in Scotland. A third of all the Conservative councillors who stood lost their seats. The Conservatives were defending the fortresses to which the poll tax local elections of 1990 had confined them but they surrendered many of these too. Outside London they retained control in only eleven out of the 162 councils being elected; in London they were swept out of hitherto invulnerable suburbs such as Barnet and Croydon, their power base reduced to Bromley, Kensington and the low-tax flagships of Wandsworth and Westminster. It was certainly the worst local election performance by a major party since at least 1945. It was probably the worst ever.

Further humiliation was heaped on the Conservatives in the European elections a month later, when five by-elections were also held. The Conservatives not only lost the one seat they were defending – Eastleigh, an affluent suburban and service sector town outside Southampton – but suffered the unique ignominy of coming third behind Labour. In the four by-election seats it was defending the Labour Party substantially increased its majorities and the Conservatives fell back to third place in three of them. The most noticeable feature of all five by-elections was the unprecedented collapse of the Conservative vote (see Table 10.7). In the lowest mid-points of the Thatcher governments, the Conservatives normally forfeited about a third of their general election vote when they lost a by-election. They had lost 58 and 54 per cent respectively in Newbury and Christchurch. In Eastleigh they lost an unprecedented 65 per cent and in the other by-elections, where their organization and support were weaker, they lost over 75 per cent. Many Conservatives switched directly to Labour or, in Eastleigh, to the Liberal Democrats. But many more simply stayed at home.

In the European elections the Conservatives were reduced to eighteen out of eighty-seven seats, losing sixteen (see Table 10.8). Conservative expectations were so low that the result was received with some relief and attributed to the dogged European campaigning of John Major and the temporary truce between anti- and pro-Europeans within the party. But the outcome did, in fact, mark another calamitous slump in the Conservatives' popularity. They won only 27.8 per cent of the vote, the lowest share obtained by either major party in any nationwide election this century. As in the county council elections a year earlier, they yielded to Labour rural and suburban areas such as Herefordshire and Shropshire, Lincolnshire, Norfolk and Suffolk which have been overwhelmingly Conservative in general elections from time immemorial. Moreover, they were lucky: of the eighteen seats they held, ten were retained with majorities of under 3 per cent and fourteen with majorities of under 5 per cent. They came within a whisker of wipe-out.

TABLE 10.8 *The European Elections of 9 June 1994*

	Seats*	Share of GB vote (%)	Change since 1989 Euro election	Change since 1992 gen. election
Conservative	18 (−16)	27.9	−6.8%	−14.9%
Labour	62 (+13)	44.2	+4.1%	+9.0%
Liberal Democrat	2 (+2)	16.7	+10.5%	−1.6%
Scottish Nationalist	2 (+1)			
Irish parties	3 (−)			

* The number of European constituencies in the UK was increased from 81 to 87 between 1989 and 1992. The change in the number of seats for each party is based on estimates of which of the 1992 constituencies the parties would have held in 1989.

The results of the June 1994 Euro-elections and by-elections were affected by the sudden death of the Labour leader, John Smith, four weeks earlier. Labour benefited from the media's eulogies for Smith, the unusually good-mannered campaign of the contenders for the succession and the widespread expectation that the moderate and modernizer, Tony Blair, would win. Blair was elected in July with an emphatic majority of all sections of the party. Labour's popular support immediately increased, although mainly at the expense of the Liberal Democrats, who were attracted by Blair's rejection of 'old Labour' thinking. The result was a steep jump in Labour's lead. In the three months before Smith's death the parties' standing in the polls was Con. 26, Lab. 48, LD 21, a Labour lead of 22 percentage points. In the three months after Blair's election the parties' standing was Con. 23, Lab. 56, LD 12, a Labour lead of 33 percentage points, a lead maintained througout 1995 (the average was 34 per cent) and early 1996.

DISASTER AT DUDLEY, WIPE-OUT IN THE 1996 ELECTIONS

The dismal showing of the Conservatives in the opinion polls was confirmed in by-elections and local elections over the following year. In December 1994 the Conservatives lost Dudley West (1992 majority 5,789) to Labour (majority 20,694) on a swing of 29.3 per cent, by far the largest since the war; in May 1995 they yielded Perth and Kinross to the Scottish Nationalists and in July 1995 Littleborough and Saddleworth to the Liberal Democrats, in both cases trailing third behind Labour. The collapse of the Conservative vote since the 1992 general election was spectacular: 56 per cent in Perth and Kinross, 58 per cent in Littleborough and Saddleworth and an astonishing 78 per cent in Dudley West. By-elections in safe Labour seats saw the Conservative vote reduced to almost nothing.

Despite the steady improvement in the economy, the May 1995 district local elections proved even more disastrous for the Conservatives than the already awful years of 1993 and 1994. The Conservative Party lost 2,000 seats and forfeited control of sixty-one councils, having won the equivalent of a mere 25 per cent of the national vote, the lowest in its history. In 1980, at the beginning of the Thatcher era, the Conservative Party controlled 200 local authorities and had 10,000 councillors. By 1995 three successive calamities in local elections left them in control of only thirteen councils throughout the country (none in Wales or Scotland) covering 4 per cent of the population, with fewer than 5,000 councillors, and virtually no representation in the council chambers of the big cities. They were no longer of consequence in local politics.

Disintegration, 1993–96: Diagnosis

Previous governments have presided over recessions, sterling crises or other national traumas and suffered mid-term electoral reverses as a result. Yet none have sunk so low and for so long in public esteem. What was different about Major's post-1992 government?

THE GOVERNMENT'S ECONOMIC PERFORMANCE

The most important cause of the Major government's downfall was Britain's ignominious withdrawal from the ERM in September 1992 which, reinforced by tax increases in 1993 and 1994, shattered overnight the Conservative Party's reputation for competent economic management.

Unlike his predecessor, John Major lacked alibis for his government's economic misfortunes. The 1980–82 recession could be partly blamed on the previous Labour government, a decade of irresponsible trade unionism and the world economy. The unanticipated high rate of poll tax could be pinned on to profligate Labour councils. The onset of the 1990 recession could be charged to the Thatcher government. But the fault for Black Wednesday, the perpetuation of the recession and the sharp tax rises lay with nobody but the government – the Major government. One year after campaigning on the promise of currency stability, low taxes and imminent economic recovery ('green shoots') sterling was outside the ERM, VAT had risen sharply, a new fuel tax was being introduced and recovery was still over the horizon. The government's credibility was in shreds.

A reputation for economic competence had been a priceless electoral asset in the 1980s, when it trumped the public's preference for Labour's social policies. Even during their mid-term doldrums the Conservatives were preferred to Labour as the party for the economy. All this changed after Black Wednesday. From 1993 onwards Labour was consistently regarded as the better party for handling

'Britain's economic difficulties' and by the largest margins ever recorded (see Table 10.9).

TABLE 10.9 *Perceived Economic Competence of the Conservative and Labour Parties*

Question: 'With Britain in economic difficulties, which party do you think could handle the problem best – the Conservative Party under John Major or the Labour Party under Neil Kinnock (John Smith/Tony Blair)?'

	1992 Jan.–Mar. %	1993 Jan.–Mar. %	1994 Jan.–Mar. %	1995 Jan.–Mar. %	1996 Jan.–Mar. %
Conservatives/ Major	42	30	25	21	23
Labour/Kinnock (Smith/Blair)	31	40	43	48	46
Con.–Lab. difference	+11	–10	–18	–27	–23

SOURCE: Gallup Polls

Despite the strong economic recovery from 1994 to 1996 the government was unable to revive its standing as the party of low taxes, sound management and prosperity and thus recapture electoral support. One reason was the markedly different character of the recovery compared with its predecessors. The recoveries of the 1980s were accompanied by a credit boom, higher wages (mainly through overtime) and rising prices, especially in housing. Together these induced in voters a sense of growing wealth, security and economic optimism. The recovery of 1994–96, by contrast, was based on low inflation, declining property prices (saddling many homeowners with negative equity), the contraction of full-time, long-term careers and increases in productivity rather than overtime. The recovery was more soundly based but, paradoxically, engendered no such 'feel good factor'; on the contrary, voters felt less wealthy, secure or optimistic. It was the first 'voteless recovery'.[30]

THE GOVERNMENT'S POLICY DIRECTION
John Major's premiership marked a change of style from his predecessor but a continuity of policy. The first priority in macro-economic strategy remained the control of inflation and to that end the government continued to look for ways of cutting public expenditure. Welfare payments were trimmed and public sector employment contracted. Defence spending was slashed. The internal market and contracting-out, first introduced in the NHS and local government, were adopted by central government. The privatization programme was extended to the railways, nuclear power and coal, and the Private Finance Initiative sought private funds for investment in roads, hospitals and other public sector projects. There was no let up, either, on Thatcher's 'popular authoritarianism'. Controls on immigration and asylum were tightened and, as part of the unceasing battle against crime, the government ordered tougher regimes for prisons and extended the power of the police at the expense of suspects in a new Criminal Justice Act.

Apart from the various tax increases in 1993–94, which were partly balanced by income tax cuts in 1995–96, there were no serious discontinuities of policy. However, one area of policy – Britain's relations with the European Union – created deep divisions within the party and became a major source of political disintegration. Thatcher's vocal opposition in 1989–90 to further measures of European integration had alienated many in her Cabinet and contributed to her own downfall. After her departure, Euroscepticism became the rallying point for disaffected Thatcherites. In their eyes supporters of a 'European Union' stood for an overweening superstate, for corporatism, vested interests, bureaucracy, waste and a diminished Britain. They stood for a sovereign, free enterprise, small-state Britain in a 'Europe of nations'. Attitudes to the Maastricht Treaty of 1993 and later the question of a single European currency (and whether it should be the subject of a referendum) became the litmus test of Euroscepticism and, by implication, adherence to the old Thatcherite cause. Every Cabinet reshuffle, internal election and ministerial speech was judged for its consequences for the anti- and pro-European cause. The issue plagued the party whips throughout the Parliament following the 1992 general election. In July 1993 the government only succeeded in obtaining parliamentary approval for the Treaty of Maastricht by daring the rebels not to support a vote of confidence. In November 1994 the whip was withdrawn from nine Euro-rebels (but restored within a year) and in July 1995, exasperated beyond endurance by sniping from the Eurosceptics, Major asked for – and secured – a vote of confidence from the parliamentary party by resigning the party leadership and standing for re-election.

The government was deeply damaged by the European issue. It preoccupied and distracted the Prime Minister, demoralized backbenchers and party activists, and alienated the public, for whom the issue was both baffling and boring. What repelled voters was not the substance of the government's European policy but the conspicuous disunity in its ranks that it exposed.

THE GOVERNMENT'S DISUNITY

It is a Conservative article of faith that splits spell electoral suicide, which is why the party traditionally conducts its quarrels in private or in code. Voters expect Labour, not the Conservatives, to brawl in public. But not since the schism over appeasement in the 1930s were factions as rife, former ministers as disloyal, and backbenchers as openly hostile to the leadership. The voters noticed. In 1981, when the fierce but contained Cabinet battle between 'wets' and 'dries' was at its height, the Conservative Party was still thought of as 'united' by 43 per cent of voters, while the Labour Party, riven by Militant, Bennites and the SDP breakaway was considered united by a mere 7 per cent. When department was pitted against department during the Westland affair in early 1986 only 32 per cent considered the Conservatives to be united, but the figure for the Labour Party, 25 per cent, was even lower. The public impact of the replacement of Thatcher and the connected division over Europe was of an altogether different order. By 1993 a mere 19 per cent of voters described the Conservatives as united, a figure that fell even further to 13 per cent in 1994 and 12 per cent in 1995. The Labour Party, by contrast, was regarded as united by 42 per cent in 1993, 54 per cent in 1994 and 53 per cent in 1995. Not since polls asked the question in the early 1970s has the party been so widely regarded as split. It was the Conservatives, not Labour, who were doing their brawling in public, and they paid for it in votes.

JOHN MAJOR'S PERSONAL STANDING

Economic mismanagement, broken tax promises and party disunity were the main culprits of the government's undoing. They not only damaged the government directly, but indirectly through their impact on the Prime Minister's personal standing.

After Black Wednesday Major became the least respected prime minister among ordinary voters since polls began. In 1993 his monthly 'satisfaction rating' averaged 23 per cent, the lowest recorded for any prime minister since Gallup first asked the question in 1947. In 1994 the figure fell further to 21 per cent, returning to 23 per cent in 1995. To the great majority of voters he was 'incompetent' (55 per cent) and 'a loser' (58 per cent), indecisive (70 per cent), 'ineffective' (71 per cent), 'not able to unite the nation' (77 per cent), and 'not really in charge' (81 per cent) or tough (81 per cent).

Asked to say which party leader would make the best prime minister, only 17 per cent of voters chose Major, who ran well behind Blair (42 per cent) and a little ahead of Ashdown (13 per cent). Comparison with Thatcher is instructive: her score never fell below 24 per cent in any quarterly period (during the Westland affair, when more-over the SDP's existence gave respondents four leaders to choose from).

Major's unpopularity was more consequence than cause of his government's unpopularity. Throughout the 1993–96 period his ratings fell in parallel with the government's but always ran above them – and by a larger margin than Thatcher's did over her government's. Disillusioned Conservatives did not place Major high on their list of reasons for defecting.[31] Polls consistently indicated that under any alternative leader the Conservatives would probably lose rather than gain votes, the only possible (and marginal) exception being Heseltine. Major's personal reputation declined less than his political one, which reflected that of the government as a whole. Between the 1992 election and July 1995, the proportion who 'liked him' fell from 63 to 47 per cent, while the proportion who 'liked his policies' fell much more sharply, from 41 to a mere 22 per cent. As a man he was still liked; but as a political leader he lost respect.

THE GOVERNMENT'S LOSS OF PRESS SUPPORT

The fourth exceptional feature of the 1993–96 period was the unprecedented hostility of sections of the Conservative press. In the 1980s, individual Conservative newspapers responded to their readers' mood and occasionally flirted with the SDP for a short period. In 1962–63 the press turned strongly against the beleaguered Macmillan government, partly out of anger at the jailing of two journalists for refus-ing to reveal their sources in the Vassall spy case. But the contempt of the Murdoch press for John Major's leadership and the partisan support for the Euro-rebels in the *Telegraph* newspapers were of a different magnitude. When he bid for re-election as party leader in July 1994, they supported his

Thatcherite and Eurosceptic challenger, John Redwood. The impact of press hostility was particularly pronounced on readers of the Tory tabloids, whose suggestibility and fickleness made them a crucial 'swing' group in the elections of the 1980s.[32]

The Conservative press turned against Major for not being Thatcherite enough, at least in style. Some prominent Thatcherites from the 1980s declared or at least hinted at their preference for Blair because his radicalism and boldness reminded them of Thatcher.[33]

As Thatcherism gradually lost its intellectual excitement and revealed its contradictions the cultural climate turned against the Conservatives. The ills of the 1990s were widely attributed to the individualist and market values championed by Thatcherites in the 1980s. Drugs and crime were blamed on the combination of long-term unemployment and a get-rich-quick culture. The growth of minor financial corruption ('sleaze') in Parliament and government agencies was attributed to the privatization of the utilities and public services. The negative equity that trapped so many young and first-generation homeowners was pinned on the deregulation of the financial services sector. 'Mad Cow Disease' was the outcome of relaxing the regulations about foodstuffs for cattle in the interests of agribusiness profits. The values of 'community' and 'public service', which resonated with the traditional right as much as with New Labour, were sung in counterpoint to the 'individualism' and 'private gain' of the 1980s. The political philosopher, John Gray, an apostle of Hayek and libertarian Conservatism in the 1980s, publicly converted to communitarian New Labour in the 1990s. *The State We're In*, a layman's critique of Thatcherite economics and manifesto for 'stakeholder capitalism' by the economics editor of the *Guardian*, Will Hutton, sold 150,000 copies in hardcover. Interests and professions normally hostile to Labour, such as the CBI and the Police Federation, warmed to Blair's attempt to ditch Old Labour, while the public sector and caring professions, such as teachers and doctors, who had in the majority voted Conservative in 1979, swung decisively to Labour by the mid-1990s. For the first time since the 1960s voting Labour was not only respectable, but fashionable.

THE OPPOSITION'S GROWING STRENGTH

This shift in the national mood was triggered by Blair's radical leadership of the Labour Party. His strategy was to recapture the voters Labour had lost to Thatcher in the late 1970s – the skilled, homeowning workers in the south – and to the centre parties in the 1980s – the public sector professionals, the well educated – by creating 'New Labour', a party that had replaced its outdated shibboleths with values and policies in tune with the post-Thatcher economic realities of the 1990s.

Armed with a decisive mandate for change from a party desperate not to lose a fifth election, Blair radically transformed the Labour Party between 1994 and 1996. There were three elements in the transformation: policy, discipline and Blair himself. Firstly, the party conspicuously severed its traditional association with trade unions, the public sector, the welfare state and tender-minded liberalism. It promoted itself as a low-tax, low-spending party of 'workfare' rather than welfare, that was 'tough on crime' but also 'tough on the causes of crime'. Under Blair's strict instructions, the party studiously avoided commitments to higher taxes or increased public expenditure, including the renationalization of industries whose privatization it strongly opposed. The trade unions, the original owners of the Labour Party, lost their bloc-voting rights at the party conference and in selecting parliamentary candidates. Most significantly of all, Clause 4 of the Labour Party constitution, which committed the party to a doctrine of public ownership, was abandoned by a ballot of members.

Secondly, these extraordinary reversals of traditional policy, unimaginable a few years earlier under Smith or Kinnock, were secured by an iron discipline imposed by

Blair's private office. Frontbenchers who wandered a fraction out of line were forced to retract or be dismissed; constituency parties selecting candidates with far-left or suspect backgrounds were required to re-select; not only the left, but all anti-'modernizers' were frozen out. United by an overwhelming need to win the election, the party looked more professional and disciplined than at any time since the war.

TABLE 10.10   *Changes in Labour's Image under Blair*

	Jan. 94	April 95	Change
Whatever one thinks of the Conservatives, it is hard to think of any really positive reasons for voting Labour (% *disagreeing*)	53%	63%	+10
Labour somehow gives the impression of being a party of the past rather than the future (% *disagreeing*)	53%	67%	+14
Labour has an attractive team of new, young leaders	49%	70%	+21
Labour is a much more moderate and sensible party than it used to be	79%	80%	+1
Whatever they may say now, taxes would go up a lot under a Labour government (% *disagreeing*)	32%	40%	+8

SOURCE: Gallop Polls

Thirdly, Blair's personal background lent itself to his ambition to create 'New Labour'. The son of Conservative-voting professional parents, a pupil at Scotland's premier public school, a churchgoer and family man, never involved in student politics, local government, left-wing causes or the trade unions, there was absolutely nothing about Blair's origins or background to remind the voter of the old Labour Party.

At Table 10.10 shows, in under a year Blair had transformed the Labour Party's image in three important respects: many more voters regarded Labour as forward-rather than backward-looking, as led by a new and attractive team and as worthy of positive support. Already under Smith the overwhelming majority accepted that Labour had become 'sensible and moderate'. In other words, for the first time since the 1960s Labour looked fit for government. The Conservatives, by contrast, did not.

'TIME FOR A CHANGE':
THE EXHAUSTION OF THE CONSERVATIVE GOVERNMENT

The ultimate reason for the Conservative election victories of 1983, 1987 and 1992 was that they looked more capable of governing than Labour did. Attempts to explain the results in terms of the parties' policies, or the personal qualities of the leaders, or the government's economic record did not work. These factors were contributory, but what they contributed to was the electorate's trust in the parties' fitness to govern in an uncertain world.

Almost every government defeated at an election in this century has lost authority before it lost office. Governments defeated at the polls forfeit votes for lack of authority, not authority for lack of votes. The Major government surrendered authority in 1996. Its parliamentary majority disappeared; its leader was barely tolerated by large sections of the party; its ministers were derided by the public; it was widely regarded as incompetent and sleazy. In the electorate, policy and ideology are mere cloaks for applying the *coup de grâce* to a government already crippled by failure, division, scandal or sheer exhaustion. Cohesion, purpose and success take precedence in voters' eyes; that is the lesson of Conservative dominance in the 1980s and Conservative failure in the 1990s.

1979 MAY 3   Conservatives win general election with majority of 43. The new prime minister is Margaret Thatcher who appoints Geoffrey Howe as chancellor of the exchequer, William Whitelaw as home secretary and Lord Carrington as foreign secretary

JUNE 12   Howe's budget cuts public expenditure by £4,000m and income tax by 3p in the pound, but doubles VAT to 15%

1980 MARCH 26   Howe's second budget cuts public expenditure by a further £1,275m and restricts the PSBR to £8,500m. Britain enters worst recession for 50 years

MAY 1   British aerospace industry privatized

AUGUST 1   Employment Bill, directed against the closed shop and secondary picketing, enacted

AUGUST 8   Housing Bill, giving local authority tenants the right to buy their homes, enacted

NOVEMBER 10   Michael Foot elected leader of

	the Labour Party in succession to James Callaghan
NOVEMBER 13	British Airways privatized
1981 JANUARY 5	Norman St John Stevas dismissed as leader of the House of Commons and succeeded by Francis Pym
MARCH 10	Howe presents a harsh budget, increasing excise duties, imposing new taxes on bank profits and North Sea oil and reducing public spending by £3,290m
MARCH 26	The SDP, a breakaway from the Labour Party, is formed
APRIL 11–13	Unemployed black and white youths riot in Brixton
JULY 4–8	Riots in Toxteth and Moss Side
SEPTEMBER 14	Cabinet reshuffle: Gilmour, Soames and Carlisle leave; Tebbit becomes employment secretary, Parkinson Conservative Party chairman, Prior a reluctant Northern Ireland secretary
1982 JANUARY 26	Unemployment reaches 3.071m
APRIL 2	Argentina invades the Falkland Islands
APRIL 5	Britain despatches a naval task force to the Falklands. The foreign minister, Lord

Carrington, and two junior ministers resign. Pym becomes foreign minister

MAY 6 — The Conservatives, boosted by the 'Falklands Factor' make big gains in the local elections

JUNE 14 — British forces capture Port Stanley in the Falklands and Argentine troops surrender

OCTOBER 28 — Enactment of Employment Bill, which provides penalties for unions involved in 'unlawful industrial action', recognizes the employer's right to dismiss strikers selectively and provides state aid for strike ballots

1983 MARCH 15 — Howe's budget raises tax allowances by 14% after the PSBR had fallen £2,000m more than projected

JUNE 10 — General election. Conservatives win with landslide majority of 144 and Labour suffers disaster. The Liberal/SDP Alliance is grossly under-represented in seats

JUNE 11 — Thatcher reforms government, with Nigel Lawson as chancellor of the exchequer, Leon Brittan as home secretary and Sir

		Geoffrey Howe as foreign secretary; Pym is left out of the government
	OCTOBER 14	Parkinson resigns; Tebbit becomes industry secretary and Tom King employment secretary
	NOVEMBER 15	Violent demonstrations by supporters of CND outside the Greenham base, where Cruise missiles are delivered
1984	JANUARY 25	Howe bans trade unions at the Government Communications Headquarters (GCHQ)
	MARCH 5	Yorkshire miners strike in protest at proposed closure of Cortonwood Colliery, setting off a bitter, year-long, national miners' strike
	APRIL 12	Telecommunications Bill, providing for transfer of British Telecom to private ownership enacted
	JUNE 26	Rate Bill, enabling the government to place a ceiling on rates, in effect rate-capping local authorities, enacted
	JULY 24	Patrick Jenkin rate-caps 18 local authorities, including GLC
	JULY 26	Trade Union Bill enacted, removing legal immunity for

	unions who hold a strike without a ballot, providing regular voting on the retention of political funds, and enforcing secret ballots for union officers
OCTOBER 12	IRA bomb planted in the Grand Hotel, Brighton, during the Conservative Party conference, explodes killing five. Tebbit badly injured and Thatcher nearly killed
MARCH 3	NUM calls off miners' strike, defeated
JUNE 16	Liverpool Council, under influence of Militant Tendency, fixes an illegal rate in defiance of government rate-capping policies
JULY 16	Local Government Bill, abolishing the GLC and the metropolitan authorities, enacted
SEPTEMBER 2	Cabinet reshuffle: Douglas Hurd becomes home secretary in place of Leon Brittan who becomes trade secretary. Norman Tebbit appointed Conservative Party chairman
SEPTEMBER 9–10	Rioting and arson in Birmingham Handsworth area

OCTOBER 6	Anti-police riot by youths in the Broadwater Farm Estate, north London
NOVEMBER 30	Transport Bill enacted, privatizing the National Bus Company
DECEMBER 13	Westland Helicopter Company rejects takeover bid by European Consortium engineered by the Defence Secretary, Michael Heseltine, in favour of a rescue deal by the US Sikorsky company and Fiat
1986 JANUARY 9	Heseltine walks out of Cabinet meeting and resigns as defence secretary over the Westland issue. George Younger replaces him
JANUARY 24	Brittan resigns, admitting responsibility for leaking letter about Heseltine and Westland. Paul Channon replaces him
JAN 86–FEB 87	Series of violent clashes between pickets and police at site of News International, Wapping
FEBRUARY 17	Britain and other EEC countries sign the Single European Act, aimed at strengthening social and economic cohesion of the European Community

MARCH 18 — Lawson's budget reduces income and corporation tax and promises tax-free personal equity plans on capital gains in attempt to encourage wider share-ownership

JULY 31 — Inflation, at 2.4%, at its lowest since November 1967. Unemployment reaches record high of 3,279,000

OCTOBER 7–10 — Successful Conservative annual conference unveils set of proposals for next Conservative government, including privatization and national school curriculum

DECEMBER 8 — British Gas privatized

1987 MARCH 17 — Lawson's budget cuts income tax by 2p in the pound

JUNE 11 — General election: Thatcher government returned for third time, with overall majority of 101

JUNE 13 — Parkinson brought back as energy secretary and John Wakeham replaces John Biffen as leader of the Commons

1988 MARCH 11 — Lawson's budget reduces higher rate of income tax to 40p in the pound and standard rate to 25p in the pound

DECEMBER 16	Edwina Currie resigns over her remarks on salmonella scare
1989 OCTOBER 29	Nigel Lawson resigns as chancellor of the exchequer over public remarks made by Mrs Thatcher's economic adviser and is replaced by John Major
DECEMBER 5	Sir Anthony Meyer challenges Margaret Thatcher for leadership of the Conservative Party. He obtains 33 votes, Margaret Thatcher 314 votes, with 27 abstentions
1990 MARCH	Riots against poll tax in London; demonstrations in many other areas
APRIL 1	Poll tax begins
JULY 13	Nicholas Ridley forced to resign over his remarks about Germany
OCTOBER 8	UK enters the Exchange Rate Mechanism
NOVEMBER 1	Howe resigns in protest at Thatcher's attitude to the European Union
NOVEMBER 20	Heseltine challenges Thatcher for the leadership of the Conservative Party and obtains 152 votes to her 204, thus forcing a second ballot

NOVEMBER 22	Thatcher resigns as prime minister and leader of the Conservative Party
NOVEMBER 27	Second round of Conservative leadership election: John Major 185, Michael Heseltine 131, Douglas Hurd 56
NOVEMBER 28	John Major becomes prime minister
1991 JANUARY 1	Major's first New Year message as prime minister promotes his vision of an opportunity society while promising to continue Thatcherite doctrine of privatization
JANUARY 17	Air strikes signal the beginning of hostilities in the Gulf War. Major's war cabinet: Major, Hurd, King, Wakeham, Mayhew
MARCH 12	Conservative Way Forward launched as new Thatcherite pressure group in the party with Thatcher as president
MARCH 21	Heseltine announces replacement of the poll tax with a council tax
JULY 22	Major reveals his Citizens Charter white paper. It includes plans for privatization of British

		Rail, end of the Post Office monopoly and a passengers' and parents' charter
	DECEMBER 9–10	Maastricht Summit. Major wins an opt-out for Britain in the later stages of the European Monetary Union. Britain rejects the social chapter which the other 11 members sign
	DECEMBER 18–19	Two-day debate on Maastricht in House of Commons. Seven Conservatives vote against the government and 20 others abstain
1992	APRIL 9	General election: Conservatives win against expectations with a majority of 21. Chris Patten, chairman of the Conservative Party, loses his seat
	APRIL 12	Major forms new government: Kenneth Baker is replaced by Kenneth Clarke; David Mellor becomes minister of the new Department of National Heritage
	APRIL 13	Neil Kinnock and Roy Hattersley resign as leader and deputy leader of the Labour Party
	MAY 21	Bill to ratify Maastricht passes its second reading in Commons,

	376–92, with 22 Conservatives voting against
JULY 14	Government announces plan to start the privatization of British Rail
JULY 18	John Smith becomes leader of the Labour Party
SEPTEMBER 16	Black Wednesday: Britain pulls out of the ERM
SEPTEMBER 17	Interest rates cut from 12 to 10%
SEPTEMBER 24	David Mellor resigns as heritage secretary because of press attacks over his affair and his undeclared acceptance of hospitality. He is succeeded by Peter Brooke
OCTOBER 7	Lord Tebbit attacks the leadership over Maastricht at the conference; Margaret Thatcher attacks Maastricht in an article in the *European*
NOVEMBER 4	Debate on Maastricht Treaty in the Commons: 26 Conservatives vote against the government. Government majority is 3, despite Liberal Democrat support
NOVEMBER 9	Three Matrix Churchill executives acquitted on charge of illegally supplying

	arms-related equipment to Iraq
NOVEMBER 10	Lord Justice Scott appointed to head enquiry into Matrix Churchill affair
1993 MARCH 8	Government defeated in division on Labour amendment to the Maastricht Bill: 26 Conservatives vote for the Labour amendment
MARCH 17	Lamont's budget announces plans for VAT on domestic fuels
MAY 6	Government loses the Newbury by-election and suffers huge losses in county council Elections
MAY 20	Commons gives third reading to Maastricht Treaty Bill by 292 votes to 112. 41 Conservative MPs vote against the bill and 5 abstain
MAY 21	Inflation at 1.3%, the lowest figure for 29 years
MAY 27	Lamont sacked as chancellor of the exchequer
JULY 22	Government defeated on Maastricht issue in Commons by 327 to 316. It calls a confidence vote
JULY 23	Major wins a vote of confidence
JULY 29	Conservatives lose Christchurch by-election on a swing of 35.4%

	OCTOBER 8	At Conservative Party conference Major launches his 'Back to Basics' campaign
	DECEMBER 15	Downing Street Declaration on Northern Ireland signed with leaders of the Irish Republic
	DECEMBER 26	'Back to basics' comes under increasing scrutiny when Tim Yeo, a junior environment minister, admits fathering an illegitimate child
1994	JAN–FEB	A number of minor sexual scandals concerning Conservative MPs undermine 'Back to Basics' campaign
	MAY 5	Conservatives suffer heavy losses in local elections
	MAY 12	John Smith, leader of the opposition, dies
	JUNE 9	Conservatives lose Eastleigh by-election and lose 14 seats in European elections
	JULY 20	Major Cabinet reshuffle: Wakeham, Patten, Brooke, Macgregor leave Cabinet; Aitken, Dorrell, Mawhinney and Lord Cranborne enter Cabinet
	JULY 21	Tony Blair becomes leader of the Labour Party
	DECEMBER 6	Government defeated in Commons on budget proposal

	to impose 17.5% VAT on fuel
DECEMBER 17	Conservatives lose Dudley West by-election to Labour on 29.3% swing, the largest since the war
1995 MAY 4	Conservatives lose over 2,000 seats in local elections, retaining control of just nine district councils in their worst election result this century
MAY 25	Conservatives lose the Perth and Kinross by-election to the Scottish Nationalists
JUNE 22	In an attempt to reassert his authority, Major announces that he will resign as leader of the Conservative Party and submit himself for re-election
JUNE 26	John Redwood resigns from the Cabinet to challenge Major for leadership of the Conservative Party
JULY 4	Major re-elected leader of the Conservative Party
JULY 27	Conservative and lose the Littleborough and Saddleworth by-election to the Liberal Democrats

This chronology draws on two useful sources: Geoffrey Foote, *A Chronology of Postwar British Politics* (Croom Helm, 1988) and Dennis Kavanagh and Anthony Seldon (eds), *The Major Effect* (Macmillan, 1994), pp. 464–80.

When Tory Governments Fail

Anthony Seldon

Why governments end, or wars finish, are matters of speculation and opinion rather than scientifically determined fact. Nevertheless, the ten preceding chapters find that the nine factors their authors were asked to weigh do provide an explanatory framework and some common diagnoses for answering the question why Tory governments end. These nine factors were: a negative image of the party leader; confusion over policy direction; manifest internal disunity; organization in the country in disarray; depleted party finance; hostile intellectual and press climate; loss of confidence by the electorate in economic management; strength of feeling of 'time for a change'; a revived and credible opposition.

Failure of leadership, and in particular a negative image of the party leader with the electorate, was the most common factor cited by authors. The conditions that led to the collapse of Tory power in 1806 are harder to divine than for any other period discussed in this book because of the lack of clarity about the meaning of 'Tory' and 'party' in the pre-Reform Act period. Nevertheless, the collapse of the Pittite system in 1806 owed much to the weaknesses of Pitt's leadership in his last years in power. The will to lead deserted him in 1801, and he was under great strain from his return in 1803 until his death in 1806. As Jeremy Black notes, George III also played his part in ensuring that the Pittites had no adequate alternative leader after Pitt's demise. Norman Gash is critical of Wellington's leadership from 1828 to 1830: a soldier rather than a politician, he was too remote and lacked tact, failing to bind together the party in the House of Commons. The political system as it evolved after 1815 demanded skilful and constructive leadership, and Wellington's failure to provide them played a large part in the collapse of Liverpool's party in 1830. Bruce Coleman also attributes the major role in the 1846 collapse, 'the greatest schism in the party's history', to Peel's failures of leadership, which were 'blind to the needs, interests and feelings of its supporters'. In 1880, John Vincent finds Disraeli to be an ill old man leading an ill Cabinet, which suffered from a deficit of talent. By 1900, Salisbury's detached and increasingly frail leadership, his judgement and his flagrant family patronage were arousing criticism. Balfour's succession in 1902, Martin Pugh argues, fared little better; he failed to galvanize the party or to give it a decisive lead in the years leading up to the 1906 election defeat. Neither Baldwin's leadership in 1929, despite its timidity on the election programme, nor Churchill's in 1945 were found by Stuart Ball and Michael Bentley to be contributory factors in defeat, but Home proved to be not a very effective successor to Macmillan. John Turner observes that Home shared the elderly, aristocratic baggage of Macmillan, but lacked his intelligence and style. Heath's approval rating was the lowest of any postwar Conservative prime minister until Major, and he lacked the ability to communicate well with either Tory MPs or the public at large. Poor though Major's standing with the public was, his unpopularity was always less marked than his government's, and polls consistently showed that under any alternative leader the Conservatives would probably lose votes.

Lack of clarity in policy direction, together with internal disunity, was the second most commonly cited factor, and was felt to have played a significant role in seven of the ten defeats. Wellington failed from 1828 to 1830 to provide other than defensive leadership, and gave his government the appearance of reverting to the impotent years of 1816– 19. The impression, if not necessarily the reality, was that 'the ministry seemed to have nothing left to offer'. Balfour's handling of the tariff reform schism after 1903 was maladroit. His dithering lost him credibility with both protectionists and free-traders: rarely can voters in any general election have been less clear about where the Tory Party stood on the key issue of the day. The Conservatives in 1924–29 were handicapped by drift and confusion in midterm. True the government rallied, and some worthwhile plans and decisions were made in 1928, but caution again prevailed, and the party's twin slogans in the 1929 election – 'Trust Baldwin' and 'Safety First' – did not inspire the electorate with a vision of a clear-sighted, still less a far-sighted, government in prospect. The Conservative failure to produce a broadly agreed policy statement for the 1945 general election owed much to Churchill's discouragement of party policy-making during wartime. Had he, however, stimulated internal party debates on postwar domestic policy, it is unlikely that a clear policy direction would have emerged. For the 1964 defeat, the Conservatives' policy direction was 'somewhat inchoate', a description that can be applied with far more force to the party's policy in the run-up to the February 1974 election. Dennis Kavanagh lists the many U-turns of the 1970–74 government, and cites Enoch Powell's question to Heath on whether, by pursuing policies so flatly in contradiction to the manifesto on which he had been elected, he had taken leave of his senses. He notes the irony that with five purposeful years in opposition under Heath this was one of the best prepared Conservative governments this century. This cannot be said of the Major government, which suffered from not having had any time to prepare for office, and which opted to continue substantially with the Thatcherite direction on policy. Clarity of policy direction was, however, obscured by the all-pervasive European issue after 'Black Wednesday' in September 1992. According to Ivor Crewe, 'It preoccupied and distracted the Prime Minister, demoralized back-benchers and party activists, and alienated the public, for whom the issue was baffling and boring.'

Manifest internal disunity was a significant factor on six occasions. As party loyalty is one of the key factors in the Conservatives' electoral success over the whole period, as discussed in the introduction, it is in some ways surprising that it is cited so often. Nevertheless, disagreements over Catholic Emancipation and franchise reform prompted the voluntary suicide of the Wellington ministry in November 1830. Government ministers' continuing lack of confidence in Wellington's leadership meant that to many the decision of the government to resign came as a relief. The 1846 schism provides the most dramatic case of a downfall being caused by disunity, between the Peelite and protectionist groups over the repeal of the Corn Laws. The split was not through all echelons of the party, but was between a ministerial cadre around Peel who wanted the repeal, and others in the government, the party majority in Parliament and the constituencies, who wanted the Corn Laws to remain. The split can be described as the most severe in the party's history, as it took twenty-eight years before it could again win a general election decisively, in 1874. In the case of the tariff reform divide of 1903–13, the split was more quickly healed, a process aided by Bonar Law playing the Orange card and by the First World War. The party was perhaps fortunate that the divisions of the interwar years, protectionism 1929–31, India 1933–35 and 'appeasement' 1937–39, with the exception of the splits over the coalition from 1921 to 1924, did not coincide with general elections. Similarly fortunate for the party was that the postwar divisions over Suez in 1956 were buried by the time of the 1959 election. The Conservatives did not escape in 1964, however. The party was disunited in Macmillan's last year

(1962–63), not least over who should succeed him. Two of his Cabinet, Iain Macleod and Enoch Powell, refused to serve under Home, and divisions over Resale Price Maintenance played a further part in a very close election in October 1964. In the 1974 defeat, the unity of the Cabinet is the striking feature, with no resignations, nor suggestions of such, despite the U-turns. As Cabinet ministers included Mrs Thatcher, Keith Joseph and Geoffrey Howe, the lack of schism is all the more remarkable. Lower down, however, division was rife, with the Heath government experiencing the highest level of revolts in the House of Commons of any government in the postwar period. Although a right-wing group was coalescing around such issues as objections to direct rule in Northern Ireland, Britain's membership of the European Economic Community and a statutory prices and incomes policy, and wanting a tougher line on immigration, it was not until after the election defeat that the opposition broke out into the open. The election victory in 1992, and Black Wednesday, again provided the spurs for dissent to emerge: by 1995, 53 per cent of voters polled regarded Labour as united, but only 12 per cent so regarded the Conservative Party. Europe in the 1990s indeed ranks in intensity with the Corn Law and tariff reform divides: no other schism in the party compares with these three episodes.

A revised opposition appears to have been a factor on six occasions. By 1830, Gash writes, 'for the first time for a quarter of a century the Whigs were a possible alternative government'. More muted was opposition recovery during 1874–80; John Vincent writes that the Liberal opposition 'remained weak and divided until the eleventh hour'. Their recovery, and its part in the 1880 election, moreover, has been exaggerated, and was confined by 1879 to little more than a Whig recovery. Liberal recovery up to 1906 rested heavily on the removal of Irish Home Rule from the top of the political agenda, allowing some of the divisions caused by Gladstone's last great project to heal. A number of factors accelerated the recovery of the Liberal Party: the Ramsay

MacDonald–Herbert Gladstone electoral pact of 1903, the Nonconformist revival, spurred by resentment at the 1902 Education Act, and the tariff reform controversy, which led to a number of defections of free-traders to the Liberals, including Winston Churchill. Henry Campbell-Bannerman's leadership from 1898, in succession to Lord Rosebery, and the increasing march of the New Liberalism through the party, also played their parts.

Stuart Ball highlights the recovery of both Labour and Liberal parties in the 1929 defeat in a close three-cornered general election. The defeat of the General Strike in 1926 removed some of the fear of left-wing extremism, and MacDonald was astute in presenting Labour as strong yet idealistic. More damage, however, was inflicted by the Liberal recovery; under Lloyd George's bracing leadership from 1926, the party offered not just a distinctive and forward-looking programme, but also utilized his long-accumulated finance to field 513 candidates. The threat from a Liberal recovery under periods of Tory government is a common feature of the century, and was seen again in 1964 and particularly in 1974 (in contrast, after periods of Labour government the Liberals do badly, as in 1924, 1951, 1970 and 1979).

In 1929, although the Liberals gained just fifty-nine MPs, in many constituencies the Liberal candidate took enough votes from the Conservatives to award the seat to Labour. Michael Bentley highlights Labour's challenge in 1945: 'it is possible to treat the Tory Party as a neutral backdrop and see the Labour Party as coming through on its own merits with a vision for the future that Conservatives lacked'. Labour muscle also resulted in the election taking place at a time of their choosing. John Turner is sceptical about Harold Wilson's leadership of Labour since 1963 having a pronounced effect on the 1964 result: it certainly cut even less ice in February 1974. But the revitalization of Labour under John Smith (1992–94) and Tony Blair has been one of the most dramatic opposition recoveries of the period under review. The latter's 'New Labour' strategy was geared to capturing the voters lost to the Tories and the centre parties in the 1970s and 1980s. Policy was brought firmly into the centre ground, links with socialism and trade unions watered down, and an iron discipline employed to ensure the success of his modernization of the party.

A hostile intellectual or media climate appears important on four occasions. The groundswell in favour of government intervention in the late nineteenth century was tangible. The Liberal Party was losing its attachment to Gladstonian *laissez-faire*, and a variety of organizations on the left were spawned, from the Fabian Society in 1884 to the Labour Party itself in 1900. A series of revelations in the 1880s and 1890s showed widespread poverty, which was moreover not the result of personal failure. The Boer War further highlighted the fact that large numbers of those applying to join up failed to meet the army's fairly basic requirements, and military setbacks prior to ultimate success in the war led to searching questions about Britain's military capability. The Conservatives seemed less well equipped than the Liberals to meet this profound *fin de siècle* questioning. To a lesser extent, the Conservatives were out of step with intellectuals in the latter 1920s also, when the economic ideas of the Liberals, and the disarmament idealism of Labour, appeared more exciting than any Tory prescriptions Baldwin dared offer the electorate. The thrust of intellectual and press thinking was very much in tune with the collectivist policies of Labour in 1945, as it was again for 1964. As John Turner writes, the Conservatives were 'not in favour with the journalists of the news media, or with the intellectual leaders of the early 1960s'. *That Was The Week That Was* and *Private Eye*, both founded at this time, were indicative of the new mood, expressed in a revulsion against the 'establishment' and its alleged values. A new right critique against Heath's policy had not been fully formulated by the 1974 election defeat, though the press became progressively disenchanted with him from 1973 onwards. If the intellectual tide ran in the Conservatives' direction from the mid-1970s to the early 1990s, it ran in Labour's favour thereafter. Intellectuals buzzed around the Thatcher honeypot in the 1980s: their sounds were scarcely to be heard in Major's No. 10 in the 1990s. Combined with an assault on a Conservative premier by the right-wing press, unprecedented in history, it made the going heavy for Major, and detracted from the image, and perhaps the reality, of a government in control of events.

Concern over the party's management of the economy, even if beyond their control to ameliorate, has been a potent negative force in some defeats. News in the 1880 budget that the deficit for the year, largely on account of the Zulu War, was over £3 million, dropped neatly into Gladstone's polemics on the incompetent and irresponsible stewardship of the nation's finances of Beaconsfieldism. The Great Depression of the late Victorian period also rebounded against the Tories in much the same way that the boom of 1868–73 had benefited the Liberals. Widespread concern about national efficiency and comparative industrial strength did not help the Tories in 1900–06. Baldwin's second government could not reduce unemployment in line with expectations: the return to the gold standard in 1925 exacerbated the lack of competitiveness, and the de-rating policy of 1928, designed to stimulate industry, proved ineffective in the time available. Disappointment at economic performance, however, was probably only a marginal factor in 1929. Criticism of the governments' economic management were features of both the 1964 and 1974 general elections and was again strongly present in the mid-1990s. According to Ivor Crewe, 'the ignominious withdrawal from the ERM in September 1992 . . . reinforced by tax increases in 1993 and 1994 shattered overnight the Conservative Party's reputation for competent economic management'. The slowness of the economic recovery to translate into a political recovery for the Conservatives shows how deep the disillusionment had gone.

Deficient organization is not a common factor in general election defeats for the simple reason that the party rarely lost the advantage. In 1859, Disraeli had set himself to win a general election by superior organization alone, and almost succeeded. In 1874, the Conservative organization, which he had done so much to create, was a significant factor in the victory. But by 1880, J.E. Gorst, the lynchpin of the 1874 success, had resigned, and a new chief whip, William Hart-Dyke, fell ill in 1879, leaving the election to be fought with little guidance from its national organization. The Liberals by contrast had in W.P. Adam a highly effective chief whip organizing them for the 1880 election. Martin Pugh shows how important the Conservatives' Chief Agent, R.W.E. Middleton, was in massaging Tory electoral success under Salisbury. But by 1905–6, the organization, with Middleton gone, was no longer as effective. The Primrose League had lost vibrancy, and was locked into wasteful internal rivalry with the organization of the Tariff Reform League; and the party was failing to mobilize its supporters effectively. Local organization was in an even worse state for the 1945 general election, with many constituencies, bereft of agents, barely continuing to operate. Organization was less effective in the early 1960s than it had become in the late 1940s, but it was not a significant factor in the defeat. By the early 1990s despite robust efforts from party chairmen Norman Fowler, Jeremy Hanley and Brian Mawhinney, membership and morale in the party's organization reached a postwar low.

Linked to organizational sclerosis is financial difficulty, creating problems for the party in funding propaganda at elections. This factor was rarely mentioned by contributors, yet it seems that inadequate funding was a factor of some significance in 1906 and 1974, and of limited importance in 1929 and 1964. Rarely had it been as much of a handicap, however, as it has proved to be to the Conservatives in the mid-1990s.

The feeling of 'time for a change', that the Tory leadership is stale, is a manifestation of a mass electorate and thus of the twentieth century. It may well have been a feature in the 1906 result, seems to have certainly been a strong factor in 1945 and again in 1964, but again has never been more apparent than in the mid-1990s, in part a reflection of the Tories being in office for a longer continuous period than at any other time this century. Other factors authors cited that accounted for defeat include prolonged bad weather (1880), fatigue of senior ministers (1974) and international economic factors so adverse as to severely handicap the government's strategy (1974).

Rarely are any of the factors mentioned strong enough alone to account for defeat. It is the combination that proves decisive: heavy defeats, as in 1832, 1906 and 1945, have indeed had more of the factors in evidence. But as stated at the outset, there is no certain knowledge about what has caused Tory defeats. Before the availability of poll data of ever-increasing sophistication in the postwar period, the weighing of factors is much more a matter of conjecture. Even in the 1990s, it is not possible to measure accurately the importance of some factors, such as the strength of the 'time for a change' sentiment, or the exact effect of organizational and financial difficulties. As the reasons for Tory defeats in the past are ultimately unknowable, the future is on the same terms unpredictable. No election is lost until polling day. I dissent therefore from my last author in believing the outcome of the next general election far from certain. Everything hinges on how well the party addresses the nine factors discussed in this book.

NOTES ON CONTRIBUTORS

STUART BALL is Reader in History at the University of Leicester.

MICHAEL BENTLEY is Professor of Modern History at the University of St Andrews.

JEREMY BLACK is Professor of History at the University of Exeter.

BRUCE COLEMAN is Senior Lecturer in History, University of Exeter, where he has served as Deputy Vice-Chancellor.

IVOR CREWE is Vice-Chancellor and Professor of Government, University of Essex.

NORMAN GASH is Emeritus Professor of History, University of St Andrews.

DENNIS KAVANAGH is Professor of Politics at the University of Liverpool.

MARTIN PUGH is Professor of Modern British History at the University of Newcastle upon Tyne.

ANTHONY SELDON is Founding-Director of the Institute of Contemporary British History and Deputy Head of St Dunstan's College.

JOHN TURNER is Professor of History at Royal Holloway and Bedford New College, University of London.

JOHN VINCENT is Professor of History at the University of Bristol.

NOTES

ONE. 1783–1806

I am grateful for comments on earlier drafts by Ian Christie, John Derry, Grayson Ditchfield, William Gibson, Jim Sack, Anthony Seldon and Tony Smith.

1. J.J. Sack, *From Jacobite to Conservative. Reaction and Orthodoxy in Britain, c. 1760–1832* (Cambridge University Press, 1993), pp. 66, 69. For Tories in the early eighteenth century, L.J. Colley, *In Defiance of Oligarchy: The Tory Party 1714–60* (Cambridge University Press, 1982), and J.M. Black, *Robert Walpole and the Nature of Politics in Early Eighteenth-century Britain* (Macmillan, 1990), pp. 89–103.

2. L.G. Mitchell, *Charles James Fox* (Oxford University Press, 1992), p. 194.

3. P. Mackesy, *War Without Victory. The Downfall of Pitt, 1799–1802* (Oxford University Press, 1984), pp. 186–201.

4. P. Kelly, 'The Pitt-Temple Administration: 19–22 December 1783', *Historical Journal*, 17 (1974), pp. 157–61; J. Ehrman, *The Younger Pitt: The Years of Acclaim* (Constable, 1969), p. 130; George III to Pitt, 23 December 1783, London Public Record Office (hereafter PRO) 30/8/103 fol. 14.

5. George III to Pitt, 13 January 1784, PRO 30/8/103 fol. 30; Lord George Germain to 3rd Duke of Dorset, 27 January 1784, Maidstone, Centre for Kentish Studies, C 192; Ehrman, *Pitt*, p. 125.

6. George III to Richard Grenville, 13 February 1784, London, British Library, Department of Manuscripts, Additional Manuscripts (hereafter BL. Add.) 70957; J. Norton (ed.), *The Letters of Edward Gibbon*, 3 vols (Cassell & Co., 1956), III, 44.

7. M.W. McCahill, *Order and Equipoise. The Peerage and the House of Lords, 1783–1806* (London, Royal Historical Society, 1978), pp. 31–6; J. Cannon, *The Fox–North Coalition. Crisis of the Constitution* (Cambridge University Press, 1969), p. 225; D. Large, 'The Decline of the "Party of the Crown" and the Rise of Parties in the House of Lords, 1783–1837', *English Historical Review*, 78 (1963), pp. 669–95. For the Lords in the preceding period, G.M. Ditchfield, 'The House of Lords in the Age of the American Revolution', in C. Jones (ed.), *A Pillar of the Constitution: The House of Lords in British Politics, 1640–1784* (Hambledon, 1989), pp. 199–239.

8. F. O'Gorman, *Voters, Patrons and Parties. The Unreformed*

Electorate of Hanoverian
England, 1734–1832 (Oxford
University Press 1989), pp.
295–6. For other factors at
work in the elections, T.R.
Knox, ' "Peace for Ages to
Come": The Newcastle
Elections of 1780 and 1784',
Durham University Journal, 84
(1922), pp. 13–15; P.D.G.
Thomas, 'The Rise of Plas
Newydd: Sir Nicholas Bayly
and County Elections in
Anglesey, 1734–84', *Welsh
History Review*, 16 (1992),
pp. 174–6.

9. Eden to Lord Sheffield,
10 April 1784, BL. Add.
45782.

10. O'Gorman, *Voters, Patrons and
Parties*, pp. 350–52, 359–68;
J.A. Phillips, *Electoral Behavior
in Unreformed England*
(Princeton University Press,
1982); J.E. Bradley, *Religion,
Revolution and English
Radicalism. Non-conformity in
Eighteenth-century Politics and
Society* (Cambridge University
Press, 1990); R. Hole, *Pulpits,
Politics and Public Order in
England 1760–1832*
(Cambridge University Press,
1989). An important recent
study of the High Church
position is F.C. Mather, *High
Church Prophet: Bishop Samuel
Horsley (1733–1806) and the
Caroline tradition in the Later
Georgian Church* (Clarendon
Press, 1992).

11. G.M. Ditchfield, 'Lord
Thurlow', in R.W. Davis (ed.),
*Lords of Parliament. Studies,
1714–1914* (Stanford
University Press, 1995),
pp. 75–6.

12. Marquis of Buckingham
to Grenville, 25 January

1806, BL. Add. 58878 f.
124–5.

13. Grenville to Earl Fitzwilliam,
26, 31 January, Fitzwilliam to
Grenville, 27 January, Fox to
Grenville, 1 February,
Grenville to Sidmouth, 31
January 1806, BL.
Add. 58878 f. 124–5, 58955
f. 26–9, 58953 f. 12, 58928 f.
54.

14. Grenville to Addington, 11
October, Grenville to Dundas,
4 October 1801, BL.
Add. 58928 f. 44–5, 58918
f. 128–9.

15. Grenville to Pitt, 8 May 1804,
BL. Add. 59909 f. 97, 95. On
his support for Emancipation,
Grenville to John Troy,
Catholic Archbishop of Dublin,
16 July 1805, BL. Add. 59256
f. 7.

16. Pitt to Grenville, 4 February
1804, BL. Add. 58909
f. 81–2.

17. Buckingham to Grenville, 13
June 1805, BL. Add. 58878 f.
83–4; M. Fry, *The Dundas
Despotism* (Edinburgh
University Press, 1992), pp.
262–71.

18. Canning to John Hookham
Frere, 9 January 1806, BL.
Add. 38833 f. 197.

19. I.R. Christie, 'The Changing
Nature of Parliamentary
Politics, 1742–1789', in J.M.
Black (ed.), *British Politics and
Society from Walpole to Pitt,
1742–1789* (Macmillan,
1990), p. 122.

20. D. Gray, *Spencer Perceval*
(Manchester University Press,
1963), p. 61.

21. Grenville to George III, 31
January, Fox to Grenville,
1 February, Wellesley to
Sidmouth, 23 January,

Wellesley to Grenville, 23 January, H. Mackenzie to Grenville, 26 March, Grenville to Thomas Grenville, January 1806, BL. Add. 58863 f. 9–10, 58953 f. 12, 37295 f. 74–5, 59381 f. 13, 58885 f. 4.

22. Wellesley to Grenville, 2 July 1806, BL. Add. 58913 f. 1.

23. Grenville to Brougham, 1 May 1810, BL. Add. 58965 f. 10–11.

24. Huntington Library, San Marino California, Montagu papers 4557.

TWO. 1812–30

1. C.D. Yonge (1812–91), professor of modern history, Queen's College, Belfast, in his *Life and Administration of the 2nd Earl of Liverpool* (London, 1868), I, pp. 3–4.

2. The number of newspapers in the UK approximately doubled between 1790 and 1820; London newspapers increased even faster between 1801 and 1821. See Table 2.1, p. 61.

3. William Wyndham, Baron Grenville (1759–1834), Pitt's foreign secretary 1791–1801, prime minister 1806–7.

4. Henry Addington (1757–1844), speaker of the House of Commons 1789–1801, prime minister 1801–4, created Viscount Sidmouth 1805.

5. George Canning (1770–1827), foreign secretary 1807–9 and 1822–27, prime minister 1827.

6. For a sample of voting patterns in the House of Commons (1822 session) see Table 2.2., p. 80.

7. Yonge, *Life and Administration of the 2nd Earl of Liverpool* , III, p. 138.

8. *Wellington Supplementary Despatches*, ed. by his son, 14 vols (London, 1858–72), IX, p. 536.

9. About a dozen people were killed when a parliamentary reform meeting at St Peter's Field, Manchester, in 1819 was dispersed by the military on the orders of magistrates. About half of them were probably trampled underfoot by horses or the fleeing crowd. The incident was ironically called Peterloo in parody of the more glorious victory of Waterloo gained four years earlier.

10. Forbidding the practice (known as 'Truck') of paying part of an employee's wages in the form of vouchers for goods in shops attached to the works or owned by the employer.

11. William Cobbett, one of the most influential radical journalists of the time, began in 1816 to issue reprints of articles in his newspaper the *Political Register* in the form of 2d pamphlets aimed at a wider working-class readership. He did more than any other single journalist to popularize the view that social distress was caused by the extravagance and corruption of government.

12. William Huskisson (1770–1830), economist, secretary to the Treasury under Pitt, minister for woods and forests 1814–23, president of the Board of Trade 1823–27.

13. Quoted by J.F. Cookson in his

Lord Liverpool's Administration
1815–22 (Scottish Academic
Press, 1975), p. 143.

14. L.J. Jennings (ed.), *The Croker
Papers*, 3 vols (John Murray,
1884), I, p. 170. J.W. Croker,
politician and journalist, was
secretary to the Admiralty
1809–30.

15. H. Twiss, *Life of Lord Chancellor
Eldon*, 3 vols (John Murray,
1884), II, p. 329.

16. Quoted by Cookson, *Lord
Liverpool's Administration
1815–22*, p. 222. Thomas
Tooke (1774–1858),
economist and free-trader,
was co-founder of the
Political Economy Club in
1821.

17. Speech in the House of Lords,
26 February 1822, later
published as a pamphlet, with
numerous appendices giving
details of revenue and
expenditure, from which the
quotation is taken.

18. For a general analysis of the
pamphlet see my *Pillars of
Government* (Edward Arnold,
1986), pp. 26ff.

19. See Table 2.3 (p. 83) for the
Cabinet changes 1821–23.

20. *Croker Papers*, I, p. 265.

21. George Peel (ed.), *Private
Letters of Sir Robert Peel* (John
Murray, 1920), p. 104. The
letter is here dated 9 January
1828 but this is probably a slip
for 10 January, the day on
which Peel had his first
interview with Wellington
about the new ministry.

22. Vansittart had been promoted
to the House of Lords as Baron
Bexley on retiring from the
Exchequer.

23. The Cabinet had agreed after
much discussion to enlarge

the corrupt borough of East
Retford rather than transfer
the seats to a town. In the
Commons Huskisson voted
for the original bill to give the
seats to Birmingham.

24. For an analysis of the 1830
general election see my essay
'English Reform and French
Revolution', in R. Pares and
A.J.P. Taylor (eds.), *Essays
presented to Sir Lewis Namier*
(Macmillan, 1956), pp. 258ff.

25. He told Vesey Fitzgerald in
September, for example, that
what was lacking was
'parliamentary talent in the
Cabinet for the service in the
House of Commons'. *Wellington
Despatches 1818–32*, ed. by his
son, 8 vols (John Murray,
1867–80), VII, p. 240.

26. For a general analysis of
Wellington as prime minister
see my chapter (pp. 117–38)
in Norman Gash (ed.),
*Wellington, Studies in the
Military and Political Career of
the 1st Duke of Wellington*
(Manchester University Press,
in association with the
University of Southampton,
1990). For his role in Catholic
Emancipation see ch. 7 by
Karen Noyce and for his
relations with the Tory press
ch. 8 by J.J. Sack.

THREE. 1841–1846

1. The preoccupation is clear in
the title of the one monograph
devoted specifically to this
government: T.L. Crosby, *Sir
Robert Peel's Administration
1841–1846* (David & Charles,
1976).

2. For all its excellence as a
political biography, Norman

Gash, *Sir Robert Peel* (Longman, 1972) stands as a culmination of this tradition. The same author's *Reaction and Reconstruction in English Politics 1832–1852* (Clarendon Press, 1965), pp. 119–56, similarly celebrates the rightness and inevitability of Peelism, as does Crosby's work detailed above. Robert Blake, *The Conservative Party from Peel to Churchill* (Eyre & Spottiswoode, 1970), pp. 49–59, is less enamoured of Peel ('with all allowances made, his conduct is puzzling') but still concludes that Corn Law repeal 'was surely as right as any major political decision has ever been'. Something of the same flavour lingers in D. Read, *Peel and the Victorians* (Basil Blackwell, 1987), though otherwise a rounded assessment of contemporary views of Peel.

3. For party organization see two articles by N. Gash, 'The Organization of the Conservative Party, 1832–1846', *Parliamentary History*, I (Alan Sutton, 1982), pp. 137–59, and II (Alan Sutton, 1983), pp. 131–52. The general development of the party is excellently covered by R. Stewart, *The Foundation of the Conservative Party 1830–1867* (Longman, 1978).

4. For electoral results 1832–52 see Table 3.1, pp. 107–10. The 1832–41 elections are analysed by D. Close, 'The Rise of the Conservatives in the Age of Reform', *Bulletin of the Institute of Historical Research*, 45 (1972), pp. 89–103.

5. Earl Spencer (Althorp of 1832) reflected in 1841 that 'in our Reform Act we gave rather too great a preponderance to the landed interest'; but he added that 'in the present state of the feelings of the country, any system of representation which ... could possibly be adopted would give an overwhelming majority to those who support what is called Protection to the land ...' (To Russell, 2 May 1841, quoted in S. Walpole, *The Life of Lord John Russell* (Longman, 1889), Vol. I, pp. 372–3.) On agricultural policies see also T.L. Crosby, *English Farmers and the Politics of Protection 1815–1852* (Harvester Press, 1977), and D. Spring, 'Lord Chandos and the Farmers, 1818–1846', *Huntington Library Quarterly*, 33 (1969–70), pp. 257–81.

6. I. Newbould, 'Sir Robert Peel and the Conservative Party, 1832–1841: A Study in Failure?', *English Historical Review*, 98 (1983), pp. 529–57, questions the extent of the party's cohesion and discipline. The argument seems to depend on more modern and exacting criteria than circumstances then permitted.

7. Gash, *Sir Robert Peel*, pp. 269–70.

8. *Hansard's Parliamentary Debates*, Third Series, LIX, 555–6, 17 September 1841.

9. Read, *Peel and the Victorians*, p. 145. The best treatment of policy towards Ireland's Catholics is D.A. Kerr, *Peel, Priests and Politics: Sir Robert Peel's Administration and the Roman Catholic Church in*

Ireland, 1841–1846 (Clarendon Press, 1982).

10. The best account of government's response remains F.C. Mather, *Public Order in the Age of the Chartists* (Manchester University Press, 1959).

11. C.S. Parker (ed.), *Sir Robert Peel from his Private Papers* (John Murray, 1899), Vol. II, p. 551.

12. On Graham's performance and standing, see A.P. Donajgrodski, 'Sir James Graham at the Home Office', *Historical Journal*, 20 (1977), pp. 97–120.

13. R. Stewart, *The Politics of Protection. Lord Derby and the Protectionist Party 1842–1852* (Cambridge University Press, 1971), p. 56.

14. Compare R. Stewart, 'The Ten Hours and Sugar Crises of 1844', *Historical Journal*, 12 (1969), pp. 35–57, and D.R. Fisher, 'Peel and the Conservative Party: The Sugar Crisis of 1844 Reconsidered', *Historical Journal*, 18 (1975), pp. 279–302.

15. *The Times*, 17 June 1844, quoted by Read, *Peel and the Victorians*, p. 100.

16. Read, *Peel and the Victorians*, pp. 146–9.

17. Gash, *Sir Robert Peel*, pp. 560–61, discusses Peel's euphoria at this juncture.

18. For the CAPS and the local societies see M. Lawson-Tancred, 'The Anti-League and the Corn Crisis of 1846', *Historical Journal*, 3 (1960), pp. 162–83, and Stewart, *The Politics of Protection*, especially ch. 3.

19. J.R. Fisher, 'Issues and Influence: Two By-elections in South Nottinghamshire in the Mid-nineteenth Century', *Historical Journal*, 24 (1981), pp. 155–65, has wider significance for this aspect than the title suggests.

20. J.W. Croker, 'Ministerial Resignations', *Quarterly Review*, 113 (December 1845), pp. 298–321. The same line was pressed by the London evening paper, the *Standard*, hitherto seen as the official Conservative organ.

21. For the case against Peel see Stewart, *The Politics of Protection*, pp. 58–62, and particularly the protest resolutions entered in the Lords by Stanley and Richmond against the third reading of the Corn Bill, *Hansard*, 3/LXXXVII, 961–4, 25 June 1846.

22. W.O. Aydelotte, 'The Country Gentlemen and the Repeal of the Corn Laws', *English Historical Review*, 82 (1967), pp. 47–60; D.R. Fisher, 'The Opposition to Sir Robert Peel in the Conservative Party, 1841–46', unpublished Ph.D. thesis, Cambridge University, 1970, especially ch. 7.

23. On the Peelite group see J.B. Conacher, *The Peelites and the Party System 1846–52* (David & Charles, 1972).

24. The best treatment of the cult of Peel is by Read, *Peel and the Victorians*, especially ch. 7.

25. This is the argument of G. Kitson Clark, 'The Repeal of the Corn Laws and the Politics of the 1840s', *Economic History Review*, 4 (1951), pp. 1–13.

26. Boyd Hilton, 'Peel: A Reappraisal', *Historical Journal*, 22 (1979), pp. 585–614.

27. *The Times*'s retrospective of 1846, quoted by Read, *Peel and the Victorians*, p. 194.
28. See Gash, *Sir Robert Peel*, pp. 526–30, on Peel's health problems, and his own comments to Graham and Arbuthnot in July 1846 in Parker, *Sir Robert Peel from His Private Papers*, Vol. III, pp. 456–7.
29. This aspect of League activity is discussed by J. Prest, *Politics in the Age of Cobden* (Macmillan, 1977). After a run of bad election results in the boroughs in 1844 the League turned to the county divisions where it sought to manufacture county voters from urban freeholds. Prest's argument (p. 133) that 'Peel surrendered in 1845–46, as soon as he saw the battle turning against him' has not been supported by other historians. It ignores Peel's clearly expressed fear of the League not as an electoral machine but as a force for agitation which might inflame popular passions during times of mass distress. Popular insurrection, not electoral organization, was his nightmare.
30. Gash, *Sir Robert Peel*, p. 614.

FOUR. 1874–80

1. But not in the same place. The growth in the Liberal majority in 1868 was considerable, from 47 to 84 in the Celtic Fringe, although its majority of 26 in England was unchanged. H.J. Hanham, *Elections and Party Management* (1959), pp. 216–17.
2. Hanham, *op. cit.*, p. 229n.

3. Gladstone's comment (3 April 1880) on the early election results was: 'It seemed as if the arm of the Lord had bared itself for work that He had made his own'. P. Magnus, *Gladstone, A Biography* (1963), p. 270.
4. Disraeli's manifesto took the unusual form of an open letter to the Duke of Marlborough, then Lord-Lieutenant of Ireland (text, *The Times*, 9 March 1880).
5. Disraeli's view, after hearing the early results only, was 'Never so great a discomfiture with a cause so inadequate. I think, as far as I can collect, "hard Times" was the cry against us. The suffering want a change: no matter what, they are sick of waiting'. Disraeli to Lady Bradford, 2 April 1880, *Letters*, ed. Zetland (1929) ii, p. 266. Disraeli took comfort in the thought that the results for populous seats 'prove that the enlightened masses are with us'. He also thought his timing was correct: 'Had the dissolution been delayed, we should have had to encounter agricultural insurrection as well as our usual foes. The farmers are discontented, but they move and conspire slowly. We have been too quick for them' (ibid.). Writing to Salisbury, also on 2 April, he gave an almost identical explanation: ' "Hard Times", as far as I can collect, has been our foe, and certainly the alleged cause of our downfall'. Trevor Lloyd, *The General Election of 1880* (Oxford University Press, 1968), p. 134.

6. The general election was the most truly general in memory:

Uncontested constituencies	
1868	140
1874	117
1880	66

Source: Lloyd, *op cit.*, p. 134.

7. The Liberals had a safe majority in English seats alone:

	England	
	Liberal	Conservative
1874	171	288
1880	255	204

Source: Lloyd, *op. cit.*, p. 134.

8. The 'Celtic Fringe' was more important than ever before:

	Wales		Scotland	
	Lib.	Cons.	Lib.	Cons.
1874	19	11	40	20
1880	28	2	53	7

	Ireland		
	Liberal	Home Rule	Conservative
1874	13	57	33
1880	15	62	26

9. Hanham, *op. cit.*, p. 156.
10. Ibid., p. 162.
11. The 'landslide' took place not in the aggregate vote, but in terms of seats in the House of Commons:

	Liberal	Home Rule	Conservative
1874	243	57	352
1880	351	62	239

Source: Lloyd, *op. cit.*, p. 134.

12. Votes cast:

	Liberal	%
1874	1,263,254	54.2
1880	1,801,208	56.1

	Conservative	%
1874	1,071,325	45.8
1880	1,410,650	43.0

Source: Lloyd, *op. cit.*, p. 134.

The small Home Rule vote is omitted. A truer comparison can be made by taking the 276 seats contested on the same basis in both 1880 and 1874:

	Liberal	%
1874	839,625	55.4
1880	1,140,652	58.7
	Conservative	%
1874	756,817	44.6
1880	819,865	41.3

Source: Lloyd, *op. cit.*, p. 135.

which warns against some of the figures in W. Saunders, *The New Parliament of 1880* (London, 1880) and J.P. Dunbabin, 'Parliamentary Elections in Great Britain, 1868–1900', *English History Review*, lxxxi (1966). Whichever method is used, more Conservative votes were cast in their great defeat of 1880, than in their historic victory of 1874.

13. Hanham, *op. cit.*, p. 228n.
14. In his first Midlothian campaign (24 November to 9 December 1880), Gladstone by his reckoning addressed 86,930 people. The Post Office told him that 800,330 words had been cabled by the media during the campaign. *The Times* printed 85,000 of his words in the first campaign, and a total

of 250,000 words of Gladstone from November 1879 to April 1880. Lloyd, *op. cit.*, p. 14.

15. Illness affected both Disraeli and his Cabinet repeatedly in the year preceding the election. 'If there had been a Cabinet today *six* would have been absent' Disraeli wrote to Lady Bradford on 29 January 1880 (*Letters*, ed. Zetland, II, p. 261). Salisbury, Disraeli's chief support, was the most seriously affected.

FIVE. 1886–1905

1. Quoted in Robert Taylor, *Lord Salisbury* (Allen Lane, 1975), p. 73.
2. Speech at Birmingham, 30 March 1883.
3. Salisbury was prime minister four times: 1885; 1886–92; 1895–1900; 1900–1902.
4. National Union of Conservative and Constitutional Associations, Annual Conference minutes, 14 December 1892.
5. See the discussion in E.H.H. Green, *The Crisis of Conservatism* (Routledge, 1995), p. 126.
6. Maurice Duverger, *Political Parties* (Methuen, 1954).
7. Robert Mackenzie, *British Political Parties* (Heinemann, 1955), pp. 146–84.
8. R.N. Kelly, *Conservative Party Conferences: The Hidden System* (Manchester University Press, 1989), and 'The Party Conferences' in A. Seldon and S. Ball (eds), *Conservative Century* (Oxford University Press, 1994).
9. N.U.C.C.A., Annual Conference minutes, 23 July

1880, 20 October 1886, 13–14 December 1892.
10. Michael Pinto-Duschinsky, *British Political Finance 1830–1980* (American Enterprise Institute for Public Policy Research, 1981), pp. 35–9.
11. Pinto-Duschinsky, *Political Finance*, p. 39.
12. Martin Pugh, *The Tories and the People 1880–1935* (Blackwell, 1985), pp. 25–42.
13. Pugh, *Tories*, pp. 38–40, 47–51.
14. Frank O'Gorman, *British Conservatism* (Longman, 1986), p. 36.
15. The latest major study of his career is Peter Marsh, *Joseph Chamberlain: Entrepreneur in Politics* (Yale University Press, 1994).
16. J.P. Cornford, 'The Transformation of Conservatism in the Late Nineteenth Century', *Victorian Studies*, 7 (1963).
17. S.E. Koss, 'Wesleyanism and Empire', *Historical Journal*, 18 (1975).
18. Pugh, *Tories*, pp. 83–5.
19. See the discussion in Peter Marsh, *The Discipline of Popular Government: Lord Salisbury's Domestic Statecraft 1881–1902* (Harvester Press, 1978).
20. For material on this theme see R. Harcourt Williams (ed.), *The Salisbury–Balfour Correspondence 1869–92* (Hertfordshire Record Society, 1988).
21. H.B. Berrington, 'Partisanship and Dissidence in the Nineteenth Century House of Commons', *Parliamentary Affairs*, 21 (1967–68), p. 342.
22. Marsh, *Discipline of Popular*

How Tory Governments Fall

Government, pp. 261–2, 271–2.

23. Frederick H. Allen, 'Constructive Unionism and the Shaping of Rural Ireland, c. 1880–1921', *Rural History, Economy and Society*, 4, 2 (1993).

24. *The Times*, 23 March 1894, quoted in Green, *The Crisis*, p. 132.

25. See for example, *The Campaign Guide* (Conservative Central Office, 1892).

26. Salisbury to A.J. Balfour, 26 July 1892, in Williams, *Correspondence*, p. 430.

27. See the discussion in: M. Fforde, *Conservatism and Collectivism 1886–1914* (Edinburgh University Press, 1990); J.A. Thompson and A. Mejia, *Edwardian Conservatism* (Croom Helm, 1988); and E.H.H. Green, *The Crisis of Conservatism* (Routledge, 1995).

28. F. Coetzee, *For Party or Country* (Oxford University Press, 1989); K.D. Brown, 'The Anti-Socialist Union 1908–49', in K.D. Brown (ed.), *Essays in Anti-Labour History* (Macmillan, 1974).

29. G.R. Searle, *The Quest for National Efficiency* (Eyre Methuen, 1971).

30. W.S. Churchill to H.H. Asquith, 29 December 1908.

31. A.J. Balfour to Lord Salisbury, 20 October 1900, Salisbury Papers.

32. See Richard Rempel, *Unionists Divided* (Macmillan, 1972); Alan Sykes, *Tariff Reform in British Politics 1903–13* (Oxford University Press, 1979).

33. John Ramsden, *The Age of Balfour and Baldwin 1902–1940*

(Longman, 1978), pp. 45–53.

34. E. Sinclair to Lady Londonderry, 11/3/11, Londonderry Papers C686; *Primrose League Gazette*, 1 March 1914.

35. *Primrose League Gazette*, 1 October 1901.

36. Grand Council Minutes, Primrose League, 19 February 1901, 27 July 1901, 12 July 1906, 31 October 1912.

37. Pugh, *Tories*, pp. 63–5.

38. *Primrose League Gazette*, 1 July 1902.

39. Pugh, *Tories*, pp. 169–73.

40. W.S. Churchill to Lord Hugh Cecil (not sent), 24 October 1903.

41. W.S. Churchill to A.J. Balfour, 25 May 1903.

42. Kelly, *Party Conferences*, pp. 233–5.

43. Austen Chamberlain, memorandum, 9 March 1901, Chamberlain Papers, AC/8/8/15.

44. Sir Arthur Steel-Maitland, quoted in Fforde, *Conservatism*, p. 147.

SIX. 1916–29

1 Memoranda by Bonar Law, Long and Curzon, circulated to Shadow Cabinet, 29 January 1915, in D.G. Boyce (ed.), *The Crisis of British Unionism: The Domestic Political Papers of the 2nd Earl of Selborne 1885–1922* (Historians' Press, 1987), pp. 119–26.

2. K.O. Morgan, *Consensus and Disunity: The Lloyd George Coalition Government 1918–1922* (Oxford University Press, 1979), pp. 16–19, 25, 29–36.

3. The nine factors are: a negative

image of the party leader, confusion over the direction of policy, visible internal disunity, disarray in the organization in the country, depleted funds, a hostile intellectual and media climate, a critical public perception of the government's economic management, a widespread sentiment of 'time for a change', and a revived or more credible opposition; see S. Ball and A. Seldon, 'Calculus of Failure', *Guardian*, 8 May 1995, p. 13.

4. Ormsby-Gore to Bonar Law, 17 October 1922, House of Lords R[ecord] O[ffice], Bonar Law MSS, 111/19/92.

5. Austen Chamberlain to Gretton, 20 July 1921, Birmingham University Library, Austen Chamberlain MSS, AC/24/3/47.

6. Austen Chamberlain to Birkenhead, 12 October 1922, in R. Blake, *The Unknown Prime Minister: The Life and Times of Andrew Bonar Law* (Eyre & Spottiswoode, 1955), p. 451; Midleton to Derby, 21 October 1921, Derby MSS, Liverpool RO, DER(17)/33.

7. D. Dutton, *Austen Chamberlain* (Ross Anderson, 1985), pp. 165–6.

8. 'The Fall of the Coalition Government', memo by Pollock, n.d., Hanworth MSS, Bodleian Library, Eng. Hist. d.432; Austen Chamberlain to Gretton, 21 February 1922, to Steel-Maitland, 23 March 1922, Austen Chamberlain MSS, AC/33/1/11 & 49.

9. Derby to Nall, 19 March 1921, Derby MSS, DER(17)/17/3; Dutton, *Austen Chamberlain*,

pp. 164–6, 175–8, 188–90, 193–9.

10. Torquay C[onservative] A[ssociation], Finance and General Purposes Committee, 3 April 1922.

11. On the government's foreign policy, and the problems of the Middle East, see G.H. Bennett, *British Foreign Policy During the Curzon Period 1919–1924* (Macmillan, 1995).

12. Younger to Law, 3 January 1920, 23 February 1921, 29 December 1922, Bonar Law MSS, 96/2, 100/2/30, 111/341/162; Derby to Selborne, 4 March 1921, Derby MSS, DER(17)/33.

13. Younger to local Conservative Association chairmen, 9 January 1922, in J. Ramsden (ed.), *Real Old Tory Politics: The Political Diaries of Sir Robert Sanders, Lord Bayford: 1910–1935* (Historians' Press, 1984), pp. 171–2; Wakefield CA, Council, 16 January 1922; Chelmsford CA, AGM, 25 February 1921.

14. National Union, Exec., 9 May 1922; Leith to Austen Chamberlain, 4 March 1922, Austen Chamberlain MSS AC/33/1/22.

15. M. Kinnear, *The Fall of Lloyd George: The Political Crisis of 1922* (Macmillan, 1973), pp. 78–85.

16. 'The Fall of the Coalition Government', memo by Pollock.

17. Viscount Templewood, *Empire of the Air* (Collins, 1957), pp. 26–7; 'List of Members present at meeting at Cadogan Gardens', 18 October 1922, Templewood MSS, Cambridge University Library, I (2).

18. Younger to Bonar Law, 21 July 1920, Sanders to Younger, 2 December 1920, Bonar Law MSS, 96/7, 99/8/4.

19. Davidson to Bonar Law, 13 January 1922, Bonar Law MSS, 107/2/2a; Torquay CA, Finance and General Purposes Committee, 30 January 1922; Dorset West CA, Exec., 5 July & 30 September 1922, Dorset RO; Stockton CA, Exec., 17 February 1922, Durham RO; Derby CA, Management Committee, 19 January & 10 October 1922, Derbyshire RO; Accrington CA, Exec., 21 March 1922, Manchester University Library.

20. Terrell to Bonar Law, 18 September 1922, Bonar Law MSS, 107/2/60; Reigate CA, Exec., 9 June, 31 July, 15 September, 18 October 1922, Surrey RO; Abingdon CA, Council, 27 April 1922; Hemel Hempstead CA, Council, 7 January 1922, Exec., 30 September 1922; Cirencester & Tewkesbury CA, Exec., 18 March 1922.

21. Sanders diary, and correspondence with Fraser, Wilson and Younger, August–October 1922.

22. Kinnear, *Fall of Lloyd George*, pp. 87–91.

23. Amery to Austen Chamberlain, 26 January 1922, Austen Chamberlain MSS, AC/42/4/1.

24. Lane-Fox to Bonar Law, 14 October 1922, Salisbury to Bonar Law, 23 September 1922, Long to Bonar Law, 6 February 1922, Bonar Law MSS, 107/2/68. 107/2/61, 107/2/9.

25. 'The Fall of the Coalition Government', memo by Pollock; Amery diary, 3 August 1922, in J. Barnes & D. Nicholson (eds), *The Leo Amery Diaries, Volume 1: 1899–1929* (Hutchinson, 1980), p. 290.

26. Sir E. Cecil to Bonar Law, 18 October 1922, Bonar Law MSS, 107/2/69.

27. R. Self, 'Conservative Reunion and the General Election of 1923: A Reassessment', *20th Century British History*, 3 (1992), pp. 249–73.

28. C. Cook, *The Age of Alignment: Electoral Politics in Britain 1922–1929* (Macmillan, 1975), p. 140.

29. Gretton to Baldwin, 24 October 1923, Cambridge University Library, Baldwin MSS, 35/28–9; West Wolverhampton CA, Exec., 20 November 1923.

30. M. Cowling, *The Impact of Labour 1920–1924* (Cambridge University Press, 1971), pp. 251–8.

31. McNeill to Baldwin, 12 November, Cecil to Baldwin, 14 November, Davidson and Herbert, memo to Baldwin, 14 November 1923, Baldwin MSS 42/133–4, 126–7, 130–31.

32. Darwen CA, Exec., 19 January 1924, Lancashire RO.

33. Amery to Baldwin, 5, 8 & 11 November 1923, Joynson-Hicks to Baldwin, 20 October 1923, Baldwin MSS, 35/60–64, 35/71–4, 42/113–16, 35/30–31.

34. Cook, *Age of Alignment*, pp. 137–44.

35. Midland Union, G.P. Sub-committee, 3 August 1923, Agent's Report (seen at West

Midlands Area Office, now at Conservative Party Archive, Bodleian Library); Tynemouth CA, Exec., 23 February 1923, Tyne & Wear RO.

36. Jackson's speech to the Conservative agents' society annual dinner, *Conservative Agents' Journal*, November 1923; Hall to Davidson, 19 October 1923, House of Lords RO, Davidson MSS, 155; Younger to Baldwin, 7 November 1923, Baldwin MSS, 35/67–70.

37. Younger to Derby, 30 November 1923, Derby MSS, DER(17)/17/2.

38. Bonar Law to Fitzalan, 24 January, Fitzalan to Bonar Law, 26 January 1923, in Lord Beaverbrook, *The Decline and Fall of Lloyd George* (Collins, 1963), pp. 298–300.

39. Cook, *Age of Alignment*, pp. 150–54; S. Koss, *The Rise and Fall of the Political Press in Britain, 2: The Twentieth Century* (Hamish Hamilton, 1984), pp. 426–31.

40. Cook, *Age of Alignment*, pp. 88–100, 125–30, 145–9.

41. See also the discussion by R. McKibbin, 'Class and Conventional Wisdom: the Conservative Party and the "Public" in Inter-war Britain', in *The Ideologies of Class* (Oxford University Press, 1990), pp. 259–93.

42. J.Ramsden, *The Age of Balfour and Baldwin 1902–1940* (Longman, 1978), pp. 207–15.

43. Davidson to Baldwin, 13 June 1927, 12 October 1928, Baldwin MSS, 36/65–70, 55/3–4; Davidson (Party Chairman) to Baldwin, 5 October 1928, Davidson MSS, 185.

44. Harrison to Worthington-Evans, 8 February 1929, Bodleian Library, Worthington-Evans MSS, Eng. Hist. c.896; Davidson to Irwin, 3 December 1928, India Office Library, Halifax MSS, EUR.C.152/18/173.

45. Macmillan to Cecil, 8 November 1928, British Library, Cecil of Chelwood MSS, Add. MSS 51166/79–80; Headlam diary, 4 & 12 November 1928, 8 February, 5 March 1929, in S. Ball (ed.), *Parliament and Politics in the Age of Baldwin and MacDonald: the Headlam Diaries 1923–1935* (Historians' Press, 1992), pp. 156–7, 164, 166.

46. Davidson to Irwin, 3 December 1928, Halifax MSS, EUR.C.152/18/173; Neville to Hilda Chamberlain, 5 May 1929, Birmingham University Library, Neville Chamberlain MSS, NC/18/1/652.

47. Croft to Baldwin, 17 September 1928, Churchill College, University of Cambridge, Croft MSS, CRFT/1/3/Ba4; Joynson-Hicks to Baldwin, 31 January 1929, Baldwin MSS, 12/560–68.

48. Steel-Maitland to Baldwin, 29 October, Churchill to Baldwin, 12 June 1925, Baldwin MSS, 27/225–8, 28/41–8.

49. Cabinet Policy Committee, draft conclusions, 16 July 1928, Worthington-Evans MSS, c. 896.

50. Headlam diary, 8 November 1928; Northwich CA, Exec., 20 December 1928; North West

Wiltshire CA, Exec., 1
February 1929, Wiltshire
RO.
51. Hoare to Irwin, 2 March,
Neville Chamberlain to Iwin,
25 August 1927, Halifax MSS,
EUR.C.152/17/1/193, 249c;
Amery to Baldwin, 3 August,
Churchill to Baldwin, 6 June
1927, Baldwin MSS, 59/
154–61, 5/125–35.
52. Eyres-Monsell (chief whip) to
Baldwin, 10 November 1927,
Baldwin MSS, 162/120–21;
Headlam diary, 19 November
1928; Neville Chamberlain to
Hoare, 26 November 1928,
Templewood MSS, V(3).
53. Horncastle CA, Exec., 13
August 1928, Lincolnshire
RO.
54. J. Barnes, 'The Making of
Party Policy', in A. Seldon & S.
Ball (eds), *Conservative Century:
the Conservative Party since 1900*
(Oxford University Press,
1994), pp. 358–61.
55. P. Williamson, ' "Safety First":
Baldwin, the Conservative
Party, and the 1929 General
Election', *Historical Journal*, 25
(1982), pp. 392–400.
56. Amery to Baldwin, 11 March
1929, Baldwin MSS, 36/
88–92.
57. Jones diary, 6 March 1929, in
T. Jones, *Whitehall Diary:
Volume 2, 1926–1930* (Oxford
University Press, 1969), p.
175.
58. Beaverbrook to Daryngton, 28
May, to Derby, 6 June 1929,
House of Lords RO,
Beaverbrook MSS, B95, C113;
Koss, *Rise and Fall of the Political
Press*, pp. 477–88.
59. Headlam diary, 22 December
1927, 18 July 1928.
60. Headlam diary, 27–28 June, 6

July, 15–18 December 1927,
13–14 June 1928.
61. Steel-Maitland to Baldwin,
reporting meeting of National
Union executive, 17 April
1926, Baldwin MSS, 59/
95–6; Chelmsford CA,
Council, 6 March 1925;
Guildford CA, Council, 1 May
1925, Surrey RO.
62. Epsom CA, Exec., 23 March
1927; Chelmsford CA, Council,
1 April 1927; St Albans CA,
Exec., 15 July 1927.
63. For rank-and-file criticisms of
the government's record after
the 1929 defeat, see S. Ball,
*Baldwin and the Conservative
Party: The Crisis of 1929–1931*
(Yale University Press, 1988),
Appendix 1, pp. 220–21.
64. Chelmsford CA, Exec., 23
January 1928, 8 March 1929;
Stafford CA, Exec., 15 March
1929, Staffordshire RO;
Headlam diary, 17, 21, 30 May
1929.
65. 'Central Office staff, Area
Agents and staff, Speakers and
organisers, Schedule of
Salaries', c. February 1928,
and annual balance sheets,
accounts and schedules,
1926–29, Davidson MSS, 184,
175–6; Ramsden, *Age of
Balfour and Baldwin*, pp.
218–62.
66. Reeve to Smithers, 2 Mar.
1929, Artindale to Smithers, 22
Mar. 1929, Baldwin MSS 55/
35–48.
67. 1929 general election, income
and expenditure accounts,
Davidson MSS, 187; for level
of party funds, see statements
of value, annual balances
1923–32, in reports from the
accountants Maxwell Hicks to
Gilmour (one of the trustees),

Scottish RO, Gilmour MSS, GD/383/19/4-40.

68. Neville Chamberlain diary, 18 April 1928, Neville Chamberlain MSS, NC/2; Neville Chamberlain to Irwin, 12 August 1928, Halifax MSS, EUR.C.152/18/114a; Headlam diary, 30 March 1928.

69. J.R. Clynes, *Memoirs* (Collins, 1937), Vol. 2, p. 251; Sankey to Baldwin, 5 February 1928, Maclean to Baldwin, 2 August 1926, Shaw to Bridgeman, 23 March 1929, Baldwin MSS, 163/242, 161/154-5, 175/52.

70. Headlam diary, 2 May 1929; Neville to Hilda Chamberlain, 5 May 1929, Neville Chamberlain MSS, NC/18/1/652; Jones diary, 1 June 1929.

71. Petherick to Baldwin, 2 June 1929, Baldwin MSS, 37/162; Cochrane to Gilmour, 1 June 1929, Gilmour MSS, GD/383/29/16.

72. For further discussion of this point, see S. Ball, *The Conservative Party and British Politics 1902-1951* (Longman, 1995), pp. 117-26.

SEVEN. 1931-45

1. See the remarkable diaries of Arnold Wilson, MP for Hitchin: *Walks and Talks* (Oxford University Press, 1934); *Thoughts and Talks* (Longmans & Co., 1938); *More Thoughts and Talks* (Longmans & Co., 1939).

2. There is no single treatment of the National Government and Churchill coalition and a good deal more has been written on the latter than the former. Biographies offer one way into the period as a whole. For National Government ministers, see in particular Andrew Roberts, *'The Holy Fox': a Biography of Lord Halifax* (Weidenfeld & Nicolson, 1991) and J.A. Cross, *Lord Swinton* (Clarendon Press, 1982). Lively backbenchers such as Macmillan and Boothby have perhaps fared best: see Alistair Horne, *Macmillan 1894-1956* (Macmillan, 1988) and Robert Rhodes James, *Bob Boothby: a Portrait* (Hodder & Stoughton, 1991).

3. See Peter Catterall, 'The Party and Religion', in Anthony Seldon and Stuart Ball (eds), *Conservative Century* (Oxford University Press, 1994), pp. 648-9.

4. James Kellas, 'The Party in Scotland' in Seldon and Ball, *Conservative Century*, p. 675.

5. For a commentary on the election see Andrew Thorpe, *The British General Election of 1931* (Clarendon Press, 1991).

6. Thomas Jones to Gwendoline Davies, 28 October 1931, in Thomas Jones, *A Diary With Letters 1931-50* (Oxford University Press, 1954), p. 20.

7. Diary, 21 October 1931, in Stuart Ball (ed.), *Parliamentary Politics in the Age of Baldwin and MacDonald: the Headlam Diaries 1923-35* (Historians' Press, 1992), p. 220.

8. The 59 Liberal MPs dwindled to 33 'Liberals' in 1931 plus a derisory 4 'Independent Liberals'.

9. C.T. Stannage, 'The East Fulham By-Election, 25 October 1933', *Historical Journal*, 18 (1971).

10. For Labour's internal

difficulties, see J.F. Naylor, *Labour's International Policy: the Labour Party in the 1930s* (Weidenfeld & Nicolson, 1969) and Ben Pimlott, *Hugh Dalton* (Cape, 1985).

11. For the background to the election, see Tom Stannage, *Baldwin Thwarts the Opposition: the General Election of 1935* (Croom Helm, 1980).

12. See Chris Cook and John Ramsden (eds), *By-Elections in British Politics* (Macmillan, 1973), pp. 140–64. For Chamberlain's perception of politicians and public, see Maurice Cowling, *The Impact of Hitler* (Cambridge University Press, 1975), pp. 303–6.

13. See Cook and Stevenson, *Britain in the Depression* (Longmans, 1994) previously published as *The Slump* (1977).

14. Note by King George V, 2 November 1931, quoted in K. Middlemas and J. Barnes, *Baldwin* (Weidenfeld & Nicolson, 1969), p. 654.

15. For the attacks on Baldwin, see Middlemas and Barnes, *Baldwin*, pp. 580–602, and the more detailed treatment in Philip Williamson, *National Crisis and National Government: British Politics, the Economy and Empire, 1926–1932* (Cambridge University Press, 1992). For Neville Chamberlain's disaffection and challenge, cf. Keith Feiling, *The Life of Neville Chamberlain* (Macmillan & Co., 1946), pp. 184–7.

16. E.g. Trevor Burridge, *British Labour and Hitler's War* (Deutsch, 1976). For a more measured recent study, see Stephen Brooke, *Labour's War: the Labour Party during the Second World War* (Clarendon Press, 1992).

17. Speech in London, 26 February 1929, extracted in Baldwin, *This Torch of Freedom* (Hodder & Stoughton, 1935), pp. 125–6.

18. Crozier Diary, 12 June 1934, in A.J.P. Taylor (ed.), *Off the Record: Political Interviews 1934–43* (Hutchinson, 1973), p. 24.

19. Quoted in Cowling, *Impact of Hitler*, p. 102.

20. 'Total unilateral disarmament in a sinful world he thought mere folly.' Middlemas and Barnes, *Baldwin*, p. 722.

21. Channon Diary, 14 September 1938, in Rhodes James, *Bob Boothby*, p. 166.

22. A sense of Chamberlain's continuing popularity in the country emerges from popular polls in the press: see Henry Pelling, *Britain and the Second World War* (Collins, 1970).

23. Taylor's calculation based on the printed division list: A.J.P. Taylor, *English History 1914–1945* (Clarendon Press, 1965), p. 473n.

24. For the context of this decision and some outraged responses to it, see Randolph Churchill and Martin Gilbert, *Winston S. Churchill* (8 vols, Heinemann, 1966–88), vol. 5, pp. 714–16.

25. Sheila Lawlor, *Churchill and the Politics of War, 1940–1941* (Cambridge University Press, 1994), ch. 4, passim.

26. Most recent among these is G.R. Searle, *Country Before Party: Coalition and the Idea of 'National Government' in Modern British Politics 1885–1987* (Longman, 1995) which carries

forward the logic of his earlier study of *The Quest for National Efficiency: a Study in British Politics and Political Thought 1899–1914* (Blackwell, 1971). But the genre is strengthened too by Kenneth O. Morgan's important study of the Lloyd George Coalition, *Consensus and Disunity: the Lloyd George Coalition Government 1918–22* (Clarendon Press, 1979) and in parts by the conclusion of Williamson, *National Crisis and National Government.*

27. Speech of November 1934, quoted in Williamson, *National Crisis and National Government*, p. 516.
28. See Paul Smith, *Disraelian Conservatism and Social Reform* (Routledge & Kegan Paul/ University of Toronto Press, 1967).
29. Quoted in Rhodes James, *Bob Boothby*, p. 136.
30. Boothby to Baldwin, n.d. (January 1934), in Rhodes James, *Bob Boothby*, p. 149.
31. Harold Macmillan: b.1894; Eton and Balliol College, Oxford; Cons. MP Stockton-on-Tees 1924–9, 1931–45.
32. This argument has been most fully adumbrated by Robert Skidelsky: see his *Politicians and the Slump: the Labour Government of 1929–31* (Macmillan, 1967) and in biographies of *Oswald Mosley* (Macmillan, 1975) and *John Maynard Keynes* (2 vols and continuing, Macmillan, 1983–).
33. Ross McKibbin defends the record of the MacDonald government of 1929–31 partly on this ground in a highly effective critique: see

'The Economic Policy of the Second Labour Government', *Past and Present*, 68 (1975). For a sophisticated analysis of Keynesian evolution, cf. Peter Clarke, *The Keynesian Revolution in the Making 1924–1936* (Clarendon Press, 1988), esp. pp. 229–310.
34. Derek H. Aldcroft, *The Interwar Economy: Britain 1919–39* (Batsford, 1970), pp. 306–7.
35. See Uri Bialer, *The Shadow of the Bomber: the Fear of Air Attack and British Politics 1932–39* (Royal Historical Society No. 18, 1980).
36. For this important term and its distinction from the idea of 'pacifism', see Martin Ceadel, *Pacifism in Britain 1914–1945: the Defining of a Faith* (Clarendon Press, 1980).
37. Quoted in Cowling, *Impact of Hitler*, p. 92.
38. Channon Diary, 10 May 1939, in Robert Rhodes James (ed.), *Chips: the Diaries of Sir Henry Channon* (Weidenfeld & Nicolson, 1967), p. 198.
39. Colville Diary, 10 May 1940, in Colville, *The Fringes of Power: Downing Street Diaries* (2 vols, Sceptre, 1985–7), vol. 1, p. 140.
40. Isaac Leslie Hore Belisha: b. 1893; Clifton and St John's College, Oxford; Liberal MP Devonport 1923–45; financial sec. to Treasury, 1932–4, minister of transport 1934–7, secretary for war, 1937–40.
41. See, for example, the unremittingly hostile observations of Alexander Cadogan, Permanent Under-Secretary at the Foreign Office, in his splenetic diaries –

especially when Hoare was denied office in May 1940 and left for Madrid: David Dilks (ed.), *The Diaries of Sir Alexander Cadogan 1938–45* (Cassell, 1971), pp. 282–7.

42. Amery Diary, 28 May 1937, quoted in Cowling, *Impact of Hitler*, pp. 224–5.

43. Chamberlain Diary, October 1939, quoted in Feiling, *The Life of Neville Chamberlain*, p. 420.

44. When the crisis came in May 1940 the realization among Labour leaders that it would have to be Churchill had become more generally current than is often remarked: see Ben Pimlott, *Hugh Dalton*, (1986 edn), pp. 275–6. This edition is published by Papermac.

45. Lord Davies to Beaverbrook and reply, 3 May and 7 May 1940, in A.J.P. Taylor, *Beaverbrook* (Hamilton, 1972), p. 407.

46. The authors included the young socialist intellectual Michael Foot. Sales of *Guilty Men* proved a phenomenon with 12 impressions appearing in the first month (July 1940).

47. Those polled who wanted Churchill to continue as prime minister never fell below 70% of the whole: see Pelling, *Britain and the Second World War*.

48. For the Common Wealth Party, see Angus Calder, *The People's War: Britain 1939–45* (Panther, 1969), pp. 631–5; and Kevin Jefferys, *The Churchill Coalition and Wartime Politics 1940–45* (Manchester University Press, 1991).

49. For the Labour administrative side, see Burridge, *British Labour and Hitler's War*, and J.M. Lee, *The Churchill Coalition 1940–45* (Batsford, 1980).

50. See Paul Addison, *The Road to 1945: British Politics and the Second World War* (Cape, 1975), pp. 238–9.

51. For the background and Woolton's approach, see Lord Woolton, *Memoirs* (Cassell, 1959), pp. 259–305.

52. A good exposition of an anti-consensual view of these years is Jefferys, *The Conservative Government*.

53. Eden's low spirits in facing an election are reflected in his memoirs: se Eden, *The Eden Memoirs: the Reckoning* (Cassell, 1965), pp. 540–51.

54. Jones to Flexner, 4 August 1945 in *Diaries*, p. 536.

55. Quoted in Michael David Kandiah, 'The Conservative Party and the General Election of 1945', *Contemporary Record*, 9 (1995), p. 23.

56. For further details see Kandiah, 'The Conservative Party', p. 26 and John Ramsden, 'Winston Churchill and the Conservative Party', ibid., p. 103.

57. Ramsden, 'Churchill and the Conservative Party', p. 105.

58. John Ramsden, *The Age of Churchill and Eden* (Longman, 1995), pp. 5–6.

59. Ramsden, *The Age of Churchill and Eden*, p. 55.

EIGHT. 1951–64

1. I am grateful to members of the Oxford University graduate seminar on Modern British

History, in particular Dr Ross McKibbin, Dr Jose Harris and Dr Brian Harrison, for comments on part of an earlier draft of this chapter which reshaped the conclusions; responsibility for the final form, warts and all, is exclusively my own.

2. Many of whom were unopposed, thus distorting the figure of total votes cast.

3. See Kathleen Burk, *The First Privatisation* (Historians' Press, 1988).

4. R.A. Butler, 'Notes of the 1945–6 session', 30 August 1946, Trinity College (Cambridge), Butler Papers RAB G18/28.

5. Oliver Poole to R.A. Butler, 28 February 1949, Butler Papers RAB H33/184. On Churchill's ineffectual tenure as leader of the opposition see John Ramsden, 'Winston Churchill and the Leadership of the Conservative Party, 1940–51', in *Contemporary Record*, Vol. IX (1995), pp. 99–119.

6. Lord Salisbury (Colonial Secretary), Harry Crookshank (Leader of the House), James Stuart (Scottish Secretary) and Patrick Buchan-Hepburn (Chief Whip).

7. Martin Gilbert, *Never Despair* (William Heinemann, 1988), pp. 989–91 and 1097; Alistair Horne, *Macmillan 1894–1956* (Macmillan, 1988), p. 353.

8. His Research department aide, Peter Tapsell, quoted in Robert Rhodes James, *Anthony Eden* (Weidenfeld & Nicolson, 1986), p. 408.

9. The Conservative Research Department had been warning

of popular concern since the middle of 1954, but to no avail. John Ramsden, *The Making of Conservative Party Policy* (Longman, 1980), pp. 177–8.

10. Mrs Beryl Platts to *The Times*, June 1956, quoted by Rhodes James, *Anthony Eden*, p. 439.

11. 'The People's League for the Defence of Freedom and the Middle Class Alliance. Report of the Committee of Investigation', November 1956, Butler Papers, RAB H38/153–85.

12. There is a huge literature on Suez. See Keith Kyle, *Suez*, for a narrative account of the campaign and Scott Lucas, *Divided We Stand: Britain, the U.S. and the Suez Crisis* (Hodder & Stoughton, 1991) for a study of policy-making. W.R. Louis & Roger Owen, *Suez, 1956: the Crisis and Its Consequences* (Oxford University Press, 1989) offers a range of expert analyses including Max Beloff, 'The Crisis and its Consequences for the British Conservative Party', pp. 319–34.

13. As peers Kilmuir (formerly Sir David Maxwell-Fyfe, responsible for the 'Maxwell-Fyfe reforms' of party organization) and 'Bobbety' Salisbury, whose lisping enquiry Kilmuir recorded, were regarded as disqualified. Lord Kilmuir, *Political Adventure: Memoirs* (Weidenfeld & Nicolson, 1964), p. 28.

14. The speech to the 1922 committee has been described ('One of the most horrible things that I remember in politics . . .') by Enoch Powell,

quoted by Anthony Howard, *RAB: the Life of R.A. Butler* (Jonathan Cape, 1987), p. 241; Salisbury's question is recorded by Lord Kilmuir (David Maxwell-Fyfe), *Political Adventure* (Weidenfeld & Nicolson, 1964), p. 28. Butler's reaction is in 'Diverse reminiscences ending with Suez', Butler Papers, RAB G31/88. Lord Home of the Hirsel, in an interview with the author, confirmed a general sentiment among ministers then of the second rank that Macmillan was more decisive. See also John Turner, *Macmillan* (Longman, 1994).

15. The 'Wind of Change' speech to the Cape Town Parliament in 1959 was written by Sir John Maud, the High Commissioner to South Africa, borrowing a phrase from Stanley Baldwin; the Greeks and Romans simile was Macmillan's own, first noticed when he was Minister Resident in Algeria during the war, but finally made public in March 1960. See Alistair Horne, *Macmillan 1957–1986* (Macmillan, 1989), pp. 193–6; Harold Evans, *Downing Street Diary. The Macmillan Years 1957–1963* (Hodder & Stoughton, 1981), p. 112.

16. Salisbury resigned over the government's policy towards Cyprus.

17. John Barnes, 'From Eden to Macmillan, 1955–1959', in Peter Hennessy and Antony Seldon (eds), *Ruling Performance* (Basil Blackwell, 1987), p. 137.

18. Ramsden, *The Making of Conservative Party Policy*, p. 190.

19. Cabinet Conclusions, 21 January 1957, Public Record Office, CAB 128/31/pt 1.

20. Boyd Carpenter in Cabinet, 30 January 1957, CAB 128/31/pt. 1; Macleod to Macmillan, 'Social Services Expenditure', 31 January 1957, PREM 11/1805.

21. Macmillan to Fraser, 17 February 1957, PREM 11/1816.

22. Peter Thorneycroft, 'The Pound Sterling' Draft memo, 4 September 1957, PREM 11/1824, finally circulated as CC (57) 195, CAB 129.

23. Ramsden, *Making of Conservative Party Policy*, p. 194.

24. Alec Cairncross, *The Robert Hall Diaries 1954–61* (Unwin Hyman, 1991), 20 November 1958, p. 179.

25. Michael Fraser, 'Some Thoughts on the Present Situation', 20 September 1957, PREM 11/2248.

26. Steering Committee minutes, January 1958, CRD papers; Harold Macmillan, 'The Middle Way, Twenty Years On', published as the introduction to a reprint of Harold Macmillan, *The Middle Way* (Macmillan, 1966), pp. xiii–xxix.

27. Butler to Macmillan, 19 December 1957, PREM 11/2248.

28. Rodney Lowe, 'Resignation at the Treasury: the Social Services Committee and the Failure to Reform the Welfare State, 1955–57', *Journal of Social Policy*, 18 (1989), 505–26; for a more nuanced view of the debate, see M.C. Jarvis, 'The 1958 Treasury Dispute and the Nature of

Conservatism', unpublished Leeds MA Thesis, 1995.

29. Macmillan's memorandum, described as 'Some thoughts which have occurred to me during my short holiday', C (57) 194, 1 September 1957, PREM 11/1824.
30. Collected in CRD 48/83.
31. Macmillan to Lloyd, 15 July 1961, PREM 11/3883.
32. E.g. in July 1962 the national figures for Approve/ Disapprove/Don't Know were 42/25/33; Conservative voters registered 51/19/30; Labour voters 33/34/33. George H. Gallup, ed., *The Gallup International Public Opinion Polls: Great Britain, 1937–1975* (Random House, 1977), p. 637. All other references in this chapter to opinion poll responses are taken from this source.
33. The Conservative majority in 1959 was 14,760; the Liberal majority in 1962 was 7,855. Although Orpington has a special resonance it was not unique: on the previous day at Blackpool North a Liberal had come from the bottom of the poll to within 1,000 votes of the Conservative victor.
34. A full account is in Keith Alderman, 'Harold Macmillan's Night of the Long Knives', in *Contemporary Record*, Vol. VI (1992), pp. 243–65.
35. CRD Paper, 'An Analysis of Political Support in Mid–1958 with some notes for speeches' (R.M. Fraser), 2 September 1958, Trinity College, Cambridge, Butler Papers, RAB H39/43.
36. CRD Paper, 'The Next Ten

Years' (G.D.M. Block), 24 April 1963, Butler Papers, RAB H50/241.
37. Parliamentary Secretary to the Ministry of Education, 'Thoughts on Meals and Means', Cabinet Papers C(61)219, PREM 11/4484. For a fuller discussion of Conservative understanding of social changes, see John Turner, 'A Land Fit for Tories to Live In: The Political Ecology of the British Conservative Party, 1944–1994', in *Contemporary European History*, Vol. IV (1995), pp. 189–205.
38. *H.C. Debs*, 1958–59, 15 December 1958, col. 892.
39. 'Transcript of Prime Minister's remarks to the Cabinet on May 28th 1962', PREM 11/3930.
40. 'Incomes Policy. Memorandum by the Prime Minister', 19 June 1962, Cabinet Papers C(62)99.
41. Macleod to Macmillan, 27 April 1962, Butler Papers, RAB H31/49.
42. After a series of abortive missile developments whose purpose was to extend the effective life of the nuclear bomber fleet, the government had obtained a promise in March 1960 that the Americans would supply the Skybolt air-to-ground missile to carry British warheads until the submarine-launched Polaris was ready.
43. The crisis began with Profumo's parliamentary denial in March that there was an 'impropriety' in his relationship with Christine Keeler, a prostitute. It ended in September with the publication of Lord Denning's

report on the risk to security posed by Keeler's simultaneous relationship with the Russian military attaché.

44. Butler, as leader of the House, was often consulted by Benn. 'By the way,' he asked on 21 November 1962, 'one thing: would your scheme permit Quintin to come back?' Benn said it would not. 'Ah, well that's all right,' replied a relieved Butler. Tony Benn, *Years of Hope: Diaries, Letters and Papers 1940–1962* (Hutchinson, 1994), p. 360.

45. Anthony Howard and Richard West, *The Making of the Prime Minister* (Jonathan Cape, 1965), p. 80.

46. Fullest published details of the final decision process are in Horne, *Macmillan*, pp. 557–60, and D.R. Thorpe, *Alex Douglas-Home* (Sinclair Stevenson, 1996).

47. Macleod to Macmillan, 27 April 1962, Trinity College, Cambridge, Butler Papers, RAB H31/39.

48. CRD Paper, 'The Next Ten Years' (G.D.M. Block), 24 April 1963, Butler Papers, RAB H50/241.

49. See John Ramsden, *The Winds of Change* (Longman, 1996), pp. 111–28.

50. National numbers were not published between 1955 and 1970, by which time numbers had dropped to half the 1951 level. There was a membership drive in the late 1950s.

51. Ramsden, *The Winds of Change*, pp. 72–7.

52. Richard Cockett, 'The Party, Publicity and the Media', in Anthony Seldon and Stuart Ball (eds), *Conservative Century*, (Oxford University Press, 1994) pp. 547–77.

53. The Liberal vote dropped again, but this time to Labour's benefit, in 1966. The full figures were Labour 13.1m (48.1%), Conservative 11.4m (41.9%), Liberal 2.3m (8.5%).

54. See e.g. University of Leeds, Brotherton Library, Boyle Papers, Michael Fraser to Boyle, 15 December 1965, 660/22550. They returned with such predictable trophies as Robert Blake, Felix Markham, Maurice Cowling and Norman Gash.

NINE. 1970–74

1. Enoch Powell, *Joseph Chamberlain* (Pimlico, 1977), p. 151.

2. Sir Keith Joseph, *Reversing the Trend* (Barry Rose, 1975), Jock Bruce-Gardyne, *Whatever Happened to the Quiet Revolution?* (Charles Knight, 1974) and Margaret Thatcher, *The Path to Power* (HarperCollins, 1995), p. 240. For a similar perspective see Martin Holmes, *Political Pressures and Economic Policies. British Government* (Butterworth, 1982).

3. For a balanced perspective see Stuart Ball and Anthony Seldon (eds), *The Heath Government 1970–74 – A Reappraisal* (Longman, 1996).

4. Richard Rose, *Do Parties Make a Difference?* (Macmillan, 1982).

5. Paul Sabatier, 'Top-Down and Bottom-Up Approaches to Implementation Research', *Journal of Public Policy*, 6 (1986), pp. 21–48.

6. Dennis Kavanagh, 'The Heath Government' in Peter Hennessy and Anthony Seldon (eds), *Ruling Performance* (Blackwell, 1987), p. 233.

7. David Butler and Anthony King, *The British General Election of 1966* (Macmillan, 1966), p. 266.

8. Douglas Hurd, *An End to Promises* (Collins, 1979), p. 149.

9. David Butler and Michael Pinto-Duschinsky, *The British General Election of 1970* (Macmillan, 1971), p. 346.

10. David Butler and Donald Stokes, *Political Change in Britain* (Macmillan, 2nd edn, 1974), p. 344.

11. For the views of Sewill, see John Ramsden, *The Making of Conservative Party Policy* (Longman, 1980), p. 278.

12. For contemporary biographies of Heath see George Hutchinson, *Edward Heath* (Longman, 1970) and Margaret Laing, *Edward Heath* (Sidgwick and Jackson, 1972).

13. See John Campbell, *Edward Heath: A Biography* (Pimlico, 1993), p. 425.

14. Keith Middlemas, *Power, Competition and the State*, Vol. 2 (Macmillan, 1990), p. 308. Heath's reliance on William Armstrong and other senior civil servants to draw up economic policy and even bypass the Treasury is a theme of Peter Hall's magisterial *The Politics of Economic Management*, a manuscript being prepared for publication.

15. Butler and Stokes, *Political Change in Britain*, Chap. 16.

16. For evidence see Richard Rose, 'A Crisis of Confidence in British Party Leaders?', *Contemporary Record*, Vol. 9 (1995), pp. 273–93.

17. See Hall, *The Politics of Economic Management*, Chap. 3, p. 38.

18. Cited in Campbell, *Edward Heath*, p. 233.

19. Philip Norton, *Conservative Dissidents: Dissent Within the Conservative Parliamentary Party 1970–74* (Temple Smith, 1978).

20. Jim Prior, *A Balance of Power* (Hamish Hamilton, 1986), and Campbell, *Edward Heath*, p. 515.

21. Campbell, *Edward Heath*, p. 216. Also see the chapter by Stuart Ball, 'The Conservative Party and the Heath Government' in Ball and Seldon (eds), *The Heath Government*.

22. Ball, 'The Conservative Party'.

23. Campbell, *Edward Heath*, p. 570.

24. Hurd, *An End to Promises*, p. 295.

25. Campbell, *Edward Heath*, p. 513.

26. Ball, 'The Conservative Party'.

27. Anthony King, 'The Election that Everyone Lost', in Howard Penniman (ed.), *Britain at the Polls* (Americal Enterprise Institute, 1974), p. 70.

28. David Butler and Dennis Kavanagh, *The Bitish General Election of February 1974* (Macmillan, 1974), and Dennis Kavanagh, 'The Fatal Decision: The Calling of the February 1974 Election' in Ball and Seldon (eds), *The Heath Government*, Chap. 14.

29. For the critical views of the Labour Cabinet ministers, see Joel Barnett, *Inside the Treasury* (Deutsch, 1982) and Edmund

Dell, *A Hard Pounding* (Clarendon Press, 1991). For Conservative fears see Ramsden, *The Making of Conservative Party Policy*, pp. 306–7.

30. Middlemas, *Power, Competition and the State*, p. 390.

31. See Correlli Barnett, *The Audit of War* (Macmillan, 1986).

32. See Richard Rose, *The Problem of Party Government* (Macmillan, 1974), pp. 410–11.

33. Lord Howe, *Conflict of Loyalties* (Macmillan, 1994), pp. 197–8.

34. Brendon Sewill, in 'Conservative Party Policy Making 1965–70', *Contemporary Record*, Vol. 3 (1990), p. 38.

35. Cited in Richard Rose, *The Problem of Party Government*, p. 413.

TEN. 1979–96

1. Parts of this chapter are drawn from two previous writings of the author: Ivor Crewe, 'Electoral Behaviour' in Dennis Kavanagh and Anthony Seldon (eds), *The Major Effect* (Macmillan, 1994), pp. 99–121; and Ivor Crewe, 'The Thatcher Legacy', in Anthony King (ed.), *Britain at the Polls 1992* (Chatham House, 1992), pp. 1–28.

2. See John Curtice and Michael Steed, 'Appendix 2: The Results Analysed' in David Butler and Dennis Kavanagh, *The British General Election of 1992* (Macmillan, 1992), pp. 322–62 and especially pp. 347–53.

3. *The Observer*, interview, 25 February 1979.

4. Peter Hennessy, 'The Secret World of Cabinet Committees', *Social Studies Review*, 1 (November 1985), pp. 7–11.

5. See David Cowling 'Detailed findings of the ITN/Harris on-the-day poll in the Mid-Staffordshire by-election (22 March 1990)', *mimeo*, March 1990.

6. Numbers Market Research poll of 14–15 March, reported in Nicholas Comfort, 'Disillusioned Homeowners and Skilled Workers Desert Thatcher', *Independent on Sunday*, 18 March 1990.

7. *Gallup Political Index*, Report No. 363, November 1990, p. 2.

8. *Gallup Political Index*, Report No. 363, November 1990, p. 3.

9. See Ivor Crewe, 'Why the Conservatives won', in Howard R. Penniman (ed.), *Britain at the Polls, 1979* (American Enterprise Institute, 1981), p. 274.

10. See Anthony King, 'Margaret Thatcher: the Style of a Prime Minister', in Anthony King (ed.), *The British Prime Minister* (2nd edn, Macmillan, 1985).

11. Labour Party, *Meet the Challenge, Make the Change* (Labour Party, 1989).

12. See Ivor Crewe, 'Values: The Crusade That Failed', in Dennis Kavanagh and Anthony Seldon (eds), *The Thatcher Effect: A Decade of Change* (Clarendon Press, 1989), pp. 239–50, at p. 242.

13. *The Economist*, 25 May 1985, p. 22.

14. Ivor Crewe, 'The Policy Agenda: A New Thatcherite Consensus?', *Contemporary Record*, Vol. 3 (February 1990), pp. 2–7 (p. 4).

15. Crewe, 'The Policy Agenda', p. 4.
16. Crewe, 'The Policy Agenda', p. 5.
17. Central Statistical Office, *Social Trends 22* (HMSO, 1992), pp. 102–3.
18. BBC/Gallup election survey, 10–11 June 1987.
19. Anthony Heath et al., *Understanding Political Change* (Pergamon Press, 1991), p. 123.
20. Labour Party, *Britain Will Win*, p. 5.
21. See Ivor Crewe, 'Labor Force Changes, Working Class Decline, and the Labour Vote: Social and Electoral Trends in Postwar Britain', in *Labor Parties in Postindustrial Societies*, ed. Frances Fox Piven (Polity Press, 1991), pp. 20–46 (p. 34).
22. See Heath, *Understanding Political Change*, pp. 106–7 and 206–7 and Government Statistical Service, *OPCS Monitor SS 90/3 (General Household Survey)* (Government Statistical Service, 1990), p. 4 (Table 10.5).
23. This is based on applying Heath et al.'s estimate of a 4.8% swing between 1964 and 1987 *pro rata* to the period 1979–91. The association between housing tenure and vote has been very steady since 1964. See Heath et al., *Understanding Political Change*, pp. 206–7.
24. In March 1990 the swing to Labour since the 1987 general election was 18% among mortgagees compared with 14.5% among council tenants. See Ivor crewe, 'Centre of Attraction', *Marxism Today*, May 1990, pp. 14–17.
25. Central Statistical Office, *Social Trends 22*, p. 113.
26. A.H. Halsey, *British Social Trends Since 1900* (Macmillan, 1988), p. 33.
27. Literally. In week 2 of November 1990, before Michael Heseltine formally challenged Thatcher for the leadership, Labour led the Conservatives by 16%. In week 3, during the leadership election campaign, that lead fell to 5%. In week 4, during which Thatcher stood down but before her successor was known, the Conservatives went into a 0.5% lead. In the final three days, after John Major became prime minister, the Conservatives leapt into an 11.5% lead. See Anthony King, 'Major restores Tories' fortunes with 2.5 per cent lead', *Daily Telegraph*, 14 December 1990.
28. See Ivor Crewe and Anthony King, 'Did Major Win? Did Kinnock Lose?', in Anthony Heath et al. (eds), *Labour's Last Chance? The 1992 Election and Beyond* (Dartmouth, 1994), pp. 125–48.
29. See, in particular, Butler and Kavanagh, *The British General Election of 1992*, especially Appendix 2; Ivor Crewe, 'Why Did Labour Lose (Yet Again)', *Politics Review*, Vol. 2 (September 1992), pp. 2–11; Ivor Crewe, Pippa Norris and Robert Waller, 'The 1992 General Election' in Pippa Norris et al. (eds), *British Elections & Parties Yearbook* (Harvester Wheatsheaf, 1992), pp. xv–xxxvi; David Denver et al., *British Elections & Parties Yearbook 1993* (Harvester

Wheatsheaf, 1993); and David Sanders, 'Why the Conservative Party Won – Again', in Anthony King (ed.), *Britain at the Polls 1992* (Chatham House, 1992), pp. 171–202.

30. See Peter Spencer and John Curtice, 'Flexibility and the Feel Good Factor', (Kleinwort Benson Securities, 24 November 1994).

31. Among deserters at the Christchurch by-election his leadership (mentioned by only 15%) ranked fifth out of nine factors, behind the 'overall state of the economy' (44%), 'VAT on fuel' (43%), 'law and order' (30%) and 'government competence' (29%). See Peter Wilby, 'Economy Will Sink Tories', *Independent on Sunday*, 25 July 1994, p. 2, reporting on NOP poll. Among Conservative deserters generally, it ranked only eighth out of thirteen factors: the government's overall record, the economy, the NHS and other public services and rising taxes were all far more important reasons. Anthony King, 'Tories Vote with Their Feet Over Economy', *The Daily Telegraph*, 21 March 1994, p. 8.

32. A comparison between the vote at the 1992 general election and the aggregate of voting intentions recorded by the monthly omnibus MORI poll for the calendar year 1993 showed that the largest falls in Conservative support occurred among readers of the Murdoch tabloids – *Today* (–17%), the *Sun* (–16%) and the *Daily Star* (–16%) – while the smallest falls (of 7–8%) occurred among readers of the non-Conservative *Mirror*, *Guardian* and *Independent*. It was notable that the drop-off in Conservative support was smallest among readers of the *Daily Express*, the one Tory tabloid to stick steadfastly by the government – and John Major. See Robert M. Worcester, 'Demographics and values: what the British public read and what they think about their newspapers', MORI, February 1994.

33. For example: Rupert Murdoch, the media owner; Andrew Neil, the former editor of the *Sunday Times*, and Lord Young, a member of Thatcher's Cabinet.

CONCLUSION

The editor would like to thank Stuart Ball, John Barnes, John Ramsden and Robert Waller for their helpful comments on both the introduction and conclusion.

INDEX

Governing Britain
Fifth Edition

A. H. Hanson & Malcolm Walles

Politically and administratively Britain is a highly developed country. For the performance of governmental functions she has well-established, clearly defined and widely respected institutions, run by men and women with a deep understanding of the roles they are expected to play. The emphasis throughout this book is on the way in which the political and administrative institutions of central government have responded to the challenge presented by the accelerating pace of social change. The result is a comprehensive account of the problems that face both people and government in Britain today.

This is the fifth edition of this book, and it has been extensively revised to take into account the particular convulsions which have altered the British political system during the 1980s.

ISBN 0 00 686208 X

Fontana Press

The English
A Social History 1066–1945

Christopher Hibbert

'Christopher Hibbert writes so well, and presents a huge amount of material with such skill, that this 900 page volume can be read more quickly and enjoyably than many novels . . . an admirable evocation of the past and a lasting analysis of the English character'
JOHN MORTIMER *Sunday Times*

'From tournaments, pilgrims and kings through to bus conductors and summer holidays, he isolates the changing habits of successive generations. His greatest – and extraordinary – success is to have extracted from this mass of material the exact character of each century he touches' *The Independent*

'Enthralling . . . Barons and peasants, contemporaries of Pepys and Boswell, a people revolutionised by technology – all leap from his pages like figures on a canvas by Lowry . . . How anyone can write as much and as well as Hibbert is a mystery. His big, rich book deserves a place on the shelves of anyone remotely interested in our history'
Mail on Sunday

'A glorious cavalcade of 900 years of life and death, work and play, sex and sensibility amongst the English . . . Christopher Hibbert blends erudition, energy and elegance to perfection . . . Get beyond the myths of history; treat yourself to this feast of a book'
ROY PORTER *The Standard*

'Compiled with flair and skill and with that flair for particularity and even oddity which no historian, "popular" or otherwise, can afford to dispense with' *Times Literary Supplement*

0 586 08471 1

HarperCollins*Publishers*

The Rise and Fall of the Great Powers

Economic Change and Military Conflict
from 1500 to 2000

Paul Kennedy

'One of the masterpieces of modern historical writing.'
CHRISTOPHER ANDREW, *Daily Telegraph*

'I doubt whether the story of the rise and fall of the great powers has ever been told so professionally, with such a command of sources, or with such close attention to the connections between economics, geography and politics.' ROBERT SKIDELSKY, *Independent*

'Paul Kennedy has written a brilliantly original book which has become a best-seller in the US and made its author a pundit to be seen and heard. It is intended for the intelligent layman as well as the academic historian, combining in Toynbee-esque manner the sweeping conception with careful attention to historical detail.'
ZARA STEINER, *Financial Times*

'Despite the irresistible fascination of the subject, Paul Kennedy's outstanding new book is the first to tackle it with any real historical rigour. He ranges across five centuries and around the whole world. He seems to have read every relevant book in every possible language. And he has produced a general argument so deceptively simple that no politician, however busy, should ignore or misunderstand it.'
DAVID CANNADINE, *Observer*

'A masterpiece of exposition. It is erudite and elegantly written.'
LAWRENCE FREEDMAN, *New Society*

'A remarkable book, reported to be compulsory reading in exalted circles in Washington and Moscow. It is long, clever, often funny, and crammed with remarkable insights; it is tinged with the genius that unravels complexity.' ANDREW WHEATCROFT, *Evening Standard*

ISBN 0 00 686052-4

FontanaPress
An Imprint of HarperCollins*Publishers*

Demanding the Impossible

A History of Anarchism

Peter Marshall

'To be governed means that at every move, operation or transaction one is noted, registered, entered in a census, taxed, stamped, priced, assessed, patented, licensed, authorized, recommended, admonished, reformed . . . exploited, monopolized, extorted, pressured, mystified, robbed; all in the name of public utility and the general good.'

So said Proudhon in 1851, and from the Ancient Chinese to today's rebel youth many have agreed – among their number Godwin and Kropotkin, Bakunin and Malatesta, Tolstoy and Gandhi, the Ranters and the Situationists, de Sade and Thoreau, Wilde and Chomsky, anarcho-syndicalists and anarcha-feminists. Peter Marshall, in his inclusive, inspirational survey, gives back to the anarchistic, undiluted and undistorted, their secret history.

'Reading about anarchism is stimulating and funny and sad. What more can you ask of a book?'   Isabel Colegate, *The Times*

'Massive, scholarly, genuinely internationalist and highly enjoyable . . . this is the book Johnny Rotten ought to have read.'
David Widgery, *Observer*

'Large, labyrinthine, tentative: for me these are all adjectives of praise when applied to works of history, and *Demanding the Impossible* meets all of them. I now have a book – Marshall's solid 700 pages and more – to which I can direct readers when they ask me how soon I intend to bring my *Anarchism* up to date.'   George Woodcock, *Independent*

'This is the most comprehensive account of anarchist thought ever written. Marshall's knowledge is formidable and his enthusiasm engaging . . . he organizes a mass of diverse material with great subtlety and skill, presenting a good-tempered critique of each position with straightforward lucidity.'   J. B. Pick, *Scotsman*

ISBN 0 00 686245 4

Fontana Press

Patriots and Liberators
Revolution in the Netherlands 1780–1813

Simon Schama

'A rare and magnificent example of total history.'
Richard Cobb, *Times Literary Supplement*

'An outstanding work of historical scholarship . . . Simon Schama writes brilliantly. He can bring a character alive in a sentence . . . This powerful book reads with the ease of a novel. Every page glitters with intelligence and perception. In every way *Patriots and Liberators* is an extraordinary achievement.'
J. H. Plumb

Between 1780 and 1813 the Dutch Republic – a country once rich enough to be called the cash till of Europe and powerful enough to make war with England – was stripped of its colonies, invaded by its enemies, driven to the edge of bankruptcy, and finally reduced to becoming an appendage of the French Empire. Out of these events Simon Schama has constructed a gripping chronicle of revolution and privateering, constitutions and coups, in a tiny nation desperately struggling to stay afloat in the seas of geopolitics. Like his *The Embarrassment of Riches* and *Citizens*, *Patriots and Liberators* combines a mastery of historical sources with an unabashed delight in narrative. The result confirms Schama as one of the most exciting and engaging historians now at work.

'This remarkable book is more than a revision, it is a revelation.'
A. J. P. Taylor, *Observer*

'A dramatic story, full of pathos and true comedy. If any book may be said to inhale without sententiousness the clear, calm and steadying air of a European ideal, this is it.' Michael Ratcliffe, *The Times*

'Schama's book is written in the grand manner, its sweep as impressive as its erudition and the constant brilliance of its style. He gives the Dutch revolution back to the people to whom it belonged – the Dutch.'
Economist

ISBN 0 00 686156 3

Fontana Press

The Rise of Respectable Society

A Social History of Victorian Britain, 1830–1900

F. M. L. Thompson

In the fifty years since the appearance of G. M. Young's brilliant survey, *Victorian England: Portrait of an Age*, a mass of new research from new perspectives, has entirely changed the landscape of the Victorian era. *The Rise of Respectable Society* offers a new map of this territory as revealed by close empirical studies of marriage, the family, domestic life, work, leisure and entertainment. In doing so it rescues the middle and working classes from the rigidity of the class stereotypes by which they have been frequently portrayed. But it also argues that the diversity of cultures within those classes was in fact the essence of Victorian society, and that as each class developed its notions of self-respect, so it adhered ever more closely to the classes above and below it, thus avoiding the revolutionary fractures which appeared in many other European countries during this period.

For the quality of its research and the clarity of its synthesis, *The Rise of Respectable Society* will gain a reputation as an outstanding reinterpretation of the Victorian period.

ISBN 0 00 686157 1

Fontana Press